# TRANSLATION AND THE TRANSMISSION OF CULTURE BETWEEN 1300 AND 1600

# TRANSLATION AND THE TRANSMISSION OF CULTURE BETWEEN 1300 AND 1600

Edited by
Jeanette Beer
and
Kenneth Lloyd-Jones

Studies in Medieval Culture, xxxv
Medieval Institute Publications

WESTERN MICHIGAN UNIVERSITY

Kalamazoo, Michigan — 1995

© Copyright 1995 by Board of the Medieval Institute
Kalamazoo, Michigan 49008-3801

**Library of Congress Cataloging-in-Publication Data**

Translation and the transmission of culture between 1300 and 1600 /
edited by Jeanette Beer and Kenneth Lloyd-Jones.
   p.    cm. -- (Studies in medieval culture ; 35)
   Includes bibliographical references.
   Contents: The continuum of translation as seen in three Middle
French treatises on comets / Lys Ann Shore -- Vernacular translation
in the fourteenth-century crown of Aragon : Brunetto Latini's Li
livres dou tresor / Dawn Ellen Prince -- Patronage and the
translator : Raoul de Presles's La cité de Dieu and Calvin's
Institution de la religion chrestienne and Institutio religionis
Christianae / Jeanette Beer -- Marot's Le roman de la rose and
evangelical poets / Hope H. Glidden -- Ronsard the poet, Belleau the
translator / Marc Bizer -- Fischart's Rabelais / Florence M.
Weinberg -- "La grécité de notre idiome" : correctio, translatio,
and interpretatio in the theoretical writings of Henri Estienne /
Kenneth Lloyd-Jones -- The French translation of Agrippa von
Nettesheim's Declamatio de incertitudine et vanitate scientiarum et
artium / Marc van der Poel -- Reading monolingual and bilingual
editions of translation in Renaissance France / Valerie Worth
-Stylianou.
   ISBN 1-879288-55-9. --  ISBN 1-879288-56-7 (pbk.)
   1. Translating and interpreting--Europe--History.  I. Beer,
Jeanette M. A.   II. Lloyd-Jones, Kenneth.  III. Series.
CB351.S83 vol. 35
[P306.8.E85]
940.1 s--dc20                                                    95-30225
[418' .02' 0940902]                                                CIP

Printed in the United States of America

Cover design by Stephen Beer

# Contents

# Introduction

*Translation and the Transmission of Culture between 1300 and 1600*
is a companion volume to *Medieval Translators and their Craft* (Medieval Institute Publications, 1989) and, like *Medieval Translators*, its aim
is to provide the modern reader with a deeper understanding of the early
centuries of translation in France. It works from the premise that
translation never was, and should not now be, envisaged as a genre.
*Translatio* was, and is, infinitely variable, generating a correspondingly
variable range of products from imitatively creative poetry to treatises of
science. In the exercise of its multi-faceted set of practices the same con-
troversies occurred then as now: creation or replication? literality or
freedom? obligation to source or obligation to public? Then as now, such
questions implied an awareness of the affinities and the differences between past and present, and a commitment to a cultural continuum, later
ages profiting from earlier ages. Nineteenth-century critics (and, indeed,
certain translators featured in this volume) would have treated this continuum as evolutionary, cultural transmission necessarily involving im-
provement because later is better. Temporal superiority, i.e., "modernity," bestows no automatic advantages, however, and the terms
"mouvance" and "différence" are more satisfactory than "evolution"
toward the objective analysis of what is preserved and what is altered in
the process of cultural transmission.

For this reason we have avoided periodization in our title, concentrating instead upon a variety of case-studies and trying to avoid such
inanities as "Renaissance translators with medieval mindset" or "medieval precursors of Humanism" (the capitalization is in itself sufficient to
reveal an evolutionary presupposition). Like *Medieval Translators*, the
volume makes no pretense at temporal exhaustiveness—the subject of
translation is too vast. It does, however, aim to shed light on several

aspects of translation that have hitherto been neglected and that, despite the earliness of the period, have relevance to our understanding of translation whether in France or generally.

The science of the stars was a common interest of kings, philosophers, and laymen, and in Lys Ann Shore's "The Continuum of Translation as Seen in Three Middle French Treatises on Comets" three works on comets are examined as examples of scientific translation. Two of the treatises were translated from Latin originals, the other was compiled from several sources. The material is more overtly technical than that of the other chapters in this volume, and the techniques required to translate it were consequently different to some degree. For example, the translators often allowed untranslatable technical terms to stand, and lacunae rather than interpolations marked the places of non-comprehension (a sure signal of respect for the integrity of the source). This translative fidelity was in no way undermined by the translators' accompanying glosses (the best explicatory technique available to bridge the gap between learned source and lay public, a technique, it might be added, which was no more inelegant than our modern footnote). Interestingly, all three translations were anonymous and the identity of their translators so effaced that the three treatises may or may not be from the same translator. (One might compare the anonymity of modern interlingual technical/scientific transfers whose only intent is to impart information.) The three treatises examined in this chapter were apparently the only works of their time to treat comets, despite the popularity of astrological and astronomical literature in France. A valuable handlist of other known manuscripts concerning the science of the stars is appended to the chapter.

Dawn Prince's "Vernacular Translation in the Fourteenth-Century Crown of Aragon: Brunetto Latini's *Li livres dou tresor* " moves outside France to examine the influence of the French Valois rulers, most especially Charles V, upon the ambitiously competitive Barcelonian dynasty. A general survey of the literary activity in Aragon between 1380 and

# Introduction

1410 leads into an analytic study of the conversion of Brunetto Latini's influential French thesaurus into Aragonese and Catalan. Transfer from one Romance language to another was inevitably simpler and involved fewer changes than transfer from the more synthetic Latin. One-to-one correspondence with the French model was frequent, and the Aragonese and Catalan translators employed with efficiency the chancellery translation techniques that were the tools-in-trade of royal scribes and notaries throughout Europe.

Jeanette Beer's "Patronage and the Translator: Raoul de Presles's *La Cité de Dieu* and Calvin's *Institution de la religion Chrestienne* and *Institutio religionis Christianae*" examines the subject of patronal influence upon the translated text. Exemplification is provided by the introductions to two popularizing works of theology: Raoul de Presles's French translation of St. Augustine's *De Civitate Dei* and Jean Calvin's French and Latin versions of his *Institutes* as seen in his introductory "Epistre" and "Epistola" to Francis I. These two translators were chosen for their disparateness. One was commissioned in the fourteenth century by a royal patron for the edification of his subjects; the other desperately begged for royal patronage two centuries later. One translator made available to Charles V's subjects the most influential church theologian of all time; the other made his own theology available. One renounced commentary on all matters theological, glossing only the source's historical and literary information in order to avoid controversy and to defend the establishment; the other sought controversy and worked precisely to undermine that same (theological ) establishment. For all their dissimilarities, however, a royal patron hovered over both works, and both were textually molded by the fact of patronage.

Hope Glidden's "Marot's *Le Roman de la Rose* and Evangelical Poetics" treats what George Steiner called in *After Babel* "internal translation." A privileged text (*Le Roman de la Rose* ) that had been held in high esteem since its appearance was, in the sixteenth century, retrans-

# Introduction

lated and, in places, reinterpreted to accommodate the nascent evangelical humanism. This modernization of an ancestral text provided "a genealogy for a vernacular in the throes of growth and self-definition."

The practice of translation was an important stage in the literary formation of Rémy Belleau. In "Ronsard the Poet, Belleau the Translator: The Difficulties of Writing in the Laureate's Shadow," Marc Bizer posits that Belleau, writing as a fledgling member of the Pléiade, decided to call his early poems "translations" as a strategy to emulate Ronsard without openly competing with him. Ultimately, however, Belleau moved from the subordinate role of translator by transposing his own poems into Latin. Translation eased him from imitation through transposition and substitution toward self-assertion.

Florence Weinberg's "Fischart's Rabelais" moves outward from France to Strasbourg with Johann Fischart's conversion of *Gargantua* into Alsacian German twenty years after Rabelais's death. If the notion of translation is regarded as a continuum from rigorous literalism to (almost) total creativity, Fischart's Rabelais would necessarily be placed near the creativity extreme (alongside *Enéas*, perhaps, but before Ezra Pound). Writing to serve a new public and a new generation (of 1575), Fischart amplified and developed, neologized and omitted, interpreted and invented. His accumulation of *ornatus* continued from one edition to the next, and ultimately his translation was two-thirds again as long as its original. Germane to his evangelically didactic purpose was the insertion of anti-Catholic propaganda, which served also as self-advertisement. Delighting in Rabelais's hilarious crudity but moving away from Rabelais's carefree mingling of the sacred and the profane, Fischart revelled in his own autonomy and, simultaneously, enriched the German language immeasurably.

"'La grécité de notre idiome': *Correctio*, *Translatio*, and *Interpretatio* in the Theoretical Writings of Henri Estienne" turns to those humanists who drew their inspiration from Budé's celebration of Greek

# Introduction

as "uberior Latina, ad sensusque animi exprimendos & felicior & significantior" [more copious than Latin, and more felicitous and more telling for the expression of meanings], most particularly the scholar-printer Henri Estienne. Kenneth Lloyd-Jones examines Estienne's presentation of the special relationship that, in Estienne's view, obtained between the French language and the Greek language. Estienne's theoretical affirmation of "la précellence de la langue françoise" was based upon that relationship and upon his conviction of the superiority of Greek over Latin. Estienne's argumentation had its scientific weaknesses and his translation theory had political overtones (anti-Italianism, for example), but his work was motivated by a genuine conviction of the importance of *correctio* and *interpretatio* as functions of translation. His musings on the doctrinal consequences of translating reflect the awareness that to translate was to interpret, and to interpret was to risk entanglement with current orthodoxies.

A different type of textual transmission is seen in Marc van der Poel's study of "The French Translation of Agrippa von Nettesheim's *Declamatio de incertitudine et vanitate scientiarum et artium: Declamatio* as Paradox." In this case the original text, which had already been translated into Italian and English during the sixteenth century, was controversial (and was ultimately judged heretical). Faced with a text that presented such intellectual and spiritual challenges, its French translator, Louis Turquet de Mayerne, intervened didactically and conceptually to shift the *Declamatio* to a different hermeneutic context. Marc van der Poel sees this contextual shift from an intellectually challenging text to a "literary trifle on a conventional theme" as an exercise in the genre of paradox.

The final chapter, "Reading Monolingual and Bilingual Editions of Translations in Renaissance France," addresses the important relationship between translator, printer, and public. Concentrating upon the "concrete artefact" itself, Valerie Worth-Stylianou examines selected works—original editions and reprints of sixteenth-century translations—to determine whether their manner of presentation (for example, parallel texts, indexes, glossaries, rhetorical/moral annotations) provides clues as to the manner in which monolingual and bilingual translations were read. With her focus upon the text and with her exploration of the question of bilingualism the volume comes full circle, from a Raoul de Presles who glossed, commented, and retained Latin quotes for a readership with varying degrees of bilingual competence to a de la Planche who retained foreign words "to ensure that readers remained aware of the difficulty." The context, the audience, and even the physical artefact may have changed from century to century, but from antiquity to the present the same range of issues continues to present itself during the translation and transmission of culture.

# The Continuum of Translation as Seen in Three Middle French Treatises on Comets

## Lys Ann Shore

Appearing suddenly, dramatically, and unpredictably in the night sky—much darker in premodern times than today—comets naturally attracted the attention of the medieval scholars who wrote on the "science of the stars" (Lat., *scientia stellarum*; Fr., *science des estoilles*). As I have pointed out elsewhere,[1] the science of the stars encompassed both what we would now call astronomy and astrology—that is, it dealt both with the nature and apparent motions of the heavenly bodies and with their presumed significance for events on earth.

According to the Aristotelian tradition, comets were, properly speaking, sublunary phenomena, created in the upper atmosphere (below the sphere of the moon) by the ignition of hot, dry exhalations as a result of the circular motion of the spheres. This explanation was accepted until the true supralunary position and planetary character of comets were definitely recognized in the late sixteenth and early seventeenth centuries.

Still, discussions of comets form a distinct part of the literature of the "science of the stars," in spite of the presumed sublunary nature of the phenomena. This is because the overwhelming importance of comets for the Middle Ages lay in their astrological significance—what sort of (usually disastrous) events they portended on earth. As astrological portents, comets resembled eclipses; in addition, they were linked to the planets and constellations because the exact nature of a comet's effect was considered to depend in part on the zodiacal sign in which it appeared and the position of the planets in the sky at the time of its appearance.

1

Lys Ann Shore

Dozens of medieval works in French exist that deal with the science of the stars. These include both translations from Latin and works composed in French. They are found in fifty or more manuscripts; a handlist of the known manuscripts is presented in the appendix to this chapter. Given the astrological importance of comets, it is surprising that, out of these numerous works in French on the science of the stars, only three deal with comets. This is all the more unexpected since discussions of comets are not uncommon in the Latin astronomical and astrological literature.[2]

These three treatises on comets, written in Middle French, form the nucleus of the present study. So far as is known, they are the only medieval works on this subject to have been written in French.[3] All three appear to date from the late fifteenth century. Two are translations based on Latin originals of the thirteenth century; the third is a compilation from more than one source. The surviving manuscripts were almost certainly produced in the Loire Valley, perhaps in the milieu of the court of René of Anjou at Angers, although the program of decoration is not sufficiently elaborate for any of them to have been produced for René himself.[4]

The first published notice, and the only detailed account, concerning these texts is that of Thorndike, published in 1950.[5] Thorndike identified the three works as: (1) a translation of the anonymous Latin *Liber de significatione cometarum*, entitled *Livre de la signification des cometes*; (2) a translation of the Latin work composed by the Dominican friar, Giles (Aegidius) of Lessines, *De Essentia, motu, et significatione cometarum*, entitled *De l'Essence et mouvement et signification des comettes*; and (3) an anonymous French work in eight chapters based in part on the *Liber de significatione cometarum* and entitled *Petit Traictié de la signification des comettes*.[6]

The techniques of translation used in these works range from literal rendering through expansion and adaptation to abridgment and omission.

2

## The Continuum of Translation

The *Petit Traictié* shows how a selective translation could be combined with new material to create an independent work. Taken together, these works display the full continuum of nonliterary translation. In the remaining sections of this chapter, sample passages of each work are analyzed in detail, with the twin purposes of glimpsing the translator at work and revealing his aims.

### Livre de la signification des cometes

According to Thorndike, the *Liber de significatione cometarum* was written in the eastern part of the Spanish peninsula during the second quarter of the thirteenth century. Its author is unknown, but Thorndike noted the writer's familiarity with Arabic language and history and his frequent references to "various rulers and places in the Spanish peninsula and northwestern Africa." Thorndike dated the work to ca. 1238, based on his identification of a comet mentioned in the text as one that appeared in the year 1238.[7] His dating was revised by Stahlman, who dated the comet in question to late in the year 1240.[8]

The sixteen chapters of the *Liber de significatione* focus exclusively on comets and consist, as Thorndike noted, of "a succession of excerpts from various authorities." These excerpts are loosely organized into topical discussions, but digressions are frequent. The author's main interest was in the astrological significance of comets, particularly in comets as signs of future events. The treatise also includes sections on cometary theory and descriptions of several historical comets. As Thorndike remarked, this work is largely based on Arabic and oriental astrological literature.[9]

The *Liber de significatione* opens with a table of contents that lists the titles of its sixteen chapters. The astrological emphasis of the entire work is evident just from reading this table, which may be translated as follows (all translations are my own unless otherwise attributed):

3

1. What is a comet?
2. What comets are made of and what they look like.
3. How many [types of] comets there are, and their names according to Ptolemy, Alquindus [al-Kindi], and the Chaldeans.
4. The shape of comets as they appear to men.
5. The meaning of comets and which planets they correspond to in their colors.
6. The meaning of comets in general.
7. The meaning of comets when they appear in any triplicity[10] of signs.
8. The meaning of comets when they appear in a particular sign.
9. The meaning of the size, complexion, and proper color of each comet and their consequences.
10. In which provinces and cities the consequences of comets will occur.
11. When these consequences will happen and how long they will last.
12. The quality of these consequences.
13. Whether the consequences will happen to men or animals or birds or fish or reptiles.
14. To demonstrate to objectors that comets are signs of future consequences.
15. What wise men have said about comets and running stars.[11]
16. Examples of comets.[12]

The French translation of the *Liber de significatione* reproduces its Latin original quite literally.[13] A fair idea of the quality of the translation can be obtained by comparing the following excerpt of the *Livre de la signification* with the corresponding passage of the Latin text. (The passage, drawn from chapter 8 of the work, was selected at random.)[14]

## The Continuum of Translation

Albumazar dit ou *Livre des conjunctions* que quant les cometes apparoissent ou signe de Aries, elles demonstrent descension qui adviendra au roy d'icelui climat et dissensions et guerres et batailles qui seront entre les roys d'icelle terre. Et en icelle apparoistront les armes des cristiens, et souffreront grans peines et paours, et moult de sang sera respandu ou lieu ou Aries domine (comme en Perse et semblables lieux). Et le roy des cristiens recevra dommaige, et esclandre sera en son royaume. Et les turcs aront grande occasion[15] et secheresse grande et souffreront douleur des yeulx. Et la mortalité sera sur les vaches et autres bestes, et adviendront morts et dissensions entre les grans gens, et les nobles s'esleveront contre les vilains et les mauvais hommes. Et pluseurs minieres d'or et d'argent seront descouvertes, et en esté sera grant chaleur. Et si elle est de la partie d'orient, elle signifie que dissension sera entre les roys d'icelle terre comme en Perse et semblables et partie des villes d'icelle terre obeira au roy de Babiloine. Et si elle apparoist de la partie d'occident, elle demonstre que les maures souffreront tristesse et desplaisance des roys. Et sera guerre entre aucuns d'eulx avecques ceulx d'occident. Et seront grans pluyes et habondance des rivieres.

Here is the same passage in the original Latin:

Dixit Albumasar in libro coniunctionum: Quando apparuerunt comete in signo Arietis, ostendit dissensiones que evenient regi illius climatis et discordias et guerras et bella que erunt inter reges illius terre. Et apparebunt in illa arma Christianorum et patientur magnos timores, et effundetur multus sanguis in locum ubi dominatur Aries, sicut in Persica et similibus. Et recipiet rex Christianorum dampnum et scandalum erit in regno suo. Et Turci habebunt magnam occisionem et siccitatem magnam, et patientur dolores oculorum. Et erit mortalitas in vaccis et in aliis pecudibus. Et evenient mortes et dissensiones inter magnos homines et nobiles, et insurgent viles homines et mali homines. Et discooperientur multe minere auri et argenti, et erit calor magnus tempore estivo. Et si fuerit a parte orientis, ostendit quod erit dissensio inter reges illius (regionis) sicut in Persia et in similibus. Pars villarum illius terre obediet regi

Babilonie. Et si apparuerit a parte occidentis, ostendit quod nigri homines patientur tristitiam et displicentiam a regibus et erit bellum inter aliquos illorum cum illis de occidente. Et erunt pluvie multe et habundantia fluviorum.[16]

[Albumasar (Abū Ma'shar) said in the *Book of Conjunctions*, when comets appear in the sign of Aries, it signifies dissension which will happen to the king of that region, and discord and fighting and wars which will occur between the kings of that land. And the arms of the Christians will appear in that land and they will suffer great fears, and much blood will be shed in the place where Aries rules, for example in Persia and such places. And the king of the Christians will receive an injury and there will be a scandal in his kingdom. And the Turks will suffer much slaughter and great drought, and they will incur illnesses of the eyes. And there will be mortality among cows and other cattle. And death and dissension will occur among great and noble men, and peasants and evil men will rise up in rebellion. And many mines of gold and silver will be discovered, and there will be great heat in the summer. And if it shall have appeared in the east, it shows that there will be dissension among kings of that region, such as in Persia and such places. Some of the cities of that land will obey the king of Babylon. And if it shall have appeared in the west, it shows that black men will suffer grief and pain from kings, and there will be war among some of them with those of the west. And there will be great rains and the rivers will rise.]

A detailed comparison between the *Liber de significatione* and its translation over the course of the entire work reveals chapter after chapter of painstaking literal, often word-for-word translation. Where possible, the translator tried to retain the exact wording of the original simply by gallicizing the Latin word. This can be seen in the sample passage in such choices as *domine* for *dominatur*; *recevra/recipiet*; and *mortalité/mortalitas*.

6

## The Continuum of Translation

The literalness of the translation, however, does not preclude occasional changes in verb tense, number, subject, or even word order (where the word order typical of Latin may be replaced by one more natural to Middle French). Some examples of these characteristic modifications are found in the sample passage: *apparoissent/apparuerunt* (present tense replacing perfect tense); *elles demonstrent/ostendit* (plural subject with pronoun replacing singular verb with understood subject); *Albumasar dit/ Dixit Albumasar* and *les cometes apparoissent/apparuerunt comete* (where the ordering subject-verb replaces the Latin order verb-subject).

Modifications such as these, however, have no effect on the sense of the original, which for the most part is conveyed quite accurately. Some differences appear to be the result of misunderstanding, as when the translation has nobles rising up against peasants and bad men, while in the original it is simply peasants and bad men who rise up. Or might this be an example of political correctness *avant la lettre*? Over the course of the entire work, the modifications and alterations pale into insignificance against the translator's overwhelming tendency to translate the original as faithfully as possible.

This concern for accuracy can be seen in the translator's retention of technical terms where no corresponding French term existed. These words were sometimes Latin, more often Arabic terms taken over into Latin. For example, in chapter 5 the translator retained the Latin word *tiphones* (typhoons), merely adding an explanatory phrase in French to help his readers: *vens qui s'appellent tiphones*. In chapter 2, the Arabic term *hayule* (matter) was retained in the translation.

More strikingly, the translator left a blank space in his translation when he came across an unclear reading or a lacuna in his exemplar. For example, in chapter 3 the translation presents only a blank space where the Latin text reads *luminosa Duamfuc*; as Thorndike notes, the name is unclear in the Latin manuscripts.[17] In the same chapter, a lacuna occurs in the listing of the various types of comets: all the Latin manuscripts omit the seventh comet-type entirely. This omission was noticed by the

7

alert translator, who accordingly inserted in his translation the phrase, *La vii^e* . . . , followed by a space of a line and a quarter—enough to fill in the missing identification. Elsewhere in the French text, a space indicates the translator's puzzlement over the meaning of an Arabic word that occurred in the Latin text: the phrase *vel in signis alnuchi* was rendered by *des signes alnuchi* . . . , followed by a space.

Comparison of the French translation with the surviving Latin manuscripts indicates that in all likelihood none of these served as the translator's exemplar. *G* contains only a fragment of the Latin text. In both *C* and *P*, the text of chapter 4 of the *Liber* contains crude drawings of comet-types. These drawings are missing in all the manuscripts of the French translation. Given the translator's careful execution of his task, it seems unlikely that he would have failed to reproduce the drawings had they been present in his exemplar. This is all the more likely since the drawings are syntactically linked to the text by the phrase (preserved in the translation) "and it is shaped like this" (*Ista est eius figura/et sa figure est telle*).

### De l'Essence et mouvement et signification des comettes

The Dominican friar, Giles of Lessines in Hainaut (ca. 1235–1304 or later), said he wrote his treatise *De Essentia, motu, et significatione cometarum* as a direct result of the consternation created among the public by the appearance of the comet of 1264. He composed it, he said, "because I heard many people say they were astonished and dumbfounded by the appearance of a certain tailed or hairy star which appeared in the kingdom of France in the east before sunrise from the third kalends of August [July 30][18] until the fifth nones of October [October 3] in the year of our Lord 1264, and because I was asked by many people both about the nature and the significance of comets."[19] His intention, he went on to say, was to gather in a single work the sayings of all the wise men—both ancient and modern natural philosophers, mathematicians, and theologians—that I have come across on this subject, to explain their arguments, uphold those that have been proven, and discard the unproven.[20]

Giles's approach to his chosen subject was both scholarly and orderly, as might have been expected of a cleric who is said to have studied under both Albert the Great and Thomas Aquinas. His interests were broad; his known works include an important treatise on usury and scientific works on geometry (now lost) and twilight, as well as his treatise on comets.[21] As Thorndike noted, Giles had access to "a remarkably extensive library";[22] he understood and utilized his sources well. As authorities, Giles drew impartially on ancient, Arabic, and modern authors, analyzing and comparing their statements.

*De Essentia, motu, et significatione cometarum* consists of ten chapters, which divide rather neatly into two parts. The first of these (chapters 1–7) discusses the origin, nature, and properties of comets. This astronomical and meteorological discussion is followed by three chapters (8–10) that discuss the astrological significance of comets and list examples of historical comets.[23]

The French translation of *De Essentia*, like that of the *Liber de significatione*, reproduces the whole of this lengthy work.[24] The translation is a literal one, often rendering the Latin into French with word-for-word accuracy. A sense of the close relationship of the translation to its Latin original can be gleaned from comparison of the two. (The following sample passage from chapter 6 was selected at random.)[25]

Pour ces choses et semblables, les comettes ne sont point veues differer si non par matiere et par accidens et non point par differences essenciales specifiques, lesquelles differences et

9

distinction aucuns ont voulu reduire par art en .v. membres pour ung mot que dit Aristote en ses *Metheores*, que on trouve cinq estoilles comees—du quel l'intencion declaire plainnement la translacion qui est du grec. La raison de la distincion d'iceulx qui suivent la translacion d'arabique est telle: que comette se peut varier en .v. manieres selon sa matiere. Ou elle est grosse et grasse ou elle est subtille ou elle est moyennement disposee. Si elle est moyennement disposee, ce peut estre en trois manieres car ou elle approche ou participe egallement des deux extremitéz ou elle participe plus de l'ung et moins de l'autre, ou au contraire. Et selon ceulx cy ceste distinction combien qu'elle soit materielle—et pource n'est elle point par art—toutesfois si est elle reduitte aucunement a art et a division formelle car les comettes qui sont de matiere subtille sont formees autrement et celles qui sont de matiere moyenne autrement sont formees, et ainsi des autres. Dont sont trouvees .v. manieres de formes de comettes, car ou la comette gette sa come de toute part, et ainsi est une forme; ou i[26] la gette a part—c'est en pluseurs manieres. Car ou i la gette en hault et c'est la seconde forme; ou en bas, ainsi est la tierce forme; ou a costé et c'est en deux manieres: ou il la gette de tous les deux costéz, et c'est la quarte forme; ou il la gette a ung costé tant seulement, et c'est la quinte forme.

This is how the same passage reads in the original Latin:

Propter hec et similia videntur modi cometarum distingui solum per materiam et accidentia et non per differentias essentiales specificias. Quam quidem distinctionem quidam conati sunt ad quinque membra arte reducere propter quoddam verbum Aristotelis in *Metheoro-logicis* suis ubi dicitur quod inveniuntur stelle habentes comas quin-que, cuius intentionem clarius habet translatio que de greco est. Est autem ratio distinctionis illorum qui translationem de arabico consequuntur quod secundum materiam potest cometes diversificari quinque modis quia materia eius in genere quidem grossa et coherens existens potest in specie considerari respectu sui generis et grossa et subtilis et medio modo, et hoc tripliciter qui medium

# The Continuum of Translation

potest esse per equalem participationem extremorum seu per approximationem ad alterum magis quam quod contingit. Item dupliciter secundum duo extrema et sic quinque modis potest variari cometas ex materia. Et secundum istos, licet hec distinctio sit materialis et ideo inartificialis, tamen quodammodo reducitur ad artem et ad formalem divisionem, quia aliter formantur cometes et figurantur et colorantur qui sunt ex subtili materia, aliter qui sunt ex grossa, aliter vero qui ex media. Unde et quinque etiam modi figurarum inveniuntur, quia aut est undique proiciens crines aut ad partem. Si undique, sic est unus modus; si ad alteram partem, aut est sursum, sic est secundus modus; aut deorsum, sic est tertius modus; si vero ad latus, aut ad duo, sic est quartus modus; aut ad unum latus, sic est quintus modus. (Thorndike, *Latin Treatises*, pp. 126–27)

[Due to these and similar things, the kinds of comets can be distinguished only through their matter and accidents, and not through specific essential differences. Some have tried to reduce this distinction to five members artificially, because of something that Aristotle says in his *Meteorologica*, where it is said that there are five stars which have hair. But the translation from Greek expresses his meaning more clearly. However, the reasoning behind the distinction made by those who follow the translation from Arabic is that comets can be divided into five types according to their matter because their matter, which is indeed of a thick and clinging kind, can be considered in its appearance with respect to its kind, thick and thin and moderate, and this in three ways because a mean can occur through equal participation in the extremes or through a closer approach to one than to the other. Likewise in two ways according to the two extremes, and thus comets can vary in five ways by matter. And according to these people, although this distinction is material and therefore not artificial, nonetheless in some way it can be reduced to an artificial and formal division, because comets which are made of thin matter are formed and shaped and colored differently from those which are made of thick matter, and differently again from those which are made of

11

moderate matter. And thus indeed the kinds of shapes are found, because it either projects its hair all around or in a direction. If it projects it all around, that is one kind; if in a direction, then either upwards, which is a second kind; or down, which is a third kind; if to the side, either to both sides, which is a fourth kind; or to one side only, which is a fifth kind.]

The translation of *De Essentia* is frequently literal even at the cost of some awkwardness. This can be seen, for instance, in the sample passage, where the phrase *du quel l'intencion declaire plainnement la translacion qui est du grec* reproduces the word-order of the Latin phrase. A similar example occurs elsewhere in the same chapter, where the Latin phrase *quarum nomina et effectus quidam astrologi scripserunt* was rendered nearly word for word as *des quelles les noms et les effectz aucuns astrologiens ont mis par escript.* The translator's concern for accuracy frequently extended to keeping the exact words of his Latin original through gallicization, as in chapter 5, where the learned French words *colloqué* and *vehemence* were used to translate the Latin *collocatur* and *vehementia.*

All this is not to say, however, that the translator was blindly faithful to his original; on the contrary, certain discrepancies can be noted between the Latin text and French translation, which reveal the translator at work. And it seems that he had a systematic procedure for his work. Discrepancies are of several kinds—the use of doublets to translate single words, the addition of brief explanations of terms, and simplifications in the syntax of the original.

*De Essentia* is a scholastic treatise, written by a university-trained philosopher. As might be expected, the style of the work is dense and complex, a kind of thirteenth-century "academese." Minor changes and simplifications of thought and syntax by the translator, then, may be seen as part of his effort to make the work more comprehensible to a French-speaking lay reader. The tendency to simplify for greater clarity by using some techniques common to French translators of Latin works can be seen throughout the sample passage. In the first sentence, *modi cometarum* was translated simply by *les comettes*, with the result that an abstract category was replaced by a concrete object. Near the end of the passage, the French phrase *car ou la comette gette sa come de toute part, et ainsi est une forme* simplified the Latin syntax somewhat by conflating two clauses into a single clause, while still preserving the author's thought.

Brief explanations added by the translator helped to clarify technical terms, such as *dyaphanum* (transparency) in chapter 2, which was explained on two separate occasions by the translator: *in dyaphano/en dyaphane c'est a dire en transparent*; *per dyaphanum/par dyaphane c'est a dire par corps transparent.*

Two pairs of doublets often occur within a single sentence of the French translation, as in chapter 3, where in the same sentence *seoir et durer* replaced the Latin verb *sedeat* and *non certain et vague* rendered *incerto*. Likewise, in chapter 6 the Latin phrase *acrior est acies aut hebetior* contains two pairs of doublets in the French translation: *les unes plus cleres et agues en lumiere, les autres plus obfusques et obtuses.*

Thorndike referred to the French translation of *De Essentia* as being "much freer" than the translation of the *Liber de significatione*.[27] A more accurate description of *De l'Essence* is that it is a faithful and even literal rendering of *De Essentia*, only somewhat simpler in syntax and style.

As in the case of the *Liber de significatione*, none of the existing Latin manuscripts of *De Essentia* appears to have served as the exemplar for the French translation. Throughout the work cases occur of disagreement between the French translation and the extant manuscripts. *P* disagrees with the translation less often than either *A* or *C*, but several cases can be noted of minor omissions in the text of *P* where the word in question is present in the manuscripts of the translation.

The French translations of the *Liber de significatione* and *De Essentia* give no clue as to the identity of their translators. Similarly, no clear evidence exists to indicate whether the two texts were translated by two individuals or were the work of a single translator. The tight codicological links between the two translations make it probable that they were the work of a single translator: they are found together and in the same order in two of the three extant manuscripts, including *R*, which is the probable exemplar of the others and may also be the author's original.[28]

Moreover, some indirect indications that one person translated both works arise from a comparison of the translations. Both, for example, show a similar concern for accuracy and precision. The translation of the *Liber de significatione* adheres more closely to the exact wording of its original than does the translation of *De Essentia*. It is possible, however, to account for this by the differing natures of the two texts: a loosely organized and nontechnical astrological work (*Liber*) and a closely reasoned, scholarly work (*De Essentia*). Somewhat different techniques of translation would naturally be called for to translate such different styles of writing.

It is also interesting to note the impersonal quality of both the translations. Many other French translations of astronomical and astrological works contain personal comments interjected by their translators.[29] All such remarks are wholly absent from the *Livre de la signification* and *De l'Essence*; both works present, instead, a sober, accurate, and completely impersonal rendering of their Latin originals.

In chapter 9 of the *Livre de la signification*, the word *conjonction* was used repeatedly and consistently—although incorrectly—to translate the Latin term *complexio*. On a single occasion in chapter 6 of *De l'Essence* the same mistranslation occurs. Thorndike noted in his edition of the *Liber de significatione* that the abbreviation in the extant Latin manuscripts might be taken to represent either *conjunctio* or *complexio*.[30]

14

It is, of course, possible that in the exemplar the word *conjunctio* was written out rather than abbreviated. If, on the other hand, the translator himself made the wrong choice in expanding the abbreviation, his misunderstanding would be odd and uncharacteristic, since his work is otherwise quite accurate. Yet such an error would help to show that a single mind was at work in the translation of the two Latin texts.

## Petit Traictié de la signification des comettes

The *Petit Traictié de la signification des comettes* is a much shorter work than either the *Livre de la signification* or *De l'Essence*. According to its rubric, it is a compilation, pieced together from "the sayings of Ptolemy, Albumasar (Abū Ma'shar), 'Haly,' Alquindus (Al-Kindi), Giles of Rome, and many other astrologers."[31] The *Petit Traictié* is almost entirely an astrological work. Its first chapter discusses the physical characteristics of comets—their substance and appearance. The remaining seven chapters fall into two sections. The first (chapters 2–4) treats the technical aspect of comets in a general way, beginning with the agreement of each of several comet-types with a different planet due to their corresponding colors (chapter 2), their general astrological significance (chapter 3), and their significance when they appear in any triplicity of signs (chapter 4). The second section includes chapters 5 through 8, all of which deal with various specific astrological topics. Chapter 5, which forms the centerpiece of the work, classifies and discusses in detail the various comet-types. Chapter 6 outlines the significance of comets when one appears in a specific sign of the zodiac. Chapter 7 briefly lists the characteristics of each of the seven planets, and chapter 8 even more briefly assigns each planet to its appropriate zodiacal house.

In his announcement of the existence of the *Petit Traictié*, Thorndike commented that this work "in large part reproduces portions of the treatise in sixteen chapters [the *Liber de significatione*]."[32] He went on to list the correspondences between the chapters of the *Petit Traictié* and those of the *Liber de significatione*; his observations are summarized in Table 1.

**Table I**
**Relationship of *Petit Traictié* to *Liber de significatione***

| Petit Traictié | Liber de significatione | Comments |
|---|---|---|
| Chapter 1 corresp. to | parts of chapters 1, 2 | |
| Chapter 2 corresp. to | part of chapter 5 | |
| Chapter 3 corresp. to | part of chapter 6 | |
| Chapter 4 parallels | chapter 7 | Quotations from "Busahen" omitted; relations to points of compass added. |
| Chapter 5 corresp. to | (part of chapter 9)[*] | Ordering changed, but much of wording identical; could be due to use of common sources. |
| Chapter 6 corresp. to | chapter 8 | Brief introduction added; otherwise reproduces chapter with only minor variations. |
| Chapter 7 | no parallel | |
| Chapter 8 | no parallel | |

[*] Thorndike, *Latin Treatises*, p. 8, neglects to give chapter number.

16

# The Continuum of Translation

The *Petit Traictié* was later characterized by Jean-Michel Massing as an "abridged version" of the French translation of the *Liber de significatione*, the *Livre de la signification*. Massing noted, however, that the *Petit Traictié* "differs somewhat in wording" from the *Livre*.[33] Both Thorndike and Massing were quite correct in recognizing that the *Petit Traictié* is closely based on the *Liber/Livre*. (I use this dual form of the name to indicate the work without distinguishing between the Latin original and the French translation.) The exact relationship, however, is harder to define, even after a close comparison of the texts. Was the compiler of the *Petit Traictié* working from the Latin text of the *Liber de significatione*? or from the French *Livre de la signification*? Was the compiler, in fact, the same individual who had translated the *Liber de significatione* (and probably *De Essentia* as well) into French? I have no firm answer for any of these questions. The text of the *Petit Traictié* often agrees in wording with the French text of the *Livre*; just as often, however, the wording of the two texts differs even while the sense remains the same. Sometimes the *Petit Traictié* appears to follow the Latin *Liber* more closely, sometimes the *Livre*. Table 2 presents an interlinear comparison of the *Petit Traictié*, the *Livre de la signification*, and the *Liber de significatione*, utilizing the sample passage given above from chapter 8 of the *Liber/Livre* (chapter 6 of the *Petit Traictié*).

## Table 2
### Comparison of *Petit Traictié*, *Livre de la signification*, and *Liber de significatione*

| | |
|---|---|
| *P.T.* | Albumazar au second livre des conjunctions des planetes . . .[a] |
| *Livre* | Albumazar dit ou *Livre des conjunctions* que |
| *Liber* | Dixit Albumasar in libro coniunctionum: |

| | |
|---|---|
| | dit que se les comectes apperent au signe de Aries, elles |
| (2) | quant les cometes aparoissent ou signe de Aries, elles |
| | Quando apparuerunt comete in signo Arietis, ostendit |

# Lys Ann Shore

*P.T.*
*Livre*
*Liber* demonstrent dissensions qui adviendront au roy de ce climat,
demonstrent descension qui adviendra au roy d'icelui climat
dissensiones que evenient regi illius climatis

(4)

discordes, guerres, et batailles qui seront
et dissensions et guerres et batailles qui seront
et discordias et guerras et bella que erunt

(5)

entre les roys de celle terre
entre les roys d'icelle terre. Et en icelle apparoistront
inter reges illius terre. Et apparebunt in illa

(6)

et auront grant paour et grant crainte;
les armes des cristiens, et souffreront grans peines et paours,
arma Christianorum et patientur magnos timores,

(7)

et avec ce y aura grande effusion de sang su lieu ou le signe
et moult de sang sera respandu ou lieu ou
et effundetur multus sanguis in locum ubi

(8)

de Aries a dominacion, comme en Perse et païs semblables
Aries domine (comme en Perse et semblables lieux).
dominatur Aries, sicut in Persica et similibus.

(9)

et recevra le roy des rommains scandale et dommaige
Et le roy des cristiens recevra dommaige, et esclandre sera
Et recipiet rex Christianorum dampnum et scandalum erit

(10)

en son royaume. Les turqs auront detriment, perte, et
en son royaume. Et les turcs aront grande occasion [*sic*]
in regno suo. Et Turci habebunt magnam occisionem et

(11)

grande secheresse et souffreront douleur aux yeulx.
et secheresse grande et souffreront douleur des yeulx.
siccitatem magnam et patientur dolores oculorum.

18

# The Continuum of Translation

*P.T.*    Il sera mortalité de vaches et d'autre bestial,
*Livre*   Et la mortalité sera sur les vaches et autres bestes,
*Liber*   Et erit mortalitas in vaccis et in aliis pecudibus.

        et se sourderont guerres et dissencions mortelles entre
(13)    et adviendront morts et dissensions entre les grans gens,
        Et evenient mortes et dissensiones inter magnos homines

        grans et nobles hommes, et s'esleveront les hommes viles
(14)    et les nobles s'esleveront contre les vilains et les
        et nobiles, et insurgent viles homines et

        et mauvais. Pluseurs minieres d'or et d'argent seront
(15)    mauvais hommes. Et pluseurs minieres d'or et d'argent
        mali homines. Et discooperientur multe minere auri et

        descouvertes. En esté regnera grant chaleur.
(16)    seront descouvertes, et en esté sera grant chaleur.
        argenti, et erit calor magnus tempore estivo.

        Et se celle comecte a regard de la partie d'orient, elle
(17)    Et si elle est de la partie d'orient, elle signifie que
        Et si fuerit a parte orientis, ostendit quod

        demonstre dissension entre les roys de celle partie,
(18)    dissension sera entre les roys d'icelle terre
        erit dissensio inter reges illius (regionis)

        comme en Perse et autres semblables.
(19)    comme en Perse et semblables . . .[b]
        sicut in Persia et in similibus . . .[c]

| | |
|---|---|
| *P.T.* | Et se de la partie d'occident celle comecte se demonstre, |
| *Livre* | Et si elle apparoist de la partie d'occident, |
| *Liber* | Et si apparuerit a parte occidentis, |

| | |
|---|---|
| | elle signifie que les hommes noirs endureront tristesse |
| (21) | elle demonstre que les maures souffreront tristesse |
| | ostendit quod nigri homines patientur tristitiam |

| | |
|---|---|
| | et desplaisir des roys, et y aura bataille entre aucuns |
| (22) | et desplaisance des roys. Et sera guerre entre aucuns |
| | et displicentiam a regibus et erit bellum inter aliquos |

| | |
|---|---|
| | d'eulx avec ceulx d'occident; sera aussi grande |
| (23) | d'eulx avecques ceulx d'occident. Et seront grans |
| | illorum cum illis de occidente. Et erunt pluvie multe |

| | |
|---|---|
| | inundacion de pluies et d'eaues et habondance de fleuves. |
| (24) | pluyes et habondance des rivieres. |
| | et habundantia fluviorum. |

[a] The *Petit Traictié* here adds part of a sentence (some thirty words) linking the subject matter of this chapter to that of chapter 4.

[b] The *Livre de la signification* continues (following the Latin), "et partie des villes d'icelle terre obeira au roy de Babiloine." This phrase is omitted in the *Petit Traictié*.

[c] The *Liber de significatione* continues, "Pars villarum illius terre obediet regi Babilonie." This phrase is omitted in the *Petit Traictié*.

Several instances occur in this passage of insignificant differences in wording between the *Petit Traictié* and the *Livre de la signification*: *a dominacion/domine* (Lat. *dominatur*, line 8); *païs semblables/semblables lieux* (Lat. *similibus*, line 8); *douleur aux yeux/douleur des yeulx* (Lat. *dolores oculorum*, line 11); *autre bestial/autres bestes* (Lat. *aliis pecudibus*, line 12); *a regard de/est de* (Lat. *fuerit a*, line 17); and *demonstre/signifie* (Lat. *ostendit*, lines 17–18). It is difficult to say why the compiler would have made such changes in wording if he had been working directly from the French *Livre* rather than the Latin *Liber*. In this context, it is interesting to note that the Latin word *patientur*, which occurs three times in this short passage (lines 6, 11, 21), was consistently translated *souffreront* in the *Livre de la signification* but was rendered variously by *auront* [*grant paour et grant crainte*] (line 6), *souffreront* [*grans peines et paours*] (line 11), and *endureront* [*magnos timores*] (line 21) in the *Petit Traictié*.[34]

On the other hand, the *Petit Traictié* significantly agrees with the Latin text in its reading of lines 13–14, against the *Livre*, where the sense of the phrase has been distorted. This might indicate that the compiler was following the Latin text only, rather than the French translation. Again, in line 21, the *Petit Traictié* reads *hommes noirs*, in agreement with the Latin *nigri homines*, against *maures* in the *Livre*. Both of these examples argue against the compiler of the *Petit Traictié* and the translator of the *Livre* having been the same individual.

In line 9, the *Livre* and *Liber* agree in reading *roy des cristiens* and *rex Christianorum* respectively as opposed to *roy des rommains* in the *Petit Traictié*. This might be seen as an indication that the compiler felt himself free to take minor liberties with the wording of his model— whether he was using the Latin or the French version of the text.

Such faint and even mutually contradictory hints provide no firm basis for judgment about the precise relations of the three texts. A more provocative hint is that in chapter 5 of the *Petit Traictié* (corresponding to chapter 9 of the *Liber/Livre*) the word *complexion* is used consistently—and correctly—for the Latin *complexio*. The same word, as we have seen, is incorrectly translated by *conjonction* in the *Livre*. While this could hint at different translators, it might mean that between completing his two projects, the translator learned the correct way to expand the Latin abbreviation for *complexio*.

It is clear that the *Petit Traictié* is closely based on the *Liber/Livre*, of which it may fairly be called an abridgment. But it must be recognized as an abridgment of a very special type. The compiler of the *Petit Traictié* had a goal beyond simply preparing a shorter version of the *Liber/Livre*. His objective, in fact, was to create a short, informative, and easily understood layman's guide to the mysterious and important phenomenon of comets. To this end, he employed a variety of techniques, including addition, omission, explanation, and reordering of material.

The compiler of the *Petit Traictié* took his reader by the hand right from the start. In the opening sentence of the work, he added no fewer than three explanatory phrases. Thus a rather dry and formulaic appeal to authority became the vehicle for introducing some half a dozen new terms to the lay reader (additions in italics): "Dit Ptholomee . . . que les estoilles courantes et celles qui ont *crins ou cheveulx ou* comes *comme sont les cometes* ensuivent les autres estoilles *c'est assavoir les fixes ou planectes que l'on nomme estoilles errantes.*"[35] Similar explanatory phrases recur throughout the *Petit Traictié*. The compiler evidently made the assumption that his reader would likely be unfamiliar with even the basic terminology relating to the science of the stars. This can be seen in chapter 4, where an explanatory phrase identifies Aries, Leo, and Sagittarius as signs of the zodiac.

The compiler likewise did not hesitate to alter the syntax of the *Liber/Livre* in order to clarify the text for his reader. Thus, in chapter 2, glosses found in the *Liber/Livre* are integrated smoothly into the syntax of the *Petit Traictié*. The compiler also supplied cross-references at several points in his text, as for example in chapter 2, where he referred the reader to a subsequent chapter: "comme il sera dit ou chapitre des couleurs des comettes" [as it will be said in the chapter on the colors of comets (chapter 5)].

The most obvious indication of the compiler's didactic intention can be seen in the freedom he took in omitting from his work passages—sometimes lengthy—of the *Liber/Livre*. These are of three types: learned references, examples, and technical material, all of which were regularly omitted by the compiler. For example, in chapter 1 he omitted a passage of some six hundred words found in chapter 2 of the *Liber/Livre*. The omitted segment includes: (a) technical material in the form of details about the "diversity and irregularity" of comets and about the different varieties of "running stars"; (b) examples of an actual comet recorded by "Jacob Alquindus" (Al-Kindi) and a comet seen "in our time"; and (c) a reference to the meaning of comets drawn from Ptolemy in the *Quadripartitum*. In chapter 4 (corresponding to chapter 7 of the *Liber/Livre*) the compiler systematically omitted the quotations from "Busahen" that occur at the end of the discussion of each of the four triplicities of zodiacal signs.[36] Citations of Busahen in other chapters, as well as references to authorities such as Aristotle and Masha'Allah, were also often omitted by the compiler.

Descriptions of comets are not the only kinds of examples the compiler chose to omit. In chapter 1 (corresponding to chapter 2 of the *Liber/Livre*), for instance, the compiler simplified his text by leaving out several examples of atmospheric phenomena (omitted portion in italics):

> *come sont les roues qui apparoissent entour le soleil et la lune et l'urc et la rougeur qui apperi devant le soleil levé et apres soleil couché en l'orizon* et toutes autres couleurs qui apparoissent en la spere de l'air.

> [*such as the wheels that appear around the sun and the moon and the rainbow and the redness that appears before sunrise and after sunset on the horizon* and all the other colors that appear in the sphere of air (the atmosphere).]

23

An example of the type of technical material the compiler evidently considered too difficult for his intended reader can be seen in chapter 1 of the *Petit Traictié*, shortly after the lengthy omission described above. After defining comets as a product of ignited vapors, the compiler left out the discussion found in the *Liber/Livre* of the way in which the vapors catch fire and burn (chapter 2 of the *Liber/Livre*). In his second chapter, the compiler similarly chose to omit a passage some 150 words in length that digressed to discuss the working (*operacion*) of eclipses (chapter 5 of the *Liber/Livre*).[37]

But the compiler of the *Petit Traictié* took greater—and more significant—liberties with the *Liber/Livre* than those already described. He freely rearranged the order of his material, omitted several chapters of his model altogether, and added two new chapters. The compiler utilized the chapters of the *Liber/Livre* in the following order: chapter 1, 2, 5, 6, 7, 9, 8. Chapters 3, 4, and 10–16 of the *Liber/Livre* were discarded. Why? The compiler may have chosen to omit chapters 3 and 4 of his model because of their rather dry and repetitive contents; the two chapters consist largely of lists of the names of various kinds of comets in Latin and Arabic. This material is repeated in chapter 9 of the *Liber/Livre*, which provided the basis for chapter 5 of the *Petit Traictié*. The final seven chapters of the *Liber/Livre* (chapters 10–16) detail the various consequences that follow the appearance of a comet and give examples of historical comets. The compiler may well have felt that this material provided more detail than necessary for his intended readers.

Chapters 7 and 8 of the *Petit Traictié* were added by the compiler. They do not correspond to any of the material included in the *Liber/Livre*. These brief chapters discuss the planets, giving the characteristics of each (chapter 7) and its zodiacal house (chapter 8). The compiler evidently felt that his readers would benefit from this information, which was basic to an understanding of the significance of comets because each comet-type was considered to correspond to a particular

24

planet. A particular comet-type's significance was determined by its planet, and the influence of the planet in turn was affected by the sign in which it was located when the comet appeared.

The compiler may have drawn these brief additions from one of the many introductory texts to the science of the stars that were quite common in the later Middle Ages. The most widely known of these works, the *Introductorium maius* of Abū Ma'shar, seems not to have been the source for these chapters, since it gives at least a full page of text to the description of each planet. Another common source for this type of material was the *Centiloquium*, but it contains no section corresponding to these chapters of the *Petit Traictié.*[38] It is possible—and even likely, in view of the brevity of these chapters—that the compiler may have composed them himself to round out the useful information in his work.

In reworking the material provided him by his model, the compiler exercised the greatest freedom—and took the most care—in his treatment of chapter 5. This chapter forms the centerpiece to the entire work, in its clearly organized presentation of the name and appearance of each comet-type. This information naturally was of central importance to any study of comets, since the determination of a comet's astrological effect depended on its identification as one of the comet-types. It is clear that the compiler viewed this chapter as the keystone of his work; the elaborate illustrations that accompany this chapter (and only this chapter) in all the manuscripts testify to this.[39]

The compiler's rearrangement of, and alterations to, his model for this chapter (chapter 9 of the *Liber/Livre*) likewise emphasizes its centrality in the work. The compiler left out a passage of three hundred words or more at the beginning of the chapter, in order to begin directly with the nine types of comets according to Ptolemy. In the description of several of the comet-types, the compiler added items of information not found anywhere in the *Liber/Livre*. It is interesting to note that many

25

of these items *do* occur in *De Essentia/De l'Essence*; thus, the compiler almost certainly utilized this work in addition to the *Liber/Livre*. In fact, Giles of Lessines could be the individual intended by the name "Giles of Rome" given in the rubric.[40] Most important, the compiler's addition of the comet-type Domina Capillorum to the list of nine comet-types, for a total of ten types, was very likely based on the discussion of Domina Capillorum in *De Essentia/De l'Essence* (chapter 9). The two passages correspond closely, with some differences in exact wording. The attribution of this comet-type in *De Essentia/De l'Essence* to "Haly in his commentary on the next-to-the-last *verbum* of the *Centiloquium*" may have influenced the compiler in his decision to include it in a list of comet-types attributed to Ptolemy.

In addition, the compiler added the derivation of the names of the comet-types Rosa and Gebea; the remark that the comet-type Veru always appears near the sun; and the description of the rays of the comet-type Pertica as large and dark. All these items of information can be found in *De Essentia/De l'Essence.* A similar instance is the addition of the well-known anecdote drawn from Seneca, concerning the appearance of a historical comet; the same anecdote is related in chapter 6 of *De Essentia/De l'Essence.*

Somewhat puzzling is the compiler's reordering of the types of comets. Aurora is second in the *Petit Traictié*, replacing Azcuna which comes second in the *Liber/Livre*; in the *Petit Traictié* Azcuna is fifth in the list, a shift that appears to be arbitrary.

The cumulative effect of the various alterations wrought by the compiler in his adaptation and abridgment of the *Liber/Livre* reveals the deliberate nature of his work. His additions, omissions, and explanations were the tools he used to craft a new work from an old one. He composed with care and deliberate intent a guide to understanding the phenomenon of comets, suitable for the lay reader of the late fifteenth century. The *Petit Traictié*, in fact, is a work of expository prose that largely eschews the jargon both of the "science of the stars" and of scholastic style. In its stylistic simplicity, the *Petit Traictié* fits into the tradition of scientific texts translated into the vernacular for cultivated and intellectually curious members of the nobility.[41] The *Petit Traictié*, then, can properly be viewed as a skillful job of popularization of a topic of compelling interest to many people in late fifteenth-century Europe—a topic normally treated in rather abstruse and thorny treatises in the learned tongue. The success of this layman's guide, complemented by its apt illustrations, can be judged to some extent by its longevity, which included at least a century of successive editions, in manuscript and print.

Taken together, the *Petit Traictié* and its companion works, the *Livre de la signification* and *De l'Essence*, embody the complex nature of "translation" in the late Middle Ages. From literal and mechanical to loose and idiosyncratic, late medieval translations can best be viewed as a continuum, the exact placement of any particular translation depending on numerous factors, from the clarity and legibility of the original to the knowledge and skill of the translator, and the translator's aim and audience. On such a continuum, the *Livre de la signification* and *De l'Essence* would be placed near one end, the *Petit Traictié* near the other. But the literalness of the two translations and the comparative freedom of the compilation do not eliminate the possibility that all might be the work of a single individual. We just cannot tell.

## Appendix

Handlist of Known Manuscripts Containing Astronomical
and Astrological Works in French

No comprehensive catalogue exists of medieval French works on astronomy and astrology, the subject matter collectively known in the Middle Ages as "the science of

# Lys Ann Shore

the stars." Yet dozens of such works are known, some translated from Latin, others seemingly composed or compiled in French. The following list is an interim attempt to fill this gap. It includes approximately fifty manuscripts of the late thirteenth through the late fifteenth centuries. The results presented, while preliminary, provide a glimpse of the wealth of material that exists.[42] The list collects and summarizes information found in secondary sources, such as histories and library catalogues. Very few of the texts contained in these manuscripts have been published or discussed; often, the only information available consists of very brief indications of manuscript contents and date, or the title and authorship of individual works.[43] I have listed under the heading "Contents" only those works in a manuscript that relate to astronomy or astrology; fuller information can be obtained from the sources noted. "Comments" refer to a specific work unless it is explicitly stated that they refer to the entire manuscript. The following source abbreviations are used in the list:

AAAS    F. Carmody, *Arabic Astronomical and Astrological Sciences in Latin Translation: A Critical Bibliography* (Berkeley: University of California Press, 1956).

AWIE    R. Levy, *The Astrological Works of Abraham Ibn Ezra, a Literary and Linguistic Study* (Baltimore: Johns Hopkins University Press, 1928).

BCV    R. Delachenal, "Note sur un manuscrit de la bibliothèque de Charles V," *Bibliothèque de l'Ecole des Chartes* 71 (1910): 33–38.

Bib. Imp.    Catalogue des manuscrits français: Bibliothèque impériale, vol. 1 (Paris: Firmin Didot, 1868).

BPD    *Catalogue général des manuscrits des bibliothèques publiques de France: Départements*, vol. 5 (Paris: Plon, 1859), vol. 7 (Paris: Plon, 1899), vol. 24 (Paris: Plon, 1894), vol. 25 (Paris: Plon, 1894).

BSG    Ch. Kohler, *Catalogue des manuscrits de la Bibliothèque Sainte-Geneviève*, 2 vols. (Paris: Plon, 1893–96).

BU E.    Chatelain, *Catalogue des manuscrits de la Bibliothèque de l'Université* (Paris: Champion, 1892).

CCB    H. Hagen, *Catalogus codicum Bernensium (Bibl. Bongarsiana)* (Hildesheim: Olms, 1974).

CM L.    Delisle, *Le Cabinet des manuscrits*, 4 vols. (Paris, 1868–81; repr. New York: Imprimerie Nationale, 1973).

# The Continuum of Translation

Coxe    H. Coxe, *Catalogus codicum manuscriptorum qui in collegiis aulisque oxon. hodie adservantur*, vol. 1 (Oxford: E. Typographeo Academico, 1852).

DSB    *Dictionary of Scientific Biography* (New York: Scribner's, 1970–80).

Duhem    P. Duhem, *Le Système du monde*, vol. 8 (Paris: Hermann, 1958).

Edgren    R. Edgren, *Mahieu le Vilain: Les Metheores d'Aristote* (Uppsala: n.p., 1945).

HLF    *Histoire littéraire de la France*, vol. 21 (Paris: Palme, 1847), vol. 25 (Paris: Palme, 1849), vol. 30 (Paris: Palme, 1888), vol. 35 (Paris: Palme, 1921).

HMES    L. Thorndike, *A History of Magic and Experimental Science*, vols. 1–2: *The First Thirteen Centuries of Our Era* (New York: Columbia University Press, 1923), vols. 3–4: *Fourteenth and Fifteenth Centuries* (New York: Columbia University Press, 1934).

IRHT    F. Vielliard, personal communication, 21 August 1981.

Lemay    R. Lemay, personal communications, 30 September 1978, 26 December 1982.

LOA    F. Carmody, *Leopold of Austria, Li Compilacions de le science des estoilles* (Berkeley: University of California Press, 1947).

Martin    H. Martin, *Catalogue général des manuscrits de la Bibliothèque de l'Arsenal*, vols. 1–3 (Paris: Plon, 1885–87).

MD    A. Menut and A. Denomy, *Nicole Oresme, Le Livre du ciel et du monde* (Madison, Wis.: University of Wisconsin Press, 1968).

NOA    G. Coopland, *Nicole Oresme and the Astrologers* (Cambridge, Mass.: Harvard University Press, 1952).

Omont    H. Omont, *Bibliothèque nationale, Catalogue général des manuscrits français (Ancien petit-fonds français II . . .)* (Paris: Imprimerie Nationale, 1902).

OSK    R. Lemay, "Origin and Success of the Kitāb Thamara . . . ," in *Aleppo University, Proceedings of the First International Symposium for the History of Arabic Science, 5–12 April, 1976* (Aleppo: University of Aleppo Institute for the History of Arabic Science, 1978).

Petau    H. Aubert, "Notices sur les manuscrits Petau . . . ," *Bibliothèque de l'Ecole des Chartes* 70 (1909): 247–302, 407–522.

# Lys Ann Shore

PLB     G. Doutrepont, *Inventaire de la "librairie" de Philippe le Bon (1420)* (Geneva, 1977).

Poulle     E. Poulle, *Un Constructeur d'instruments astronomiques au XV$^e$ siècle: Jean Fusoris* (Paris: Champion, 1963).

RCV     C. Sherman, "Representations of Charles V of France (1338–1380) as a Wise Ruler," *Mediaevalia et Humanistica* n.s. 2 (1971): 83–96.

Scott     J. Scott, *Index to the Sloane Manuscripts in the British Museum* (London: British Museum, 1904).

SGP     L. Delisle, *Inventaire des manuscrits de Saint-German-des-Prés . . .* (Paris: Durand, 1868).

SHS     S. Ayscough, *A Catalogue of the Manuscripts Preserved in the British Museum . . .* (London: J. Rivington, 1782).

Skeat     W. Skeat, *A Treatise on the Astrolabe . . . by Geoffrey Chaucer* (London, 1872; repr. New York: Johnson, 1967).

Sherman     C. Sherman, personal communication, 29 November 1982.

Trinity     M. James, *The Western Manuscripts in the Library of Trinity College, Cambridge: A Descriptive Catalogue*, vol. 3 (Cambridge: Cambridge University Press, 1902).

UI     "Inventario dei manoscritti regin. (Bibl. Apost. Vat.)," microfilm, Pius XII Memorial Library, St. Louis University, St. Louis, Mo.

VDG     J. Van den Gheyn, *Catalogue des manuscrits de la Bibliothèque royale de Belgique*, vol. 4: *Jurisprudence et philosophie* (Brussels: Lamertin, 1904).

Wisdom     R. Levy, ed., *Abraham Ibn Ezra, The Beginning of Wisdom* (Baltimore: Johns Hopkins University Press, 1939).

| Shelfmark | Contents | Comments |
|---|---|---|
| Paris, Arsenal 1037 (Martin 2) | Begins fol. 8$^v$, William of Saint-Cloud, *Directorium* (*L'Adrescoir*). Inc. "Presens ingenium" ("Tres haute dame"). | Lat. text followed by Fr. tr. |
| Paris, BN fr. 1353 (anc. 7485) (AAAS, 49ff.; Lemay; Bib. Imp. 1; Duhem 3: 130; 8: 401ff.) | Fols. 7–66, Anon., *Introductoire d'astronomie* (in verse). Inc. "Por ce que la science." | Dedicated to Baldwin of Courtenay. |
| | Fols. 66ff., Abu'l-Hasan 'Ali, *Le Livre des nativités des enfanz*. Inc. "Ou nom de Nostre Segnor, dist Abu Ali." | Tr. of *De judiciis nativitatum*. Based on Lat. of Plato of Tivoli. |
| | Fols. 80ff., Māshā'Allāh, *Epistre des choses des eclipses*. Inc. "Cist premiers capitles, dist Messehalah." | Tr. of *Epistula de lunae eclipsis et planetis*. |
| | Fols. 83ff., Abū Ma'shar, *Li Livres des flors de Albumaxar*. Inc. "En cest livre commencerons." | AAAS does not list this text among MS contents. |
| | Fols. 95ff., Anon., *Le Livre des corruptions de l'air*. Inc. "Entre les jugemenz." | |
| Paris, BN fr. 24276 (anc. Sorbonne 1825) (HMES 2: 926; DSB "Henry Bate"; Omont; AWIE 20f.; LOA 51; AAAS 95; Wisdom) | To fol. 66, Ibn Ezra, *Li Livres du commencement de sapience*. | Tr. by Hagin the Jew, 1273. Ed. Wisdom. |
| | Fols. 66–100, Ibn Ezra, *Livre des jugemens des nativités*. | |
| | Begins fol. 100, Abū Ma'shar, *Le Livre Even-Masar des revolucions du siecle*. | Frag. (2 chaps. and part of a third). |
| | Fols. 104–13, Ibn Ezra, *Livre des élections*. | Sections bound in incorrect order. |
| | Fols. 113–25, Ibn Ezra, *Le Livre des interrogations*. | |

| Shelfmark | Contents | Comments |
|---|---|---|
| Bern, Bib. Bongarsiana 310 (MD; CCB) | Fols. 1–27, Nicole Oresme, *Traitie de l'espere* | Fragment. |
| | Fols. 28–152, Nicole Oresme, *Le Livre du ciel et du monde.* | Tr. of Aristotle, *De caelo.* Ed. MD. |
| Brussels, Bib. roy. de Belgique 2903 (11200) (VDG 4; Edgren) | 102 fols., Mahieu le Vilain, *Les Metheores.* | Tr. of Aristotle, *Meteorologica.* Ed. Edgren. MS made for Charles V. |
| Brussels, Bib. roy. de Belgique 11203–04 (2305) (PLB 109f.; VDG 3) | Fols. 56–74, Nicole Oresme, *Le Livre de divinacions.* | Ed. NOA, 49ff., but this MS is not discussed. |
| Cambridge Univ., Trinity 1313 (2 vols.) (Trinity 3; HMES 2: 221n) | 1. On divination. | Perh. an extract from *Kyranides.* |
| | 2. Treatise on numbers. | |
| | 3. On geometry. Inc. "Un sage autour de geometrie dist." | |
| | 4. Hermes Trismegistus, *Le Livre Hermes le Philosofre parlaunt des 15 esteilles greyndres fixes . . .* | Tr. of *De quindecim stellis.* |
| | 5. Fols. 25–28, *Lunarie* (in verse). Inc. "Cy comence vne sommarye / que lem apele la lunarie." | Followed by a table of lucky and unlucky days. |
| | 6. Vol. 2, Treatise on medicine in Latin & French. Inc. "Quoniam omnia vicia a capite procedunt." | Fr. begins fol. 3b, with no break in text. |

| | | |
|---|---|---|
| Cambridge Univ., Trinity 1447 (Trinity 3; HMES 2, 120n) | Fols. 1–112, William of Moerbeke, *Livre de geomancie.* Inc. "En lonor de dieu pere filz et saint esperit." | Tr. by Walter of Brittany, 1347. MS belonged to Charles V in 1373. |
| | Fols. 132–38, *Le Livre eufrate.* Exp. "et puet passer et avoirfilz. Explic t." | |
| | Fols. 138–39, *La Raison de l'espere pictagoras iadis philosofre.* Exp. "Et saturne du samedi. deo gracias." | |
| Oxford Univ., St. John's College 164 (Lemay; HMES 3: 586f; Coxe 1; NOA 184f; CM 3: 336f; Sherman; RCV) | Fols. 1–32, Nicole Oresme, *De l'espere.* | MS belonged to Charles V. Dated to 1377 on the basis of horoscopes of royal family. |
| | Fols. 33–111, Pèlerin de Prusse, work on astrology in 3 parts. Inc. "En nom du tres misericors et piteos." | |
| | Fols. 111–19, Pèlerin de Prusse, *Tractatulus de usu astrolabii.* Inc. "La science du firmament et du mouvement des estoiles." | |
| | Fols. 119–58, al'Qabīsī, *Introductorium.* Inc. "Require de notre seigneu prolixité de vie." | From the Lat. tr. by John of Spain. |
| Paris, Arsenal 2872 (101 S.A.F.) (Martin 3; BCV; MD 5n; HLF 35: 628; LOA 50; AAAS 66) | Fols. 1–21, William of Saint-Cloud, *Kalendrier.* Inc. "Si come Vegesce tesmoigne en son livre." | Tr. by William of Saint-Cloud from his own Lat. text. |
| | Fol. 21$^v$, William of Saint-Cloud, *L'Adrescoir.* | Tr. by William of Saint-Cloud from his own Lat. text. |
| | Begins fol. 22, *L'Agregacion des secrés de nature ajoustéz des livres des sages philozophes.* Inc. "Le glorieus Dieux de nature fit le monde." | |

| Shelfmark | Contents | Comments |
|---|---|---|
| Paris, Arsenal 2872 (cont.) | Fols. 38–57, *Le Livre des secréz de nature sur la vertu des oyseauls et des poissons, pierres et herbes et bestes*. Inc. "Le glorieus Dieux devant toutes choses fist nature de sa benigne grace." | Tr. of *Kiranides*. |
| | Fols. 57–79, *Le Livre de Ypocras sur la conjunction de la lune es 12 signes*. Inc. "Le tres sage Ypocras de touz les mirez expert et soutil." | |
| | Fols. 79–83, Mâshâ'Allâh, *Epistre sur la nature et signification des 12 signes*. Inc. "En nom de Dieu Nostre Seigneur commence l'espitre Messahala." | |
| | Fols. 83–84, *Le Livre de Seni le philozophe*. Inc. "Ou nom du puissant Seigneur qui a tout fait et fourmé." | |
| | Fols. 84–85, *Le Livre que les philozophes de Rome firent sur l'entree du jour de l'an*. | |
| | Fols. 85–309, *Le Livre des 9 anciens juges de astrologie*. Inc. "La fourme du ciel qui est ronde." | Tr. Robert Godefroy, 1361. Tr. of *Liber novem judicum*. |
| | Fols. 394–97, *Le Livre des mansions de la lune*. Inc. "Ce sont les 28 mansions de la lune." | |
| | Fol. 397, *Doctrine de Socrates prise sur la nature des 12 signes*. | |
| | Fol. 398–400, *Le Livre de l'influence de la lune sur les XII signes*. Inc. "Cant la lune sera ou signe de Aries." | |

| | | |
|---|---|---|
| Paris, BN fr. 613 (anc. 7095) (LOA; Bib. Imp.; HLF 35: 630ff.; AAAS 74, 96, 152) | Fols. 1–86, Leopold of Austria, *Li Compilacions de le science des estoilles*. Inc. "Li glorieus dieus et li tres haus." | Tr. of Leopold of Austria, *Compilatio*, Bks. 1–8, followed without break by tr. of "Ali ibn Abi'l-Rijāl, *De judiciis astrorum*, Bk.7, labeled "traité neuf." Ed. LOA. |
| | Fols. 87–133, *Introductoires d'astronomie*. Inc. "Ch'est uns introductoires d'astronomie que uns philosophes traita por un empereur de Romme." | End of *Introductoires* is lost (LOA). |
| | Fols. 135–38, *Le Figure et le machine dou monde*. Inc. "Li entencions de nous si est de descrire en che traitié le figure et le machine doue monde." | Attrib. in MS to Robert Grosseteste. End of text is lost (LOA). |
| | Fols. 138–44, *Les Images cooriens en 12 signes*. Inc. "Li commencement des quartes est horoscopus." | Partial tr. of a Gr. work attrib. to Hermes Trismegistus. |
| | Fols. 144–45, *Centiloges Bethem*. Inc. "Chi commenche li centiloges Bethem. Je commencheroy le livre des coustumes et des jugemens des estoilles." | Based on the Lat. tr. of Plato of Tivoli or Peter of Abano (AAAS, 74). |
| | Fols. 145–47, Abū Ma'shar, *Elections*. Inc. "Chi commenche Albumazar des Elections selonc les regars et les conjonctions de le lune as planettes." | Tr. by Arnoul de Quinquempoix. |
| | Fols. 147–49, tract on climates. Inc. "Sachiés que li planettes ont .iii. lius." | |
| Paris, BN fr. 1082 (anc. 7350) (MD; Bib. Imp.) | Fols. 1–203, Nicole Oresme, *Le Livre du ciel et du monde* | MS served as base MS for edn. (MD). |

| Shelfmark | Contents | Comments |
|---|---|---|
| Paris, BN fr. 1349 (anc. 7483$^{2-2}$ Colbert 988) (OSK 105n; LOA 47n; Lemay; Bib. Imp.) | Begins fol. 1, Ptolemy, *Quadripartitum*. Inc. "Ci commence le prologue Giles de Thebaldes, lombard, qui translata cest livre. Savoir et entendre est glorieuse chose." | Fr. tr. of *Quadripartitum* based on Lat. of Aegidius de Tebaldis; based on Sp. tr. of Arabic comm. of 'Ali ibn Ridwan. MS owned by Charles V in 1373. |
| | Begins fol. 215, Ptolemy, *Centiloquium*. Inc. "Ptholomé dist: Iesure ie tai ia escrit livres de que les estoiles font." | Fr. tr. based on Latin of Plato of Tivoli. |
| | Begins fol. 245, William of Aragon, Sentence on *Centiloquium*. Inc. "Si come dit Ptholomé ou proverbe del Almages." | |
| Rennes, Bib. Mun. 593 (BPD 24; HLF 35: 628n) | Fols. 1–8, Peter Philomena, *La Lettre a savoir le vrai cours de la lune par le qualendrier mestre Pierre de Dace, dit Rosignol* and William of Saint-Cloud, *La Lettre a savoir le novel Kalendrier que mestre Guillaume de St Cloot fit*. | MS dated 1303. |
| | Fols. 41–43, Ibn Tibbon, *Almanach*. Inc. "Si conmenche le canon sus l'almenach au juif." | |
| | Fols. 167–70, *Le Lunaire de Salmon*. Inc. "Salmon, qui ot toute la saingnorie d'escripture et de clergie." | |
| | Fols. 170–284, Brunetto Latini, *Li Livres dou Tresor*. | |
| | Fols. 320–471, *Le Livre de Sydrac*. | |

| Shelfmark | Contents | Comments |
| --- | --- | --- |
| Dijon, Bib. Mun. 447 (Poulle 7; BPD 5) | Fols. 82–97, Jean Fusoris, *Le Traictie de l'astrolabe*. Inc. "En l'astrolabe sont diverses choses." | Dedicated to Pierre de Navarre. Ed. Poulle. MS also incl. astronomical texts in Latin. |
| Dijon, Bib. Mun. 449 (270) (LOA 47n; HMES 3: 263n; AAAS 144ff.; BPD 5) | Fols. 65–97, al'Qabīsī, *Abbreviationes Alkabicii*. Inc. "Albumasar dist que quant l'astronomien voldra d'aucune chose jugier." | Fr. tr. of John of Saxony's comm. on al'Qabīsī, *Isagogus*. |
| | Begins fol. 97, Ptolemy, *Centiloquium*. Inc. "Ptolomeus dist: Jhesure je t'ay ja escript." | Copied by Pierre Pevidic, med. student, Univ. of Dole, dated 14 Feb. 1459. MS contains several astrological texts in Latin. |
| Geneva, Lat. 80 (Petau 53) (Petau 290ff.; Poulle 7) | Fols. 46–59, Jean Fusoris, *La Pratique de l'astrolabe*. | Treatise on the use of the astrolabe. Ed. Poulle. |
| Grenoble, Bib. Mun. 814 (HMES 2: 256n; BPD 7; AAAS 29) | Fols. 1–24, *Le Livre de jugemens d'astrologie selon Aristote* (in 4 parts). Inc. "Le prologue du derrenier translateur. Aristote fist un livre de jugemens." | Compare MS contents with MS Paris, BN fr. 1083. |
| | Fols. 24–34, Māshā'Allāh, *Des conjonctions et receptions et interrogations*. Inc. "Un des sages trouva un des livres." | Tr. for Charles V, 1359. |
| | Fols. 34–40, Māshā'Allāh, *Le Traitié Messahallac arabes pour scavoir la pensee et la cogitation d'aucun qui veut demander d'aucune chose*. Inc. "Le premier chapitre: Messahallac commanda." | Based on tr. by John of Spain. |

| Shelfmark | Contents | Comments |
|---|---|---|
| Grenoble, Bib. Mun. 814 (cont.) | Fols. 40–66, Sahl, *Le Livre des jugemens d'astrologie*. Inc. "En nom de Nostre Seigneur plain de pitié et de misericorde, Zehel, homme du peuple d'Israel." | Tr. for Charles V, 1359. |
| London, BL Sloane 314 (HMES 2: 120n; Scott; SHS; Skeat xii) | Fols. 2–64, *Filia astronomiae*. Inc. "Et est Gremmgi Indyana, que vocatur filia astronomie quam fecit unus sapientum Indie." | Geomancy, in Lat. & Fr. MS also contains Chaucer's *Treatise on the Astrolabe*. |
| London, BL Sloane 420 (Scott; SHS) | *Livre de duze signes*. | This is the sole Fr. text in a coll. of Lat. medical works. |
| Moscow, Lenin State Libr., Western European MSS, Fond 183, no. 357. | Fols. 1–15, *Petit traictié de la signification des cometes*. | |
| Paris, Arsenal 2911 (208 S.A.F.) (HLF 35: 629f.; LOA 40n; Martin 3) | Guido Bonati, astrological and meteorological treatises. | Tr. by Nicolas de La Horbe, 1327. |
| | Begins fol. 16, *La premiere partie de ce livre nommé Introductoire*. Inc "... ou impossible et non sur ce qui est possible n'est pas vraye." | Incomplete at beginning. |
| | Fols. 99–156, *La deuziesme partie de ce livre laquelle est des Interrogations*. Inc. "Savoir devez que se le seigneur de l'ascendent." | Compare MS contents with MS Valenciennes, Bib. de la ville 348. |
| | Begins fol. 156, *La troiziesme partie de ce livre laquelle est des Elections*. | |
| | Begins fol. 185, *La quatriesme partie de ce livre laquelle est des Revolutions tant du monde comme des nativités ou interrogations universelles*. | |

| | | |
|---|---|---|
| Paris, Arsenal 2911 (cont.) | Begins fol. 259, *La cinquiesme partie de ce livre laquelle est des Nativitéz.* | |
| | Begins fol. 344, *La viͤ et derniere partie de ce livre, divisee en trois traictéz: 1° Des pluyes et mutacions de l'air.* | MS is incomplete; stops after opening lines of chap. 40 of *Des pluyes.* |
| Paris, Arsenal nouv. acq. 10020 (AAAS 151) | 'Alī ibn Abi'l-Rijāl, *De judiciis.* | Fr. tr. based on Lat. of Aegidius de Tebaldis. |
| Paris, Bib. Sainte-Geneviève 2521 (Z.f. in-4° 17) (HMES 4: 146f.; BSG; Poulle 7) | Fols. 37–57, Jehan de Bruges, *Le Livre des grandes conjonctions et mouvemens du ciel et des jugemens sur iceulx, fait et compillé par maistre Jehan de Bruges, medicin et astrologien estudiant en l'Université de Louvain.* Inc. "Le premier chapitre qui fait mention de la nature de l'escorpion." | Composed in 1444. |
| | Begins fol. 73, Tract on astronomy & astrology. Inc. "Zodiaque est ung cercle ou ciel, divisé en xii parties." Exp. " . . . et quant il estincelle fcrt en yver et est fort cler, c'est signe de forte gellee. Finis." | |
| | Begins fol. 91, Jean Fusoris, Treatise on the use of the astrolabe. Inc. "En l'astrolabe sont diverses choses." | Ed. Poulle. Treatise is incomplete in this MS. |
| | Begins fol. 113, Treatise of astral horoscopy. Inc. "Comme il soit ainsi que toutes choses de ce monde soient gouvernees par la vertu." Exp. "tant l'omme comme la femme viveront loyaulment." | |
| Paris, Bib. de la Sorbonne 571 (MD; BU) | Fols. 1–226, Nicole Oresme, *Le Livre du ciel et du monde.* | Tr. of Aristotle, *De caelo.* Ed. MD. |

| Shelfmark | Contents | Comments |
|---|---|---|
| Paris, BN fr. 565 (anc. 7065) (MD; Bib. Imp.) | Fols. 1–22, Nicole Oresme, *Traitié de l'espere*. | |
| | Fols. 23–168, Nicole Oresme, *Le Livre du ciel et du monde*. | Tr. of Aristotle, *De caelo*. Ed. MD. |
| Paris, BN fr. 612 (anc. 7094) (LOA 50; Bib. Imp.) | Fols. 1–162, Jehan de Beauvau, *Livre de la figure et de l'imaige du monde*. Inc. "Ainsi que le philozophe dit en son premier livre De anima avoir certainement la science." Exp. "du rivaige de laquelle est attaint deux fois par an le terme d'Ynde par navigacion." | Composed in 1479 and dedicated to Louis XI. |
| Paris, BN fr. 1083 (anc. 7350², Colbert 3230) (MD; LOA 50f.; AAAS 27; Bib. Imp.) | Fols. 1–122, Nicole Oresme, *Le Livre du ciel et du monde*. | Tr. of Aristotle, *De caelo*. Ed. MD. |
| | Fols. 126–47, Nicole Oresme, *Traitié de l'espere*. | |
| | Fols. 146–71, *Le Livre des jugemens d'astrologie selon Aristote*. Inc. "Des signes les uns sont appelléz masculins ou de masculin gendre." Exp. "des planetes et par les eclipses qui aviennent en l'annee." | Tr. for Charles V (while still dauphin). Compare MS contents with MS Grenoble, Bib. mun. 814. |
| | Fols. 171–82, Māshā'Allāh, *Le Livre Messehallac astrologien des conjoncions et recepcions es interrogacions*. Inc. "Un des saiges trouva un des livres des secréz des estoiles." Exp. "c'estoit l'aversaire contraint a ce, du plaisir de Dieu." | Tr. 1359. Tr. of Māshā'Allāh, *De recepcione*, based on Lat. of John of Seville. |
| | Fol. 183, Māshā'Allāh, *Traité Messehallac arabe pour savoir la pensee et la cogitacion d'aucun qui veult demander d'aucune chose*. Inc. "Messehallac commande que tu constitues." Exp. "et avec les significacions des figures." | Tr. of Māshā'Allāh, *De occultis*. |
| | Fols. 184–86, Māshā'Allāh, *Livre des choses occultes et mustees*. Inc. "Ou nom de Dieu commence le livre des interpretacions." Exp. "qui estoient moins saiges en ces ars." | |

| Paris, BN fr. 1083 (cont.) | Begins fol. 186, Māshā'Allāh, *Le Epistre Messehallac des choses des eclipses de la lune et du soleil*. Inc. "Dist Messehallac que le treshau t Seigneur fist la terre." Exp. "c'est ce derrenier que nous avons prononcé en cest livre." | Tr. of Māshā'Allāh, *Epistula de lunae eclipsis et planetis*. |
|---|---|---|
| | Begins fol. 189, Sahl, *Le Livre que fist Zehel des jugemens d'astrologie*. Inc. "Ou nom de Nostre Seigneur, plain de pitié et de misericorde, Zehel, homme du peuple d'Ysrael." Exp. "ou telles autres choses le moiteur ou moilleur." | Tr. 1359. Tr. of Sahl, *De judiciis astrorum*. |
| Paris, BN fr. 1339 (anc. $7482^2$, Bigot 145) (Poulle 7, 14; Bib. Imp.) | Fols. 115–28, Jean Fusoris, Treatise on the use of the astrolabe. | Ed. Poulle. |
| | Fols. 128–39, Jean Fusoris, Composition of the astrolabe. | Ed. Poulle. |
| Paris, BN fr. 1348 (anc. $7483^2$: (BCV 37–38; LOA 47n; NOA 181n; Bib. Imp.; RCV) | Ptolemy, *Quadripartitum*. Inc. "Anciennement le commun langage du peuple romain estoit latin." Exp. "ce sont les reglez et racines et principes parquoy ceste art est composee." | Tr. Guillaume (or Nicole?) Oresme. |
| Paris, BN fr. 1350 (anc. $7483^6$, Colbert 4270) (NOA; Bib. Imp.) | Fols. 1–38, Nicole Oresme, *Traitié de l'espere*. | |
| | Fols. 39–61, Nicole Oresme, *Le Livre de divinacions*. | Ed. NOA. MS served as base MS for edn. |
| Paris, BN fr. 1351 (anc. 7484) (Bib. Imp.; AWIE, 30ff.) | 1. Ibn Ezra, *Le Livre des jugemens d'astronomie, des nativitéz, et des élections*. Inc. "Commencail de sapience, c'est cremeur de Dieu." Exp. "a cellui sire qui a estandu les ars. Amen." | Tr. Hagin the Jew. Compare contents of MS Paris, BN fr. 24276. |

| Shelfmark | Contents | Comments |
| --- | --- | --- |
| Paris, BN fr. 1351 (cont.) | 2. Ibn Ezra, *Le Livre des jugemens des nativités*. Inc. "Ce dist nostre maistre Abraham le sage l'advertissant." Exp. "et ou signe deux 2 et es chevilles." | |
| | 3. Ibn Ezra, *Le Livre des élections*. Inc. "Les sages de la loy s'octroient que l'omme a bien povoir." Exp. "le lieu de Venus ou de Jupiter ainsidirent les anciens." | |
| | 4. Ibn Ezra, *Le Livre des questions de Abraham Ibn Ezra*. Inc. "Les chiefs d'astronomie furent deulx." | Dated 1477 by scribe Viennot Pingot, Paris. |
| Paris, BN fr. 1352 (anc.) 7484³ Colbert 1911) (Bib. Imp.; LOA 48) | Begins fol. 3, 'Ali ibn Abi'l-Rijāl, *Le Grant livre des jugemens de astronmie*. Inc. "Je rens graces a Dieu qui est un seul." Exp. "qui scet toutes les choses passees, presentes et futures, lequel soit loé et glorifié. Amen." | Tr. of 'Ali ibn Abi'l-Rijāl, *De judiciis astrorum* (opening books only, through Bk. 7). Bk. 7 is also found in MS Paris, BN fr. 613. |
| Paris, BN fr. 1354 (anc. 7485³, Colbert 2150) (Bib. Imp.) | Treatise on astrology. Inc. "V. Boins jours pour amender aucune chose aux princes, et parler as rois et aquerre bestes." Exp. "ce senefie larons et reubeurs d'avoir." | |
| Paris, BN fr. 1355 (anc. 7485³·³, de Boze 16) (Bib. Imp.) | 1. Treatise on judicial astrology. Inc. "Pour avoir le congnoissance des nativités, nous traicterons de le nutricion de l'effant." Exp. "juge qu'il vient pour chose perdue." | MS dated 1469. |
| | 2. Begins fol. 73, *Le Livre des passions astrologiques*. Inc. "Ou nom de la tres glorieuse et tres beneoitte Trinité." Exp. "en toutes couleurs fors en noires." | By Nicholas Monvel de Blaringhem? See MS Paris, BN fr. 2074. |
| | 3. Begins fol. 181, *Le Senefiance de la lune*. Inc. "Aries est ung signe cault et secq." | Followed in MS by "quaedam astrologica" (Bib. Imp.) |

| Paris, BN fr. 2071 (anc. 7942) | Fols. 3–19, *Petit traictié de la signification des comectes.* <br><br> Fols. 2 –72, Giles of Lessines, *De l'essence et mouvement et signification des cometes.* | Tr. of Giles of Lessines, *De essentia, motu et significatione cometarum.* |
|---|---|---|
| Paris, BN fr. 2074 (anc. 7944) (Bib. Imp.) | Nicolas Monvel de Blaringhem, *Le Livre des passions astrologikes.* Inc. "On non de la tres glorieuse et tres beneoitte sainte Trinité de paradis." | Text incomplete. |
| Paris, BN fr. 2078 & 2079 (anc. 7945 & 7945²) (Bib. Imp.) | 1. *Theorica planetarum.* Inc. "A icelle oevre des mouvemens des planettes, tant en longitude comme en latitude, aveuc leurs figures proporcionnellez." Exp. "qui est tout le tamps que la demeure se fait." <br><br> 2. Begins fol. 16, *Du nombre sollaire.* Inc. "Dieu, nostre createur, qui par sa grant puissance tout le monde estably, premièrement le ciel, le soleil, les estoilles, la lune." Exp. "jusques en la fin du monde. Et l'esprouva le philozophe certainement. Amen. Explicit." | |
| Paris, BN fr. 2080 (anc. 7946) (Bib. Imp.) | Robert du Herlin, *Ung petit tractié qui se intitulera et appellera Influencia celi.* Inc. "lequel contiendra xvi questions et xvi chappitres avec deux petites tables." Exp. "preste seurement a celluy, il te rendra." | Autograph MS, dated 1481. |
| Paris, BN fr, 2081 (anc. 7947) (Bib. Imp.) | Frere Jehan Thenaud, *La Science poeticque.* Inc. "Pource que plusieurs sont en cestuy monde, qui autre chose ne demande fors longue vie." Exp. "Pectus et ora lee, caudam serpentis habebat." | |
| Paris, BN fr. 12289 (anc. suppl. fr. 2467) | Fols. 1–24, *Petit traictié de la signification des comettes.* | |

| Shelfmark | Contents | Comments |
|---|---|---|
| Paris, BN fr. 12289 (cont.) | Fols. 25–86, Giles of Lessines, *Traittié de Frere Gile de l'ordre des freres prescheurs de l'essence et mouvement et signification des comettes.* | Tr. of Giles of Lessines, *De essentia et motu et signification cometarum.* |
| | Fols. 87–133, *Ung autre livre de la signification des cometes.* | Tr. of *Liber de signification cometarum.* |
| Paris, BN fr. 24278 (St. Victor 221) (MD; Omont) | Fols. 1–135, Nicole Oresme, *Le Livre du ciel et du monde.* | Tr. of Aristotle, *De caelo.* Ed. MD. |
| | Fol. 140, Nicole Oresme, *Traitié de l'espere.* | Fragment (chaps. 37–50). |
| Paris, BN lat. 7287 (Poulle 109) | Fols. 92–99, Jean Fusoris, Treatise on the use of the astrolabe. | Ed. Poulle. This is an abbreviated version. |
| Paris, BN lat. 7321A (anc. 128, 4776, 7316B) (Lemay; IRHT) | Fols. 53–125, Ptolemy, *Quadripartitum* | |
| | Fols. 132–71, Ptolemy, *Centiloquium.* | Extracts only (IRHT). |
| | Fols. 173–81, Ps.-Hippocrates, *Libellus de medicorum astrologia.* | |
| | Fols. 183–84, Ptolemy, *De cometis.* Inc. "Thollomee dit que les estoilles cometes sont 9." Exp. "es roys et es riches hommes." | Tr. of *Stelle cum caudis.* |
| | Fols. 184–88, Astronomical/astrological tract. Inc. "Affin qu'on ait la congnoissance." | |
| | Fols. 212–13, Astronomical tract on the mansions of the moon. Inc. "Sachiés que les jugemens du siecle." | |
| | Fols 225–26, Astronomical/astrological tract. Inc. "Affin qu'on ait la congnoissance." | |

| Reference | Contents | Notes |
| --- | --- | --- |
| Paris, BN lat. 7405 (Poulle 7) | Fols. 43–57, Jean Fusoris, *La Pratique de l'astrolabe.* | Treatise on the use of the astrolabe. Ed. Poulle. |
| Paris, BN lat. 11252 (SGP 117; Lemay) | | Contains astronomical/astrological texts in Lat. & Fr. |
| Paris, BN nouv. acq. lat. 595 (Poulle 7) | Fols. 41–49, Jean Fusoris, *La Pratique de l'astrolabe.* | Treatise on the use of the astrolabe. Ed. Poulle. |
| Vatican City, Bib. Apost. Vat. Reg. Lat. 1330 | Fols. 1–11, *Petit traictié de la significacion des comettes.* | MS also contains several astronomical/astrological texts in Lat. |
| | Fols. 13–38, Giles of Lessines, *Traictié de Frere Gile de l'ordre des freres prescheurs de l'essence et mouvement et significacion des comettes.* | Tr. of Giles of Lessines, *De essentia, motu et significatione cometarum.* |
| | Fols. 39–57, *Ung autre livre de la significacion des cometes cometarum.* | Tr. of *Liber de significatione cometarum.* |
| Vatican City, Bib. Apost. Vat. Reg. Lat. 1337 (UI; Poulle 7, 14) | 1. Astronomical tract, on the course of sun & moon. Inc. "Qui savoir." | |
| | 2. Treatise on the sphere. Inc. "La figure." | Probably the *Traictié de l'espere* of Nicole Oresme. |
| | 3. Pelerin de Prusse, Treatise on judicial astrology in 2 books Inc. "En nom." | Probably the treatise on astrology in 3 parts, tr. 1361 for Charles V. See MS Oxford, St. John's College 164. |

| Shelfmark | Contents | Comments |
|---|---|---|
| Vatican City, Bib. Apost. Vat. Reg. Lat. 1337 (cont.) | 4. Tract on the use of the astrolabe. Inc. "la science." | Probably the tract on the use of the astrolabe of Pelerin de Prusse, 1362. See MS Oxford, St. John's College 164. |
| | 5. Fols. 111–20, Jean Fusoris, Treatise on the use of the astrolabe. | Composed for Pierre de Navarre. Ed. Poulle; this MS served as base MS for edn. |
| | 6. Fols. 121–35, Jean Fusoris, Treatise on the composition of the astrolabe. | Ed. Poulle; this MS served as base MS for edn. |
| | 7. Fols. 135–36, *Nocturlabe.* Inc. "Se voulez savoir les heures de la nuyt." | |
| | 8. Fols. 137–38, description of the zodiac. Inc. "Il est assavoir que le zodiaque du soleil." | |
| | 9. Fols. 138–39, description of the astrological man. Inc. "Le mouton tient le chief." | Description only; no figure. (Poulle). |
| | 10. Abū Ma'shar, *On elections.* Inc. "Ce dist." | Tr. of Abū Ma'shar, *De electionibus.* Probably tr. by Arnoul de Quinquempoix; see MS Paris, BN fr. 613. |
| Valenciennes, Bib. de la ville 348 (335) (HLF 35: 629f.; BPD 25) | Guido Bonati, astrological treatises. | Tr. by Nicolas de La Horbe. Compare contents of MS Paris, Arsenal 2911. |

| Valenciennes, Bib. de la ville 348 (cont.) | | | Begins with third treatise of first part, incl. fourth & fifth. |
|---|---|---|---|
| | 1. | Introductorium. Inc. "Le iii^e traité de ceste premiere partie qui est de l'accidentel estat du zodiaque." | |
| | 2. | Begins fol. 49, On interrogations. Inc. "La ii^e partie de ce livre, an quelle est des interrogations, contient deux traitiéz. | |
| | 3. | Fols. 101–18, *Advertissement pour jugement de astrologie pour so·· garder de erreur et choses chy apres declairiés*. Inc. "P·imes que aux signes de la commune espece." | |

# Lys Ann Shore

## Notes

1. Lys Ann Shore, "A Case Study in Medieval Nonliterary Translation: Scientific Texts from Latin to French," in Jeanette Beer, ed., *Medieval Translators and Their Craft* (Kalamazoo: Medieval Institute Publications, 1989), pp. 297–98.

2. For an overview of the French works, see Shore, "Case Study." For the Latin texts, see Lynn Thorndike and Pearl Kibre, *A Catalogue of Incipits of Medieval Scientific Writings in Latin*, rev. ed. (Cambridge, Mass.: The Medieval Academy of America, 1963), s.v. *comet*.

3. There also exists a French translation of the final *verbum* of the *Centiloquium* (which circulated independently under the title *De cometis*), found in a single fifteenth-century MS: Paris, Bib. Nat. lat. 7321A, fols. 183d–84d. A description of the MS was provided to me by Mme. Françoise Vielliard of the Institut de Recherche et d'Histoire des Textes (section romane), Paris. Personal communication, 21 August 1981.

4. A critical edition of one of these texts, the *Petit Traictié de la signification des comettes*, can be found in Lys Ann T. Shore, "Three Treatises on Comets in Middle French: A Study in the Development of a Vernacular Scientific Tradition" (Ph. D. diss., University of Toronto, 1983), chap. 6. The other two treatises remain unpublished. The possible attribution of the manuscripts to the milieu of René of Anjou's court is based primarily on an analysis of the decoration of the manuscripts; see ibid., pp. 128–36.

5. Lynn Thorndike, *Latin Treatises on Comets Between 1238 and 1368 A.D.* (Chicago: University of Chicago Press, 1950).

6. Critical editions of the two Latin works have been published by Thorndike, *Latin Treatises*. The editions are based on all the known MSS of the Latin texts and include many variant readings from the MSS of the French translations. The *Liber de significatione* survives in three MSS: Cambridge, University Library MS Kk.IV.7, fols. 101$^{rb}$–107$^{ra}$ (*C*); Basel, Offentliche Bibliothek der Universität MS F.II.15, fols 112$^v$–113$^v$ (*G*) (fragment only); and Cambridge, Pembroke College Library MS 227, pp. 228a–250b (*P*). *De essentia* also survives in three MSS: *C*, fols. 96$^{ra}$–101$^{ra}$; *P*, pp. 250b–282a; and Oxford, Bodleian Library, Ashmole MS 341, fols. 61$^r$–76$^r$(*A*). The *Livre de la signification des cometes* and *De l'Essence et mouvement et signification des comettes* are both

found in two MSS: Paris, Bibliothèque nationale fr. 12289 (anc. suppl. fr. 2467, suppl. fr. 324) (*R*), fols. 25$^r$–86$^v$ (*De l'essence*) and 87$^r$–133$^v$ (*Livre de la signification*); Vatican City, Bibliotheca Apostolica Vaticana, Reg. Lat. 1330 (*Vc*), fols 13$^r$–38$^v$ (*De l'essence*), fols. 39$^r$–57$^r$ (*Livre de la signification*). In addition, *De l'essence* exists in a third MS, Paris, Bibliothèque nationale fr. 2071 (anc. 7942) (*T*), fols. 21$^r$–72$^r$. The *Petit traictié de la signification des comettes* is found in *R*, fols. 1$^r$–24$^r$; *T*, fols. 3$^r$–19$^v$; *Vc*, fols. 1$^r$–11$^v$; and also in a MS in the Lenin State Library, Moscow (Western European MSS, Fond 183, no. 357, fols. 1$^r$–15$^v$).

In this paper, the *Liber de significatione/Livre de la signification* and *De essentia/De l'essence* will be referred to by short title in Latin or French, according to whether the Latin original or the French translation is intended.

7. Thorndike, *Latin Treatises*, p. 9.

8. William D. Stahlman, "On the Date of a Comet Ascribed to A.D. 1238," *Isis* 43 (1952): 348–51. Stahlman's dating was accepted by Brian G. Marsden in his *Catalogue of Cometary Orbits*, 3rd ed. (Cambridge, Mass.: Smithsonian Astrophysical Observatory, Central Bureau for Astronomical Telegrams of the International Astronomical Union, 1979), p. 12.

9. Thorndike, *Latin Treatises*, pp. 10, 15.

10. The twelve zodiacal signs were divided into four groups of three signs each, with each group characterized by one of the four elements. Thus the triplicity of earth signs included Taurus, Capricorn, and Virgo; air signs were Gemini, Libra, and Aquarius; fire signs were Aries, Leo, and Sagittarius; and water signs were Cancer, Scorpio, and Pisces.

11. *Stelle currentes*: presumably meteors. Thorndike translated this phrase as "coursing stars." It is not included in the list of technical terms compiled by Umberto Dall'Olmo, "Latin Terminology Relating to Aurorae, Comets, Meteors and Novae," *Journal of the History of Astronomy* 11 (1980): 10–27.

12. Thorndike, *Latin Treatises*, pp. 16–17. "Et est capitulum primum ad sciendum quid sit cometa. Capitulum 2m ad sciendum ex quo fiunt comete et cuius figure sunt. Capitulum 3m ad sciendum quot sunt comete et nomina eorum secundum Ptholomeum et Alquindum et Caldeos. Capitulum 4m ad sciendum figuras cometarum secundum quod

apparent hominibus. Capitulum 5m ad sciendum significationem cometarum et cum quibus planetis conveniunt in suis coloribus. Capitulum 6m ad habendum generalem cognitionem cometarum. Capitulum 7m ad habendum cognitionem quam habent comete quando apparent in quacumque triplicitate signorum. Capitulum 8m ad habendum cognitionem cometarum quando apparent in quocumque signo. Capitulum nonum de significatione magnitudinis et complexionis et coloris proprie cuiuscumque comete et quid habent pro se. Capitulum 10m ad sciendum in quibus provinciis et in quibus civitatibus contingunt accidentia sequentia cometas. Capitulum 11m ad sciendum in quo tempore contingent accidentia et quanto durabunt. Capitulum 12m ad sciendum qualitatem accidentium. Capitulum 13m ad sciendum in quo genere sive hominum sive bestiarum sive avium sive piscium sive reptilium debent contingere hec accidentia. Capitulum 14m ad probandum effectus signorum contradicentibus. Capitulum 15m de eis que dixerunt sapientes de cometis et stellis currentibus. Capitulum 16m de exemplis cometarum."

13. The French translation has not been published, but I have transcribed it from all the known MSS.

14. The text is that of MS *R* (fol. 105ᵛ). The distinction between *i* and *j*, *u* and *v* has been supplied, and punctuation has been normalized.

15. Thus in both MSS (*R* and *Vc*). Both Latin MSS (*C, P*) read "occisionem."

16. Thorndike, *Latin Treatises*, pp. 34–35.

17. Thorndike, *Latin Treatises*, p. 24.

18. Thorndike's reading, "*tertio* kalendas Augusti," in one of the MSS of the work is conjectural: As he himself declares the word is illegible, as far as can be determined from examination of a microfilm of the MS (*A*, fol. 61ʳ). Thorndike prudently refers to the date in his introduction as "sometime in July" (*Latin Treatises*, p. 90). The other MSS read *xix kalendas*, apparently a corrupt reading.

19. "Quoniam multorum animos audivi stupefactos ac intellectus suspensos occasione cuiusdam stelle caudate sive crinite qui apparuit in regno Francie in oriente ante solis ortum a tertio kalendas Augusti usque quinto nonas Octobris in anno domini 1264 et a multis interrogatus fuerim tam de eius natura quam de eius significatione. . . ." Thorndike,

*Latin Treatises*, p. 103.

20. ". . . omnium sapientum tam antiquorum quam modernorum naturalium, mathematicorum et theologorum sententias et scripta, que videram circa hanc materiam, in unum tractatum colligere et eorum dicta et rationes explanare, approbata vero tenere et inprobata spernere." Thorndike, *Latin Treatises*, p. 103.

21. William A. Wallace, O.P., "Giles (Aegidius) of Lessines," *Dictionary of Scientific Biography* (New York: Scribner's, 1970–80).

22. Thorndike, *Latin Treatises*, p. 95. He went on to remark that "some of [Giles's] authorities were not accessible to me under recent conditions nearly 500 years after the invention of printing."

23. Although the second part of the treatise consists of only three chapters, it is actually somewhat longer than the first part. An analytical table of contents (in English) is provided by Thorndike, *Latin Treatises*, pp. 100–03.

24. Since the translation has not been published, I have transcribed it in its entirety from all known manuscripts.

25. The text is that of *Vc*, fol. 21$^r$; the distinction between *i* and *j*, *u* and *v* has been supplied, and punctuation normalized.

26. *i la gette*: This unusual form, *i*, of the pronoun *il* is explained by Christiane Marchello-Nizia, *Histoire de la langue française aux XIV$^e$ et XV$^e$ siècles* (Paris: Bordas, 1979), p. 87, as the result of final implosive *l* becoming mute after *i*. She also notes examples of the reverse notation, *quil* for *qui*.

27. Thorndike, *Latin Treatises*, p. 100.

28. For a detailed codicological analysis of the three manuscripts (*R*, *T*, *Vc*,), see Shore, "Three Treatises on Comets," chapter 5.

29. See Shore, "Case Study," pp. 309–10.

30. Thorndike, *Latin Treatises*, p. 41.

31. All references to the text of the *Petit Traictié* are to the edition that forms chapter 6 of my dissertation: Shore, "Three Treatises on Comets."

32. Thorndike, *Latin Treatises*, p. 7.

33. Jean-Michel Massing, "A Sixteenth-Century Illustrated Treatise on Comets," *Journal of the Warburg and Courtauld Institutes* 40 (1977): 320.

34. There are some indications in this passage of different linguistic patterns between the *Petit Traictié* and the *Livre*, such as *au/ou* (lines 1, 2, 7); *apperent/apparoissent* (line 2); *auront/aront* (line 10); *ce, celle/icelui, icelle* (lines 3, 5). The morphological and orthographical variation characteristic of Middle French, however, makes it extremely difficult to ascertain the significance of these differences for the textual relationship of the two works.

35. "Ptolemy says . . . that running stars [i.e., meteors] and those which *are hairy or have hair or* a head of hair *such as comets* follow the other stars, *that is to say the fixed [stars] or planets, which are called wandering stars. . . .*"

36. Busahen: Abū'l Wafā (al-Buzajani) (940–98), identified in the *Liber/Livre* only as "a sage of India."

37. I owe to astrophysicist Steven N. Shore the insightful observation that an omission such as this shows how tightly the compiler focused on his subject matter, concentrating on comets to the exclusion of other phenomena such as eclipses. Dr. Shore has also provided invaluable help in understanding medieval theory and observations of comets; indeed, it was his interest in this subject that first drew my scholarly attention to it.

38. Richard Lemay, letter received December 26, 1982.

39. For a detailed study of the illustrations, see Shore, "Three Treatises on Comets," appendix 2.

40. The two Gileses have occasionally been confused in modern scholarship; see Thorndike, *Latin Treatises*, p. 87n.

41. For examples, see Shore, "Case Study," pp. 307–10.

42. I am actively continuing research on this project, with a view to publication of a more complete listing, based on personal examination of the MS sources.

43. An example of the difficulties that can arise from this situation is the case of Paris, Bibliothèque de l'Arsenal, MS 534. Several sources list this MS as containing on fols. 91–107 the *Calendarium* of William of Saint-Cloud in Latin, while one scholar who had personally examined the MS maintained that it held the French translation of this text (*Le Calendrier la royne*). Most recently, at my request Claire R. Sherman perused the MS; she found it to contain only the Latin text of the *Calendarium*, beginning on fol. 91 (letter received Nov. 29, 1982). As a result, I have eliminated this late thirteenth-century MS from the present list.

# Vernacular Translation in the Fourteenth-Century Crown of Aragon: Brunetto Latini's *Li livres dou tresor*

## Dawn Ellen Prince

In the fourteenth century the Barcelonese dynasty, under the initiative of Pere III the Ceremonious (Pedro IV of Aragon), launched a conscious policy to consolidate royal authority, develop a sense of national unity, and encourage imperialist expansion.[1] The cornerstone of the extensive royal operations was a cohesive royal parliament or "corts," and a distinguished royal chancellery, which used Catalan, Aragonese, and Latin alike. These institutions were to give the Crown of Aragon the intellectual and political leadership of Spain for nearly a century. It was during this lengthy period, spanning the reigns of Pere III (1336–87), Joan I (1387–96), and Martí I (1396–1410), that humanistic tendencies first emerged in the peninsula, centering around the royal patronage of literary translations.[2]

An intimate relationship with the Valois rulers of France appears to have roused the nationalistic (and undoubtedly competitive) spirit of the bibliophile Pere III during the early years of his rule. It was Pere's contemporary, the French ruler Charles V the Wise (1338–80), who first realized the value of establishing a royal library.[3] Not unlike Alfonso X, Charles appears to have been inspired by political, not esthetic, motives, based on the notion of public usefulness, and many texts collected by Charles were ordered translated from Latin into French.[4] The French scholar-prince, praised by his contemporaries, sponsored such practical ventures as Denis Foullechat's translation of the *Policraticus* by John of Salisbury (1372); Jacques Bauchant's translation of Seneca's *De remediis fortuitorum*; the *Liber de proprietatibus rerum* of Bartholomaeus Anglicus, translated by Jean Corbechon (1372); Petrarch's *De remediis*

55

*utriusque fortunae,* translated by Jean Daudin (ca. 1377); Jean Golein's translation of the *De regimine principum* by Giles of Rome (1379); Raoul de Presles's version of St. Augustine's *De civitate Dei* (1371–74); the *Memorabilia* of Valerius Maximus translated by Simon de Hesdin and Nicolas de Gonesse (ca. 1375); Evrat de Conti's translation of the pseudo-Aristotelian *Problemata* (1372); and Nicole Oresme's *Ethics* (1370), *Politics* (1372), *Economics* (1372), and *On the Heavens* (1377).[5] This immense translation enterprise reinforced the role of French as a language of learning.[6] And, as we shall see, many of these French versions were used as models by the scriptorium of Pere III, who understandably envied the extensive array of literary material owned by Charles V.

The Aragonese maintained close contacts with their northern neighbors during the course of the fourteenth century for a multitude of reasons, including the Aragonese annexation of the county of Roussillon in 1344 and the establishment of a university in the city of Perpignan six years later. The residence of the antipopes in Avignon during much of the fourteenth century resulted in the founding of a rich pontifical library and scriptorium, under the direction of Pope Clement VII (1378–94). Both Aragonese and French monarchs took advantage of the situation by sending emissaries in search of valued codices.[7] As testified by the findings of Rubió i Lluch (see n. 2), a cultural partnership, based on the acquisition of texts, evolved between the two kingdoms.

The most fervent literary activity in Aragon corresponds to the period 1380–1410, spanning the last years of Pere III's rule and focusing on the patronage of his sons, Joan I and Martí I. The Aragonese royal chancellery and the initiative of Juan Fernández de Heredia's school of translators in Avignon (1382–96) account for the majority of translations produced in Catalan and Aragonese during these three decades.

As part of his administration, Pere III employed protonotaries, secretaries, and scribes to attend to the royal correspondence.[8] These men, who also served as the king's translators, appear to have been versed in both literary Catalan and Aragonese.[9] The most influential scribes in the chancellery were Jaume Conesa (1351–66), Ferrer Sayol (1350–85), Bernat de la Torre (b. ca. 1349), Bernat Descoll (1331–91), Joan de Barbastre (1362–86), and the clerics Jaume Domenech (1351–84) and Arnau Estanyol (1341), as well as several Jewish writers.[10] Juan Fernández de Heredia (1308–96) served as counsellor to both Pere III and the young prince Joan.

The king's literary interests, though vast in scope, were in particular related to the consolidation of political power. History, oratory, legislative works, and, of course, astrology were of prime interest. Historical works translated at the king's request—or at least during his reign—that merit mention are the *Croniques de Saint Denis* of the monk Primat; the *Suma de les histories del món,* requested in Catalan (1362) and in Aragonese (1370); the *Speculum historiale,* prepared by Jaume Domenech (1360); and the *Libre historial compilat de diversos autors per D. Alfonso dit lo Savi (General Estoria).* Of a more political nature were the translations of Giles of Rome's *Regiment de princeps* by Arnau Estanyol (before 1381) and fragments of Alfonso X's extensive legislative work *Les partides,* translated by Matheu Adrià (before 1365). In addition to his more serious interests, Pere III also sought chivalric romances such as *Lancelot,* the *Taula rodonda,* and the *Sifar.*

Correspondence reveals that during his lengthy reign Pere III bought, borrowed, and requested manuscripts from many members of the Aragonese royal family (including his sons Joan and Martí, daughter María, the countess Urgell, Queen Alionor, and Jaume d'Aragó the Bishop of Valencia) and from an assortment of foreigners (principally Charles V, Jean de Berry, Charles's daughter, the countess of Foix, and the count of Terranova). Called in his time *afrancesat,* Joan I (1350–96) was even more imbued with French culture than his father, principally because of his two marriages to French noblewomen, Matha d'Armanyac

(1372–78) and Violant de Bar (1380–96). During his reign French influence was felt most profoundly, and many translations were based on French-language models, thanks to the accessibility of French-language manuscripts. French culture served as an attractive model for the citizens of the Aragonese kingdoms, and the ambitious Catalonian society was undoubtedly eager to profit from the cultural gains of its northern neighbor. Little could be gained from contact with its neighbor to the south, for Castile was embroiled in political conflict with the Aragonese kings for much of the fourteenth century, culminating in the war of the two Pedros (Pere III of Aragon and Pedro the Cruel of Castile). The Catalans preferred to align themselves culturally and linguistically with the more sophisticated French.

For at least one century translators had complained of the many obstacles posed by Latin originals, particularly in questions of syntax and lexis. In 1282, the French translator Jean d'Antioche, in the epilogue to his translation of the *Rettorique de Marc Tulles Cyceron,* summed up the consensus of frustration toward the difficulties posed by Latin works: "ne les proprietez des paroles ne les raisons d'ordener les araisonemenz et les diz dou latin ne sont pas semblables a celes dou françois" [neither the properties of the words, nor the rationale for ordering the arguments and the expressions of Latin are similar to those of French].[11] The accessibility of French-language manuscripts and the relative ease with which Catalano-Aragonese writers understood Francien, Provençal, and other Gallo-Romance dialects reinforced the flow of material from north of the Pyrenees. Later writers sometimes criticized Romance-based translations as superficial and of limited literary value.[12] But, while this type of textual transmission may have debilitated the grace of the original Latin prose, and multiplied scribal errors, it nonetheless provided the peninsula with an invaluable cultural and linguistic legacy.[13] It was through these early translations that the ancient and medieval literary classics were made accessible to a large number of literate men and women. Furthermore, the flurry of translations afforded Catalan and Aragonese writers the opportunity to stylize their own prose through the manipulation of the lexical, morphological, and syntactical complexities inherent in the translation process. The following is a partial listing of the nearly eighty translations (cited in Rubió i Lluch, *Documents per l'história*, 2: xxii) requested or completed during the reigns of Pere III and Joan I. All are cited in the royal correspondence; many are no longer extant. The list attests to the vast domain covered by the royal collection.

**Table 1: Translations during the reigns of Pere III and Joan I**

| TITLE | TRANSLATOR | DATE |
|---|---|---|
| Aben Ezra *Libre dels juhis de les esteles* | Anonymous | ? |
| Alfraganus (Alfergani) | Anonymous | 1381 |
| Ali Aben Rasen | Anonymous | 1386 |
| Antolin *Libre de laurar* | Anonymous | ca. 1370 |
| Augustine *De civitate Dei* (*La ciutat de Deu*) | Anonymous | ca. 1387 |
| Avicenna *Canon* | Anonymous | 1386 |
| Beauvais *Speculum historiale* | Jaume Domenech, Antoni Ginebreda | ? |
| Bersuire *Dictionarium morale bibliorum* | Anonymous | 1376 |
| Boethius *De consolatione* | Pere Saplana, Antoni Ginebreda | ? |
| *Breviloquium* (*Breu parlament de les virtuts dels antichs philosophs*) | Anonymous | ad quem 1387 |
| Cicero *Paradoxes* | Ferran Valenti | ? |

| | | |
|---|---|---|
| *Disticha Catonis* (*Libre de Cató*) | Anonymous | ? |
| Egidius Romanus (*Regiment de princeps*) | Arnau Estanyol | ad quem 1381 |
| Frontinus *Stratagemata* | Jaume Domenech | 1367 |
| Gregory the Great (*Dialegs y morals*) | Bernat Oller | 1344 |
| Guido delle Colonne *Historia destructionis Trojae (Histories troyanes)* | Jaume Conesa | 1367 |
| John of Wales *Communiloquium* (*Suma de collacions*) | Joan de Prohomen | ? |
| Josefus *De bello judaico* | Anonymous | ca. 1384 |
| Justinian | Anonymous | ca. 1386 |
| Koran (*El Corà*) | Pons Saclota | 1381 |
| *Lancelot* | Anonymous | ca. 1346 |
| *Llibre moresc* | Francesc Roys | 1349 |
| Maimonides *Drets hebraics* | Anonymous | 1383 |
| Ovid *Metamorphosis* (*Métamorphoses*) | Francesc Alegre | ? |
| Ovid *Heroides* | Anonymous | ? |
| Palladius *De re rustica* | Jaume de Vedrinyans, Ferrer Sayol | 1377 1380–85 |
| *Postilles* | Bertrán de la Tour | 1374 |
| *Proverbis aràbics* | Anonymous | ? |
| *Secret de secrets* | Anonymous | 1377 |

## Brunetto Latini's *Li livres dou tresor*

| Seneca *De providentia* | Antoni Canals | 1396–04 |
|---|---|---|
| Seneca *Moralia* | Anonymous | ? |
| Seneca *Tragediae* | Antoni de Vilaragut | ? |
| Sydrac (*Libre de Sidrac*) *L'infant Epitus* | Anonymous | ? |
| Valerius Maximus | Anonymous | ad quem 1395 |

Classical holdings, such as Ovid, Cicero, Boethius, and Seneca, were complemented by Arabic and Christian religious pieces and more contemporary texts, such as Guido delle Colonne's account of the destruction of Troy.

Brunetto Latini's *Li livres dou tresor* aimed to educate the wise ruler, affording him all the knowledge necessary to speak and judge effectively. Begun ca. 1262, the *Tresor* is representative of the general encyclopedic tradition that arose in thirteenth-century Europe. It is the first true encyclopedia in a vernacular language, namely French. Likened to a "treasure" by its author, the encyclopedia is divided into three books: the first, like *deniers contans* [currency], treats practical knowledge (biblical and secular history, geography, the bestiary, astronomy); the second discusses vices and virtues, described as *prescieuses pieres* [precious stones], and contains a translation of part of Aristotle's *Ethics;* the third book, like *fin or* [fine gold], is the most valued and teaches one to speak and govern effectively, offering its readers selections from Cicero's *De inventione.* Brunetto's high appraisal of the art of rhetoric is expected, if we take into consideration his background as both a politician and notary. In classical times, rhetoric was recognized as the means by which one could obtain political power, by verbally defeating an adversary. During the Middle Ages, rhetoric was still valued, but primarily as a tool for embellishing written discourse, including translations. The concept of rhetoric as the source of political power was to be revitalized only with the onset of the Italian Renaissance. Brunetto's interest in this art was twofold: he utilized the rhetorical arts as a political orator and as a vulgarizer of classical texts.

In contrast with the Latinate encyclopedias of his contemporaries, for example, the *Speculum majus* of Vincent of Beauvais, Brunetto's *Tresor* is written in the vernacular for the new middle class, composed primarily of wealthy merchants. Brunetto alludes to his intended audience by referring in his title to *tresor* [treasure, wealth]. The *Tresor* emphasizes practical matters, including contemporary history, domestic architecture, ethics, vice and virtue, rhetoric, and politics. Such a practical tool was well suited as an instructional manual to be digested with little difficulty by its readers. The pragmatic use of French in place of Latin underscores Brunetto's objective:

> E se aucuns demandoit pour quoi cis livres est escris en roumanç, selonc le raison de France, puis ke nous somes italien, je diroie que c'est pour .ii. raisons, l'une ke nous somes en France, l'autre pour çou que la parleure est plus delitable et plus commune a tous langages. (*Tresor* 1.1.7)

> [And if someone were to ask why this book is written in Romance, in the French language, when we are Italian, I would say it is for two reasons, one, that we are in France, the other because that language is more delightful and more common to all languages.]

The popularity of the *Tresor* in medieval Spain is attested by the many peninsular translations made of the text. Three different Catalan translations are preserved in five manuscripts.[14] The Castilian *Tesoro,* translated in 1292 by Alfonso de Paredes at the request of Sancho IV, survives in thirteen manuscripts.[15] And a solitary Aragonese translation, prepared during the late fourteenth century, survives in a unique fifteenth-century manuscript.[16] This unique codex of the Aragonese *Libro del trasoro* (Gerona Cathedral, MS 20, a, 5—henceforth referred to as "G"), an apparent copy of an earlier translation, can be dated to the mid-fifteenth century based on its watermark and cursive Gothic hand.[17] MS G comprises an interpolated version of Brunetto's text, designated version Δ by Carmody in his Bédierist edition and stemma of the French *Tresor*.[18] The Aragonese text appears to be related to French MSS M (Paris, B.N. fr. 568), O (Paris, B.N. fr. 569)—both owned by Jean de Berry, brother of Charles V—, R (Paris, B.N. fr. 726), and V (Paris, B.N. fr. 1113). The contemporaneous Catalan translation (Barcelona, Biblioteca de Catalunya, MS 357) prepared by Guillem de Copons (1418) reveals that it, too, is an interpolated text showing great affinity to G.[19]

Translated in the last quarter of the fourteenth century or the first of the fifteenth (ca. 1375–1425), the *Trasoro* appears to have been prepared at the request of a member of the Aragonese ecclesiastical community, quite possibly the Bishop of Gerona, Dalmau de Mur, an ally of the royal family, who traveled on several occasions to the French royal court and was a known patron of the arts. The Aragonese ecclesiastical community was highly politicized and powerful during the fourteenth and fifteenth centuries; its members stood to benefit greatly from the eclectic approach of the *Tresor*. Although the *Tresor* reflects upon thirteenth-century Italian politics, it was of extreme cultural interest to fourteenth century French and Aragonese rulers.

As a member of the religious community, the *Trasoro*'s benefactor was undoubtedly well versed in Latin and thoroughly familiar with Biblical and secular history; thus the translator does not seem compelled to gloss names of historical figures and places. One may also assume that this patron solicited a translation of the *Tresor* for its didactic, not literary, value, given the lack of any stylistic embellishment in the

Aragonese text. This limited purpose notwithstanding, many difficulties confronted the Aragonese translator who aimed to provide a literal interpretation of his French prototype. In light of the fact that the model was not a Latin, but rather a Romance, text, this choice of methodology was sensible: the translator was not faced with the many difficulties posed by a Latin original. Problems of interpretation caused by complicated Latinate syntax were avoided; the paratactical sentence structure so typical of medieval vernacular prose was effortlessly imitated.[20] The common stock of Romance culture and lexis circumvented the need for the lengthy glosses and commentaries that were almost always necessary for the comprehension of Latin prose. The translator's literalism can be seen in the following example from the *Tresor* 1.118.1:[21]

Ch.      *Nous lison en la Bible que au commencement dou*
G         *Nos leemos en la Biblia que al començamjento del*
[We read in the Bible that in the beginning of the]

Ch.      *siecle quant Nostre Sires crea et fist toutes*
G         *mundo, quando Nuestro Senyor creo e fizo todas*
[world, when Our Lord created and made all]

Ch.      *choses, que toutes les estoiles furent faites*
G         *cosas que todas las strellas fueron feytas*
[things, that all the stars were made]

Ch.      *au quart jor, ce est xj jors a l'issue*
G         *al quarto dia, yes a saber, el xjo dia ala exida*
[on the fourth day, that is, the eleventh day at the beginning]

Ch.      *dou mois de mars.*
G              *de març.*
[of March].

The Aragonese translator does not react personally to the material in his text, nor does he present the reader with an extensively commented version. Rather, he limits himself to brief clarifications of confusing or ambiguous passages, as exemplified by the following additions (underlined) taken from the Aragonese bestiary chapters:

| | |
|---|---|
| 1.167.2 | *lur dreyta madre, <u>aquella quelos auja paridos</u>* (67va33)[22] |
| | [their true mother, <u>she who had given birth to them</u>] |
| 1.167.2 | *la lur falsa madre, aquella quelos auja furtados gueuos* (67va35–36) |
| | [their false mother, <u>she who had stolen them as eggs</u>] |
| 1.186.1 | *Por que y a <u>cauallos</u> de muytas maneras* (73va11) |
| | [because there are <u>horses</u> of many types] |

Taken from the chapter on partridges, the first two additions serve to clarify what is meant by *dreyta madre* [true mother] and *falsa madre* [false mother], which is an unusual distinction to make. The addition in the third example restates the subject of the preceding sentence, *cauallos* [horses], in order to provide a smoother transition to the next sentence, which will elaborate on types of *cauallos*.

To facilitate the readers' comprehension, the translator makes use of the formula *clamada* [called] in several chapter rubrics, particularly when referring to little known animals, as may be the *alerion* [eagle] or the *ardea* [heron]:

| | | |
|---|---|---|
| 1.151 | Fr. | *De alerion* [On the eagle] |
| | G | *De <u>au clamada</u> alerion* |
| | | [On <u>the bird called</u> the eagle] |
| 1.152 | Fr. | *De ardea* [On the heron] |
| | G | *De la <u>au clamada</u> ardea* |
| | | [On <u>the bird called</u> the heron]. |

Despite the fact that these chapters form part of the section on birds, the translator forces the inclusion of *au* [bird].

Occasionally single words in the source are glossed by two terms in the translation, when the translator determines one translation to be insufficient for his reading public (e.g., 1.125.1, 1.125.11, 1.131.1, 1.147.2, 1.148.1, 1.162.4, and 1.163.6). Three examples are offered here as illustration:

| | | |
|---|---|---|
| 1.125.1 | Fr. | *estanc* [pond] |
| | G | *balsa o laguna* [pool or lake] |
| 1.131.1 | Fr. | *maisselle* [cheek] |
| | G | *maxiella de jus, yes a saber, las bariellas susanas* [upper cheek, that is, the upper jaw] |
| 1.148.1 | Fr. | *esperviers* [sparrow-hawk] |
| | G | *esparuers o gaujlan* [sparrow-hawk or hawk]. |

In these instances, the translator provides the reader with two dialectal names for the same object. In the first example, Fr. *estanc* [pond] is initially translated by *balsa* [pool], an Aragonese term etymologically related to Cat. *bassa* "hueco de terreno que se llena de agua" [a cavity in the earth that is filled with water].[23] The translator then expands this gloss with the addition of Cast. *laguna* [lake] (*DCECH* 3:558). In the second example, the translator first gives a Castilian calque of Fr. *maisselle* [cheek], namely *maxiella (de jus)* [upper cheek] (*DCECH* 4:18), with the superfluous *de jus* [above] in imitation of Cat. *(barra) de dalt* [upper (jaw)].[24] The Castilian translation is subsequently glossed by the Arag. *barriellas susanas*. The third example, Fr. *esperviers* [sparrow-hawk], mirrors the first; the translator initially uses the etymologically related Arag. *esparvers* [falcon-like bird].[25] Cast. *gavilan* [hawk] (*DCECH* 3:127) is then provided for those readers unfamiliar with the Gallo-Romance word stock.

These synonymic dialectal variants are of particular interest to the field of medieval translation because, by studying their textual context, one can extrapolate which areas of the lexis witnessed greatest divergency among cultures. The examples of geographical variants extracted from the Aragonese *Tresor* are concentrated in the chapters on animals and domestic life. While widely disseminated traditions such as biblical history or astrology showed greater unity among neo-Latin cultures, names of plants, animals, and terrain must have varied from one geographical area to another. For this reason, medieval translators saw the need for intervention in the contexts noted above.

These dialectal glosses differ from synonymic pairs in that they incorporate two dialectal translations of the French source word, one Catalan and the other "Castilianizing."[26] The sequence of Catalan and "Castilianizing" terms chosen by the translator may very well indicate that our translator was bilingual.[27] It is more likely, however, that he provided these glosses for his readers, who spoke either a variety of Aragonese closer to Catalan (an older variety) or the rapidly expanding Castilian (diluted) variety. Additional examples of dialectal variants from a variety of fourteenth-century sources must be examined in order to determine what linguistic service they provided.

A comparison of the Aragonese *Trasoro* with Guillem de Copons's Catalan translation is instructive in further clarifying medieval translation practices. Copons appears to be more conscious of style than his Aragonese counterpart. A well-known translator, he openly identifies himself in the dated dedication of the Catalan *Tresor* and again refers to his role as translator in 1.1.7. A more evident preoccupation with style, a mainstay of later humanistic translations, is revealed as Copons takes liberties with Brunetto's text: he suppresses superfluous prose by systematically abbreviating the recapitulary formulas with which Brunetto typically joins sections and chapters:

|         | Fr.                                                                  | Cat.                                                                       |
|---------|----------------------------------------------------------------------|---------------------------------------------------------------------------|
| 1.21.4  | *mais de lui se taist ore li contes, ke plus n'en dira en ceste parti.* | *lexa a parlar d'ell.* [stops speaking of him.]                        |
| 1.27.3  | *de qui li contes a devisé ça en arieres*                            | *que és dita detrás* [which was said previously]                          |
| 1.131.1 | *selonc ce ke li contes a devisé ça en arieres*                      | *segons la ystòria ha dit dessús* [as the story said previously]          |

By omitting the repeated references to *li contes*, Copons alters one of Brunetto's characteristic chapter connectors. He also replaces the wordy conjunctive phrases *c'est a savoir* and *c'est a dire* [that is to say] with *ço es* [that is], or omits them altogether:

|        | Fr.                                                       | Cat.                                                                              |
|--------|-----------------------------------------------------------|-----------------------------------------------------------------------------------|
| 2.45.9 | *vivre solitairement, c'est à dire, tout seul*            | *viure solitari* [to live alone]                                                  |
| 3.1.2  | *rectorique, c'est à dire la science du parler*           | *rethòrica, ço és sciència de parlar* [rhetoric, that is the science of speaking] |

Much like his Aragonese contemporary, the Catalan translator intervenes primarily to clarify difficult readings (e.g., 2.66.3, Fr. *sourcis* [eyebrow] > Cat. *la volta de les celles* [the curve of the eyebrow]; 3.1.11, Fr. *esmeraudes* [emeralds] > *safirs d'orient* [sapphires of the Orient]. Wittlin cites a few instances of more substantial intervention by Copons, for example:

> 1.122.24, Fr. *les Ictiofagi, une gent ki ne manguënt se poisson non; mais quant Alixandres les conquist, il lor vea k'il ne les mangaissent*

*jamés* [the Ichthiophagi, a people that ate only fish; but when Alexander conquered them, he forbade that they ever eat them (the fish) again]

1.122.24 Cat. *Los gerjofagis mejen sinó pexos e en lo francès hi ha 'poyssons', qui vol dir 'pexos' e 'metzines'. E quant Alexandre los conques, los vedà que no.n menjassen e creu que.u diga per les metzines* (emphasis added) [the Ichthiophagi ate only fish, *and in French there is the word "poyssons" which means both "fish"* [*i.e., Fr. "poisson"*] *and "venom"* [*i.e., Fr. "poison"*]. And when Alexander conquered them, he forbade them to eat it, *and I think that he meant the "venom".*]

Here Copons is baffled by the fact that Alexander would forbid people to eat fish, because Copons himself was a native of the Mediterranean port of Valencia. He is compelled to offer an alternate interpretation of the passage, based on his misunderstanding of Fr. *poisson,* which he confuses with its near homophone *poison* [venom, drug]. Our Aragonese translator does not react so personally and follows the Fr. model.

The common parent of the Aragonese and Catalan translations appears to have been plagued by a good number of homeoteleuta, which were propagated into the peninsular renditions. The twenty-three instances in which the Aragonese and Catalan texts coincide in their omissions in Book One alone are a strong indication that the omissions go back to the French model.[28] In addition, the translator (or scribe) of G adds thirty-two homeoteleuta to those already present in Book One, which may make one speculate as to the conditions under which the translation was prepared (lack of light, poor materials, etc.).[29]

The French prototype used by the peninsular translators appears to have been written in a late thirteenth-century Gothic book script, similar to that of French *Tresor* MS M[3] (El Escorial, MS L.ii.3). This thirteenth-century codex typically lends itself to paleographic confusion of certain letters.[30] These confusions most often occur between the minuscule letters *c/t, c/e, s/f,* and *n/u,* or in combinations such as *mi, nu, un, im,* etc., particularly in the case of unusual and exotic proper names, where the translator is unfamiliar with the context. A number of paleographic misreadings of this type are shared by G and Cat., due to a prior corruption of their French model, sporadically documented in Chabaille:

|  | Fr. | G | Cat. |
|---|---|---|---|
| *c/e:* | *Declam* | *de Elam* (17ra11) | *de Elam* |
|  | *Eridaine* | *Cridanya* (51vb25) | *Cridine* |
| *c/t:* | *Cecrops* | *Cetrops* (19vaå) | *Etrops* |
| *n/u:* | *Inde* | *Judea* (50rb29) | *Judea* |
| *f/s:* | *Faramont* | *Sericiot* (22vb8) | *Seremont* |
|  | *grise* | *grifa* (63vb10–11) | *grifa* |

As in the case of the homeoteleuta, MS G offers a considerable number of additional paleographical errors sprinkled throughout the text that are not evident in Cat. Whether it was the Aragonese translator or the scribe of G who was hindered by the Gothic script of his model is unclear, but an alarming number of added faults did slip into the text.

A restricted number of errors can be attributed to misinterpretation of abbreviations in both French and Aragonese models. One of the most common Latin abbreviations for final *-m,* namely *-z,* was imitated by French scribes in their vernacular works.[31] This symbol was twice copied by the scribe of G, who quickly realized and emended his error: G *Adaz,* replaced by *Adam* (16ra6–7); G *ylez,* replaced by *ylem* (11va27–28).

A second pair of errors may also be tentatively attributed to the scribe of G. Twice the French text reads *qui ne* [who not], which is translated in G as *quando* [when] (14va20, 24va2). This lapse originated in the misinterpretation of the model $\bar{q}$ *no* (=*que no* [which not]), as *qño* (=*quando* [when]).

At least one error of abbreviation was already present in the French codex used for the Aragonese and Catalan *Tresor.* The peninsular translations read as follows: G *lipesa duenna* (21va4) in which only *duenna* [lady] is recognizable; and Cat. *li pe sa dona,* in which only *sa dona* [his lady] is Catalan. Both erroneous translations are modeled on Fr. *le pere sa feme* [the father of his wife]. It is evident that the mistake is based on a French codex in which the usual abbreviation of *pere,* namely *pe* with a super- or subscript stroke of abbreviation, is erroneously copied without the abbreviation, i.e., *pe.* Neither translator discerns the omission, and each simply copies his model.

An internal metathesis plagued the scribe of G since with some regularity he inverts syllables within a word.[32] This internal metathesis at times takes on the appearance of simple paleographic confusion, i.e., of *c* and *t*: G *Costana* (21vb35, 52ra15, 52ra18–19) vs. Fr. *Toschane* [Tuscany]. One might also cite metathesis of liquid consonants: *Grabiel* (15va6, 28ra16) vs. Fr. *Gabriel; fuulio* (48vb25) vs. Fr. *fleuves* [river]. A handful of cases in Book One, however, are clearly examples of syllable inversion, based not on the French but, rather, on the original Aragonese translation:

| Fr. | Original Aragonese MS* | G |
|---|---|---|
| *Gomorre* | for *Gomorra* | *Mogorra* (49va35) |
| | cf. 17ra19, 25va2 | |
| *tache* | for *\*tachada* [spotted] | *chatada* (75vb1) |
| *vapor* | for *\*vapor* [vapor] | *bafor* (38vb25) |
| *Garesmans* | for *Garramanos* | *Marraganos* (54va3–4) |
| | | cf. 54va16–17 |

The scribe's internal dictation of his model as part of the copying process may have caused such shifts.[33]

Sometimes the translator misreads his model, either because of his unfamiliarity with the word or language or because of paleographic confusion, creating false union and separation of words. Given the paleographic difficulties discussed above, the complications posed by a French model, and the high frequency of exotic proper names, one would expect many faults of this type in a copy or translation of the *Tresor*; and such, indeed, is the case with G. Examples of false separation are:

| Fr. | G |
|---|---|
| *Elespons* | *los puentes* [the bridges] (52vb24–25) |
| *encharnées* [fleshed] | *e carnes* [and flesh] (34vb32) |
| *Evilmeradap* | *aquel Meradabel* [that Meradabel] (19ra12–13) |

One instance of erroneous word division appears to have been already present in the French manuscript tradition, although correctly represented in Carmody's base text: Fr. *Lotiers* [Lothar] > F *li tiers* [the third] > G *el tercero* [the third] (33va13). Copons, noting the miscalculation in the enumeration of the sons of Charlemagne (1.90.1), corrects *li tiers* to *lo segon* [the second] in Cat., for *Lotiers* was the French prince listed in the model.

Examples of false union are:

| Fr. | G |
|---|---|
| *as poulains* [to the Poles] | *aspoliens* (52va17) |
| *outre le Rin* [beyond the Rhine] | *ultra Lorin* [beyond Lorin] (53rb1) |
| *Constantinople* | *Costantin Noble* [Noble Constantine] (30va14) |
| *Saba, Ophir* | *Saluophir* (17ra12) |
| *Et Valach* | *Eualach* (17ra27) |
| *Salon as athenes,* | *e Saciel Satanas el goloso alos* |
| *Ligurgus as troienes* | *troyanos* (15ra20) |
| [Salon to the Athenians, Ligurgus to the Trojans] | [and Saciel Satanas, the greedy one, to the Trojans] |

Since these instances of false union involve proper names, the mis-readings are due primarily to unfamiliarity with the subject matter, and do not necessarily reflect a less than adequate knowledge of French.

Numerals appear to have caused great distress among French and foreign scribes alike. A good many of the figures and calculations cited by Brunetto in the *Tresor* were corrupt in his Latin source manuscripts. Carmody corrects some of the errors supposedly inherent in Brunetto's text by going to modern editions of these Latin sources. A few samples suffice to illustrate the confusion found in the various French manu-scripts of the *Tresor*. Note that G and Cat. are usually in agreement with the variant offered in Chabaille:

| Fr. MSS | G |
|---------|---|
| Fr. *v*, Ch. *v*, T *vii* | *vij* (19ra35), Cat. *vii* |
| Fr. *iii*, Ch. *iiii* | *quatro* (19rb34), Cat. *iiii* |
| Fr. *iiic et xxxii*, F *ccccxxxii* | *ccccxxxiii* (23rb2), Cat. *ccccxxxii* |

Many of the errors in calculation undoubtedly occurred in the copying process. As a general rule *x* and *v* were easily confused (e.g., Fr. *lxxv*, G *lxxx* [17vb29]), as were the number of minim strokes. On the whole, G does not present an excessive number of unique errors of this type.

Up to this point, we have examined external errors or those of a mechanical nature, including paleographical and scribally originated errors. We now turn our attention to internal difficulties encountered by the Aragonese translator. These typically encompass problems of French grammar and syntax. Old French, together with Old Provençal, is unique among the medieval Romance languages in that, until the last quarter of the thirteenth century, it maintained a functional two-case declension system, composed of a nominal case (*cas sujet*) and an oblique case (*cas régime*) for nouns, adjectives, and articles. Even before the twelfth century this system had already begun to show signs of decay, as analogical tendencies began to surface, tendencies that grew stronger in the thirteenth century. Third declension nouns were modified by analogy with first declension nouns, for example, *li sire* > *li sires*. The language utilized by Brunetto in the *Tresor* shows signs of this trend.

Aware of the existence of a case system, and aided by the presence of conjugated verbs, the Aragonese translator manages a good amount of fidelity to his source, despite the lack of a comparable case system in Aragonese, Catalan, or Castilian. Nevertheless, he experiences occasional lapses, interpreting the final *-s* of the singular nominative noun as a standard Hispano-Romance plural marker and, therefore, translating incorrectly:

| Fr. (sg.) | G (pl.) |
|---|---|
| *jaans* [giant] | *gigantes* [giants] (24rb9–10) |
| *li sires* [lord] | *los senyores* [the lords] (57rb29–30) |
| *li homs* [man] | *los omnes* [the men] (59vb35) |
| *millors* [better] | *mjllores* [better] (62ra12–13) |
| *pelerins* [pilgrim] | *pelegrines* [pilgrims] (63va1) |
| *fiz* [son] | *fillos* [sons, or sons and daughters] (67ra25) |
| *peres* [father] | *padres* [fathers, or parents] (67ra26) |

In two instances a plural noun is converted into a singular, because the masculine plural noun correctly lacks a final *-s* in the *cas sujet:* Fr. pl. *arteil* [joints] > G sg. *artillo* [joint] (63va20). The interpretation of Fr. pl. *les gens* [peoples] > G sg. *el omne* [the man] is more difficult to explain and should most logically be attributed to a reading similar to the pl. *li hom* [the men] in the unknown French model, which to the Aragonese translator would appear to be singular.

Irregularities in the forms of proper names in the Aragonese *Tresor* do not seem to have been caused by the French case system. They appear, rather, to be due to the translator's vacillation between Latinate and vernacular reflexes: *Iohan/Juan*; *Julius/Juljo*; *Luch/Luchas*; *Octaujanus/Octaujano*; *Priamus/Priamo*; *Saturnus/Saturno*; and *Tulius/Tulio*.

Of a more serious nature are those instances in which the translator corrupts a name, sometimes in various forms:[34] *Demetrius Creticus* 18va22, *Njntrion Creticon* 18va28 [Demetrius Creticus]; *Efesun* 29ra9, *Efesio* 50ra37, *Esenesun* 30vb18–19 [Efesun]; *Loys* 33va32, *Locis* 33va15 [Louis]; *Mont Causo* 49rb34, *Mont Chasso* 49vb17 [Mod. Fr. *Mont Casse*]; *Patimos* 31ra5, *ysla de Pannos* 29ra6 [island of Patmos]; and *Rose* 53rb6, *Royne* 51vb27 [Rhone river]. Generated by multiple interferences, as well as false union and separation, these errors are indicative of a lack of comprehension of the source material on the part of the translator.

Characteristic of medieval vernacular prose is its paratactic format, which involves the coordination of sentences through the repetition of the copulative conjuction Lat. *et* [and] > Cast., Arag. *e/et.* Hypotactic constructions and subordinated clauses were less common, and many medieval vernaculars employed only a meager range of conjunctions (e.g., in OCast.: *que* [that], *mas* [but], *como* [as], *assi como* [such as], *si* [if]).[35] Among the conjunctions used in the *Trasoro* (some in imitation of their French model) are: *car* [for], *otrosi, por esto*, and *por exo* [for this] (for Fr. *parce que* [because], as well as *porce/por ce* [for this reason]), *por que* [because], *pero* [but], *sino* [but rather], *si* [if], and *assi que* [thus].

There are many instances in which the syntax of G is faulty, rendering sentences and even entire passages unintelligible, particularly in the *mappamundi* and the bestiary. One may be quick to accuse the Aragonese translator of inadequacy in his task, and some errors may, indeed, be due to his lack of comprehension of the French text. However, the *Tresor* is plagued by the paratactic overuse of copulative conjunctions, which makes for lengthy sentences. Further deterioration of logical progression in the prose is a result of the corrupted manuscript tradition. For these reasons, it is clear to see why the translator of G often loses track of the sense of a sentence.

In those instances where the translator of G misunderstands the syntax of his French model, he inserts the copulative conjuction *e/et* between the principal and dependent clauses, as illustrated by the following examples: "tanto como la cosa yes mas grosa e de mas espesa materia, (e) de tanto si toma el fuego mas fuerte" [as much as the thing is bigger and of thicker material (and so), it burns stronger] (39ra25–28) and "por que alla do la luna deue star judgada de xxxa dias, segunt las epactas, (e) ella es prima" [because there, where the moon ought to be judged at 30 days, according to the phases, (and) it is prime] (46va9–12). In contrast to this tactic, the translator at times omits a conjunction where it is necessary; he has either failed to comprehend the OFr. original or has been affected by external factors such as poor lighting or inattention caused by exhaustion: "E su contrario [son] la tierra, mal enconja [e] aptupno" [and its opposite [is] the land, melancholy, [and] autumn] (34vb15–16) and "Es tal manera que lexa la mar e toda la tierra de Africa ala diestra, [e] Espanya e toda Eoropa a sinjstra" [It is such that it leaves the sea and all the land of Africa on the right, [and] Spain and all Europe to the left] (53va14–17).

Frequent omission of the verb *ser* occurs throughout the text, another indication that the translator did not logically follow his model with ease "Alla es la tierra de Dite, en do [es] el monte de Samaria que de nueyte fa grant frio" [There is the land of Dite, where the mountain of Samaria [is], which is very cold at night] (50ra33–35); and "Pues [es] de dentro la nuestra mar la isla de Grecia" [So, inside our sea [is] the island of Greece] (52vb3–4).

The foremost problem faced by vernacular translators has always been posed by the lexis. Medieval prologues repeatedly complain that the Romance tongues are so lexically impoverished as to provide only rudimentary possibilities for translation. Early translators point out that while their predecessors were challenged by translations from Greek to Latin, "esa misma o mayor dificultad sea tornar de latin en fabla castellana que de griego en latin" [it is an equal or greater difficulty to translate from Latin into Castilian as from Greek into Latin] (Alonso de Madrigal, in Schiff 1905, p. 41).[36]

One popular medieval translation device was the binary construction or replacement of one word in the source text by two in the translation, the latter usually being synonyms joined by the copulatives *e* [and], *o* [or], or *ni . . . ni* [neither . . . nor]. Lacking the rich lexical resources of Latin, vernacular scribes were often forced to use two terms to express the full sense of the Latin. Burgundius, the thirteenth-century translator of the *Vie de St. Jean Chrisostome,* explains this practice: "verbum ex verbis statui transferendum, deficienciam quidem dictionum intervenientem duabus vel etiam tribus dictionibus adiectis replens" [I have decided that a word should be translated with several words, supplementing any deficiency in expression between them by adding two or even three expressions].[37] Raoul de Presles echoes Burgundius's statement, contending that in Latin works there are "plusieurs mos qui ne se peuent pas bonnement translater en françois sanz adition ou declaration" [several words which cannot be well translated into French without addition or clarification], obliging the translator to procede "par une maniere de circonlocution ou autrement" [by a manner of circumlocution or otherwise.][38] The Aragonese *Trasoro* is replete with these multinomial formations.

## Foreign Term + Gloss

In a number of instances, the Aragonese translator replaces a French word with an item etymologically related to it, but which is uncommon in his native Aragonese. An additional term of a more familiar nature is then added as a remedy:

| Fr. | G |
|---|---|
| *noiens* [nothing] | *nient o no Res* [nothing or no thing] (12vb16) |
| *art* [burns] | *arde e crema* [burns] (13ra24) |
| *maint* [remains] | *manexe o esta* [remains or is] (44va14–15) |
| *mont* [mountain] | *mont o montanyas* [mount or mountains] (53ra15–16) |
| *gorge* [throat] | *gorga o cuello* [throat or neck] (70rb19) |

## Synonymic or Approximative Translation

The translator sometimes replaces his source by two equally valid translations. Each choice conveys part of the contextualized meaning of the source word, since neither suffices alone in the mind of the translator:

| Fr. | G |
|---|---|
| *apeticent* [get smaller] | *achiquecen et mjnguan* [grow smaller] (45rb26–27) |
| *ostée* [thrown] | *tirado o sacado* [thrown and taken out] (56ra7) |
| *bek* [beak] | *pico o rostro* [beak and face] (58ra3–4) |
| *fuit* [fled] | *fuye o se slenga* [flees or distances himself] (58ra16) |
| *gorge* [throat] | *la bocha ela gola* [the mouth and the gullet] (58rb31–32) |
| *hain* [hate] | *yra e desplazer* [anger and displeasure] (65ra10) |

Somewhat rarer is the opposite tendency of simplifying or replacing two French terms with one Aragonese term, either because the translator deems his model superfluous (e.g., *nés et les narilles* [nose and nostrils]) or because he does not understand his model (*tantalus o hairon* [woodstork or heron]):

78

| Fr. | G |
|---|---|
| *dous et soués* [sweet and tender] | *bueno* [good] (64ra9) |
| *tantalus o hairon* [woodstork or heron] | *tantalus* [woodstork] (64ra16) |
| *nés et les narilles* [nose and nostrils] | *narizes* [nostrils] (62rb17) |

## Binary Formulas

Certain binary constructions become so commonplace that they take on the characteristics of a formula. Many of these pleonastic groups are considered carryovers from the bureaucratic or chancellery style prose, which today still lingers in legalistic formulas.[39] These usually signal a dissatisfaction with the first translation and indicate deficiencies in the vernacular of the translator. The *Trasoro* offers several instances of what may be considered formulas:

| Fr. | G |
|---|---|
| *mestier* [trade] | *officio o menester* [profession or trade] (10rb26–27) |
| *mestiers* [trade] | *oficios o mesteres* [professions or trades (10rb35) |
| *tozjours* [always] | *todos dias o tiempos* [every day or time] (40va24) |
| *tozjors* [always] | *todos dias o tiempos* [every day or time] (42ra11–12) |
| *signal* [sign] | *senyal o signo* [signal or sign] (44va14; 47rb10–11) |
| *tour* [rotation] | *torno o buelta* [turn or rotation] (43vb29) |
| *tornie* [turns] | *mueue e rueda* [moves and circles] (47ra22) |
| *tornie* | *mueue e gira en torno* [moves and turns around] (47va9–10) |

It is unlikely that the examples offered above are mere coincidence; however, a glance at other Aragonese translations of the period would furnish a more accurate account of whether widely accepted formulas existed and the frequency with which they were used.

One word that troubled our translator, Fr. *tost* [soon, quickly], is replaced now by a single word, now by a formulaic pair:

| Fr. | G |
|-----|---|
| *tost* | *luego* [presently] (24rb19) |
| *tost* | *ayna* [quickly] (39vb5; 41ra31) |
| *tost* | *en vn punto o ayna* [immediately or quickly] (11rb21) |
| *tantost* | *lugo o en vn punto* [presently and immediately] (49va27–28) |
| *tost* | *ayna e en vn punto* [quickly and immediately] (62vb3) |

Whether this is symptomatic of the birth of a formula or its demise is not clear; it is evident, however, that some change in the translator's system is in progress.

## Semicorrections

Semicorrections are binary constructions in which the translator, for external or internal reasons, incorrectly interprets his source word, and, realizing his mistake, supplies a corrected translation. The error is left in the text, joined to the correction by the conjunctions *e/et* or *o*. Wittlin describes the process as such:[40] the translator dictates a first vague or faulty translation, and immediately corrects or betters this first choice. His scribe writes and leaves both forms, perhaps not wishing to mark his copy with erasures, or not realizing that the dictator has corrected himself. The process could also occur by means of internal dictation; Wittlin documents the regularity of this practice among medieval translators and scribes.[41] Nearly three dozen instances of semicorrection have been documented in Book One of the *Trasoro,* of which I provide a few examples:

| Fr. | G |
|---|---|
| *choses* [things] | *questiones o cosas* [questions or things] (9rb9) |
| *ne set la fin* [doesn't know the end] | *no sabe la fin nj supo* [doesn't know the end nor knew it] (16va1) |
| *fu* [went] | *era o fue* [was going or went] (27rb1) |
| *l'espois* [space] | *los poderes o spacios* [the powers or spaces] (38vb6) |
| *cours* [course, route] | *cuerpo o curso* [body or course] (40vb31–32) |
| *comme* [how] | *quanto o como* [how much or how] (41ra32–33) |
| *e mont Martel* [and Mount Martel] | *e mont Moral e mont Martel* [and Mount Moral and Mount Martel] (50vb25–26) |
| *home* [man] | *padre o omne* [father or man](51va5–6) |
| *quex* [which (pl.)] | *que o quales* [what or which (pl.)] (55rb10) |
| *le fosse* [ditch] | *la tierra ela fuesa* [the land and the ditch] (56vb9) |

Some of the above pairs reveal the translator's process of mental association in his own language (e.g., *padre o omne*), while others signal an initial lack of recognition of the French source word (*l'espois, cours, quex*).

## Mistranslations and Changes in Meaning

Instances of inaccurate or mis-translations are sprinkled throughout the *Trasoro* for a variety of internal and external reasons. In the majority of cases, the translator did not recognize his model and incorporated into his text something that looks similar and that may even make some sense in the context:

| Fr. | G |
|-----|---|
| *passion* [passion] | *la presion de Jhesu Xristo* [the arrest of Jesus Christ] (29va18–19) |
| *unité* [unity] | *humanjdat delas .iij. personas* [humanity of the three persons] (31rb34) |
| *monda* [cleans] | *era mudado de la lebrossedat* [was converted from the leprosy] (32ra29) |
| *eternité* [eternity] | *nj de entendimjento, mas de naxenc'a* [not of reasoning, but rather of birth] (35ra25) |
| *ensamble* [together] | *fizo todas cosas en senblança* [made all things in the image] (35ra27–28) |

Certain words caused repeated problems for the translator:

| Fr. | G |
|-----|---|
| *neis* [still] | *nj encara* [not even] (60vb36); *Delos* [of the] (34va18) |
| *boches* [humps] | *bocas* [mouths] (70vb30, 73ra9) |
| *es* [in the] | *elas* [and the] (35ra10); *las* [the] (35ra11) |

The Aragonese translator was evidently competent in his task and appears to have made most of his errors through inattention, or simple ignorance of the peculiarities of Old French (*es* = contracted form of *en les; neis* < L. *nec ipsum*).

Brunetto Latini's *Li livres dou tresor*

In this examination of the specific translation techniques used by the Aragonese translator of the *Tresor,* it has become clear that the author adhered to the practical methods employed by his contemporaries. A one-to-one correspondence with the French model is maintained and stylistic embellishment is avoided. One may hypothesize that the almost formulaic use of synonymic pairs or binomials, while common to most medieval translations, stems from the chancellery language so well known to the royal scribes and notaries who produced so many literary translations in France and Aragon. Certainly the *Tresor* exemplifies the fourteenth-century Crown of Aragon's awakening interest in vernacular translation, cultural enhancement, and political enrichment.

The stream of French translations of Graeco-Roman and Semitic texts across the Pyrenees into Aragon inspired prominent patrons such as Pere III, Joan I, Juan Fernández de Heredia, and Martí I to gather and carefully preserve these works in their own languages (Aragonese and Catalan), in emulation of the French monarch, Charles V, and his royal court. As a postscript, it should be mentioned that the Aragonese texts produced during this period were subsequently used as source material by Castilian authors decades later. Vernacular humanist translation in Spain thus traces its roots from the late medieval Crown of Aragon to royal literary patronage in fourteenth-century France.

## Notes

1. Antoni Rubió i Lluch, "La cultura catalana en el regnat de Pere III," *Estudis Universitaris Catalans* 8 (1913–14): 221.

2. Of fundamental importance to the study of this period is the work of Rubió i Lluch, *Documents per l'història de la cultura catalana mig-eval,* 2 vols. (Barcelona: Institut d'Estudis Catalans, 1908–21), which provides a carefully sifted selection of chancellery documents from the Archivo de la Corona de Aragón. The raw data are analyzed in two significant articles by Antoni Rubió i Lluch that deal with the reigns of Pere III ("La

cultura catalana") and Joan I ("Joan I Humanista i el primer període de l'humanisme català," *Etudis Universitaris Catalans* 10 [1917–18]: 1–116). The equally significant question of fourteenth-century Catalan humanism is treated in Martín de Riquer, "Medievalismo y humanismo en la Corona de Aragón a fines del siglo XIV," in *VIII Congreso de Historia de la Corona de Aragón: Ponencias, 1–8 de octubre de 1967, Valencia* (1969–73), pp. 221–35; Lola Badia, "L'humanisme català: Formació i crisi d'un concepte historiogràfic," in *Actes del V Col.loqui Internacional de Llengua i Literatura Catalanes, Andorra, 1–6 d'octubre de 1979,* ed. J. Bruguera i J. Massot i Muntaner (Santa Creus: Publicacions de l'Abadia de Montserrat, 1980), pp. 41–70; and Francisco Rico, "Petrarca y el 'humanismo catalán'," in *Actes del Vi Col.loqui Internacional de Llengua i Literatura Catalanes, Roma, 28 setembre–2 octubre 1982,* ed. Giuseppe Tavani i Jordi Pinell (Santa Creus: Publicacions de l'Abadia de Montserrat, 1983), pp. 257–91.

3. All four sons of Jean II the Good of France were avid bibliophiles: along with Charles there was Louis d'Anjou (1339–84); Jean de Berry (1340–1416) (see Leopold Delisle, *Recherches sur la librairie de Charles V,* 2 vols. (Paris: Honoré Champion, 1907); and Philippe, duc de Bourgogne (1342–1404) (see Patrick M. de Winter, *La Bibliothèque de Philippe le Hardi, duc de Bourgogne (1364–1404)* (Paris: Centre National de la Recherche Scientifique, 1985). The holdings of Charles's library (listed as ca. one thousand volumes), carefully inventoried in 1373, 1411, 1413, and 1424, have been published by Delisle (*Recherches sur la librairie de Charles V*).

4. A closer evaluation of Charles's motivation can be found in Jacques Monfrin, "Humanisme et traductions au Moyen Age," in *L'Humanisme médiéval dans les littératures romanes du XII^e au XIV^e siècles,* Actes et Colloques 3, ed. Anthime Fourrier (Paris: C. Klincksieck, 1964), pp. 232–34.

5. The king is lauded for his patronage of the arts by Christine de Pisan in *Le Livre des fais et de bonnes meurs du sage roy Charles V,* and by Raoul de Presles in his French translation of St. Augustine's *De civitate Dei*; see Peter Dembowski, "Learned Latin Treatises in French: Inspiration, Plagiarism and Translation," *Viator* 17 (1986): 261, and Jeanette Beer, "Raoul de Presles's *La Cité de Dieu* and Calvin's *Institution de la religion Chrestienne* and *Institutio Christianae religionis*" in this volume.

6. See Nicole Oresme's comment in the prologue to his translation of Aristotle's *Ethics* (1370): "Et, pour certain, translater telz livres en françois et baillier en françois les arts

et les sciences est un labor moult profittable; car c'est un langage noble et commun a genz de grant engin et de bonne prudence" [And, of course, to translate such books into French and to put these arts and sciences into French is a very profitable task; for it is a noble language and one common to people of great intellect and of true competence]. Cited from the Menut edition of Oresme's translation (p. 100), in Dembowski, "Learned Latin Treatises in French," p. 263.

7. Holdings of the pontifical collection are described in Francisco Ehrle, *Historia Bibliothecae Romanorum Pontificum tum Bonifatianae tum Avenionensis,* Biblioteca dell'Academia Storico-Giuridica 7 (Rome: Typis Vaticinis, 1890); Anneliese Meier, "Der Katalog der päpstlichen Bibliothek in Avignon vom jahr 1411," in *Ausgehendes Mittelalter: Gesammelte Aufsätze zur Geistesgeschichte des 14. Jahrhunderts,* vol. 3, Storia e Letteratura 138 (Rome: Edizione di Storia e Letteratura, 1977); and Daniel Williman, *Bibliothèques ecclésiastiques au temps de la papauté d'Avignon,* Documents, Etudes et Répertoires publiés par l'Institut de Recherche et d'Histoire des Textes (Paris: Editions du Centre National de la Recherche Scientifique, 1980).

8. According to Rubió i Lluch (*Documents per l'història,* 2:xix), the Archivo de la Corona de Aragón in Barcelona preserves close to two million pieces of correspondence dating from the reigns of Jaume II (1291–1327) to Alfonso V (1416–58). Approximately 2,100 deal explicitly with literary translations made under Pere III.

9. Riquer, "Medievalismo y humanismo," addressing the question of linguistic unity in the kingdom, finds evidence to support the existence of a standard literary Catalan in the Aragonese court in the writings and correspondence of Bernat Metge and Francesc Eiximenis. Many translators appeared to be bilingual; see Ferrer Sayol's dual translation of Palladius's *De re rustica* into Aragonese and Catalan (Thomas Capuano, ed., *Obra de agricultura, traducida y comentada en 1385 por Ferrer Sayol,* Dialect Series 10 [Madison: Hispanic Seminary of Medieval Studies, 1990]).

10. Rubió i Lluch, "La cultura catalana," p. 232.

11. Peter Russell, *Traducciones y traductores en la Península Ibérica (1400–1550),* Monografías de Cuadernos de Traducción e Interpretación 2 (Bellaterra: Universidad Autónoma de Barcelona, 1985), p. 14.

12. In the second part of *Don Quijote* (2:63), Cervantes has his protagonist reproach translators who used Romance versions of Latin originals as their models, asserting that "traducir de las lenguas fáciles ni arguye ingenio ni elocución" [to translate from simple languages requires neither intelligence nor eloquence]. Lope de Vega also attacked the fraud perpetrated by some later writers who utilized Italian models: "No sabiendo latin bastantemente copian y trasladan de la lengua italiana lo que se les antoja, y luego dicen: traducido de latin en castellano" [Not knowing Latin well enough, they compose and translate from the Italian language whatever they please, and then they say: translated from Latin into Castilian] (from *El desdichado por la honra*, in Curt J. Wittlin, ed., *Las décadas de Tito Livio de Pero López de Ayala*, 2 vols. (Barcelona: Puvill Libros, 1982), 1: 91.

13. Pero López de Ayala's translation of the *Decades* of (Titus) Livy is a prime example of, in this case, a Castilian translation modeled on a French translation of a Latin original. Wittlin's edition of the Castilian translation provides a thorough comparison of all three versions, pointing out the types of deficiencies that crept into each vulgarization; see Wittlin, *Las décadas de Tito Livio de Pero López de Ayala*, vols. 1–2.

14. The only complete version extant is the 1418 translation by Guillem de Copons; see Curt J. Wittlin, ed., *Llibre del tresor: versió catalana de Guillem de Copons*, 4 vols. (Barcelona: Barcino, 1971–89).

15. See Spurgeon Baldwin, ed., *Libro del tesoro* (Madison: Hispanic Seminary of Medieval Studies, 1989).

16. See Dawn Prince, ed., *Text and Concordance of the Aragonese Translation of Brunetto Latini's 'Li livres dou tresor' Gerona Cathedral, MS 20, a, 5*, Dialect Series 11 (Madison: Hispanic Seminary of Medieval Studies, 1990) [booklet and microfiche].

17. Prince, *Text and Concordance,* pp. 5–6.

18. Francis J. Carmody, ed., *Li livres dou tresor de Brunetto Latini*, University of California Publications in Modern Philology, 22 (Berkeley: University of California Press, 1948).

19. Although the Aragonese *Trasoro* has been specified with certainty as a member of the interpolated Δ family of manuscripts, the exact French codex used in its preparation has

yet to be identified, if indeed it is extant. Without the translator's precise model, it is difficult to determine with accuracy which innovations and modifications in G are to be attributed to the Aragonese translator and which originated in his source. This causes some difficulty in conducting an analysis of the translation technique used in its preparation. Fortunately, the existence of a Catalan translation using the same source codex offers a reliable control text. See Dawn Prince, "The Textual History of *Li livres dou tresor* of Brunetto Latini: Fitting the Pieces Together," *Manuscripta* (forthcoming), for a more detailed study of the textual relationship between G and *Cat.*

20. Joaquín Rubio Tovar, *La prosa medieval*, Lectura crítica de la literatura española, 3 (Madrid: Playor, 1982), pp. 50–54.

21. G is compared to Polycarpe Chabaille's edited text (*Li Livres dou tresor par Brunetto Latini* [Paris: Imprimerie Impériale, 1863, here designated Ch.]; it is an eclectic edition, based on MS F (Paris, B.N. fr. 12581). Chabaille's French version is consistently closer in content to the Aragonese than Carmody's *Li Livres dou tresor*, based on MS T (Paris, B.N. 1110). All references to the *Tresor* indicate book, chapter, and section, observing the system established by Carmody. Because of its philological rigor, Carmody's edition will serve as the standard French text (labeled Fr.) in this chapter.

22. References to passages are listed in the following order: page number, indication of v (verso) or r (recto), column indication (a or b), then line number(s).

23. Juan Corominas with José Pascual, *Diccionario crítico etimológico castellano e hispánico*, 2nd ed., 6 vols. (Madrid: Gredos, 1980), 1: 479, "balsa." Subsequent references to the *Diccionario* appear in the text abbreviated as *DCECH*.

24. A[ntoni] Griera, *Tresor de la llengua, de les tradiciones i de la cultura popular de Catalunya*, 2nd ed., 14 vols. (Barcelona: Ediciones Poligráficas, 1966–70), 2: 73, "barra."

25. Griera, *Tresor*, 6: 251.

26. Juan A. Frago Gracia, "La sinonimia textual y el proceso castellanizador de Aragón," in *La Corona de Aragón y las lenguas románicas. Miscelánea de homenaje para Germán Colón,* ed. Günter Holtus, Georges Lüdi, and Michael Metzeltin (Tübingen: Gunter Narr Verlag, 1989), pp. 215–25.

27. Of interest in this respect is the case of the Aragonese *Libro de Paladio*, translated in 1385 by the Catalan notary Ferrer Sayol, author of a Catalan translation of the same work. According to Capuano (*Obra de agricultura*, p. vi), Sayol's Aragonese version is characterized by a hybrid language, as a result of interference by the translator's native language.

28. These omissions as documented in the Aragonese text, cited from Dawn Prince, "An Edition and Study of Book One of the Unique Aragonese Translation of Brunetto Latini's 'Li livres dou tresor'" (Ph.D. diss., University of California—Berkeley, 1990), are: 9ra34, 10va11, 10vb6, 11vb16–17, 12rb7, 12va16, 15va31, 16ra21, 22vb1, 22vb20, 22vb36–23ra1, 25va14–15, 35rb18, 42va25–28, 43ra15, 47va27, 70rb30, 70rb31 (twice), 71rb28–29, 73vb12–13, 74rb18–19, and 76rb6.

29. The additional omissions, cited from Prince, "An Edition," are: 14ra35, 17rb12–13, 19va17, 21va8, 24vb17–18, 25ra32, 25rb4, 27vb18, 29ra3, 29ra17, 30ra27, 30vb7–8, 30vb23, 32rb1–2, 42ra16, 42va14–15, 46ra22, 46va26, 47ra28–29, 49rb12, 50ra37–50rb1, 52rb20–21, 53va21, 53va34–35, 54vb1, 54vb6, 54vb25, 61va27–28, 63vb2–3, 70rb6, 74va5, and 74vb19–20.

30. See Conrado Morterero y Simón, *Apuntes de iniciación a la paleografía española de los siglos XII a XVII*, 2nd ed., Instituto Luis de Salazar y Castro (CSIC) (Madrid: Hidalguía, 1963), p. 59.

31. Adriano Cappelli, *Dizionario di abbreviature latine ed italiane*, 6th ed. (Milan: Ulrico Hoepli, 1979), pp. xxxii–iii.

32. Alberto Blecua, *Manual de crítica textual* (Madrid: Castalia, 1983), p. 24.

33. Blecua, *Manual*, p. 17.

34. Purely phonological vacillation in the target language of the type *Fredrich/Fradrich/Fadrich* reflects the instability of the nascent vernacular and is not considered as corruption.

35. Af Geijerstam, *La Grant Cronica de Espanya*, libros I–II (Uppsala: Almquist and Wiksells, 1964), p. 126, lists the conjunctions found in Heredia's *La Grant Cronica de*

*Espanya,* subdividing them acording to function (disjunctive, adversative, temporal, conditional, etc.). She briefly outlines the use of each in the accompanying vocabulary (pp. 162–365). Gunnar Tilander, ed., *Vidal Mayor. Traducción aragonesa de la obra 'In excelsis Dei thesaurus' de Vidal de Canellas*, 3 vols., Legas Hispanicae Medii Aevi, 4 (Lund: Hakan Ohlssons Boktryckeri, 1956), pp. 85–90, also comments on subordination in the *Vidal Mayor.*

36. Alonso de Madrigal, in Mario Schiff, *La Bibliothèque du Marquis de Santillane*, Bibliothèque de l'Ecole des Hautes Etudes, Sciences historiques et philologiques, 153 (Paris, 1905; repr. Amsterdam: G. I. Van Heusden, 1970), p. 41.

37. Curt J. Wittlin, "Traductions et commentaires médiévaux de la *Cité de Dieu* de saint Augustin," *Travaux de Linguistique et de Littérature* 16 (1978): 546 n. 19.

38. See, in this volume, Beer, Appendix, lines 187–88 and 183–84.

39. Wittlin, *Las décadas*, p. 120.

40. Curt J. Wittlin, "Semicorrections en traduccions medievals," in *Estudis de llengua i literatura catalanes oferts a Ramon Aramón i Serra en el seu setantè aniversari*, ed. Manuel Jorba, Estudis Universitaris Catalans, 23 (Barcelona: Curial Edicions Catalanes, 1979), p. 55.

41. Wittlin, "Semicorrections en traduccions medievals," pp. 599–604.

# Patronage and the Translator:
## Raoul de Presles's *La Cité de Dieu* and Calvin's *Institution de la religion Chrestienne* and *Institutio religionis Christianae*

### Jeanette Beer

In an age when patronage has virtually disappeared[1] it is not easy to appreciate the complexity of the role of earlier translators who attempted to fulfill their responsibilities towards a public, a source, *and* a patron.[2] This chapter looks at patron-translator interaction from the textual evidence of the prologue to Raoul de Presles's *La Cité de Dieu*[3] and the "Epistre" and "Epistola" prefacing Calvin's *Institution de la religion Chrestienne*[4] and *Institutio religionis Christianae*.[5] The two translators could not have been more different. Raoul de Presles, an advocate by profession, was converting one of the most important texts in Christendom from Latin into French by the request of his sovereign, Charles V of France. During the translation process the king initially paid him four hundred *livres* per annum, and subsequently the king paid six hundred *livres* per annum for the task. In addition, the king allowed Raoul the use of several volumes from his personal library.[6] The commissioned task began in 1371 and ended with Raoul's presentation to the king of two weighty volumes on September 1, 1375. In the prologue Raoul commented on his royal commission, used traditional protestations of incompetence to reveal his competence, and named several of the works he had translated. His new assignment, as he saw it, was to make available to the king's subjects an edifying, instructive, and interesting translation of a key work that would certainly enhance the reputation of his most Christian Majesty without precipitating disputes over orthodoxy.

His identity as a translator was visibly defined in relation to the diverse set of constituencies that he mentioned in his prologue: his patron ("Vous tres excellent prince, Charles le Quint, roy de France"); his source ("monseigneur saint Augustin"); contemporary scholars, especially the theologians ("les soverains clers de vostre royaume"); the translated product ("ce livre"); and his public ("chascun qui ce livre lira"). The primary interest of this chapter is the first constituency, but an examination of the interaction between Raoul and Charles V will necessarily involve occasional consideration of the other contexts.[7]

Calvin also had a legal training, and he played a substantial role in producing a vernacular translation of the Bible, sometimes called "The Calvin Bible," but the resemblance between him and Raoul de Presles ends there. First, Calvin was his own source, and his reasons for producing a Latin and a French version of his theological treatise, the *Institutes,* were personal, not regal. Variations between the *Institutio* and the *Institution* derived from his calculated effort to convince disparate publics. (The possibility of a "traduttore e traditore" situation was, of course, eliminated in self-translation, and the variations between the versions were never due to Calvin's misinterpretations of the source!) Unlike Raoul, who wished to avoid disputes with orthodox Catholicism, Calvin's aims were precisely to precipitate such disputes and to undermine the religious establishment. The fact of patronage remained crucial in the sixteenth century, however, and Calvin desperately sought against all odds to win royal support for this first important manifesto of Protestantism in France. Calvin's efforts in the *Institutes* to reassure and instruct the faithful, justify his cause to the theologians, *and* persuade the king of Protestantism's viability were a brilliant display of versatility. If they had succeeded, the whole religious scene in France would have changed irrevocably from that moment onward.

## Raoul de Presles

The fact that the decision to have St. Augustine's *De civitate Dei* rendered into French was a royal decision explains Raoul's proper posture of servitude in the prologue's dedication: "A vous tres excellent prince, Charles le Quint, roy de France, je Raoul de Praelles, vostre humble serviteur et subjet, tout vostre et tout ce que je sai et puis faire a vostre commandement" [To the most excellent prince, Charles the Fifth, king of France, I Raoul de Presles, your humble servant and your subject, totally yours, whose every skill and ability is yours to command].[8] Of course the "servitude" of patronage was never as extreme as the conventions of patronal homage suggested, and in the *La Cité de Dieu* Raoul managed, despite his official hiring, to establish for himself a discrete identity, neither idiosyncratically dominating the enterprise nor allowing himself to be dominated by it. But the relation of commissioned to commissioner remained one of close understanding and of mutual trust throughout. Raoul, a lawyer by profession, was happy to perform this literary service of translation for the king, and Charles knew that Raoul could be relied upon to fulfill the charge appropriately.

In homage to his monarch Raoul provided a short history of the monarchy in France, beginning with a mention of the line of Roman emperors who bore the eagle (lines 45–46), then proceeding from the divinely anointed Clovis (line 54 and lines 63–78), through Charlemagne whose divine aid, miraculous vision, and noble victories over the Saracens were listed (lines 94–111), down to that great emperor's living namesake (112 ff.).[9]

> Et ces choses, mon tres redoubté seigneur, denottent et demonstrent par vraye rayson que par ce vous estez et devés estre le seul principal protecteur, champion, et defenseur de l'Esglise comme ont esté vos devanciers. Et ce tient le saint siège de Romme qui a acostumé a escripre a vos devanciers et a vous singulièrement en l'intitulation des lettres: "Au Tres Crestien des Princes." (lines 131–35)

[And these things, my very revered lord, truly demonstrate and reveal that through this you are and must be the sole and principal protector, champion, and defender of the Church as were your ancestors. And this is maintained by the Holy See of Rome whose custom it has been to address your forebears and you uniquely by entitling letters "To the Most Christian of Princes."]

It is notable that, by a happy coincidence of protocols, Raoul's "Tres Crestien des Princes"—Charles V—*and* Charlemagne *and* St. Denis *and* St. Augustine *and* St. John the Evangelist gloried together in the venerable title of "monseigneur." The suggestive affinities linking St. Augustine, St. Charles "jadis empereür et roi de France" [former emperor and king of France], and Charles V were, in fact, the unifying theme of the prologue at a time when Charles V's astute rule was repairing past damages to the image of French monarchy. In lines 12–14 Raoul established a useful comparison between St. Augustine and the eagle whose properties were:

1) to soar above all others—as St. Augustine soared above all the doctors of the Church;

2) to gaze unblinkingly at the Sun—that is, the Holy Trinity; and

3) to rid itself of those of its young who cannot do similarly—as the saint condemned heretics.

Those theologically interpreted bestiary similes were transferred without delay from St. Augustine to the king, "estrait du lignaige des empereurs rommains qui portent l'aigle" (lines 45–46) [descended from the lineage of the emperors who bear the eagle]. Significantly, the exposition of the eagle simile for the *monarch* occupied 182 lines, not the mere 36 that Raoul's saintly source had received.

Raoul also established with explicitness the connections between the fourteenth-century Charles and that other Most Christian of Princes, Charlemagne. The latter, who had enjoyed the dual honor of ruling France and protecting the faith of the Holy Roman Empire, had preferred

St. Augustine over all books, and it was with obvious political intent that Raoul reminded the king publicly of the cultural tradition to which the monarchy was heir:

> Et tieng que en ceste partie vous avez voulu ensuivre monseigneur saint Charles, qui entre touz les livres que il estudioit et veoit volontiers, il lisoit les livres de monseigneur saint Augustin, et sur tous les autres le livre *De la Cité de Dieu.* (lines 148–50)

> [And I believe that in this respect you wanted to follow the example of St. Charles who, of all the books he studied and enjoyed, preferred the books of St. Augustine and, in particular, the book of *The City of God.*]

Raoul was not the first to remark upon the king's veneration of Charlemagne, for, even before Charles's ascendancy to the throne, his veneration of Charlemagne was celebrated. For example, there is a striking similarity (which can hardly be coincidental) between Raoul's comment and the earlier observation of Yves de St.-Denis in his *Vie de Saint Denis* that Charles "historia [*sic*: "historiam"] et antiquorumque [*sic*: "antiquorum"?] gesta libenter audiebat, in libros diurnis perpetue beati Augustini qui *De civitate Dei* intitulantur non mediocriter delectatus."[10]

Raoul's explicit charge was to translate the *De civitate Dei* as a service to Charles's kingdom, Charles's subjects, and all Christendom: "Vous [l]'avez voulu estre translaté de latin en françois pour le proufit et utilité de vostre roiaume, de vostre pueple, et de toute crestienté" (lines 145–47) [You wanted it to be translated from Latin into French for the profit and utility of your kingdom, your people, and the whole of Christendom]. Raoul referred again to this public in his prologue to the second half of the translation, where he described *La Cité de Dieu* as "non pas pour ceulx qui entendent et l'un et l'autre mais pour ceulx qui sont purs lais" [not for those who understand both (French and Latin)

Jeanette Beer

but for those who are complete laymen]. The phrase "purs lais" was not equivalent to our "total illiterates," which signifies both an absence of certain quantifiable skills and also an absence of cultural pursuits. By the fourteenth century a substantial segment of the French public could both read and write in the vernacular; a more substantial segment could read it without being able to write it; and there were even laypersons who could read and understand some Latin without being "litterati" in the clerical sense. Raoul's manner of translation revealed the level of sophistication of this lay public.

Raoul's treatment of Latin quotations even presumed an interest in that source-language for its own sake. Augustine's original preface had contained quotations from the Psalms, from the Epistle of St. James, and from Vergil's *Aeneid.* Raoul converted the Scriptural quotations into French, but the one-liner from Vergil—"Parccrc subiectis et debellare in superbos" [to spare the humble and subdue the proud]—remained in Latin, made comprehensible by Raoul's careful handling of the surrounding text. In chapter two another one-liner from Vergil remained in Latin, but two other Vergilian quotations that were only slightly longer went into French. In the next four chapters Raoul opted for French in all quotations, but Latin continued to emerge sporadically throughout the work.

One may conclude that individual lines that were easily understandable in their context were retained, as were technical (usually legal) phrases, and *sententiae* with epigrammatic qualities. There were even occasional transcriptions of certain familiar Greek words such as "angelos." The selective retention of Latin sentences should probably be interpreted as a didactic device. By titillating his public with easy citations, the translator whetted their cultural appetites. Raoul's gift for exposition can be seen in this commentary on St. Augustine's remarks on Fortuna:

Voye Alain en *Anticlaudiano* en son VII$^{me}$ livre dequel Maistre
Jehan du Mehun ou livre de la rose ou chapitre de Fortune print son

96

texte et sa sentence, et semble qu'il ne fist que le translater en ce pas. Car ou Alain dit: "Est rupis in medio maris quem verberat equor" Maistre Jehan du Mehun dit: "Une roche est sur la mer seans ice," en poursuivant le latin de Alain.

[See Alain in the seventh book of *Anticlaudianus* from which Master Jean de Meun took his text and his sentence in the *Book of the Rose*'s chapter on Fortune. And he seems merely to have translated Alain at this juncture. For where Alain says, "Est rupis in medio maris quem verberat equor," Master Jean de Meun says, "Une roche est sur la mer seans ice," following Alain's Latin.]

Raoul concluded the didactic commentary with a suggestion for further reading: "Et qui vouldra veoir belle disputacion de Fortune, voye Boece *De Consolacion* en son ii^e livre" [And for a fine disputation concerning Fortune see Boethius's *Consolatio*, book two].

One section of the public that needed no help with the intermittent snatches of Latin discourse was the *clergie*. Raoul was careful in the prologue of his vernacular enterprise to pay homage to the theologians in Charles's kingdom, marveling with somewhat ostentatious humility at the royal selection of a Raoul de Presles over such learned men:

Je doi estre esmerveillé, et non sans cause, de ce que delaissiez les souverains clers de vostre roiaume dont il en y a tant et de si grans que en toute crestienté n'en a tant ne de telz, et ausquiex tele euvre appartenoit et leur estoit deüee a translater, il puet estre cheü en vostre pensee de le moy baillier, qui au regart de culx ne suis que poudre et cendre. (lines 155–60)

[I must, however, marvel and with cause, that you pass over the sovereign *clercs* in your kingdom, whose numbers and whose excellence are unsurpassed in all Christendom; that when to them such a work belonged and its translation was their due, it occurred to you to give it to me who in their regard am but dust and ashes.]

The phrase "au regard de eulx" was brilliantly ambiguous. Its more obvious meaning was "in comparison with them I am nothing," a genuine confession of inferiority spoken, it would seem, from an objective point of view. The phrase might also mean "from their point of view I am nothing," a loaded rather than factual observation that implied no necessary endorsement from Raoul. Raoul subsequently added further disingenuous protestations of unworthiness, all of which only served to emphasize the opposite.[11] He urged the king to remember how long he had resisted the royal offer and played "hard to get":

> Et pour ce que l'en ne cuide pas que par arrogance ou par moy ingerer je l'aie voulu entreprendre, je appelle Dieu a tesmoing et vous le savez assez comment et par quel temps je l'ay refusé et differé a entreprendre, et les excusacions que je y ai pretendues. (lines 162–65)

> [And lest it be thought that I decided to undertake it through arrogance or to put myself forward, as God is my witness, you well know how and for what length of time I refused and delayed the undertaking, and the excuses I proffered to avoid it.]

He re-asserted his inferiority, his awareness of the honor done to him, and his age: "Je savoie et sai la foiblesse de mon engin, la grandeur de l'euvre et la age dont je sui qui me deüsse, si comme il me semble dorenavant reposer" (lines 165–67) [I knew and know the smallness of my ability, the greatness of the work, and my age, which should, in my view, have entitled me to rest from now on]. Noting his professional commitments as an advocate, "la grant charge du fait de mon avocacie qui est office publique et qui requiert labour continuel" (lines 176–77) [the great responsibility of my advocacy, which is a public office requiring constant labor], he gratuitously enumerated his previous works, ostensibly as another good reason *not* to accept the translative endeavor:

## Patronage and the Translator

Il me sembloit que je avoie assez labouré en mon temps tant a faire le livre qui se apelle *Le Compendieux moral de la chose publique* et le livre qui se apelle *La Muse* la quele il vous plut a recevoir en gré pour ce que je l'avoye entitulé a vouz, comme *Les Croniques en françois contemporisees du commencement du monde jusques au temps de Tarquin l'orgueilleux et du roy Cambises qui regnerent en un temps*, avecques aucunes *Epistres*. (lines 170–76)

[It seemed to me that I had labored enough in my lifetime, writing the book entitled *The Moral Compendium of the Republic*, the book called *The Muse*, which you were gracious enough to accept when I had dedicated it to you, and *Modernized French Chronicles from the Creation of the World to the Era of Tarquin the Proud and King Cambises*, together with a book of *Letters*.]

Raoul's detailed list of indisputably scholarly accomplishments provided public justification for the scholar-king's taste in translators. Perhaps it also served to advertise items with which Raoul's public was not particularly familiar. In addition, however, there was private empathy between the elderly lawyer and the infirm monarch because of their similar ages, tastes, and shared experiences during France's difficult years preceding Charles's accession. Raoul's cooperation with the king's political interests could be counted upon, and the mutually beneficial interaction of patron and translator never faltered throughout the work. It was not only the monarch's interests but also the translator's interests in the monarchy that induced Raoul's lengthy inclusions explaining royal symbolism: the monarch's thaumaturgical powers, the *fleurs de lis*, the details of the monarch's anointing and coronation, and the legend of the *oriflamme:*[12]

Et si portez seul roy et singulièrement l'oriflamme en bataille, c'est assavoir un glaive tout doré ou est atachiee une baniere vermeille la quele vos devanciers et vous avez acostumé a venir querre et prendre en l'eglise de monseigneur saint Denis a grant solempnité, reverence, et devotion, si comme vous le savez. (lines 79–82)

99

[And, sole king and singularly, you carry into battle the oriflamme, which is a golden lance with crimson banner attached that, as you know, you and your ancestors have customarily received with great solemnity, reverence, and devotion from the Church of St. Denis.]

There was no question but that the king was aware ("si comme vous le savez," said Raoul unnecessarily) of every heraldic fact in that loyalist exposition. The public homage was serviceable nevertheless, both to stroke the patron and to encourage patriotism in the patron's subjects.

As for the monarch's concern for his own edification, that, like his concern for his subjects, was genuine.[13] Charles's love of letters was greater than Raoul's quip on Sallust or a translator's compliment could convey,[14] and both were aware that this particular translation assignment was a monumental one. There was the most obvious difficulty of length, a difficulty that was compounded by the complexity of Augustine's argumentation and the technicalities in his lexicon. Furthermore, Paris of the fourteenth century bore no resemblance to Roman Africa of the fifth. The latter had desperately needed relief from schism within the Church—a relief that unfortunately the saint could not provide—and, more generally, it had needed resolution of the conflict between Christian and pagan—which the saint could provide even less. It was those needs that the Bishop of Hippo had tried to address in his monumental volumes on faith and unbelief. Fourteenth-century France had more immediate concerns than the destruction of false idols: its perpetrators of discord were no longer a Donatus or a Pelagius. Besides, it now possessed a powerful politico-religious structure, the Church, whose many theologians were professionally trained to explain with skill and authority the divine mysteries of predestination and grace. Of those "sovereign clerks whose numbers and whose caliber are unmatched in all Christendom" Raoul was carefully solicitous. They were the most dangerous and unpredictable part of an equation that for him comprised patron, translator, source, and a public anticipated by Raoul but as yet unseen.

## Patronage and the Translator

The complexity of the assignment is, therefore, apparent. Hired by an enlightened king to translate the most influential theological text yet written in Europe, chosen for his linguistic, scholarly, and patriotic qualities over a number of experts whom he was anxious not to offend or decry, and realizing the political and theological usefulness of his *La Cité de Dieu*, Raoul did not intend to jeopardize its future. Cognizant of his personal worth, he nevertheless assumed the pose of overworked "avocat" whose monarch had unfortunately read Seneca and had consequently seen fit to preserve Raoul from the unlettered idleness that, according to Seneca, was death to a man's vitality: "Je croi que vous aviés leüe celle parole de Seneque qui dist que ociosité sanz lettre est mort et sepulture de homme vif" (lines 177–79) [I believe you had read that dictum of Seneca's that inactivity without letters is like burying a man alive]. Whether as a result of his unpretentiousness or because of the quality of his translation—or both—Raoul succeeded with all the constituencies mentioned above, and copies of his work multiplied.[15]

So far no mention has been made of that most personal of interactions for a translator, that of the translator with his source. Whatever his protestations, Raoul de Presles was an excellent craftsman as he worked on Augustine. With an abundance of scholarship and an unmistakable elegance of style, he rendered the saint's text clearly and intelligently into French. Accountable to his literary patron *qua* literary patron as well as king, he effectively did homage to Charles's cultural sophistication by discussing translation methodology with him. Even more, *he made his royal patron responsible for them.* Apologizing for deviations from literality, for circumlocutions, and such, he attributed their presence to Charles's instruction to render the *real* meaning:

> Si supplie a vostre roial magesté que aussi comme simplement a
> vostre commandement j'ai ceste euvre entreprise, il vous plaise a la
> recevoir en gré et supporter mes defaultes dont je sai bien que il en
> y aura pluseurs. Et se je ne ensuy en ceste translation les propres

moz du texte, et que je y voise aulcune fois par une maniere de circonlocution ou autrement, il me sera pardonné pour ce que vous m'avez commandé pour la matiere esclarcir que je ensuive la vraie, simple, et clere sentence et le vrai entendement sans ensuivir proprement les mos du texte. (lines 180–86)

[And I beg your royal highness that inasmuch as I have with simplicity undertaken this work, it may please you to receive it favorably and to bear with my defects of which I am sure there will be several. And if I do not in this translation follow the exact words of the text and if I approach it sometimes with a sort of circumlocution or other device, I shall be forgiven because you told me, in order to make the material clear, to follow the plain, simple, obvious meaning and the real intent without meticulously following every word of the text.]

The explanation was not a new one, nor was the professed methodology; the connection between paraphrase and exegesis dated back to antiquity, as did the discussion of free versus literal translation. Raoul's inclusion of the king as both party to and also sponsor of the "sentence" method of translation reveals the degree of Charles's influence upon his translators, so that many of Raoul's contemporaries discussed their translation aims and achievements in similar terms, for example:

Aucunes foiz, où l'aucteur du livre et les docteurs et philosophes ont, pour le plus bel rectorique latin querir, transporté les dictions, pourquoy le françois ainsi ordené seroit pesant et moins cler à entendre, j'ai la sentence mise rez a rez, si comme j'ay pensé que il l'eusent dit eulz meismes, se il parlassent françois.[16]

[Sometimes, when the author of the book and the doctors and philosophers have, to achieve the finest Latin rhetoric, rearranged the phrases, with the result that the French, if ordered in this way, would

be ponderous and less easily understood, I have put each sentence in
the order I think they themselves would have said it if they had
spoken French.]

While invoking well-known debates and well-known solutions, however,
Raoul remained always a meticulous cooperator with his source-text,
which he treated as reverently as if it were Holy Scripture.[17] The greatest
liberty that Raoul allowed himself was the smoothing away of syntactic
infelicities in the original, clarifying, for example, that first sentence of
*De civitate Dei* which Augustine had lifted so awkwardly out of his *Retractiones* 2: 69 to re-use as an introduction to the new work: "Interea
Roma Gothorum inruptione agentium sub rege Alarico atque impetu
magnae cladis eversa est, cuius eversionem deorum falsorum multor-
umque cultores, quos usitato nomine paganos vocamus, in Christianam
religionem referre conantes solito acerbius et amarius Deum verum
blasphemare coeperunt"[18] [Meanwhile Rome has been overturned by an
inrush of Goths led by King Alaric and the violence of a great disaster;
the worshippers of the many false gods tried to blame this reversal on
the Christian religion and began more sharply and bitterly than usual to
blaspheme the true God]. Raoul tidied up the clumsy opening with
minimal syntactic change—the addition of a main verb to the loosely
hanging "interea"—and without change in the substance. *His* introduction
was: "Pendant ce que Romme fu affaiblie, prise, trebuchee et destruite
des Goths qui estoient soubz le roi Alaric . . . des payens . . .
s'efforcerent de mettre sus a la religion" (fol. 7ʳ) [While Rome was
weakened, captured, ravaged, and destroyed by the Goths under King
Alaric . . . pagans attempted to set upon the true religion]. In this
important introductory sentence, as throughout *La Cité de Dieu*, Raoul
succeeded remarkably well in the syntactic transference from synthetic
to analytic style, dividing long sentence units into halves or even
quarters and reworking clumsy juxtapositions or unwieldy chunks of
syntax into smoothly comprehensible sequences. The changes were made

with respect and with awareness. Raoul described his Latin source as "[un livre] compilé de diverses et haultes matieres et de hault stile et de ancienne gramaire, chargé de grans sentences suspensivez en brieves paroles" (lines 188–90) [(a book made up of) diverse lofty matters, high style, and ancient grammar, laden with long, suspended sentences, succinctly worded]. Underlying his description of Augustine's "high style" was, presumably, Cicero's classification of the "tria genera, quae genera nos figuras appellamus . . . gravis . . . mediocris . . . attenuata" (*Ad Herennium* 4. 8. 11). The contemporary translator Pierre de Bersuire used similar terminology in his description of Livy's "tres haute maniere de parler" and "les constructions . . . si trenchiees et si brieves, si suspensives et si d'estranges moz."[19] Clearly, the lexical and syntactic disparateness of French and Latin and the notion of differing stylistic "levels" were translators' discussion-pieces at the court of Charles V. Raoul's brief stylistic homage to his source reveals also the profundity of his respect for the text that had been and would continue to be one of the most influential theological works in Christendom. This respect would prevent him from taking excessive substantive liberties during the translative shift from Latin to French. Nor were his stylistic shifts so great as to produce a *rapprochement* of St. Augustine to the colloquial French of Raoul's time. (In this regard, I find an interesting difference between the style of the translation proper and Raoul's prologue or even his commentary, both of which were written in more conversational style with the king and the king's subjects in mind. I venture to guess that the prologue at least was dictated orally, while the translation of the saint's work was done more deliberately and in private.)

A significant decision in the production of *La Cité de Dieu* was Raoul's renunciation of theological comment (whether by the king's suggestion or not will probably never be determined). The detailed expositions that Raoul appended to each chapter were restricted to cultural items in *De civitate Dei*. He culled them (perhaps in Charles V's own library) from Isidore of Seville; from the three Latin commentators of *De civitate Dei* (Thomas Waleys and Nicolas Trevet's *Expositiones* and François de Meyronne's *Flores Augustini*); and from the wide range of authors who were part of Raoul's own reading experience. In matters of theology, however, the saint was the *auctor* supreme. Raoul's reverence for him was unmistakable, and he humbly described his task of translating the theological giant as "si petite main si grant mole tourner" (line 161) [such a little hand to turn so great a mill].

Raoul had reason for caution. In the fourteenth century the proper commentators for theological disputation were the doctors of the Church, a Church that was striving for a Gallican future and whose interests were protected by the new Charlemagne, "rex christianissimus." Raoul was not inclined to jeopardize either his patron or the French Church by tendentious additions to the theology of Augustine, that most "reverentissimus" of the Church fathers. He explained what the nature of his commentary would be at the beginning of the translation proper: "Nostre intention ne fut onques de mettre principalement ces paroles fors en ce qui seroit d'histoire et de poeterie . . . ayens pour principe qu'il n'est licite a aucun a disputer publiquement de la foy crestienne" (fol. 1) [Our intention was never to put forward these words (i.e., his commentary) except in what concerned historical or poetic material . . . on the principle that it is illicit for anyone to dispute publicly concerning the Christian faith]. By this modest renunciation of personal comment on all things theological Raoul was serving his patron, his Church, and, of course, his source, whose integrity would thereby be protected from gratuitously idiosyncratic glossing.[20]

There was a unique context in which Raoul's individual (i.e., legal) interests appeared to protrude to the degree of arguing with his source. The unusual intervention occurred after St. Augustine's reference to the *lex Voconia* (*De civitate Dei,* 3:1), a law forbidding female inheritance. The *lex Voconia* was introduced at the time of the Punic Wars. Augustine had reported Sallust's view that at this period of Roman history morality was at its highest peak. The saint had disagreed with Sallust, saying that Asiatic decadence ("Asiana luxuria") was still cultivated; those high morals ("mores optimos") touted by Sallust were merely a matter of degree. At all events, during the period of "Asiana luxuria" between Rome's second and last war with Carthage, said Augustine, "lata est etiam lex illa Voconia, ne quis heredem feminam faceret, nec unicam filiam" [that (infamous) Voconian law was passed forbidding anyone from naming a woman as heir, even an only daughter]. Lest his disapproval of the law had not been adequately conveyed by the scathing "illa," Augustine commented: "Qua lege quid iniquius dici aut cogitari possit, ignoro" [If anything more iniquitous than this law could be imagined, I do not know what it might be]. Raoul's opinion of the law was different. He explained first the intent of his source:

> Quant il parle de la loy qui s'apelle *lex Voconia* et dit que il nen estoit nulle plus inique pour ce que selon celle loy nulle fille ne venoit a succession de pere ne de mere, supposé que il n'y eüst autres enfans, l'entent a proprement parler des successions des privees personnes et non pas des puissans hommes comme des roys et autres grans seigneurs qui ont le gouvernement de la chose publique, si comme dit Thomas Walencis, à quoy s'acorde Franciscus de Maronis. (fols. 150ʳ–150ᵛ)

> [When he speaks of the law called the *lex Voconia* and says that there was none *so iniquitous* because according to this law no daughter could inherit from father or mother supposing there were no other children, properly speaking he is addressing the successions of private persons and not the successions of powerful men like kings and other great lords who have the government of state in their hands, as Thomas Waleys says and François de Meyronnes confirms.]

Raoul followed this clarification with a lengthy exposition of the subject of female succession and its implications as he saw them. He frankly disagreed with St. Augustine's "Qua lege quid iniquius dici aut cogitari possit, ignoro" and used Biblical history and patristic commentary to justify his anti-female stance. Thus, no woman in the Old Testament succeeded to the kingdom of Judah. "Ne il ne se treuve en tout le Viez Testament que oncques fame succedast ou roiaume de Juda ne ou roiaume d'Israël" (fol. 151$^r$) [Nor in the whole of the Old Testament can there be found a single case of a woman succeeding to the kingdom of Judah or to the kingdom of Israel]. The unusual career of Athaliah was the exception that proved the rule because "elle n'i demoura point longuement. Mais aussi comme elle y estoit entree mauvaisement aussi fu elle boutee hors honteusement et mise hors du temple et tuee si comme il se treuve ou iiii$^e$ livre des Roys en l'onzieme chapitre (fol. 150$^v$) [She did not stay there long. Just as she had acquired the succession in evil fashion, she was thrown out also in disgrace, driven from the temple, and killed. This can be found in the fourth book of Kings, chapter eleven].

Raoul's arguments and exempla were reinforced with citations from the Church fathers, for example Gellius's *De noctibus Atticis* and Gregorius's *Morales* XXXV. The sources were carefully chosen to demonstrate the weakness of women and to support Raoul's view that men were inherently more suited, by their physical strength, to wield power than were women. Customs in Britain and Vermandois were adduced. After detailed explication and discussion Raoul introduced citations in Latin from legal statutes concerning succession, which, to ensure total comprehension, he translated also into French. And he underlined all the unfamiliar information that, as a lawyer, he had been able to provide by repeating the name of the little known law and noting its plebeian origins:[21] "Ceste loy fu trouvee par un qui avoit a nom Voconius qui la fist par l'acort de tout le pueple qui s'apele 'plebiscitum'" (fol. 151ᵛ) [This law was invented by one Voconius who created it by the general agreement of the people, which is called a "plebiscite"].

A seemingly gratuitous comparison reveals the translator's underlying motivation for the lengthy legalistic expansion. The intent of the Voconian law was similar, Raoul commented, to that of the Salic Law: "A ceste loy s'acorde une loy pareille qui fut appellee *lex Saliqua* (fol. 151ʳ) [With this law, another law called "The Salic Law" is in agreement]. Political correctness obligated all right-thinking French lawyers in the fourteenth century to be staunch supporters of the Salic Law. Otherwise the benighted English (who maintained that succession to a throne could be transmitted by a woman) might win their claim that Edward III of England, because the closest relative of the late French king, was owed territory in France through his mother Isabella.[22] No wonder Raoul used his commentary to urge that men were bound to preserve their rights to inherit: "les hommes qui sont plus abiles a deffendre que les fames qui sont moles et frailes de leur nature, tenissent les heritages" [men, who are more able at defense than women, who are soft and frail by nature, should inherit]. Open disagreement with his source was necessary to defend his monarch by defending the Salic Law:

> Ceulz qui firent celle loy furent ceulx qui premierement firent et ordonnerent les loys de France ou de ceulz de qui les Françoys descendirent, afin que la chose publique feüst mieux et plus puissamment deffendue par les malles que par les famelles. (fol. 151ʳ)

> [Those who made this law were those who in the beginning made and ordained the laws of France or of those from whom the French descended, in order that the state could be better and more powerfully defended by males than by females.][23]

Thus even this isolated intervention, which appeared to be an individual outburst from an impassioned lawyer indulging his professional interests, was actually the supreme manifestation of patronage's influence upon a commissioned translator. Raoul's exposition of the little known *lex Voconia* and his comment about its similarity to the Salic Law were part of his devoted service to his king, which, in this rare instance, caused him even to argue with his revered source. Translators established discrete identities for themselves by expert re-presentation of their sources, but seemingly individual features may still have derived from the fact of their hiring.

## Jean Calvin

The circumstances of patronage were very different for the *Institutio religionis Christianae* and *Institution de la religion Chrestienne*.[24] It was not that royal sponsorship of translators had diminished in France since the enlightened reign of Charles V.[25] The reign of Francis I provided the most lavish encouragement to cultural activities that France had ever seen. However, after *l'affaire des placards*, the chameleon king had withdrawn his support from all dissenters from Catholicism.[26] Some Reformers were convinced that this disfavor was only temporary and that the king would be willing to look favorably on them if only he had enough information to separate out the various dissenting groups one from another. Sturm's letter to Bucer in May 10, 1535, for example, analyzed the situation as follows: "Nihil interest inter Anabaptismam, Erasmianum, Lutheranum; omnes sine discrimine coërcentur et educuntur; nemo tutus nisi Papista. Regis verò aliam sententiam esse puto contra seditiosos et eos qui de Eucharistia secùs sentiunt quàm assolet"[27] [No distinctions are made between the Anabaptist, the Erasmian, and the Lutheran; all indiscriminately are being coerced and summoned, no-one but a Papist is safe. But I believe the king judges the seditious differently from those who hold divergent views on the Eucharist]. Calvin and Beza shared this view[28] and therefore the *Institutes*, originally intended as catechetical, became an apology for, and defense of, the Protestant cause.[29]

The stakes could not have been higher. The French *Institution* must rally the Protestant faithful with reassurance and comfort. The Latin *Institutio* must persuade/combat the theologically sophisticated ("illos"). Hovering above all of this was a king who was now potentially hostile and must be won over. Indeed, the persuasion, patronage, and propitiation of the king was now as urgent as the instruction of the faithful, and Calvin's prefatory letter to the king took on the appearance of a legal brief.[30] Consideration will be concentrated in this chapter upon the two earliest versions of this letter, sketching the differences between the Latin and French versions, then examining Calvin's attitude to the king as reflected therein.

The chronology of the two versions, the Latin "Epistola" and the vernacular "Epistre," has not been definitively established. The first edition of the *Institutes* was, of course, the Latin edition of 1536, while the first French edition appeared only in 1541. However, within the French edition the "Epistre" bears the date of August 23, 1535. This mystery has been variously explained by the following hypotheses: a separate 1535 production of the "Epistre"; a simultaneous 1535 production of "Epistre" and "Epistola"; and the production of an early French edition of the *Institutes* that was subsequently lost.[31] My own assumption is that the *Institutes* developed from three initial chapters— "De lege," "De fide," and "De oratione"—written as a catechism for the faithful. When Calvin decided to combine instruction with apology, he wrote for the work a prefatory letter in French (the king had no Latin), then in 1536 converted this "Epistre" into the "Epistola" at Bâle. Following Calvin's 1535 dating, I assume that the French "Epistre" preceded the "Epistola," although the *Institutio* preceded the *Institution*. But while opting for the chronological precedence of the French over the Latin version, I shall not discuss the matter further in this chapter, since my primary purpose is to examine the textual implications of patronage in the "Epistre" and the "Epistola." The order of the French and Latin quotations should not, therefore, be interpreted chronologically: it is determined solely by the substantive context.

The French and the Latin "Epistles" courted two different audiences, necessitating two different rhetorical strategies. Immediately apparent, for example, is the differing length of many sentences in the two versions, the French usually being longer than the Latin. This difference was due less to substantive changes between the two versions[32] than to the fact that the "Epistre" was conceived in analytic mode, the "Epistola" in synthetic mode—Calvin had equal facility in the two languages.[33] Simple examples are the sentence units: "Nous avons la victoire en main" (p. 12); "In manibus est victoria" (p. 10) [Victory is in our hands]. Even this briefest of examples demonstrates that, barring substantive modifications, the sentence-units in the "Epistre" necessarily would have been longer than those in the "Epistola" through the sheer mechanics of vernacular usage, pronoun subjects necessarily accompanying French verbs and definite articles necessarily accompanying French substantives.

Other semantic inevitabilities for which Calvin was not personally responsible explain the greater length of the vernacular text. For example, the Latin "Dominus" was consistently rendered in French as "Nostre Seigneur," and the names of the saints were prefaced with "saint" in the vernacular ("Saint Paul," "Saint Augustin," "Saint Jerome," and "Saint Pierre" for the Latin "Paulus," "Augustinus," "Hieronymus," and "Petrus"). In this regard it is interesting to note, in passing, the degree to which such syntactic inevitabilities reinforced the directly personal nature of the French *Institutes*. The involvement and confidence of "nous avons la victoire en main" as compared with the abstraction of "in manibus est victoria," and the personal conviction implied by "Nostre

Seigneur" as compared with the bleaker "Dominus" surely did no harm to the Reformers' faith that a personal God was on their side! More calculated examples of difference (in that they imply translative choices) were "qui aliquo religionis studio tanguntur" (p. 3) [those who are moved by some zeal for religion]; "ceux qui seroient touchez d'aucune bonne affection de Dieu" (p. 7) [those who might be moved by some good affection for God]; and "propitium patrem" (p. 11) [propitious Father] or "pere doux et benign" (p. 12) [kind and loving Father]. Such stylistic reinforcements leave little doubt that the "Epistre" was conceived to reinforce the Reformers' faith that God was with them, while the *Epistola* was intended to conciliate theologians.

Obviously, when "nos" and "nostri" occurred in the *Latin* "Epistola," Calvin continued to be part of the group designated as "nos," from which the Latin *clercs* were excluded. He knew, however, how to speak the Catholic theologians' language and could mirror briefly their scorn of the Reformers by a selective deployment of derogatory Latin diminutives: "Nos quidem, quam pauperculi simus et abiecti homunciones, probe nobis conscii sumus" (p. 9) [However minuscule, whatever abject homunculi we may be, we truly know ourselves]. The French version, intended not only to comfort but also to strengthen the faithful, did not play with stylistic odium here, nor did it employ diminutives. Instead Calvin wore the factually simple and effective phrase "povres gens et de mespris" [humble and despised folk] as a Reformers' red badge of courage: "Certes nous recongnoissons assez combien nous sommes povres gens et de mespris" (p. 11) [We know full well what humble and despised folk we are].[34]

Calvin's identification with the "povres gens" may have precipitated two dialectisms in the "Epistre." The first occurred when Calvin, addressing the king, spoke of the "horribles raportz" with which the Reformers' adversaries had filled Francis's ears, and momentarily

Picardized those august body parts as "aurailles": "Bien scay-je de quelz horribles raportz ilz ont rempli tes aurailles" (p. 10) [I know well the horrible reports they have poured into your ears]. He then proclaimed the Reformers' innocence of the charges of treason, denied that their loyalties were personal and local, and urged the king to hear their worthy cause, reverting to the usual Francien orthography of "aureilles": "Or à toy appartient, Tres gratieux Roy . . . de ne destourner tes *aureilles*" (p. 10) [Now it behooves you, o most gracious King, not to turn a deaf ear].[35] The other Picardism occurred after Calvin's identification of himself as one of the "povres gens" (see above) when his explanation of "povres gens et de mespris" used a Picard spelling, "c'est à scavoir, devant Dieu miserables *pecheus*" (p. 11) [that is to say, before God miserable sinners]. The momentary departure from the standard language symbolized the Reformers' alterity. And while the subject of dialectisms must be treated with care—universality rather than dialectism was Calvin's overall purpose, and the orthographical variant may anyway have been a choice of his printer—the textual results of the dialectisms are noticeable.[36] For whether they came from the polemicist (Calvin's temporary and perhaps unconscious reversion to the familiar language of populist dissent?) or whether they came in fact from the printer, this flaunting of a provincial spelling that was no longer in vogue at the court graphically conveyed the Huguenots's lack of status with the king.

Calvin's more important linguistic goal in the *Institution* was, of course, to mold the standard language into an appropriate theological medium and thereby "servir à noz François, desquelz j'en voyois plusieurs avoir faim et soif de Jesus Crist, et bien peu qui en eüssent receu droicte congnoissance" (p. 7) [to be of service to our people, many of whom I saw hungering and thirsting after Jesus Christ, and very few of whom had received true knowledge of Him].[37] A frequent technique to this end was his deployment of synonymic binomials, the translator's traditional recourse when confronted with lexical non-equivalence:

"force et violence . . . fraude et trahison" (p. 8)
    ["vis . . . fraus" (p. 5)];
"l'analogie et similitude de la Foye" (p. 12)
    ["fidei analogiam" (p. 10)];
"contemnez et déjectez" (p. 11) ["despectissimi" (p. 9)];
"plus prodigieux et admirables" (p. 16)
    ["valde prodigiose" (p. 16)];
"raviz et transportez" (p. 9) ["correpti" (p. 6)];
"par une modération et gravité judiciaire" (p. 9)
    ["legitima gravitate" (p. 6)]; and
"la clemence et mansuetude" (p. 8) ["clementia" (p. 4)].[38]

Sometimes lengthier and more specific explanations were employed for the benefit of the French faithful than for the *litterati*. Calvin's Latin paraphrase of Pope Gelasius's pronouncement on the Eucharist might be appropriate for the readers of the "Epistola," who were well versed in the technicalities of sacramental doctrine. A slightly expanded and more explicit formulation was chosen in the French version: "Ex patribus erat, qui negavit in sacramento coenae esse verum corpus, sed mysterium duntaxat corporis" (p. 18) [It was one of the Fathers who denied that the Real Body was present in the sacrament of the Lord's Supper, but only the mystical Body] is, in the French version, "Cestuy estoit au nombre des Pères, qui a nyé qu'au Sacrement de la Cène, soubz le pain, feust contenu le vray corps de Christ, mais que seulement c'estoit un mystère de son corps" (p. 21) [It was one of the Fathers who denied that in the sacrament of the Lord's Supper beneath the bread the Real Body of Christ was contained, but only a mystery of His Body]. If Calvin employed expansion in the "Epistola," it usually served to reinforce the abusive arguments with which Calvin liked to jab at his Catholic adversaries. His didactically factual French definition of the Church Fathers as "les anciens Pères, j'entends les escrivains du premier temps de l'Esglise" (p. 19) [the early Fathers, I mean the writers of the first era of the Church] was, for example, supplemented in the Latin version by the gratuitously nasty addition "antiquos *et melioris adhuc saeculi* scriptores intelligo" [I mean the early writers *of a better age than this* (p. 16), emphasis added]. And for the benefit of the Catholic theologians he added several examples in the Latin "Epistola" to his collection of patristic contradictions. The word "patres" occasioned, in fact, several attacks in the "Epistola," and Calvin always chose weapons that were appropriate to the target audience. A striking example was his deployment of Greek, which he used rarely but always to good effect in the *Institutes*. Attacking the Catholic Church's misguided interpretation of the word "father," Calvin launched this Greek missile into the Latin discourse: "Quod si tantopere gestiunt 'allygorizein' cur non apostolos potius quam alios quosvis patres interpretantur?" [Why don't they interpret the Apostles rather than anybody else as their "Fathers" since they do adore so to "allégoriser?" (p. 20)[39]]. The unexpected Greek script, complemented by the composite fussiness ("tanto" plus "opere") of "tantopere" and by "gestiunt"'s suggestion of unrestrained passion ["they passionately lust for/adore"] conveyed stylistically *and* graphically Calvin's accusation of the theologians' alien excesses. (The French version employed the French substantive "allégories" in "puis qu'ilz ayment tant *les allégories*" (p. 20), thus conjuring up a range of different connotations in the French-speaking audience, and associating the writings of Catholic theologians with such "allegories" as were part of the popular experience, viz., medieval romances.

Calvin was to employ a similar technique in the second edition of the "Epistola" when he derided the follies of the Latin episcopate with its "horned bishops." His rhetorical question "Quid autem hodie in cornutis suis Episcopis mundus veneratum?" (Tholuck, p. 16) [What filth must today be worshipped in its horned bishops?] was followed by a dismissive Graecism "*Apage sis* ergo tam stupidam aestimationem" [Forget such stupid reckoning!]. The un-Ciceronian phrase would conjure up for the learned unflattering reminiscences from Plautus and Terence as Calvin relegated the current episcopate, reverenced not as spiritual leaders but as administrators of big-city bishoprics, to a world of satiric comedy. The French is less colored: "Ostons donc une si folle estime" (p. 27) [Let us do away with such foolish esteem].

Calvin's intemperate abuse of his enemies—priests, bishops, cardinals, popes, and all the trappings of ecclesiastical authority—did not, of course, extend to the king. Francis may not have been included among "nos" but neither was he one of the infamous "those others" ["illos"], and it is time to look at the manner of Calvin's address to his monarch. The letter began formally and, however, flatteringly, with multiple superlatives of homage: "Très Hault, Très Puissant, et Très Illustre Prince . . . Roy de France Très Chrestien" [Potentissimo illustrissimoque monarchae . . . Regi Christianissimo]. Other such superlatives were strewn through the opening pages: "Très noble Roy" [Rex clarissime]; "Très excellent Roy" [Rex nobilissime]; "Très illustre Roy" [Rex invictissime]; "Très gratieux Roy" [Serenissime Rex]; and "Roy Très vertueux" [Fortissime Rex]. As the petitioner in a prayer invokes in the deity those attributes that he most desires for his circumstance, Calvin used the semi-formulaic tags of flattery to elicit desired responses from his monarch.[40] Such stroking was as old as literary patronage itself— except that the princely generosity Calvin sought for his group of *personae non gratae* was on a wider scale. Favor to the Huguenots at that juncture could have cost the king his throne, a possibility that to Francis would surely be more persuasive than all of Calvin's eloquence in determining royal actions![41]

The formal homage of the early pages did not prevent Calvin from immediately lecturing the king with frankness and directness. It had been the traditional role of the translator (as, for example, Raoul de Presles) to serve as cultural mentor to the king and his court. Calvin preferred the role of an Old Testament prophet, exposing with vatic enthusiasm Francis's real significance in the eternal scheme of things and hurling dire predictions of impending disaster and destruction if God's (i.e., Calvin's) words were not heeded by the merely mortal monarch: "Car l'édict celeste ne peut mentir: par lequel il est dénoncé que le peuple sera dissipé quand la Prophétie défauldra" (p. 11) [quando coeleste oraculum excidere non potest, quo edictum est: dissipatum iri populum, ubi defecerit prophetia (Prov. 29)[42] (pp. 8–9)]. The king was instructed in what to think and how to think it: "Mais tu as à reputer, selon ta clemence et mansuetude, qu'il ne resterait innocence aucune, n'en ditz n'en faictz, s'il suffisoit d'accuser" (p. 8) [Sed id tibi pro tua Clementia perpendendum est, nullam neque in dictis neque in factis innocentiam fore, si accusasse sufficiat (p. 4)]. He was forced into taking responsibility for the persecution of the faithful in "his" kingdom: "J'entreprens la cause commune de tous les fidèles, et mesme celle de Christ; laquelle aujourd'huy . . . est descirée et foullée en *ton* Royaume" (p. 10) [Christi causam complector, quae . . . hodie in regno *tuo* proscissa et protrita (p. 7)]. He was forced to listen to a reprimand that verged on the abusive by its suggestion that "real" monarchs reflect wisely: "O matière digne de tes aureilles, digne de ta jurisdiction, digne de ton Thrône Royal! Car ceste cogitation faict un vray Roy" (p. 11) [Digna res auribus tuis, digna tua cogitatione, digna tua tribunali. Siquidem et verum regem haec cogitatio faci (p. 8)]. He was lectured, cajoled, and commanded with vigorous imperatives that barely concealed Calvin's impatience: "Considère, O Roy Très vertueux, toutes les parties de nostre cause; et nous juge estre les plus pervers des pervers, si tu ne trouves manifestement que nous travaillons et recevons injures et opprobres" (p. 13) [Consider, o most virtuous King, all parts of our case and judge us to be the wickedest of men if you do not find that we are laboring and being harassed]; "Percurre, Fortissime Rex, omnes causae nostrae partes, et quovis sceleratorum hominum genere nequiores nos existima, nisi plane comperias in hoc laborare et probris affici" (p. 12). Again, "Contemple d'autre part noz adversaires (je parle de l'estat des Prestres), à l'aveu et appétit desquelz tous les autres nous contrarient; et regarde un peu avec moy de quelle affection ilz sont menez" (p. 14) [Just contemplate our adversaries (I'm speaking of the priesthood at whose wish, nod and desire the others persecute us) and consider a while with me what sort of zeal motivates them]; "Intuere iam in adversarios nostros (de ordine sacrificorum loquor, quorum nutu et arbitrio alii nobiscum inimicitias exercent) et mecum paulisper reputa, quo studio ferantur" (pp. 12–13). There was even a veiled sneer as Calvin suggested that Francis sacrifice some of his leisure time, however brief, to do some serious (i.e., Huguenot) reading:[43] "Mais si tu veux departir un peu de ton loysir à lire noz enseignemens, tu congnoistras clairement que leur doctrine mesme . . . est une cruelle Géhenne[44] et boucherie des âmes" (p. 30) ["Ipsam, ipsam doctrinam, cui id deberi aiunt, quod sunt ecclesia, exitialem animarum carnificinam, facem, ruinam, et excidium ecclesiae esse non obscure cognosces, si legendis nostris aliquantum otii tui *decidas*" (p. 33)].

Once the serious catechetical exposition of "nostre doctrine" began, however, Calvin textually abandoned his (leisured) king for the flock (at p. 15 of the "Epistre," p. 14 of the "Epistola"). Moreover, when he returned, he pointedly highlighted the fact of the abandonment and the fact, therefore, that the king was not one of the elect. His blunt signal for Francis to re-enter his stage was: "Mais je retourne à toy, o Roy Très magnanime" (p. 33); "sed ad te revertor, o magnanime Rex" (p. 37) [But I return to you, o most magnanimous King]. The suddenness of the transition was barely eased by Calvin's fulsome invocation of the king's magnanimity, an invocation that once more forced Calvin's expectations upon his beleaguered monarch.

At least in the remainder of the letter the king's status was upgraded from that of witness or accused to that of judge: "s'il te plaist une fois, hors d'indignation et courroux, lire ceste nostre confession, laquelle nous voulons estre pour deffense envers ta Majesté" (p. 35); "si hanc confessionem, quam pro defensione apud tuam maiestatem esse volumus, placidus compositusque semel legeris" (p. 39) [If it please you when you are cool and calm in spirit to read (just) once this confession which we wish as our defence to Your Majesty]. During the final "confession" the king was urged to consider the ridiculousness of the charge that the Protestants aimed to overthrow his kingdom and was assured that, although "chased out of their homes," they neverthless persisted in praying for the prosperity of the king. (The pointedness of the reminder and the condescension of Calvin's homage here was barely tactful!): "Et maintenant, chassez de noz maisons, nous ne laissons point de prier Dieu pour ta prosperité, et celle de ton Règne" (p. 34) [And now, chased from our homes, we do not cease from praying to God for your prosperity and the prosperity of your reign]; "Qui nunc etiam, domo profugi, tibi tamen regnoque tuo fausta omnia precari non desinimus" (p. 37) [Who even now, having fled our homes, do not cease from praying that every prosperity be visited on you and on your kingdom.]

The pointing finger of the accusing Prophet was finally lowered when Calvin resorted to what constituted a bribe. In expectation—or pretended expectation—of the king's favor, Calvin administered a benediction and serenely promised the French king a blessing from the King of Kings: "Le Seigneur Roy des Roys veuille establir ton throsne en justice, et ton Siège en équité, Très illustre Roy" (p. 36) [May Our Lord, the king of Kings, establish your throne in justice and your seat in equity, most illustrious King]; "Dominus, Rex Regum, thronum tuum iustitia stabiliat, et solium tuum aequitate, Fortissime ac illustrissime Rex"[45] (p. 41) [May Our Lord, King of Kings, establish your throne with justice and your seat in equity, most powerful and illustrious King.]

The two versions of Calvin's letter to Francis were subject to far fewer revisions than the text they introduced.[46] Even more interesting is the fact that Calvin retained the eloquent letter in its place even after its historical usefulness was over. "Elle figurera en tête de chaque édition comme pour dire: regardez donc à quel touchant appel le roi n'a pas voulu prêter l'oreille."[47] Thus, unlike Raoul's exemplary prologue hymning the beneficence of patronage, Calvin's preface has become a symbolic example of patronage denied, and from these two brilliant but disparate texts the disparate faces of patronage emerge. For Raoul patronage provided an ideal context for the instruction of a sophisticated lay public. Adopting publicly the stance of servant, the translator was, in fact, the acknowledged mentor of a king, a court, and a kingdom. With Calvin the situation and the personalities were different. Royal patronage had been removed, and the king's sympathies for the Evangelicals were (it subsequently became apparent) irrevocably lost. These tough political circumstances, combined with Calvin's temperamental inability to accept human authority and with his predilection for apocalyptic rhetoric, made him exchange the translator's traditional role of royal mentor for that of Biblical prophet. Viewed from a literary perspective, both translators made significant contributions to the development of French culture. Their prefatory texts show that those significant contributions would, however, have been very different without the determining factor of patronage.

# Patronage and the Translator

## Appendix

A vous tres excellent prince, Charles le Quint, roy de France, je Raoul de Praelles, vostre humble serviteur et subjet, tout vostre et tout ce que je sai et puis faire a vostre commandement.

Mon tres redoubté seigneur, les naturiens comme Plyne, Adelin, Aristote, Bede, et
5  autres qui firent les livres des proprietez des choses, metent l'aigle roy souverain de touz les oysiaus. Et entre ses proprietés dont elle a pluseurs li en attribuent trois principalx:

La premiere est que elle seurmonte par son vol touz autres oisiaux.

La seconde que elle regarde directement et sans flechir le soleil.
10  La tierce que ses faons elle preuve, et ceus qui ne peuvent regarder le soleil plainement sans flechir elle les gette hors de son ny et renie.

Et quant j'ai bien considéré et ymaginé ces trois hautes proprietez y me semble que je ne les puis miex comparagier ne plus proprement a nul de touz les docteurs de Sainte Eglise, especialment de l'Eglise primitive que a monseigneur saint Augustin.
15  Car premierement en la doctrine de la foy, en la confutation ou reprobation des herites en la declaration de la benoite Trinité, onques nuls de touz iceux docteurs de l'Eglise primitive ne vola si haut ne n'entreprist si haultement a ces choses enseigner, declairer et demonstrer; de ce sont les livres tesmoings. Dont un docteur appelé Possidonius en son epythaphe dist qu'il fist trois mille volumes,
20  et que celui ment qui afferme que touz ses livres il ait leüs.

Secondement, en ce que il regarde directement le soleil sans flechir, c'est assavoir la benoite Trinité, et en a traitié, pour en avoir la cognoissance d'icelle, si haultement et si parfondement que nuls desdiz docteurs n'y a peu veoir si parfondement comme il a fait.
25  Mais tiercement, en ce que aussi comme l'aigle preuve ses faons et gette ceus qui ne peuvent pas de droit regarder le soleil, aussi monseigneur saint Augustin ceus qui ne veulent regarder directement le vray soleil, c'est assavoir la benoite Trinité et la vraie foy crestienne sans varier comme font les hirittes dont il en i a de plusieurs manieres, il les confute et repreuve, dampnez et condampnez, si comme il appert
30  par ses livres que il fist *Contra Faustum, Contra Manicheos, De heresibus* et en pluseurs autres livres qui sont assez nottoires, et en ce livre meïsmes *De la Cité de Dieu.*

Et par ces causes, tout aussi comme monseigneur saint Jehan l'Evangeliste, pour ce que il comprist et senti plus haultement de la divinité que nulz des autres

121

35  evangelistes, est comparé a l'aigle, pareillement monseigneur saint Augustin entre
les docteurs de l'Eglise primitive y puet et doit estre comparé et clamé roy aussi
comme l'aigle est reputé roy et souverains des oisiaux.
Et aprés ce, quant j'ay bien tout consideré et avec ce avisé et regardé vostre
haute nativité, la noblesce et grandeur de vostre personne, et en aprés vostre estude

(fol. 4ʳ) 40  et continuele occupation, et sus toutes ‖ ces choses la haute pensee qui est cheüe en
vostre cuer et qui vouz a pleü a moy declairer, tout consideré et mis ensemble, il me
semble que je vouz puis et doi encore assez convenablement comparer a l'aigle.
Car premierement a prendre vostre nativité: il est certain que vouz estes filz de roy
de France, et qui plus est, roy de France qui est le plus grant, le plus haut, le plus

45  catholique, et le plus puissant roy crestien. Et avec ce, estes estrait du lignaige des
empereurs rommains qui portent l'aigle pour ce que fu le premier signe rommain.
Secondement, en ce que vous estes le plus digne roy crestien: car avec ce que en
vostre baptesme vouz estes enoint du saint cresme comme est un chascun
bon crestien, encore par excellence estes vouz roy consacré et si dignement enoint

50  comme de la sainte liqueur que un coulon, que nous tenons fermement que ce fu
le Saint Esprit mis en celle forme, apporta du ciel en son bec, en une petite
empole ou fiole, et la mist, veant tout le pueple, en la main de monseigneur
saint Remy, lors arcevesques de Rains, qui tantost en consacra les fons et en
enoint le roy Clovis, premier roy crestien. Et en ceste reverence et pour ce tres

55  noble mistere, touz les roys de France qui depuis ont esté a leur premiere creation
ont esté consacrez a Reins de la liqueur de celle sainte empole.
Et ne tiengne nous ne autre que celle consecration soit sans tresgrant, digne, et
noble mistere, car par icelle vos devanciers et vouz avez tele vertuz et puissance qui
vous est donnee et attribuee de Dieu que vous faites miracles en vostre vie, teles si

60  grans et si apertes que vous garissez d'une tres horrible maladie qui se appelle les
escroelles de la quele nul autre prince crestien ne puet garrir fors vous.
Et si portez les armes de trois fleurs de lys en signe de la benoite Trinité qui de Dieu
par son angle furent envoiez au dit Clovis, premier roy crestien, pour soi
combatre contre le roy Caudat, qui estoit Sarrazin et adversaire de la foy crestienne

65  et qui estoit venu d'Alemaigne a grant multitude de gens es parties de France, et qui
avoit fait, mis, et ordené son siege a Conflans. Dont combien que la bataille
commençast en la valee, toutevoies fu elle achevee en la montaigne en la quele est a
present la tour de Mon Joie, et la fu pris premierement et nommé vostre cri en
armes, c'est assavoir *Mont Joie Saint Denis*.

70  Et en la reverence de ceste victoire et de ce que ces armes Nostre Seigneur envoia

122

du ciel par un angle et demonstra a un hermite qui tenoit en icelle valee decoste une
fontaine un hermitage, en lui disant qu'il feïst raser les armes des trois croissans
que Clovis portoit lors en son escu et feïst mettre en ce lieu les trois fleurs de lys
en icelles et se combatist et il avroit victoire contre le roy Caudat. Le quel le revela a
75 la reine Clovis, qui reperoit au dit hermitage et apportoit souvent au dit hermite sa
recreation. La quele les emporta et deffassa les croissans et y mist les trois fleurs de
lys. Fu fondé un lieu religier qui fu et encore est appelé l'abbaye de Joie-en-Val, en
la quele l'escu de ces armes a esté par lonc temps en reverence de ce.
Et si portez seul roy et singulierement l'oriflamme en bataille, c'est assavoir
80 un glaive tout doré ou est atachiee une baniere vermeille la quele vos devanciers et
vous avez acostumé a venir querre et prandre en l'eglise de monseigneur saint Denis
(fol. 4ᵛ)   a grant solempnité, ‖ reverence, et devotion, si comme vous le savez. Car
premierement la procession vous vient a l'encontre jusques a l'issue du cloistre,
et aprés la procession sont atains les benois corps sains de monseigneur saint Denys
85 et de ses compaignons et mis sur l'autel en grant reverence, et aussi le corps saint
monseigneur saint Louys, et puis est mise ceste baniere ploiee dessoubz les
corporaux ou est consacré le corps de Nostre Seigneur Jesus Crist le quel vous
recevez dignement aprés la celebration de la messe, si[t] fait celui auquel vous
l'avez esleü a baillier comme au plus preudomme et plus vaillant chevalier.
90 Et ce fait, le baisiez en la bouche et lui baillés et la la tient entre ses mains par grant
reverence, a fin que les barons assistens la puissent baisier comme relique et chose
digne. Et en li baillant pour le porter li faites faire serement solempnel de la garder et
porter en grant reverence et a l'onneur de vous et de vostre roiaume. Ainsi la prinst
ce souverain protecteur et deffenseur singulier de l'Esglise monseigneur saint
95 Charles, jadis empereür et roy de France, quant il ala a secours a l'empereür
Constentin qui estoit empereür de Constantinoble pour delivrer son païs des
Sarrasins qui l'occupoient et aussi la terre sainte de Jerusalem, et le quel empereür
de Constantinoble le manda par la vision que il avoit veüe devant son lit qui fu tele
selon les croniqueurs et anciennes hystoires: c'est assavoir que devant icelui em-
100 pereür au piez de son lit il se apparu un chevalier armé de toutes armes et monté à
cheval, tenant une hante toute doree du bout de la quelle [sic] hante yssoit flambe a
merveilles grande. Et comme il fust en grande perplexité de savoir quele
signification ce estoit et que telle chose signifioit, un angle s'apparut a luy qui
li dist que celui qu'il avoit veü c'estoit celui qui delivreroit le pays de Sarrasins. Si
105 congnut Constantin par ce que il avoit veü que ce estoit le roy Charlemaigne, a
present nommé monseigneur saint Charles, et tantost le manda, qui entendit le

123

mandement et la vision, tantost ala à Saint Denys et prist la baniere vermeille en tele

reverence comme vous m'avez oÿ raconter, mist la coronne sur l'autel, laissa le

roiaume de France en la protection de monseigneur saint Denis et, ceste baniere

110    vermeille ainsi reveremment prise et en tele devotion, sc parti et ala a Constantinoble

et vainqui les Sarrasins et en delivra le pays.

Et en ceste reverence tant dc cellc saintc vision comme de la noble victoire que il ot,

l'ont aussi acoustumé a prendre vos devanciers et vous, et si portés hante doree. Et

pour ce est il appelé oriflambe pour la flambe qui apparu au bout de la hante doree.

115    Et est la baniere vermeille en la remembrance du glorieux martyr ou martyrs

monseigneur saint Denys et de ses compaignons qui premier apporta la foy

en France pour la quele il fu martyrés, luy et ses compaignons. Et doit estre

atachiee ceste baniere, comme dist est, en une hante doree pour avoir

tous jours vraie recordation et memoire de celle haute et noble vision de nostre foy et

120    de leur glorieuse passion.

Et ont tenu vos devanciers que elle ne doit point estre desployee sanz tres grand

(fol. 5$^r$)    nécessité et, qui plus est, que, la victoire faite, elle doit estre rap ‖ portee a grant

devotion et reverence en l'esglise de monseigneur saint Denys et rendue sur son

autel en remembrance de la victoire, ainsi comme fist Challemaigne. De ce me

125    croy je, car je en ay veü deux de mon temps sur l'autel des glorieux martyrs, de

chascune partie de l'autel une, et estoient enhantees de deux petites hantes d'argent

dorees ou pendoient a chascune une baniere vermeille dont l'une estoit apelee la

baniere Challemaine, et se portoit par reverence par un des religieux a certaines

processions. Et c'est ce que l'en apele proprement "l'oriflambe" et dont

130    elle vint, de ce qui en peut estre venu a ma petite congnoissance.

Et ces choses, mon tres redoubté seigneur, denottent et demonstrent par vraye

rayson que par ce vous estez et devés estre le seul principal protecteur, champion, et

defenseur de l'Esglise comme ont esté vos devanciers. Et ce tient le saint siège de

Romme qui a acostumé a escripre a vos devanciers et a vous singulièrement en

135    l'intitulation des lettres: "Au Tres Crestien des Princes."

Tiercement, en ce que des le temps que vous eüstes premierement congnoissance,

vous avés tousjours aimé science et honoré les bons clers, et estudié continuelment

en divers livres et sciences se vous n'avez eü autre occupation, en avez fait faire et

translater pluseurs livres tant pour plaire a vous comme pour proufiter a voz

140    subges. Et en ce, avez eschivé le reproche du sage qui dit: "Roy sanz lettre est un

asne coronné." Et, par especial, en ce que la haultesse de vostre engin et entendement a

si hault volé et esté si haultement eslevé que la plus grant euvre d'un livre, part hors

celui que il fist de la benoite Trinite, et qui plus traitte de matieres grandes, haultes, subtilles, et diverses, et qui apaines peuent cheoir en entendement humain pour la
145 haultesse et profondité des matieres, vous avez voulu estre translaté de latin en françois pour le proufit et utilité de vostre roiaume, de vostre pueple, et de toute crestienté, c'est assavoir le livre de monseigneur saint Augustin *De la Cité de Dieu*. Et tieng que en ceste partie vous avez voulu ensuivre monseigneur saint Charles, qui entre touz les livres que il estudioit et veoit volentiers, il lisoit les livres de
150 monseigneur saint Augustin, et sur tous les autres le livre *De la Cité de Dieu*, si comme il est trouvé en sa vie et es croniques.

Pour toutes les queles trois choses il me semble que je vous puis comparagier a l'aigle de toute noblesse, grandeur, et bonne volenté. Et tieng que ceste volenté vous est venue principaulment par droite inspiration divine mais, mon tres
155 redoubté seigneur, de ces choses ne sui je point esmerveilliez. Mais je doi estre esmerveillé, et non sans cause, de ce que delaissiez les souverains clers de vostre roiaume dont il en y a tant et de si grans que en toute crestienté n'en a tant ne de telz, et ausquiex tele euvre appartenoit et leur estoit deüee a translater, il peut estre cheü en vostre pensee de le moy baillier qui au regart de eulx ne suis que poudre et
160 cendre, et comment vous avez voulu a moy qui sui de si feible entendement baillier si fort fessel, et a si petite main si grant mole a tourner.

(fol. 5ᵛ) Et pour ce que ‖ l'en ne cuide pas que par arrogance ou par moy ingerer je l'aie voulu entreprendre, je appelle Dieu a tesmoing et vous le savez assez comment et par quel temps je l'ay refusé et differé a entreprendre, et les excusacions que je y
165 ai pretendues tant pour ce que je savoie et sai la foiblesse de mon engin, la grandeur de l'euvre, et la age dont je sui qui me deüsse, si comme il me semble dorenavant reposer. Si ne tiengne vous ne autre moy avoir esté si hardi ou si oultrecuidié de l'avoir entreprist de moy, car se je ne cuidasse avoir commis plus grant offence et que l'en me tenist plus oultrecuidié de le vous avoir refusé que
170 de avoir obeÿ a vostre commandement, je l'eüsse a plain refusé. Car il me sembloit que je avoie assez labouré en mon temps tant a faire le livre qui se apelle *Le Compendieux moral de la chose publique* et le livre qui se apelle *La Muse* la quele il vous plut a recevoir en gré pour ce que je l'avoye entitulé a vouz, comme *Les Croniques en françois contemporisees du commencement du monde jusques au*
175 *temps de Tarquin l'orgueilleux et du roy Cambises qui regnerent en un temps,* avecques aucunes *Espistres*, consideré encore la grant charge du fait de mon advocacie qui est office publique et qui requiert labour continuel. Mais je croi que vous aviés leüe celle parole de Seneque qui dist que ociosité sanz lettre est mort et sepulture de homme vif.

125

180 Si supplie a vostre roial magesté que aussi comme simplement a vostre
commandement j'ai ceste euvre entreprise, il vous plaise a la recevoir en gré et
supporter mes defaultes dont je sai bien que il en y aura pluseurs. Et se je ne ensuy
en ceste translation les propres moz du texte, et que je y voise aucunes fois par
une maniere de circonlocution ou autrement, il me sera pardonné pour ce que vous
185 m'avez commandé pour la matiere esclarcir que je ensuive la vraie, simple, et clere
sentence et le vrai entendement sans ensuivir proprement les mos du texte. Et si y a
plusieurs mos qui ne se peuent pas bonnement translater en françois sanz adition ou
declaration car, comme dessus est dit, ce livre est compilé de diverses et
haultes matieres et de hault stile et de ancienne gramaire, chargé de grans sentences
190 suspensivez en brieves paroles, pluseurs et diverses hystoires abregees de divers et
anciens aucteurs dont les originaux ne peuent pas bonnement estre trouvés en cest
païs pour y avoir recours es pas et es termez qui desirent declaration,  toutevoies est
mon entention d'y mettre aucunes declarations et expositions pour donner
declaration au texte es parties et pas ou il aura doubte ou oscurité.


[To the most excellent prince, Charles the Fifth, king of France, I Raoul de
Presles, your humble servant and your subject, totally yours, whose every skill and
ability is yours to command.
My most revered lord, the naturalists like Pliny, Adelin, Aristotle, Bede and
others, who wrote the books on the properties of things, make the eagle sovereign
king of all the birds. And among its several properties they attribute to it principally
three:
The first is that in flight it soars above all the other birds.
The second that it looks directly and unflinchingly at the sun.
The third that it tests its young, and throws out of its nest and abandons those that
cannot look full at the sun unflinchingly.
Considering well and pondering those three noble properties, it seems to me that of
all the doctors of our Holy Church, especially of the early Church, there is none to
whom I can better or more appropriately apply them than to Saint Augustine.
For firstly, in Christian doctrine, in refuting or correcting heretics in
affirmation of the Blessed Trinity, none of all those doctors of the early Church
soared so high nor undertook in such exalted fashion the teaching, affirmation, and
demonstration of these matters; to this the books bear witness. For which reason
a doctor named Posidonius said in his epitaph to St. Augustine that the latter wrote
three thousand volumes and that no one can truthfully claim to have read all the
saint's books.

# Patronage and the Translator

Secondly, in that he looks directly and unflinchingly at the sun, that is the Blessed Trinity and, having knowledge of it, has written about it with such depth and such profundity that none of the above-mentioned doctors has succeeded in matching it. Further, thirdly, in that as the eagle tests its young and throws out those which cannot gaze directly at the sun, so St. Augustine refutes and reproves those, damned and condemned, who are unwilling to gaze directly at the true Sun, that is the Blessed Trinity and the true Christian faith without wavering, like the diverse kinds of heretics. This is evident in the books he wrote *Against Faustus, Against the Manicheans*, *On Heresies*, in several other equally significant books, and in this book in particular *On the City of God*.

For these reasons, just as St. John the Evangelist, because he had more profound understanding and experience of the Divinity than any other evangelist, is likened to the eagle, similarly among the doctors of the early Church St. Augustine can and must be compared to it and designated king, as the eagle is considered king and sovereign among birds.

And when I have pondered everything, considering and weighing your high birth, the nobility and grandeur of your person, your study and unceasing industry, and above all those things that noble thought which came to you and which it pleased you to reveal to me, putting and weighing all this together I feel I can and must very appropriately compare you also with the eagle.

First in regard to your birth: you are unquestionably son of the king of France and, further, the greatest, noblest, most catholic and most powerful Christian king. Also you are descended from the lineage of the Roman emperors who bear the eagle as the first symbol of Rome.

Second, in this you are the worthiest Christian king for, as well as having been anointed with the holy chrism as are all good Christians, you are as king supremely consecrated as to be anointed with the liquid which a dove, who we truly believe was the Holy Spirit in that form, brought in its beak from heaven in a tiny phial or ampulla and, in the view of all the congregation, placed in the hand of St. Rémy, then archbishop of Rheims, who immediately used it to bless the fonts and anoint King Clovis, the first Christian king. And in honor of this and for this most noble mystery all subsequent kings of France have at the moment of their consecration been blessed at Rheims with the liquid from this holy ampulla.

Nor must you nor any other doubt that this consecration is imbued with the greatest, worthiest, noblest of mysteries. For by this consecration you and your ancestors have such virtue and power, given and bestowed by God, that you work

127

miracles in your lifetime, miracles so great and so spectacular that you can cure a horrendous malady called scrofula—no other Christian prince but you can cure this disease.

Also you bear the arms of three fleurs de lis as symbol of the Blessed Trinity. The fleurs de lis were sent from God by his angel to the above-mentioned Clovis, first king of the Christians, to [help him] fight against the Sarracen King Caudat, enemy of the Christian faith, who had come from Germany to French territory with a large horde of soldiers, and had arrived, set up, and established his headquarters at Conflans. That is where your battle-cry "Mont Joie St. Denis" was first adopted and took its name. So although the battle began in the valley, it was neverthless concluded on the mountain where the tower of Montjoie stands today. A religious house, which was and is still called the Abbey of Joyenval was founded in that place. In it the shield with the arms of fleurs de lis has long been worshipped in honor of that victory and of those arms that Our Lord sent from heaven through an angel, who showed them to a hermit who had a hermitage in that valley beside a fountain, telling the hermit that he should have the three crescents that Clovis then bore on his shield erased and replaced with the three lilies; then if Clovis did combat, he would have victory over King Caudat. The hermit revealed this to Clovis's queen who often went to the said hermitage with food for the hermit. She carried away the fleurs de lis, erased the crescents, and put the fleurs de lis in their place.

And, sole king and singularly, you carry into battle the oriflamme, which is a golden lance with crimson banner attached that, as you know, you and your ancestors have customarily received with great solemnity, reverence, and devotion from the Church of St. Denis. First the procession comes right through the cloister toward you. After the procession the blessed holy relics of St. Denis and his companions are taken and placed on the altar with all reverence, together with the relics of St. Louis, and then that folded banner is placed under the corporals containing the body of Our Lord that you solemnly receive after the celebration of the Mass, as does he whom you have selected to receive it because he is your most valuable and worthy knight. This done, you kiss it and hand it to him. Then he holds it most reverently in his hands so that the attendant barons may kiss it as a relic and thing of worth. You give it to him to carry, making him swear a solemn oath to guard it and bear it with great reverence in your honor and that of your kingdom.

# Patronage and the Translator

Thus did that sovereign protector and sole defender of the Church, St. Charles, former emperor and king of France, receive the oriflamme when he went to the aid of the emperor Constantine of Constantinople to deliver that emperor's country from the Saracens who occupied it along with the holy territory of Jerusalem. The emperor of Constantinople sent for him because of the vision that appeared at his bedside. The chroniclers and early histories narrate it thus: at the foot of his bed there appeared before the emperor of Constantinople a knight in full armor, mounted on horseback. He held a golden shaft from the end of which issued a wondrously great flame. And as the king was greatly perplexed to know what sign this was and what such a thing might signify, an angel appeared to him and told him that the man he had seen was the one who would deliver the country from the Saracens. Constantine realized from what he had seen that it was the king Charlemagne, now called St. Charles. He immediately sent for him, Charlemagne learned of the summons and the vision, went forthwith to St. Denis, and took the crimson banner in that same reverence you have heard me describe, set the crown on the altar, and left the kingdom of France in the protection of St. Denis. Having received that banner with such reverence and devotion he departed for Constantinople, conquered the Saracens, and freed the country from them.

In honor of that holy war and of the noble victory he won, your ancestors and you also by custom receive the banner, and you carry a golden lance called "oriflamme" on account of the flame that appeared at the end of the golden lance. The banner is crimson in memory of the blessed martyr or martyrs St. Denis and his companions. He first brought the faith to France and for it he and his companions were martyred. This banner, as has been said, must be attached to a golden shaft to preserve the true remembrance and memory of that high and noble vision of our faith and of their glorious suffering. Your ancestors maintained that the banner must be deployed only at a time of dire necessity and, what is more, when the victory is won, the banner must be returned with great reverence and devotion to the Church of St. Denis, and restored to its place on the altar in memory of the victory, following Charlemagne's example.

I feel confident in this, for in my lifetime I have seen two on the altar of the glorious martyrs, one on each side of the altar. They were equipped with two small shafts of gilded silver and a crimson banner hung from each. One was called the banner of Charlemagne and it was carried reverently by one of the monks in certain processions, and this is the one that is properly called the oriflamme and whence it came, in so far as I have been able to discern from my limited experience.

# Jeanette Beer

And these things, my very revered lord, truly demonstrate and reveal that through this you are and must be the sole and principal protector, champion, and defender of the Church as were your ancestors. And this is maintained by the Holy See of Rome whose custom it has been to address your forebears and you uniquely by entitling letters "To the Most Christian of Princes."

Thirdly, because from the time when you reached an age of understanding, you have always loved learning, honored the good *clercs*, and, if you had no other occupation, studied constantly in diverse books and disciplines, you arranged to have several of those books written down amd translated both for your own pleasure and for the profit of your subjects, thus avoiding the reproach of the sage who said: "An unlettered king is an ass in a crown"; and especially because the loftiness of your intelligence and understanding has soared so far and reached such heights that his greatest work (apart from the one he wrote on the Blessed Trinity) which deals with serious, sublime, subtle, and diverse matters, and which scarcely reaches down to human understanding because of the loftiness and profundity of its subject-matter, you wanted this book, namely St. Augustine's book on the *City of God*, to be translated from Latin into French for the profit and utility of your kingdom, your people, and the whole of Christendom. And I believe that in this respect you wanted to follow the example of St. Charles who, of all the books he studied and enjoyed, preferred the books of St. Augustine and, in particular, the book of *The City of God*, as is attested by his life and by the chronicles.

For all these three things, it seems to me, I can compare you in all your nobility, grandeur, and goodwill, to the eagle, and I believe that this goodwill came to you principally by direct inspiration from God. But, my most revered lord, at these things I do not marvel. I must, however, marvel and with cause, that you pass over the sovereign *clercs* in your kingdom, whose numbers and whose excellence are unsurpassed in all Christendom; that when to them such a work belonged and its translation was their due, it occurred to you to give it to me who in their regard am but dust and ashes; and that you decided to give such a heavy assignment to me who am endowed with such limited understanding—such a little hand to turn so great a mill!

And, lest it be thought that I decided to undertake it through arrogance or to put myself forward, as God is my witness, you well know how and for what length of time I refused and delayed the undertaking, and the excuses I proffered to avoid it because I knew and know the smallness of my ability, the

130

greatness of the work, and my age, which should, in my view, have entitled me to rest from now on.

May neither you nor any other think I was so bold or arrogant as to undertake this of my own accord. If I had not thought I would have been considered more presumptuous to have refused it than to have obeyed your command, I would have refused it outright. It seemed to me that I had labored enough in my lifetime, writing the book entitled *The Moral Compendium of the Republic*, the book called *The Muse,* which you were gracious enough to accept when I dedicated it to you, and *Modernized French Chronicles from the Creation of the World to the Era of Tarquin the Proud and King Cambises*, together with a book of *Letters;* taking into account also the great responsibility of my advocacy, which is a public office requiring constant labor. I believe you had read that dictum of Seneca's that inactivity without letters is like burying a man alive.

And I beg your royal highness that inasmuch as I have with simplicity undertaken this work, it may please you to receive it favorably and to bear with my defects of which I am sure there will be several. And if I do not in this translation follow the exact words of the text and if I approach it sometimes with a sort of circumlocution or other device, I shall be forgiven because you told me, in order to make the material clear, to follow the plain, simple, obvious meaning and the real intent without meticuously following every word of the text. And if there are several words which do not translate well into French without expansion or exposition for, as was said above, this book comprises diverse lofty matters, high style, and ancient grammar, laden with long, suspended sentences, succinctly worded, many and diverse narrations abridged from diverse ancient authors, whose originals cannot readily be found in this country in order to check on the parts and the terms that require clarification, nevertheless it is my intention to insert clarifications and expositions to shed light on the text in the those parts and places where there is doubt or obscurity.

Jeanette Beer

Notes

1. Translators continue to be commissioned in such contexts as commerce and advertising, but their responsibilities to such "patrons" and to the text are now more clearly defined than were those of their earlier conterparts.

2. The following provide useful contextual background: Léopold Delisle, *Le Cabinet des manuscrits de la Bibliothèque Nationale*, vol. 1 (Paris: Imprimerie Impériale, 1868), pp. 18–46; Claire R. Sherman, *The Portraits of Charles V of France (1338–1380)* (New York: New York University Press, 1969); Suzanne Solente, *Christine de Pisan* (Paris: Imprimerie Nationale and Librairie Klincksieck, 1969), pp. 41–47; Marcel Thomas, *La Librairie de Charles V* (Paris: Bibliothèque Nationale, 1968); Franklin J. Pegues, *The Lawyers of the Last Capetians* (Princeton: Princeton University Press, 1962); Paul Pradel, "Art et politique sous Charles V," *Revue des Arts* 1 (1951): 89–73; Norma L. Goodrich, *Charles, Duke of Orléans* (New York: Macmillan, 1963); Karl J. Holzknecht, *Literary Patronage in the Middle Ages* (1923; repr. New York: Octagon, 1966); Henri I. Marrou, *Saint Augustin et la fin de la culture antique* (Paris: Boccard, 1937); Curt J. Wittlin, Jr., "Traductions et commentaires médiévaux de la *Cité de Dieu* de saint Augustin," *Travaux de linguistique et de littérature* 16 (1978): 531–55; Christine de Pisan, *Le Livre des fais et bonnes meurs du sage roy Charles V*, 2 vols., ed. Suzanne Solente (Paris: Champion, 1936, 1940); and Roland Delachenal, *Histoire de Charles V*, 5 vols. (Paris: Picard, 1909), vol. 5. I should like here to acknowledge also the generous help of a living repository of fifteenth-century information, Charity Cannon Willard. It was her chapter, "Raoul de Presles's Translation of Saint Augustine's *De Civitate Dei*" (*Medieval Translators and their Craft*, ed. J. Beer [Kalamazoo, Mich.: Medieval Institute Publications, 1989], pp. 329–46) that first interested me in the subject of Raoul's translation.

3. My source for the text was Bib. Nat., fr. 22912, which I checked against the excellent but later manuscript British Library RO 17 F iii. Until now the only version available has been that of Le Comte A. De Laborde in vol. 1 of *Les Manuscrits à peintures de la "Cité de Dieu" de Saint Augustin*, 3 vols. (Paris: E. Rahir, 1909). Unfortunately, Laborde's only interest was the manuscript's illuminations:

> Cette transcription aura du moins cet intérêt que le texte de ce prologue a servi de thème à beaucoup de peintures et que les détails qu'il contient sur l'histoire de Clovis, l'écu fleurdelysé, l'oriflamme, l'aigle et le saint Chrème ont inspiré le pinceau des artistes qui ont

132

# Patronage and the Translator

décoré un certain nombre de manuscrits, surtout de l'école flamande. (p. 63)

There are many mistakes in his text, of which the most egregious, perhaps, is his conversion of Augustine's role from "la *confutacion* ou reprobation des herites" [*confuting* or reproving heretics, my emphasis] to "la *confortacion* ou reprobacion des herites" [*comforting* or reproving heretics]. More recently, portions of BN fr. 22912, fols. 3ᵛ–4, were transcribed by William Hinkle in an Appendix (William Hinkle, *The Fleurs de Lis of the Kings of France, 1283–1488* [Carbondale and Edwardsville: Southern Illinois University Press], pp. 162–65). Unfortunately, this anyway incomplete transcription is full of inaccuracies, and it seemed imperative, therefore, to provide a new transcription of the text under discussion as a service to readers. See the Appendix to this chapter.

4. Jean Calvin, *Epistre au Roy,* in *Oeuvres complètes de Calvin: Institution de la religion Chrestienne*, vol. 1, ed. Jacques Pannier (Paris: Belles Lettres, 1961), pp. 7–36.

5. *Ioannis Calvini Opera quae supersunt omnia*, ed. J. W. Baum, A. E. Cunitz, E. Reuss, and A. Erichson, vol. 1, Corpus Reformatorum series, vol. 29 (Brunswick: Schwetschke, 1863). Also used (for the second Latin edition of Calvin's text) was *Ioannis Calvini Institutio Christianae religionis*, ed. A. Tholuck (Berlin: Eichler, 1834).

6. The nature of Raoul's assignment was, therefore, to translate not only the *De Civitate Dei* but also such glosses as might make comprehensible to a modern age the alien history and mythology of a previous one. It is important to realize that it was Charles V who determined the nature of Raoul's assignment and to avoid anachronism in the assessment of Raoul's translated commentaries. C. Wittlin, for example, faults Raoul's *modus operandi* and suggests that Raoul was appropriating other people's commentary for his own purposes:

> Résultat de presque quatre ans de travail! Mais ce temps apparaît long finalement quand, perçant le secret que Raoul savait si bien garder devant le roi et la postérité, nous découvrons que son commentaire n'est qu'une traduction des *Expositiones* de Thomas Waleys, augmentée des gloses de Nicolas Trévet et de quelques citations auxquelles Augustin ou Waleys ne faisaient qu'allusion. ("Traductions et commentaires de la *Cité de Dieu*," *Travaux de linguistique et de littérature* 16 [1978]: 535–36)

Even if Raoul *had* done nothing but translate Waleys's commentary without acknowedgement—and one has only to look at any sample paragraph of Raoul's commentary to see the multiple references to Waleys and to realize how much more complex than this were his compilation procedures—the "secret" would hardly have distressed a royal patron who had actually commissioned Raoul to make the almost sacred text available, using such commentaries as would make it more accessible. Glossators had no copyright, and their translators were not seeking credit for authorship. Raoul's principal concern was to launch an authoritative text upon an interested lay public, using whatever materials the king saw fit to provide to him.

7. Compare the modern translator for whom such multi-faceted responsibilities no longer exist and who frequently sees translative difficulties differently, for example, as a Sisyphean struggle between two forces, the authority of the source and the individuality of the source's re-creator: "Translation is really what we might call transformation. It is a form of adaptation, making the new metaphor fit the original metaphor, and in a bad translation the results can be most procrustean" (Gregory Rabassa); "We cannot translate until we 'do violence' to the original work. We must destroy—de-struct—(and we must make the obligatory disclaimer: no reference is intended to the terminology of Derrida, who has pre-empted a word I should like to use) before we can re-*con*struct" (Margaret Peden). Both quotations are from John Biguenet and Rainer Schulte, eds., *The Craft of Translation* (Chicago: University of Chicago Press, 1989), pp. 2 and 14.

8. All translations are mine unless otherwise noted.

9. The numbers refer to the line numbers of the Appendix.

10. Quoted by Hinkle, *The Fleurs de Lis*, p. 191.

11. The practice of combining antiquity's modesty topos with an Old Testament formula of self-disparagement was not, of course an invention of Raoul's; see E. R. Curtius, *European Literature and the Latin Middle Ages*, trans. Willard R. Trask (New York: Pantheon, 1953), p. 84. The Old Testament source for "dust and ashes" was Genesis 18: 27 where Abraham used it in a comparison of himself with God. One may assume there was a touch of irony in Raoul's use of the same phrase for a comparison of himself with the lofty theologians!

# Patronage and the Translator

12. For the development of the triple *fleurs de lis* and of the *oriflamme* legend see Hinkle, *The Fleurs de Lis*.

13. Cf. Jacques Monfrin's view in "Humanisme et traduction au moyen âge," *L'Humanisme médiéval dans les littératures romanes du XII^e^ au XIV^e^ siècles*, Actes et Colloques 3, ed. Anthime Fourrier (Paris: Klincksieck, 1964), pp. 217–64, that the political advantage Charles gained from his encouragement of scholarship dominated any personal interest in scholarship that he may have had.

14. With his enthusiastic cultivation of scholars and artists, his embellishment of the Louvre, and his establishment of the royal library, Charles V was one of France's most lavish royal patrons. For another testimony (among many) from his subjects, see Christine de Pisan's *Livre des fais*, ed. Solente, 1:19–48 and *passim*.

15. The statistics for the *illustrated* MSS alone are phenomenal. "Before [Raoul's] translation, there had been only four known illustrated copies of St. Augustine's text, but by the beginning of the sixteenth century there were fifty-seven, forty-five of which were copies of Raoul de Presles's translation" (Willard, "Raoul de Presles's Translation," p. 333).

16. See Léopold Delisle, *Recherches sur la librairie de Charles V*, 2 vols. (Paris: Champion, 1907), p. 116.

17. Raoul had some interest in scriptural translation also, but his translation of substantial portions of the Bible was subsequent to *La Cité de Dieu* and is not, therefore, relevant here.

18. St. Augustine followed this passage from the *Retractiones* with a brief *praefatio* introducing chapter one.

19. Jacques Monfrin, "La traduction française de Tite-Live," *Histoire littéraire de la France* 39 [n.d.]: 360.

20. It is interesting to find a similar renunciation and disclaimer in another fourteenth-century translator, Oresme. Oresme, like Raoul, was commissioned by Charles V and, although a bishop, decided to discuss ecclesiology "comme pur philisophe": "mes discuter

# Jeanette Beer

de puissance qui vient de Dieu sans moien et qui est donnee par miracle divin, ce est une chose qui transcende et passe ceste science si comme je touchay ou .xiiii$^e$ chapitre du tiers," quoted by Susan Babbitt in *Oresme's "Livre de Politiques" and the France of Charles V* (Philadelphia: American Philosophical Society, 1985), p. 104, n. 37. Babbitt comments, "Even in this restricted role he [Oresme] doubted the worthiness of his opinions, and subjected himself (though not, perhaps, without a certain irony) to the correction of those with better knowledge of the subject" (p. 105).

21. The *lex Voconia*, passed in 169 B.C., was instigated by the tribune of the plebs Quintus Voconius Saxa.

22. Isabella was a sister of Louis X.

23. See also Shulamith Shahar, "Traduction et commentaire de la 'Cité de Dieu' par un penseur politique sous Charles V," *L'Information Historique* 39.1 (Jan.–Feb. 1977): 48–49.

24. *Epistre au Roy*, ed. Pannier, pp. 7–36; and *Epistola ad Regem Galliae*, ed. Baum et al.

25. See the acknowledgement to Louis XII in the 1509 preface of *Histoires universelles de Trogue Pompee translatees par Messire Claude de Seyssel* or Joachim du Bellay's eulogy of Francis I's patronage in the 1549 *Deffense et illustration de la langue française*.

26. The statement of François I to the Parlement of Paris on December 10, 1538 was:

> *Nous sommes Très-marris et desplaisans de ce que en nostre bonne Ville de Paris, chef et capitalle de nostre Royame, et où y a Université principale de la Chrestianté, cette maudite secte hérétique Luthérienne pullule, où plusieurs pourront prendre exemple. Et pour ce voulons et entendons que telle et si griefve punition en soit faicte, que ce soit correction aux maudits Hérétiques, et exemple à tous les autres* (A.-L. Herminjard, *Correspondance des Réformateurs dans les pays de langue française . . .* [Geneva: H. Georg; Paris: Michel Levy, 1870], vol. 3, no. 440, pp. 114–15).

27. Herminjard *Correspondences*, 3:273.

# Patronage and the Translator

28. Beza provides the following valuable information about the appearance of the *Insitution* and, more particularly, the "Epistre"/"Epistola":

Calvin ne pouvant souffrir que la véritable religion fut ainsi noircie, crut qu'il devait faire imprimer son *Institution* afin de réfuter les calomnies des ennemis de la vérité, et il dédia ce livre incomparable au roi François I$^{er}$ lui écrivant une lettre si belle et si excellente, que si ce grand prince l'eût voulu lire, l'église romaine eût alors sans doute reçu une plaie mortelle. Car ce roi était si bien différent de ceux qui lui succédent; il avait le goût admirablement bon, et un jugement exquis, il aimait les savans et les gens de lettres, et même son inclination le portait à ne pas hair les personnes de notre créance. Mais par un effet de la justice de Dieu, que les péchés de ce monarque et de ses sujets avaient justement irrité, leurs plaintes ne parvinrent pas jusques à ses oreilles, et il ne lut jamais cette admirable préface (*Les Vies de Jean Calvin* [*trad. par Théodore de Bèze*] *et de Théodore de Bèze* [*par Antoine de la Faye* (?)], [*trad. par Antoine Teissier*] [Geneva: Guers; Paris: Servier, 1830], p. 17).

29. "Cum huic operi manum primum admoverem, nihil minus cogitabam, rex clarissime, quam scribere quae Maiestati tuae offerrentur. Tantum erat animus rudimenta quaedam tradere, quibus formerentur ad veram pietatem qui aliqui religionis studio tanguntur" ("Epistola," p. 3).

30. See, for example, Calvin's manner of conducting the defense/confession: his syntactic hyper-specificity, his adversarial confrontations and *ad hominem* attacks, his rhetorical questions, and his rigorously argued sequences, reinforced by strategically placed examples. His lexicon is also rich with individual legalisms: "At cuius criminis?"—"Mais de quel crime?"; and "legitimate gravitate"—"par une modération et gravité judiciaire"; "omnes leges abrogat"—"les loix abolies"; "criminatibus"—"detractions"; "humanae impietatis crimen"—"le crime en est a imputer à l'impiété des hommes."

31. J. M. V. Audin summarized the situation thus:

According to Beze, the first edition of the Christian *Institutes* appeared in 1535, at Bâle, where Calvin was residing. Gerdes *(Scrinium antiquarium sive miscellanea Groeningana,* t. 11, p. 453) also speaks of an edition of 1535, of which no copy can be found. He

137

## Jeanette Beer

remarks that printers had a custom to antedate the title of their works. It is pretended that the edition of 1536 is not the first, for Calvin in it names himself on the title page, in the commencement of the preface, and at the head of the first chapter. Whereas, from the reformer's own testimony, we know that the work did not appear under Calvin's name. The edition of 1536 is in the Brunswick library and at Geneva. M. Turretin, in a letter of 1700, says "the most ancient edition to be found at Geneva, is one in 8vo. of 514 pages, printed at Bale, per Thomam Platterum et Balthaserem Latium, m. martio, ann. 1536. At the end of the book is the representation of Minerva, with these words: Tu nihil invita faciesve ne dicesve Minerva. The beginning is wanting, as far as page 43." Sponde admits a French edition of Bale, August 1535: Bayle, art. *Calvin.*

Paul Henry thinks that there must have been a French edition of 1535, the same that appeared under the Pseudo-name of Alcuin, and a Latin edition of 1536, which bore the name of Calvin. In the French edition of the *Institutes* of 1566, the preface is dated Bale, August 1st, 1535. It remains to be explained, how no copy of the original edition has reached our times.

In the Royal Library at Paris there exists a very rare edition of this work, (1565) of which this is the title: "Institution de la religion Chrestienne nouvellement mise en quatre livres: augmentée aussi de tel accroissement qu'on la peut estimer un livre nouveau; par Jean Calvin." (*History of the Life, Works, and Doctrines of John Calvin,* trans. John McGill [Louisville: B. J. Webb & Brother, n. d.], pp. 80–81, n. 6)

The complexity of the question may be gauged by the conflicting opinions of Pannier (*Institution,* p. xiv); J.-W. Marmelstein, *Etude comparative des textes latins et français de "L'Institution de la religion chrestienne" par Jean Calvin* (The Hague and Groningen: J. B. Wolters, 1921), pp. 25–30; and Hards's reconstruction of the history of the *Institutes* in his unpublished dissertation, "*A Critical Translation and Evaluation of the Nucleus of the 1536 Edition of Calvin's Institutes*" (Princeton Theological Seminary, 1955). Although Marmelstein inclines in the direction of the "Epistola"'s precedence, he points out the impossibility of reaching a definitive conclusion without new evidence:

> Les matériaux dont nous disposons ne nous permettent pas de dire laquelle des deux a été composée la premiere: la lettre latine ou la française. Ce que nous savons sur la plupart des autres ouvrages de

> Calvin parus en français et en latin, nous amènerait à admettre que la lettre française présente la traduction de la latine. (*Etude comparative*, p. 30)

32. Two sections—on miracles and on patristic authority—are actually more developed in the Latin than in the French version.

33. Calvin's Latin scholarship is evidenced by the fact that he had just (in 1532) produced a massive commentary on Seneca's *De Clementia*. This happened on the eve of the conversion that was destined to divert him in the future from purely humanistic pursuits.

34. Calvin's avoidance of French diminutives here is, therefore, in my view a demonstration of his stylistic sensitivity to the different nuances of stylistic usage in Latin and the vernacular. While the Latin diminutive frequently had derogatory overtones, the French diminutive more frequently added charm, lightness, affection and sometimes pathos as, for example, in Ronsard's epitaph "A son âme": "Amelette Ronsardelette, / Mignonnelette, doucelette, etc." On one occasion, where such connotations were useful in the French, Calvin did in fact match up diminutives, using a "paupercula ecclesia" in the "Epistola" (7) and a "povrette eglise" in the "Epistre" (10). Given the projected audiences and their unambiguous views on the subject of the "true" Church, it may safely be assumed, of course, that "paupercula" was interpreted derisively by Catholic theologians, and "povrette" was interpreted affectionately by the Protestant faithful.

35. See also, on the same page, "O matiere digne de tes aureilles!" [O subject worthy of your ears!].

36. On the subject of Picardisms in Calvin's overall style, see Charles Guerlin de Guer, "Sur la langue du Picard J. Calvin," *Le Français Moderne* 5 (1937): 303–16. Francis Higman, in *The Style of John Calvin in his French Polemical Treatises* (Oxford: Oxford University Press, 1967), pp. 57–58, downplays the importance of Calvin's dialectisms, however. For the printing of the *Institutes*, see Albert Autin, *L'Institution chrétienne de Calvin* (Paris: E. Malfère, 1929), pp. 47–57.

37. That Calvin was aware of the suggestiveness of Picardisms is clear from his derisive imitation of the Libertine Quintin, "ceste grosse de Quintin," in his 1545 treatise "Contre la secte phantastique et furieuse des Libertins qui se nomment Spirituelz."

# Jeanette Beer

38. Although synonymic expansiveness is more frequent in the "Epistre" than in the "Epistola," the latter contains "timor et pavor" for "crainte," "consentiant et conspirant" for "conspirent," and "mille ignibus et crucibus" for "gibbetz."

39. In my English translation I have rendered the Greek infinitive into French in an effort to reproduce Calvin's satire of preciosity with some degree of accuracy.

40. It will be noted that, while the phrases used in both versions are all known and frequently used formulae, the two versions do not always match up exactly: "Très illustre Roy" is not a translation of "Rex invictissime," and "Très gratieux Roy" is not a translation of "Serenissime Rex." It is my impression that Calvin often reserves the more power-fraught terminology for the "Epistola." For example, the implications of "invictissime," with its homage to the "always unconquered, always invincible" status of the monarch, might have sounded particularly threatening to the insecure "faithful" who had just been deprived of royal support.

41. In point of fact, the king never read the letter addressed to him. The idealistic reformer Beza believed that if the king *had* read it, patronage would have been forthcoming (see n. 29 above). There was, of course, another potential royal patron, the king's sister Marguerite de Navarre, and it is interesting to speculate what would have happened if Calvin had managed to remain within her circle of intimates. But the very reasons that motivated Calvin to educate his king in the *Institution* about the various Evangelical sects caused a rift with the Evangelical Royal when Calvin wrote his scathing work against the Anabaptists. According to Beza, Calvin

> composa un livre pour réfuter les erreurs des anabaptistes et des libertins, lesquels ont renouvelé les hérésies les plus monstrueuses de l'antiquité, et il les combattit avec des raisons si fortes qu'il est impossible de les lire avec attention sans avoir de l'horreur pour une doctrine si détestable. Cependant cet écrit irrita la reine de Navarre contre Calvin; car, bien qu'elle ne fût pas infectée de leurs erreurs, toutefois elle était si préoccupée du mérite de Quintin et de Pocquart les chefs ples plus fameux de cette secte que Calvin avait nommés dans son livre, qu'elle les croyait les plus gens de bien du monde, et elle avait tant d'affection pour eux, qu'on ne pouvait les attaquer sans lui faire une plaie profonde." (*Vies de Calvin et de Théodore de Bèze*, pp. 49–50)

# Patronage and the Translator

42. "Prov. 29" occurs in the "Epistre" also, but has been placed differently (as a footnote) in Pannier's edition. The identification of source-versions for the Scriptural references in the two epistles is not always easy, especially since Calvin often quoted spontaneously from memory and, in addition, employed what I call "Scriptural reminiscences." Thus no single French source matches every detail of the French Scriptural references (which means that Calvin did not even use *his own* translations of the Vulgate consistently). A further complication is the didactic intent of many cited references. In the "Epistre" (although not in the "Epistola"), for example, Calvin appended "Romans 8" to "Dieu, duquel la dilection s'est tant estendue envers nous, qu'il n'a point espargné son propre Filz, qu'il ne l'ayt livré pour nous." The text as given was obviously a rendering of John 3: 16, which, however, was not mentioned. Instead, Calvin referred the faithful to the chapter in Romans where salvation was linked to the predestination and persecution of the elect. Here in the "Epistre," therefore, Calvin was not identifying a text but was recommending a significant cross-reference for their instruction. (John 3: 16's "*Whosoever* believeth" ["quiconque croit"] may have been too indiscriminate in a context of Divine election and predestination!) Unfortunately, further discussion of Calvin's biblical translation cannot be justified in this chapter since it is not relevant to the subject of royal patronage. For obvious historical reasons, neither Charles V nor Francis I was as influential in France as were Henry VIII and James I in England for the royal sponsorship of Bibles.

43. One might compare Raoul de Presles's different presentation of royal leisure when he complimented Charles's "estude et continuele occupation" (lines 39–40 in the Appendix to this chapter) and, with courteous respect for the king's other obligations, observed "vous avés tousjours aimé science et honoré les bons clers et estudié continuelment en divers livres et sciences, *se vous n'avez eü autre occupation*" (pp. 138–39, emphasis added).

44. For the French Protestants, Calvin here added to his description of the Catholic Church "butcher of souls" ["exitialis animarum carnifica"], the designation of Gehenna, netherworld beyond the Hebrew pale, dedicated to Baal and Moloch. The metaphor was congruent with his appropriation of other Old Testament imagery, most notably that of the Hebrew elect, to serve French Protestantism. Thus the "Epistre" used "l'ydolatrie *des Gentiles*" to castigate Roman abuses, whereas the "Epistola" used merely "idolatria" and omitted the opposition of the elect to "Gentile" idolatry.

45. See n. 40.

46. See Marmelstein, *Etude comparative*, pp. 25–26.

47. Marmelstein, *Etude comparative*, p. 26.

# Marot's *Le Roman de la Rose* and Evangelical Poetics

## Hope H. Glidden

*Car, tout ainsi que le Feu l'Or affine,*
*Le Temps a faict nostre langue plus fine.*
Marot, *Rondeau XVIII*

The vitality of the *Roman de la Rose* in the first decades of the six-teenth century is attested by the publishing history of its successive editions.[1] Between 1481 and 1538, twenty-two editions of the poem appeared, seven of which were published during the years 1526–38. According to F. W. Bourdillon, few books were edited and commented upon as persistently as the *Roman de la Rose,* with the exception of the Bible.[2] Other evidence confirms the poem's popularity during this period, notably, imitations, plagiarisms, prose versions, and the survival of over three hundred manuscripts, many of which are sumptuously illuminated with miniatures glossing its allegorical and mythological figures.

Of the seven editions from the period 1526–38, five are attributed to the poet Clément Marot. While definitive attribution remains a matter of some critical disagreement, the bulk of contemporary opinion supports attribution to Marot, and it should be noted at the outset that the debate over the poem's attribution to Marot will not be taken up in the pages that follow. The editions in question were published anonymously, and not explicitly attributed to Marot until after his death, by Etienne Pasquier. This has understandably led some scholars to withhold positive attribution, largely on the grounds that the prefatory "Exposition moralle" is pedantic and lends the text a distinctly "un-marotic" tone. In this essay, a distinction is drawn between the authored text and the poem's textuality, the latter understood in terms of the interpretive choices visible in the 1529 edition aimed at adapting it to its early

Renaissance audience. Since the primary purposes here are to examine the translation of the *Roman de la Rose* into sixteenth-century French and, in particular, to observe how the poem's ironic view of love was made meaningful to a post-medieval readership, I shall adhere to the working hypothesis of Marot's "authorship," not because debate is closed on the question but because positing authorship has the pragmatic advantage of focusing attention on the poem's language itself.[3] To the degree that aspects of the adaptation will be seen to be congruent with what we know of other aspects of Marot's poetic evolution during the late 1520s, the thesis of Marot's authorship will of necessity be reinforced. My principal interest here is less to prove authorship, however, than to demonstrate that this version of the *Rose* merits scholarly attention because of its serious engagement with the poetics and worldview of its predecessor. Specifically, the evangelical poetics of Marot and his generation may be seen to derive inspiration from the *Rose*'s critique of courtly discourse and exegetical practice, two points of relevance to the characterization of Renaissance writing as "natural."

Marot's *Rose* is not a translation in the usual sense but is an "internal translation," or one which revives and adapts a work for a later generation of readers.[4] Introduced by Marot as a "plaisant livre" composed by "deux nobles aucteurs dignes de l'estimation," the *Roman de la Rose* of Guillaume de Lorris and Jean de Meung was celebrated as a foundation text, one that provided a genealogy for a vernacular in the throes of growth and self-definition in the humanist France of the 1520s.[5] Nevertheless, the language of the *Roman* had become quaint, in places even archaic, and it is to the task of updating it that Marot applied himself in his 1529 edition.

Internal translation aims to provide access to texts by removing archaisms that stand in the way of clear understanding; it may thus be construed as a modernization that attends to formal, syntactic, and lexical updating of a source text. But Marot's translation also interrogates the premise that poetic language is translatable, that is, able to signify in the maximal conditions of transparency pertaining within stages of the same language. In a sense, internal translation constitutes a zero degree of translation, and some might dispute the claim that it is translation at all, rather than a modernization designed to render an outmoded text more readable. On the other hand, Marot's translation of the *Roman de la Rose,* like other internal translations, does not simply reinscribe the language of its predecessor but interprets it, an operation that is all the more subtle given the absence of linguistic difference that characterizes bilingual translation.

In the "Exposition moralle," which precedes the poem, Marot states his motives for undertaking the translation project:

> réintégrer et en son entier remettre le livre qui par long temps devant ceste moderne saison tant a esté de tous gens d'esprit estimé que bien la [*sic*] daigne chascun veoir et tenir au plus hault anglet de sa librairie pour les bonnes sentences propos et ditz naturelz et moraulx qui dedans sont mis et insérez. (p. 89)

> [reintegrate and restore in its entirety the book which for a long time before this modern season has been so esteemed by all intelligent people of learning that each one deems it worthy to be seen and kept in the premier place of his library for the good dicta, remarks, and natural and moral sayings which are contained therein.]

The "Exposition" positions the great courtly poem squarely between the ancient *auctores* and the ideological lens of a nascent sixteenth-century evangelical humanism. Its "bonnes sentences," or *sententiae,* correct the poem's allegorical apparatus; its lessons are deemed "moraulx," a recognition of the long tradition of moralization of pagan myths best exemplified by the *Ovide moralisé* but also complexly related to the status of allegory in the changing world of evangelical hermeneutic practice. Finally, its "ditz naturelz" anticipate the privileging of un-adorned speech in poetic theory and in biblical translation.

Marot was not the first in his century to translate this classic of medieval verse. Prior to Marot's 1526 edition, Jean Molinet had pro-duced a *Roman de la Rose* printed by Vérard in 1500, and that edition was reprinted in Lyon (1503) and again in Paris (1521). Molinet's ver-sion has been called eccentric by critics who note its "imposed alle-gories," the *moralités* he added to each chapter to gloss their Christian doctrinal significance.[6] The poem's erotic meander becomes, in Molinet's contrivance, an antetype of the life of Christ, with events in the poem finding parallels with the Incarnation, the virgin birth, and the Crucifixion, to name a few. The Marot edition eliminates such free associating but is, nevertheless, not free of the didacticism of its prede-cessor.

In the "Exposition moralle" cited above, Marot adumbrates four levels of meaning of the quest for the Rose, interpreting the Rose as wisdom and the Virgin Mary. As a result, the poem's erotics undergo ostensible transformation into an apology for orthodox Catholicism. Not-withstanding, from all that is known of Marot's anti-clericalism, it is difficult to believe that the "Exposition" could be a sincere confession of belief. Critics have speculated that it may have been affixed to placate the censors already too eager to find Marot guilty of the charge of Lutheranism that "Monsieur Bouchart, Docteur en Théologie," had brought against him.[7] Marot's stake in the translation, his rationale, and even his authorship have been unexplored for another reason, however, and that is the simplified view that the *Roman de la Rose* translation belongs to Marot's *rhétoriqueur* past, a past having no relevance to his mature vocation as an evangelical poet.[8] And yet to call his translation a "potboiler" or dismiss such poems as the "Temple de Cupido" as mere pastiche is to accept uncritically the outdated notion that Marot saw no ideological content in *fin' amors* as an institution relevant to the evangelical cause of the 1520s. In point of fact, the *Rose* translation coincides with Marot's imprisonment in the Châtelet in Spring, 1526 and, hence, with the arrest occasioned by his having broken the fast during Lent. Positioned in the midst of competing ideologies and, hence, language used and abused for political ends, Marot's translation of the *Rose* has been overlooked as a document germane to the poet's self-awareness as an evangelical writer.[9]

Before moving to the translation itself, a word may be said about the original poem's reception in the first decades of the sixteenth century. Was it regarded as an *ars amandi*? a *querelle des femmes* tract? a treatise on fortune? friendship? theology? Was it classified generically as an *imitatio* of Ovid? as an encyclopedia? a compendium of *sagesse*? There is support for each of these suggestions in the various uses to which the poem was put in polemical and lyrical writing in the late Middle Ages and the sixteenth century. Moreover, the question entails a further conjecture about how the poem was read. Was it read as a complete work and assumed to be thematically unified? or as a discontinuous patchwork of set pieces, many of which, including the discourses of Raison, Nature, Amys, la Vieille, and Génius, could stand as autonomous philosophical formulations?[10]

To answer these questions, the apparatus of the Marot edition is of crucial importance. There can be little doubt that Marot recognized the difficulty presented by a poem of such length and complexity. To thread his readers through the labyrinth of text, often dauntingly convoluted, he inserted marginalia to mark off passages of especial interest. The marginalia are of different kinds. "Nota" signs solicit the reader to pause and reflect. There are also capsule summaries of exempla, mythological names, and other unfamiliar material, and these function as glosses and thematic guideposts. The apparatus also includes rubrics functioning as dividers, so as to break the text down into manageable segments. Finally, Marot's edition attributes a name to each speaker, thereby observing the precedent of fourteenth- and fifteenth-century scribes. The apparatus of the Marot edition is part of the editorial history of the poem and is regarded here as part of the poem's translation strategy.[11]

The length of the *Roman de la Rose*—surpassing 22,000 lines—defies exhaustive treatment here. Four passages will serve as examples: the myth of Narcissus in Guillaume de Lorris's part of the poem; the opening lines of Jean de Meung's continuation; a passage from the counsel of "la tres belle Raison" [very lovely Reason], the poem's first allegorical speaker in Jean de Meung's version; and a passage from Faus Semblant's speech to the God of Love's assembled army, also from Jean de Meung's part. These passages are chosen to illustrate the degree to which "internal translation" reveals the mark of doctrinal change in a text heretofore considered of marginal relevance to the evangelical ferment of the 1520s.[12]

In the first passage depicting the "Garden of Déduit" [the Garden of Delight], the Lover comes upon the fountain of Narcissus, the "fontaine perilleux," and fears to look into its waters. The desire to do so overcomes him, and he experiences the desire for the rosebush that will become his obsession throughout the remainder of the poem. Guillaume de Lorris's allegory begins to wear thin at this point because the sexual nature of the arousal, the lust for the rose, is evoked in explicit terms. To critics accustomed to viewing Jean de Meung as the ironic poet of eroticism, the bluntness of Lorris's text is unexpected. Lorris writes openly of the urge that propelled the Lover toward his beloved:

> Quant cele *rage* m'ot si pris,
> dont maint autre ont esté sorpris,
> vers les rosiers tantost me trés. (lines 1621–23, emphasis added)[13]

> [When this madness, by which many other men have been seized, had captured me, I straightaway drew near to the rosebushes.]

## Le Roman de la Rose and Evangelical Poetics

The urgency of sexual passion is marked by the *rage* that overtakes the lover. Compare Lorris's rendition with that of Marot in which the lover in the same passage is surprised not by desire (*rage*) but by the Rose itself. Marot's translation of the Guillaume passage above follows:

> Quant celle *rose* m'eut surpris
> Dont maint autre a esté espris
> Vers le rosier tost me retrays. (lines 1633–35, emphasis added)

> [When this rose, by which many another man has been inflamed, had captured me, I straightaway drew near to the rosebush.]

In place of the *rage* marking the rose's effect on the lover, Marot substitutes *rose*, a way to sustain the allegory with its veil of doubleness. The erotic meaning of the rose as flower is thus contained within its conventional symbolism and not allowed to become sexually explicit. The scenario is further de-eroticized when Marot renders "rosiers" by the singular "rosier," again emphasizing the referential, particularized object, rather than the sensual atmosphere created by Guillaume de Lorris's plural.

Marot's translation of another passage of the Narcissus myth suggests that he did not imagine eroticism to be the driving form of the Lover's quest. We read in the Narcissus episode how the youth arrived at the fountain, the treacherous "mirouër périlleux" [perilous mirror] (1583–1648). The narrator describes how wise and chivalrous men see their boldness dissolve when they look into the fountain and contemplate its crystals. Guillaume de Lorris expresses their condition as a "noveile rage" [new madness] (line 1581) and underscores its power to make men forget all else:

> li plus saive,
> li plus preu, li mieuz afetié

149

> i sont tost pris et agaitié.
> Ci sort as genz noveile *rage*,
> ici se changent li corage,
> *ci n'a mestier sens ne mesure*
> *ci est d'amer volenté pure,*
> ci ne se set conseiller nus. (lines 1578–85, emphasis added)

[the wisest, most noble and sophisticated are quickly surprised and captured here. Out of this mirror a new madness comes upon men: here hearts are changed; intelligence and moderation are useless, here is only the pure will to love, here no-one can get advice.]

The same passage is rendered by Marot as follows:

> le plus saige
> Le plus preux et plus affecté
> Y a esté prins, et guetté
> Illec sur tres mauvais oraige,
> Car trop tost change le couraige.
> La ne se vont conseiller nulz. (lines 1592–97)

[the wisest, noblest and most sophisticated has been surprised and fallen victim here to a very violent storm: for the heart changes very quickly, there no-one asks for counsel.]

Lines 1583–84 of Guillaume's version express love's tyranny but were deleted from Marot's edition, and the characterization of love as "rage" was omitted, with "oraige" substituted to preserve the end rhyme *oraige / couraige*. Marot's rewriting and substitution bespeak a voluntary suppression of the Ovidian view of love as madness, conceiving love instead as a tempestuous force that buffets the victim, just as boats at sea are pitched and tossed in a storm. The storm conjures up an image of divine wrath, a vague reference that nevertheless locates the Lover within a classical universe ruled by Fortune, rather than a psychologically fraught inner landscape of personified vices. Moreover, Narcissus is characterized in Marot's version as "tresorgueilleux" [very prideful] (line 1584), whereas he had been merely "li orgueilleus" [the prideful one] (line 1570) in Lorris's text. His folly is underscored by the addition of the intensified adjective.

A final example from Guillaume de Lorris's part of the *Rose* will serve to demonstrate the chastened character of Marot's text. When the poet-dreamer approaches the rosebush, the delicious odor of the roses penetrates his body, impressing itself on his senses as comparable to no other fragrance. In Guillaume's version, the encounter is expressed viscerally:

> l'odor des roses savoree
> m'entra jusques en *la coree*
> que por noiant fusse enbasmez. (lines 1625–27, emphasis added)

> [the delicious odor of the roses penetrated right into my heart, more than if I had been embalmed.]

The seat of romantic madness is, not surprisingly, the heart (*la coree*). Marot's translation defines sensual experience as intellectual, locating it in the more disembodied realm of thought:

> L'odeur de la plus savourée
> Rose, m' entra en la pensée
> Et en fuz [si] fort odoré. (lines 1637–39)

> [The odor of the most fragrant Rose penetrated right into my mind, and I was [so] completely perfumed by it.]

Did Marot intend by his substitution of *pensée* for *coree* to intellectualize the power of sensual arousal? The change of wording is substantive and may suggest a predilection for "reasonable" love rather than the irrational sexual longing that marks the source text. Did Marot's translation seek as well to minimize the violence preciously hidden by the so-called plucking of the rose, in fact, a thinly veiled allegory of rape? In his earlier "Temple de Cupido," a youthful imitation of Guillaume de Lorris's *Garden of Déduit,* Marot phrased the sexual encounter as a gracious invitation: "Lors Bel acueil m'a le buisson ouvert / Du cueur du Temple, estant ung pré tout verd" [Then Fair Welcoming opened the hedge of the Temple's heart, it being a lovely green meadow].[14] A first reading of Marot's *Roman de la Rose* translation, then, suggests that his readers might be resistant to the poem's celebration of courtly love—a reading that argues the pre-eminence of Lady Reason as the ultimate moral authority. Accordingly, the *Roman*'s Lover is "an emblematic *jouvenceau* under the deleterious influence of *voluptuosité charnelle* or *amour desordonnée.*"[15] To be sure, Marot sustains the idea of romantic love inspired by the rose in the crystal fountain, but his substitutions attenuate Love's erotic charge, transmuting it into fatality instead. Translation is the interpretive strategy through which the source's ethical values are re-invented for consumption in a new, more civic-minded, age.[16]

The *Roman de la Rose* has the distinction of a double authorship, its second part being a vastly expanded and ironic version of the courtly love conceits of the first. Whereas Guillaume de Lorris presented the Lover as a reader and mythologizer of his own experience, Jean set his protagonist in a bookish landscape where such figures as Dame Raison, Génius, and Nature discourse on scientific, mythological, and theological issues. But as a mirror for lovers, Jean's *summum* also refracts these speeches through the prisms of ambiguity and ironic displacement, one aspect of which, the doubleness of language, will concern us in the final section of this essay. To explain Jean's linguistic play, critics have pointed to the complexity of a scholasticism questioning its own philosophical foundations. By the time that Jean de Meung wrote his part of the *Roman de la Rose,* High Scholasticism was in the throes of change and debate over its doctrinal and Aristotelian foundations: St. Louis had died in 1270, St. Bonaventure and St. Thomas in 1274, and persecutions were visible following the excommunications of 1277. As Panofsky has noted, "the doctrines of 'classic' High Scholasticism either stiffened into school traditions, or were subjected to vulgarization in popular treatises."[17] Jean's continuation of Guillaume's courtly poem reflects the attempt by an intellectual world to communicate not only with its clerkly readers but with lay readers as well. Among the issues in the *Roman de la Rose,* the reading of texts would hold interest for the sixteenth-century public, which wondered, along with Erasmus, how meaning was related to its outer expression, its figural *écorce.* In the opening lines of Jean de Meung's part, perplexity is the dominant motif in the Lover's response to Love. Let us begin there and then move to Raison's speech on language.

Marot's version introduces Jean's part of the poem with a rhymed heading inserted before line 4070:

> Apres plus de quarante ans
> Parfit Chopinel ce rommant
> Qui a bien faire s'efforca
> Et cy son oeuvre commenca.

> [After more than forty years, Chopinel completed this romance, who labored to do it well, and here his work began.]

Soon thereafter, a marginal note (*Note bien*) calls attention to a couplet whose wisdom summarizes in aphoristic form the lesson to be drawn from love: "Car l'on ne doibt croire fol homme / De la value d'une pomme" [For one must not believe a foolish man, any more than the worth of an apple] (lines 4147–48). The Renaissance reader found in this moral denouncing romantic love the caution already expressed by

153

Guillaume de Lorris in his part of the poem. The marginal note in Marot's edition gives prominence to this theme. Raison will once again claim center stage, amplifying her earlier warnings against love with lengthy discussions of Fortune's role in human affairs. But early in Jean's part, in the short passage fusing the poem's two parts, the Lover is found in a vague space of self-pity and despair concerning Love's stewardship of his cause. The following comparison of Marot's text with Jean's original raises this question: did Marot intentionally rewrite his predecessor to make the text more consonant with the new evangelical humanism? Let us examine this striking passage, first in Jean de Meung:

> car quantel [Amors] fet bon sillogime,
> si doit l'en avoir grant peeur
> qu'*el* ne conclue le *peeur,*
> qu'aucune foiz l'a l'en veü,
> s'en ont maint esté deceü. (lines 4054–58, emphasis added)

> [for when [Love] constructs a good syllogism, one must be in great fear lest he [Love] draw the worse conclusion; it has been often seen that many have been deceived by him.]

Jean de Meung's passage uses a vocabulary inspired by Aristotle, Porphyry, and Boethius, the function of which is to formalize the movement in a syllogism from known to unknown truths. Specifically, logic requires that if one of the premises of a syllogism is negative or particular, the conclusion of the syllogism cannot be affirmative or universal; it too must be negative or particular.[18] Applied to the Lover's dilemma, this law dooms the hope of possessing the Rose, because that hope is predicated on a negative proposition.

Let us turn now to Marot's version:

> Car quant on faict bon silogisme

154

L'on doibt bien lors avoir grant peur
Qu'*on* ne conclue le *meilleur*
Lequel souvent on a bien veu
Et maint en a esté déceu. (lines 4090–94, emphasis added)

[for when one constructs a good syllogism, one must be in great fear
lest one draw the better conclusion, something which has often been
seen, and many have been deceived in this way.]

For the medieval reader, Jean de Meung demonstrates his craftsmanship
when he puns at the rhyme: *peeur* / *peeur*. Might we see in Marot's
substitution of *meilleur* a reflection of that effort to distance himself
from the outdated nature of *rhétoriqueur* poetics that characterizes his
literary undertakings in the late 1520s?[19] Or should the substitution of
*meilleur* be read as a mistranslation that owes its genesis to Marot's
ignorance of (or discomfort with) Scholastic logic? A full account of
translation in theory and practice must question its own procedures and,
among them, the grounds on which it assigns intentionality to acts of
translation. The apparent mistranslation by Marot will serve as an
occasion to theorize the notion of "discrepancy" when applied to
translation and, beyond that, to interrogate what is meant by the very
concept of "mistranslation" itself. If it may be agreed with Lucien
Febvre that all persons—including translators—possess an *outillage
mental* [mental equipment] that is time-bound in its lexical resources,
then it may be assumed that certain blindspots produce gaps but also
options for remotivating signifiers whose efficacy has waned with time.[20]
In other words, translation is a dialectic between the given and the
linguistically possible, and it is in this spirit that the Marot translation of
*meilleur* may perhaps be best understood.

Now it may, of course, be objected that the substitution of *meilleur*
for *peeur* was an error having no justification outside its obvious source
in carelessness. However, the concept of "error," too, needs to be

theorized as an "interference" stemming from the translator's lack of receptivity to language that no longer suits a world-view that is past. If Marot's reading is inadvertent, it is nevertheless deeply motivated by a new discursive practice that reads the source text in terms of its own ideological priorities. In his "corrected" reading, Marot expresses caution lest the Lover conclude the best, i.e., deceive himself as to Amors's good offices. Marot's investment in such a cautious attitude would ally him with philosophical indifference to Fortune, a humanist commonplace.

The case for Marot's deliberate choice of *meilleur* over *peeur* may be strengthened by discussion of a second substitution in the same passage—the subject of Meung's line 4054, "car quant *el* [Amor] fet bon sillogime," translated now by the indefinite pronoun *on.* It can be hypothesized that this substitution is philosophically, as well as grammatically, motivated. Initially, *el* referred to *Amors,* who had offered to be the Lover's guardian: "Amors, por mieuz mes maus porter / me dist qu'*el* me garantiroit" [Love, to help me bear my troubles better, told me he would protect me] (lines 4036–37). Marot's version had substituted the unambiguously masculine pronoun *il,* modernizing the line and avoiding confusion with Espérance, also named along with Amors as the Lover's guardian. To differentiate further between the two forces, both designated by *el* in Meung's text, Marot amends *el* to read *elle* when Espérance is the subject: "Las mais que ay je alors que faire / S'elle est courtoise et debonnaire?" [Alas, but what can I do about this, if she (Hope) is courteous and kindly-disposed?] (lines 4079–80). Indeed, even the *Rose*'s modern translator has made Hope the subject of "fet bon sillogime," reading Espérance as the subject throughout. Confusion is further augmented by the vague pronoun reference in line 4053 immediately preceding the reference to the syllogism, "Por ce est fos qui trop s'en aprime" [For this reason, he is a fool who draws too close to Love], also taken by the modern translator to refer to Espérance: "He who draws too near to Hope is a fool."[21]

Marot's reading, "*on* faict bon silogisme," not only evinces his desire to promote grammatical clarity but also reveals his awareness of the philosophical implications of the point at issue. Arguably, the use of *on* wrests the making of syllogisms away from personifications of abstract forces (here, Amors), shifting the location to a human subject, albeit indefinite. Such a move, from passivity to a more active role, further suggests that human beings themselves are capable of constructing syllogisms, that is, thinking philosophically. In light of the widely attested "mespris des choses fortuites"[22] [contempt for what occurs by chance] that characterizes so much of Renaissance humanism, Marot's reading might well be seen as consonant with the active desire to master Fortuna understood as the embodiment of the forces of unreason.

Finally, the transitional passage has an overall message, that of perplexity. This is just the sort of dilemma-laden language that Panurge elevates to a high art in Rabelais's *Tiers Livre* and that is found both in the *Roman de la Rose* and in Marot's version. First, the Lover speaks in Jean's text:

> Promesse sanz don ne vaut gueres.
> Avoir me let tant de contreres
> que nus n'en peut savoir le nonbre. (lines 4067–69)

> [A promise without a gift is worth little, and possession leaves me with so many contraries that no one can know their number.]

Here is Marot's adaptation:

> Promesse sans don ne vault gueres
> *Quant el me laisse sans manieres*
> Tant et tant avoir de contraires,
> *Tres mauvais et non débonnaires*
> Qu'aulcun n'en peult scavoir le nombre.
>
> (lines 4103–07, emphasis added)

157

[A promise without the giving is worth little, when it leaves me without favors experiencing so many contraries, very unpleasant and disagreable ones, that no one can know their number.]

Marot amplifies the Lover's perplexity by adding two lines whose sole purpose is to enlarge the expression of despair arising from conflicting desires. Here we may agree with Maxwell Luria, who claims that fifteenth-century readers regarded the *Roman de la Rose* as a poem denouncing folly through satire of its love-sick protagonist.[23] Is love, then, disparaged in favor of the evangelical conception of marriage as a partnership, thus marking a cultural shift from love to marriage previously absent from medieval representations of male/female relations? The Lady Reason discourse, to which we now turn, betrays an even more pronounced philosophical objection to love, with, however, a defense of language that is highly pertinent to evangelical poetics.[24]

Marot's first poems reflect the still cherished idyll of a *locus amoenus,* in particular the "Temple de Cupido" poem quoted above, in which virtues and vices are personified in a springtime of eternal pleasure. The rhetoric of courtliness in that early poem contrasts sharply with the colloquial idiom of his later *Epistres,* a collection noted for its familiar, anti-rhetorical tone. For Gérard Defaux, this shift marks a transition to the "simplicité," "sincérité," and "dépouillement" [stripping away] that define Marot's poetics as evangelical.[25]

The view of Marot's mature verse as evangelical, indeed logocentric, hinges on the presence of the Word in *la lettre,* a view that confirms language as a bearer of meaning rather than of proliferation and deferral.[26] The centrality of the "literalist temper" is also established by Glyn Norton, for whom translation is a force of "naturalization" ideologically allied with an anti-rhetorical linguistic norm that mirrors the confidence expressed elsewhere in the literal reading.[27] In the theologico-courtly context of Jean de Meung's "Discourse of Lady

Reason," language is described as functioning in one of two antagonistic ways: as God-given, hence reasonable, because shared by conventional language users; or as courtly, hence artificial and rhetorically convoluted. In the "Discourse of Lady Reason," Marot found a comic dramatization of Reason's defense of common speech, understood by her as "naturalness." Her discourse is a mixture of mythography and vulgarity that draws on Ovid, and, equally, on the gross humor of the *fabliaux* with its disembodied organs circulating as signs of arbitrary linguistic reference.[28]

Readers of the *Roman de la Rose* recall that Lady Reason uses the myth of Saturn to raise issues of linguistic decorum, specifically the propriety of using vulgar words to call things by their colloquial names. Lady Reason shocks the Lover by calling the testicles that Saturn lost at the time of his castration by the vulgar name *coilles* [balls], whereas the Lover demands that euphemism be employed to gloss the dirty word. Her indiscretion, comically denounced by the Lover, opens up a debate on poetic license, myth, and, ultimately, *plein texte,* Reason's term for the speech that grounds them. Critics of the *Roman de la Rose* have noted that Reason refers to *gloses, integumanz, espondre,* and *paraboles,* terms routinely applied to medieval mythography and its moralization. Reason's boldest claim, and one that underwrites evangelical poetics as well, is that plain speech is indispensable as an access to poetic truth.

Several aspects of Lady Reason's monologue anticipate Marot's poetic practice. First, Lady Reason's preference for *plein texte* over courtly speech announces the vernacular's movement toward the natural; moreover, the nature of poetic language is theorized using a lexicon that anticipates the silenic hermeneutics of Erasmian writing noted above. But Marot's handling of Lady Reason's monologue is remarkable for another reason, and that is the way in which he reassigns allegorical reading protocols to a devout purpose: the reading of the Scriptures. This evangelical imperative would be honed and perfected in the later translations of the *Psaumes* and in devotional verse; it was formulated at its inception by contact with Jean de Meung's poem. Here is Lady Reason's text:

> Et qui bien entendroit la letre,
> le sen verroit *en l'escripture,*
> qui esclarcist la fable occure. (lines 7132–34, emphasis added)

> [And he who would understand the letter would see in the writing the sense which might clarify the obscure fable.]

Marot subtly amended the lesson to apply to scriptural exegesis, his way of updating the text to express evangelical belief:

> Et qui bien entendroit la lettre
> Le sens voirroit *en l'Escripture*
> Esclarcissant la fable obscure. (lines 7292–94, emphasis added)

> [And he who would understand the letter would see in the Scriptures the sense which clarifies the obscure fable.]

As modern scholars have noted, Marot initially adopted a somewhat *laissez-faire* attitude toward the actual publication of his writings, but was later to involve himself increasingly in their material production. His version of the *Rose* was brought out by Galliot du Pré, his publisher between 1526 and 1533, and Marot's complaints about errors and carelessness during this period are a matter of record.[29] Accordingly, while caution is called for when drawing interpretive conclusions from the material evidence of typesetting, it may be argued that the capitalization of "Escripture" reshapes the text to confirm its relevance to biblical interpretation, whereas for Jean de Meung, *l'escripture* applied to the accepted body of authors, ranging from the pagan poets to Church Fathers and Holy Scripture. Of particular note is the insistence of both poets on *la lettre* which stands for the literal reading of a text, the first step in the sequence leading to tropological and anagogical senses. In Jean de Meung, *la letre* also bears the connotation of simplicity of speech. Just as Lady Reason stresses the literal meaning as integral to a full understanding of poetic truth, she also advocates *plein texte* as a language stripped of its artificiality, unlike courtly diction, which prohibits vulgar words. According to Lady Reason, to embrace ordinary language is an act of piety insofar as God would create neither words nor things that were evil. Moreover, Reason's claim is anchored in the belief that ordinary language is fully adequate to describe the world, its naturalness serving as the guarantee of its truthfulness. When speech is understood first in its literal sense ("tout proprement, sanz glose metre"; line 7153 [strictly according to the letter, without gloss]), it then can provide access to deeper meaning—to *sen*. Indeed, poetic truth can be known only through the path of the literal.

The relevance of Lady Reason's meditation on language cannot be overestimated as a foundation for what Michel Jeanneret calls "l'absence de toute recherche ornementale" in Marot and his successors.[30] Moreover, when Rabelais later invited the discovery of a *sustantificque moelle* beneath the surface of his epic *Gargantua,* he also celebrated the materiality of the Word in its literal presence. As a translator, Marot understood that modernizing the language implied a "naturalization" of its archaic elements, so that literality would "speak" to an audience of sixteenth-century readers. Evangelical poetics could thus discover itself in the *Roman de la Rose,* a text built upon "ditz naturelz," as Marot had called its texture of erudition culled from the great antique and medieval encyclopedia. Was Marot's reading a self-fulfilling prophecy, one that mirrored his own poetic identity unexpectedly in a text of High Scholasticism? If so, translation as movement between "peer" or "same" languages might hold a curious affinity with the myth of Narcissus upon which the opening scene was itself structured. In Ovid's telling,

Narcissus's gaze into the reflecting pool brought recognition but also produced an Echo that, in terms of translation, would allow difference to be expressed only within the narrow parameters of repetition. From this perspective, internal translation would always run the risk of being only a copy of the original. I think rather that the *vieil roman* and the needs of modernity found surprising *conjointure* in *la letre*, understood by both poets as a paradoxical fusion of low speech and transcendent spiritual values. The devotion of Marot to *la lettre* anticipates Du Bellay's anti-rhetorical stance in the *Deffence et illustration de la langue françoyse* (1549); it also celebrates the simplicity of a vernacular tongue that has both put down roots and "s'elevera en telle hauteur & grosseur, qu'elle se poura egaler aux mesmes Grecz & Romains" [will rise to such a height and fullness that it will be able to equal the Greeks and Romans themselves].[31]

A final series of passages concerns the figure Faus Semblant, the hypocritical friar who, along with his consort, Astinence Contrainte, joins Love's army to help mount the final assault on the Rose. In allegorical terms, the ugly pair is the equivalent of the Lover's double standard through which he institutionalizes hypocrisy by using polite, that is devious, speech. Moreover, in a poem whose vernacular is self-consciously contrasted with classical *auctoritas,* Faus Semblant is a figure of disruption. His very name suggests deceit; yet, as a friar, he is close to institutional norms of preaching, confession, and, most crucially, interpretation of the Scriptures. At one level, this charlatan is a prototype of the Villonesque thief who finds reincarnation in Rabelais's Panurge, the rogue who makes a mockery of speech by equivocating. Notably, Faus Semblant became for sixteenth-century grammarians, among whom Palsgrave, a metaphor for language in its arbitrariness, as for example in the case of words whose genders are variable depending on whether they are used in the singular or the plural.[32] Just as translation is etymologically related to crossing and crossing over, Faus Semblant incarnates the instability of a language that refuses to conform to neat grammatical and scholastic rhetorical categories, exhibiting instead the movement associated with fallen speech in the post-lapsarian world.

Marot's translation shows sensitivity to Faus Semblant on precisely that ground which was most controversial in doctrinal terms, and that is exegesis. In a first passage taken from Jean de Meung's version, Faus Semblant claims a straightforward reading of the Scriptures based on Pauline hermeneutics:

> Or vos ai dit du sen l'escorce,
> qui fet l'entencion repondre;
> *or en veill la moële espondre.* (lines 11828–30, emphasis added)

> [Now that I have told you the rind of the sense, which hides the intent, I want to explain its marrow.]

Compare this with Marot's translation of the inner *moële* by *la nouvelle:*

> Je vous ay dit du sens l'escorce
> Qui fait l'intention musser
> *La nouvelle vous vueil noncer.* (lines 12233–35, emphasis added)

> [Now that I have told you the rind of the sense, which hides the intent, I want to announce the new one to you.]

Marot's modernity, as noted above, comprises a reworking of language to reflect evangelical belief, and this, in turn, requires that scholastic paradigms be rewritten to conform to Reformation theology. Marot deletes the word *moële* and substitutes in its place *la nouvelle,* the good news of the Gospels. This is an indication that Marot understood perfectly the exegetical language of scholasticism and the need to adapt it to evangelical reform. Collateral evidence for the obsolescence of the word *moële* to mean inner truth is found as well in the farcical

163

*sustantificque moelle* of Rabelais's Prologue to *Gargantua,* itself a sign that exegetical language and, hence, ideologies of interpretation were in a state of flux.

Other passages reflect the anti-clerical stance of Marot and may be noted here as illustrations of his stern denunciation of the Orders for their impieties. The marginalia accompanying Faus Semblant's speech in Marot's version, too, are telling in this regard. Amour remarks to Faus Semblant: "Grant desloyaultez apertes / Ne crains tu donc pas Dieu[?]" [you show a great disloyalty, do you not then fear God?] (lines 11904–05), to which Faus Semblant answers: "Non certes" [Certainly not]. His answer is marked off by a *Nota* highlighting it for special attention. Other marginal notes provide a running commentary on the sinfulness of Faus Semblant's dissembling. To a passage stating that Faus Semblant collects his silver and gold with pleasure (lines 11938–39), for example, the marginal note reads: "Le délit des usuriers" [the delight of usurers]; similarly, Faus Semblant's neglect of the poor, "n'ay cure de povre gent" [I care not for poor people] (line 11952) is linked to feigning: "Les dissimulateurs n'ayment que les riches" [Dissemblers like only the rich]. Other notes cite the vices *orgueil, ambition,* and *dissimulation,* and still another ventures to define a hypocrite: "Hipocrite est envieulx du bien d'autruy" (lines 12018–20) [The hypocrite is envious of another's possessions]. Still another, twice repeated, shows impatience with the friar's proclivity for inserting himself where he does not belong: "Faulz Semblant de tout se mesle" (lines 12058–60) [False Seeming interferes in everything].[33] The marginalia contribute actively to shape the text's reception, making visible through moralizing words the deeds that are described but go unnamed in the text. A tension is therefore set up between the text and the marginal notes, in which the text's resistance to simplification is pitted against the notes in their eagerness to pass judgment.

Was Marot responsible for the marginalia with their closural effect? Or were they affixed by an editor cognizant of the poem's daunting length and eager to supply shortcuts of a moralizing type? Regardless of authorship, the notes merit study for what they tell us about contemporary responses to the poem. But one final example of translation may serve to confirm Marot's own reception of Faus Semblant's speech. In Jean de Meung's version, hypocritical friars are lumped together with their Old Testament forebears:

> Seur la chaiere Moÿsi
> (car la glose l'espont isi:
> c'est le Testament Ancien)
> sidrent scribe et pharisien
> (ce sunt les fausses genz maudites
> que la letre apele ypocrites). (lines 11575–80)

> [Upon the chair of Moses (the gloss explains that this is the Old Testament) the scribes and Pharisees have sat. These are the accursed false people that Holy Writ calls hypocrites.]

Marot's version deletes the lines referring to the gloss, the Old Testament, and to Pharisees. Moreover, it adds an interpolation (emphasized below) to gloss the word *ypocrites:*

> Dessus la chaire de Moyse
> Ce sont assis par grant devise
> Les faulces gens et les mauldictes
> Que la lettre nomme ypocrites
> *Qui bien preschoient, mais mal vivoient*
> *Et ainsi les trésors suyvoient.* (lines 11982–87, emphasis added)

> [Upon the chair of Moses are seated through great deception false and accursed people whom Holy Writ calls hypocrites; who preached well, but lived wickedly and in so doing sought after treasure.]

Hope H. Glidden

Numerous examples of satire against the Orders could be added to this list, but these will suffice to demonstrate Marot's explicit critique of ecclesiastical abuses. Why did the Faus Semblant speech elicit such translative activity? It cannot be doubted that, in theological terms, the hypocrisy of friars undermined the veracity of the Word as embodied in God's gift to man. At the level of humanist culture Erasmus, among others, had delivered stinging denunciations of the Orders for their willful cult of ignorance, extending even to their hypocritical repudiation of Christ's own *auctoritas*:

> When they bawl about the vices of the secular clergy, and preach revolt, and incite the ignorant mob to stone them, they never think of rousing the anger of Christ, the Founder of *that* order—for he was a priest, but not a Dominican.[34]

The *Antibarbari* defended learning as an expression of piety, whereas the Orders argued that humane letters would estrange them from God by corrupting their hearts.

But Faus Semblant was subversive for another reason, and that was his doubleness, that faculty of deceit which acknowledged language's propensity to equivocate by means of trope and figure. As custodians of the written word in Scholastic culture, the Orders had presided over literacy, and it was thus particularly dangerous for the stability of meaning to entrust exegesis to fraudulent speakers.[35] Faus Semblant avows his treachery: "Sanz faille traïstres sui gié / Et por larron m'a Diex juigié" (lines 11139–40) [Without fail, I am a traitor, and God has judged me a thief]. Moreover, Faus Semblant traces his genealogy back to the mythical Proteus, the Ovidian exemplar of mutability whose many forms gained him entry to all places, accessible to him because he could make himself invisible:

> car Protheüs, qui se soloit
> muer en tout quan qu'il voloit,

ne sot onc tant barat ne guile
con je faz. (lines 11151–54)

[For Proteus, who was accustomed to change into whatever form he
wished, never knew as much fraud or guile as I practice.]

In a biblical context, this mutability takes on the sinister cast of turning
Pauline imagery inside-out, thus destabilizing the strict paradigm of
literal and figurative readings that authorize the truth of parables: "mes
de religion sanz faille / j'en lés le grain et pregn la paille" (lines
11185–86) [But, without fail, I leave the kernel of religion and take the
husk]. Faus Semblant confuses inside and outside in contempt for the
clear distinction between truth and fable. It is vital to remember,
however, that Faus Semblant is not a character with a past and a
psychology so much as a discursive function whose linguistic role is to
undermine the clear-cut distinctions between truth and falsehood.[36] Faus
Semblant is false but is all the more treacherous in that he sometimes
uses Pauline imagery properly and, thus, escapes consistency one way
or the other. Ultimately, it is the truth interwoven with subterfuge, i.e.,
art, that thwarts the status of language as transparent; moreover, his very
invisibility proclaims the presence (at least potentially) of doubleness in
any linguistic utterance. With Faus Semblant, Jean de Meung betrayed
the unease of a language community freeing itself, however tentatively,
from the solid, exegetical practices that guaranteed stability of meaning
in a clerical culture. By extension, Faus Semblant is also a figure of
secularization, one consequence of which was an attitude of irreverence
toward language as framed by Lady Reason in terms of order and
transparency.

In Marot's translation, artful language is "naturalized," as we have
seen, by a substitution of *la nouvelle* for the dated *moële* of medieval
practice. The Proteus myth was rewritten, moreover, to fuse the antique

167

god with God's word, thus showing that the Scriptures are alive and change over time, the modern time of evangelical humanism. Mythography "translated" into Christian doctrine was practiced by Erasmus and by Guillaume Budé, who had elaborated it in *De transitu* (1535) as the very ground of evangelical doctrine:

> Proteus enim est propriè sermo dei, omnia transformans sese in miracula rerum. Quem sermonem si fide tenere, si studio colere, si amore complecti institerimus: docebit nos ille omnia quae sint, quae fuerint, quae mox ventura trahantur. Sed vinculo triplici vinciendus est hic Proteus arctissimè, fidei, spei, & charitatis Christi.[37]

> [The word of God is truly a Proteus figure which is continually changing itself into all sorts of marvelous things. If we take it as our duty to safeguard this word with faith, to cultivate it with fervor, to embrace it with love, it will teach us about the present, the past and the immediate future. But this same Proteus must be securely kept in check by the tripartite bond of faith, hope and the love of Christ.]

In this brief study, we have observed how the *Roman de la Rose* contributed to the emergence of the French vernacular in significant ways. Plain speech as a humanist and evangelical ideal finds underpinning in the *Discourse of Lady Reason,* as does naturalness as a style in Marot's own later verse. At the same time, the *Rose* thematized the artfulness of language in the person of Faus Semblant, as well as warning that art could be impious in its departure from strict exegetical reading. Marot's translation of the great medieval poem invites further study, not as a dated imitation of *rhétoriqueur* verse, but as a positive sign that "internal" translation offered a paradigm of choices reflecting new spiritual and political realities.

## Notes

1. The most detailed work on the *Rose*'s earlier fortunes is by Pierre-Yves Badel, *Le Roman de la Rose au XIV<sup>e</sup> siècle: Etude de la réception de l'oeuvre* (Geneva: Droz, 1980); however, no comparable study exists for the sixteenth century.

2. F. W. Bourdillon, *The Early Editions of the Romance of the Rose* (London: The Bibliographical Society at the Chiswick Press, 1906). The classic study of manuscripts is E. Langlois, *Les manuscrits du Roman de la Rose: description et classement* (Lille: Tallandier, 1910). See also Maxwell Luria, *A Reader's Guide to the Roman de la Rose* (Hamden, Conn.: Archon Books, 1982), pp. 14–25 and 203–06.

3. Pasquier's attribution emphasizes the two authors' longstanding popularity; see his *Oeuvres*, 1723 ed., vol. 1, col. 690: cited in Nathan Edelman, *Attitudes of Seventeenth-Century France toward the Middle Ages* (New York: King's Crown Press, 1946), p. 388:

> Aussi ont-ils [Guillaume de Lorry, Jean de Mehum] conservé, et leur oeuvre, et leur memoire jusques à huy, au milieu d'une infinité d'autres, qui ont esté ensevelis avec les ans dedans le cercueil des tenebres. Clement Marot les voulut faire parler le langage de nostre temps, afin d'inviter les esprits flouëts à la lecture de ce Roman.

Among other modern scholars for whom the authorship question is of indirect (which is not, of course, to say secondary) importance, see the work of Gérard Defaux, who, while quoting the "Exposition moralle" as evidence for his thesis that Marot is writing against the erotic current of late medieval verse, nevertheless notes that the poem is, in fact, only "attributed" to Marot: Clément Marot, *Oeuvres poétiques complètes*, ed. Gérard Defaux, vol. 1 (Paris: Classiques Garnier [Bordas], 1990), *Introduction,* pp. xxxix–xl. Defaux's working assumption of Marot's authorship reflects the widely held scholarly position on the question. For a summary of the debate, see Silvio Baridon, ed, *Le Roman de la Rose dans la version attribuée à Clément Marot,* 2 vols. (Milan: Istituto Editoriale Cisalpino, 1957), 1:56–80. Ph. A. Becker was the first modern scholar to argue against Marot's authorship; see his "Clément Marot und der Rosenroman," *Germanisch-Romanische Monatsschrift* 4 (1912): 684–87. For a more recent discussion, see Bernard Weinberg, "Guillaume Michel, dit de Tours, the editor of the *Roman de la Rose*," *Bibliothèque d'Humanisme et Renaissance* 11 (1949): 72–85. The text of reference used here is Baridon's edition of the 1529 text. Quotations from the *Roman de la Rose* in Marot's translation refer to this edition, unless otherwise noted.

169

# Hope H. Glidden

4. The phrase is from George Steiner, *After Babel: Aspects of Language and Translation* (London and New York: Oxford University Press, 1975), p. 28.

5. See Pierre Fabri, *Le Grant et vray art de pleine rethorique* (Paris: P. Sergent, 1534), who conceives the authorship of the poem in terms of genealogy and paternity. Speaking of rhetoric, he notes (fol. iiii$^v$):

> la science est tres antique & par chacun siecle maintenue jusques à nostre vulgaire françoys de descendue & de noz peres tres notablement retenue ainsi que voyons par de Lorris & de Meun tres anciens compositeurs du romant de la rose.
>
> [the learning is very old, and maintained by each century, and handed down to our French vernacular, and upheld most remarkably by our ancestors, as we can see thanks to our fathers Lorris and Meung, the very old composers of the *Romance of the Rose*.]

6. See Rosemond Tuve, *Allegorical Imagery. Some Medieval Books and Their Posterity* (Princeton: Princeton University Press, 1966), pp. 219–85.

7. See Marot's "Marot à Monsieur Bouchart, Docteur en Theologie," *Les Epîtres,* ed. Claude-Albert Mayer (London: University of London, The Athlone Press, 1958), pp. 124–27.

8. See Michael A. Screech, *Marot évangélique* (Geneva: Droz, 1967). Screech's study does not draw any connection between the early Marot of *rhétoriqueur* formation and the evangelical poet.

9. See Eugene Vance, "Chaucer, Spenser, and the Ideology of Translation," *Canadian Review of Comparative Literature* 8/2 (Spring 1981): 217–38. Glyn Norton's *The Ideology and Language of Translation in Renaissance France and Their Humanist Antecedents* (Geneva: Droz, 1984) also foregrounds ideology as inseparable from theories of translation.

10. The "classic" status of the poem is attested by numerous contemporary references. See, for example, Thomas Sébillet, *Art poétique françois* (1548), ed. Félix Gaiffe and Francis Goyet (Paris: Nizet, 1988), p. 26: "Si le voeil-je bien aviser que l'invention, et le jugement compris sous [l'art de Rhétorique] se conferment et enrichissent par la

lecture des bons et classiques pöetes françois comme sont entre les vieux Alain Chartier et Jan de Meun" [I wish to advise that the invention and the judgment contained within the art of rhetoric are confirmed and enriched by the reading of good and foundational French poets among whom our old forebears Alain Chartier and Jean de Meung].

11. On the *Rose* manuscript tradition, see Sylvia Huot, *The Romance of the Rose and its Medieval Readers: Interpretation, Reception, Manuscript Transmission* (Cambridge: Cambridge University Press, 1993).

12. Passages having doctrinal resonance must be distinguished from editorial corrections, or substitutions intended simply to update an older word with a current one, for example *mye* for the out-of-date *drue*. In addition to the passages discussed here, there are many more examples of evangelical emphasis in the 1529 edition, e.g., lines 1829–30 (on love); lines 12515–17 (interpolated into Faux Semblant's speech to mock the religious orders); and in Faux Semblant's speech, lines 12710 and 12739, both in connection with Malle Bouche.

13. Italicizing is intended to facilitate the comparison of Marot's text where it diverges from its predecessor in terms of omissions, substitutions, and phraseology. French quotations from the medieval *Roman de la Rose* are from the following edition: *Le Roman de la Rose,* ed. Félix Lecoy, 3 vols. (Paris: Champion, 1965–70). English translations derive from *The Romance of the Rose,* trans. Charles Dahlberg (Princeton: Princeton University Press, 1971), and are modified where appropriate. Line numbers are incorporated into the text of the essay.

14. "Le Temple de Cupido," lines 517–18, in *Oeuvres lyriques,* ed. Claude-Albert Mayer (London: The Athlone Press, 1964), p. 112.

15. This characterization is found in the gloss of the Collins manuscript dating from the first years of the sixteenth century. See Maxwell Luria, "A Sixteenth-Century Gloss on the *Roman de la Rose,*" *Mediaeval Studies* 44 (1982): 341.

16. See Norton, *Ideology and Language*, pp. 26–31, for discussion of translation as an interpretive process.

17. Erwin Panofsky, *Gothic Architecture and Scholasticism* (New York: Meridian Books, 1957), p. 10.

18. Gérard Paré, *Les Idées et les lettres au XIII<sup>e</sup> siècle. Le Roman de la Rose* (Montréal: Centre de Psychologie et de Pédagogie, 1947), pp. 35–36.

19. For discussion of this aspect of Marot's poetic evolution, see Claude-Albert Mayer, *Clément Marot* (Paris: Nizet, 1972), p. 148 and following.

20. Lucien Febvre, *Le Problème de l'incroyance au XVI<sup>e</sup> siècle. La religion de Rabelais* (Paris: Albin Michel, 1968), pp. 353–90.

21. Dahlberg, *Romance of the Rose.* p. 91.

22. François Rabelais, Prologue to the *Quart Libre* (1552).

23. Luria, "A Sixteenth-Century Gloss," p. 340.

24. The relation between courtly love and evangelical *agapé* is too complex to be generalized about here. See my "Rabelais, Panurge, and the Anti-Courtly Body," *Etudes Rabelaisiennes* 25 (Geneva: Droz, 1991): 35–60, for a satirical view of courtly love from Rabelais's standpoint.

25. See Gérard Defaux, "Rhétorique, silence et liberté dans l'oeuvre de Marot," *Bibliothèque d'Humanisme et Renaissance* 46/2 (1984): 312.

26. See Gérard Defaux, *Marot, Rabelais, Montaigne: L'Ecriture comme présence* (Paris-Geneva: Champion-Slatkine, 1987). Essentially, Defaux argues for the priority of the literal, i.e., its logical anteriority: "les richesses inestimables dont ce sens, ce sens voulu par l'Esprit, est porteur, ne sont accessibles qu'à ceux qui ont d'abord su se rendre maîtres du sens littéral" [the priceless riches of which this meaning, this meaning intended by the Spirit, is the vehicle, are only accessible to those who have first known how to master the literal meaning], p. 141.

27. Norton, *Ideology and Language,* pp. 113–38 and 302–22.

172

28. See R. Howard Bloch, *The Scandal of the Fabliaux* (Chicago: University of Chicago Press, 1986).

29. See Nina Catach, *L'Orthographe française à l'époque de la Renaissance* (Geneva: Droz, 1968), pp. 145–46.

30. Michel Jeanneret, *Poésie et tradition biblique au XVIe siècle. Recherches stylistiques sur les paraphrases des psaumes de Marot à Malherbe* (Paris: Corti, 1969), p. 169.

31. Joachim Du Bellay, *La Deffence et illustration de la langue françoyse*, ed. Henri Chamard (Paris: Didier, 1948), p. 28.

32. See John Palsgrave, *L'esclarissement de la langue françoise* (London: s.l., 1530), Book Three, in which he notes words that promote confusion, among them, words of "uncertayne and doutfull gendre . . . some tyme of the masculine gendre and some tyme of the feminyne." The word "Evangille" is cited as one of six such words and glossed as follows: "Evangille. le Romant de la Rose, parlant de faulx semblant, sur mame je vous dis sans guille se festoit, le saint evangile. Idem, tant surmonte ceste evangille, in the plurell nombre [all authors use] evangille in the femynin gendre" (fol. iiiiᵛ) [Scripture. The Romance of the Rose, speaking of False Seeming, upon my word I tell you truly he used to play different gender roles. Moreover, this word Scripture so much overrides grammatical categories, that in the plural all authors use Scripture in the feminine gender].

33. The marginalia do not, of course, have line numbers. They may be located with reference to the lines opposite which they are found, as noted.

34. *Antibarbari,* trans. Margaret Mann Phillips, in *The Collected Works of Erasmus,* vol. 23 (Toronto: University of Toronto Press, 1978), p. 49.

35. See Paul Zumthor, "Y a-t-il une 'littérature' médiévale?," *Poétique* 17 (1986): 134: "C'est autour de l'idée et, en français, du terme de clergie, issus des milieux scolaires du XIIe siècle, que s'opéra la première cristallisation d'éléments qui, beaucoup plus tard, contribueraient à la formation de l'idée de 'littérature'" [It is round about the idea, and, in French, the term "clergie," emanating from the scholarly circles of the twelfth century, that we first find chrystallizing those elements which, much later, were to contribute to forming the idea of 'literature'].

Hope H. Glidden

36. See Paolo Valesio, *Novantiqua: Rhetorics as a Contemporary Theory* (Bloomington: Indiana University Press, 1980), p. 48.

37. Guillaume Budé, *De Transitu Hellenismi ad Christianismum,* ed. M. Lebel (Sherbrooke: Editions Paulines, 1973), fol. 261$^v$.

# Ronsard the Poet, Belleau the Translator: The Difficulties of Writing in the Laureate's Shadow

## Marc Bizer

Like other Pléiade poets, Rémy Belleau did not show total devotion to his mother tongue; he too had been seduced by the prestige of composing Latin poetry.[1] Belleau's French translations of the Anacreontic odes were more numerous and better known than his translations of French sonnets into Latin. Yet both types of translations reveal Belleau's reverence for Ronsard's works and his evolving confrontation with Ronsard's authority and prestige.

Published when he was a fledgling poet, Belleau's French translations of Anacreon were not always more faithful to their source than Ronsard's imitations of Anacreon, which were printed as his own poems in the *Bocages* and *Meslanges* of 1554. His decision to call them "translations" may, however, have been a strategy to emulate Ronsard without openly competing with him, a translator's status being subordinate to that of an author.[2] Belleau continued the *agon* with Ronsard throughout his activities as a translator. He first translated three *Amours* sonnets into Latin and placed them at the end of the *Odes d'Anacréon Teïen*. He later wrote a commentary on the second book of Ronsard's *Amours* (1560) which was, to a considerable extent, a prose adaptation of Ronsard's poetry. The commentary was a mixture of translation and competitive imitation that used the same techniques as those used in his translation of the *Amours*. At the same time, the commentary also subtly questioned Ronsard's status as an author when it showed that certain of his poems were translations.

Belleau's last translations, transposing his own poetry into Latin (1573), overturned the subordination of translation to composition.

175

## Ronsard the Poet, Belleau the Translator

Belleau consecrated his status as an author by substituting his own works for Ronsard's and Anacreon's as source texts and transcended the subservient relationship between Ronsard the poet and Belleau the translator established by earlier translations. Furthermore, since self-translations give the translator true "authority," they freed Belleau to creatively recompose as he translated.

Belleau's use of translation in his earliest work confirms the inferior status of translation with respect to *inventio*.[3] The first edition (Paris: A. Wechel, 1556) of the Anacreontic odes in French does not consist wholly of his translations, as the title indicates: *Les Odes d'Anacréon Teïen, traduites de grec en francois, par Remi Belleau de Nogent au Perche, ensemble quelques petites hymnes de son invention.* Almost after the fact ("ensemble"), and quite timidly, Belleau adds a few works that he dares to present as coming directly from himself. The Anacreontic odes are, thus, a prestigious buffer between his public and the "petites inventions," lending credibility to his first attempts as a poet in his own right. The translator is introduced, and he, in turn, presents the author. This delayed entrance is accomplished under the authority of the recognized poet Ronsard, who, in his preface to the translations, clearly states that Belleau chose the identity of a translator before appearing as an author:

> Mais avant que vouloir te declarer au monde,
> Tu as daigné tanter d'exprimer la faconde
> Des Grecs en nostre langue, & as pour ton patron
> Choisy le doux archet du vieil Anacreon.[4]

> [But before wanting to show yourself to the world,
> You have dared to try to express the eloquence
> Of the Greeks in our language, and you have for your model
> Chosen the sweet bow of old Anacreon.]

176

Belleau's perspective changes in the new preface to Jules Gassot in the third edition of his translation (1573);[5] by that time a proven author, Belleau confirms that the translation was more or less a first test of his abilities under the auspices of the "Autheur" Anacreon: "je fis chois de cest Autheur, qui servit lors d'avant-coureur aux labeurs de ma premiere jeunesse" [I chose this Author, who served then as a precursor to the labors of my early youth]. Whereas in the title the odes, "traduites," contrast with the "hymnes de son invention," Belleau, now ashamed of the former as frivolous and incompatible with his age, no longer seems to differentiate between the translations, termed "une infinité de folles & jeunes inventions," and the "petites inventions." In the new preface, Belleau seems to consider the adaptations as much a part of his own poetry as the "petites inventions": "si i'osois, le [Anacreon] desavoüerois volontiers, pour une infinité de folles & jeunes inventions mal seantes à l'âge où ie suis" (1: 5) [If I dared, I would readily disown him on account of countless foolish and early inventions ill-befitting my present age].

Ronsard prefaced Belleau's book not only in order to introduce a new poet[6] but also to legitimize Belleau's choice of "patron": Anacreon had already had a considerable influence on his own poetry. After Henri Estienne's discovery of the pseudo-Anacreon in 1552, Ronsard himself had translated two Anacreontic odes in the *Livret de folastries* (1553) even before Estienne published his edition with Latin translations in 1554. Ronsard then included in his *Bocages, Meslanges,* and the third edition of his *Odes* (1554–55) thirty-one poems whose Anacreontic origins were clearly visible.[7] The publication of the *Anacreontea* and their introduction in French poetry through Ronsard set off a long vogue of imitations.[8]

Critics have been sensitive to the close relationship between Ronsard's imitations and Belleau's subsequent translations of Anacreon. Alexandre Eckhardt, for example, declares that Belleau's translations depend completely on Ronsard's Anacreontic poetry.[9] Marcel Raymond notes that certain words and rimes from Ronsard appear in Belleau's texts.[10] However, unduly influenced by the fact that the poems are presented as translations, no critics have asked whether there are fundamental differences between Belleau's translations and Ronsard's imitations. Nolhac does at one point describe Ronsard's technique as paraphrase, but without drawing any conclusions for the distinction between imitation and translation.[11] Laumonier, when discussing the different types of imitation found in Ronsard's works, includes translation among them.[12]

It is instructive to compare Belleau's translation entitled "D'Amour picqué d'une mouche à miel" with Ronsard's "Le petit enfant Amour" from the fourth book of the *Odes,* along with their common source, Anacreon (see Appendix A[13]). While in general Ronsard's poem reveals a considerable amplification of the Greek epigram, the opening stanza is characteristic of his approach: using barely a suggestion from Anacreon, who only describes a bee lying among the roses, Ronsard focuses on Cupid and creates a whole scene. In addition, he quickly establishes the delicate atmosphere of a child's world by using diminutives, which frequently appear in the rime position throughout the entire poem (lines 3, 4, 7, 8, 27, 28, 31, 32, 39, 40). The small fragile world is colored by other pathetic accents: in Ronsard's poem, Venus's maternal solicitude for her son is dramatized by the fact that she kisses him and blows on his wound (lines 18–19), a detail that is absent from the Anacreontic ode; furthermore, it is she, and not Cupid, who identifies the winged serpent as an "avette" (line 32). Her tenderness is also tinged with mockery, since she teases Cupid by asking him if he has been wounded by the pinpricks of her Graces (lines 21–24).

There is a particularly consistent mocking tone in a similar poem by the Pseudo-Theocritus (*Idyll* 19; see Appendix A[14]), which has a tight thematic structure based on the playful idea of the stinger being stung.

At the very outset of this poem, foreshadowing Venus's evocation of the pain he inflict on others, Cupid's wound is presented as just punishment for the theft of honey, and the description of the bee as nasty ("kaká mélissa") mocks Cupid's naïveté even before his speech betrays him. Ronsard, while borrowing the detail of the beehive, insists initially, however, on the innocence of the child who happened to be picking flowers near a hive. Similarly, to Theocritus is owed the detail of the swollen hand, although in Theocritus's more cruel poem Cupid has to blow on his own hand instead of having his mother do it, as in Ronsard's ode. Finally, Venus laughs ("gelásasa") at her son who alleges he is dying. This could have prompted the invention of Aphrodite's line about her Graces (lines 23–24) by Ronsard, who otherwise does not adopt Theocritus' irony.

Ronsard's ode thus appears to be a skillful conflation of two Greek poems. The presence of the hive, along with the mention of the flowers that Cupid picks, seems to come from a creative mixture of the beginnings of Theocritus's and Anacreon's poems respectively. Even when Ronsard introduces new details, such as the "montaigne d'Hymette" (line 31), they add at least as much bucolic charm as erudition and, thus, remain faithful to the genre of its sources.[15] Ronsard also adopts the epigrammatic structure of Anacreon's and Theocritus's poems, while enlarging on certain episodes. In spite of the length of his poem, which cannot help but diffuse the concision of its models, Ronsard seems to compensate by intensifying the ending: he describes Cupid's arrows as lethal ("tes homicides sagettes"). More generally, applying Theocritus to Anacreon, he brings out pastoral details implicit in the Greek, completes the depiction of maternal affection tinged with irony, and adds a stroke of his own erudition.

While Belleau's adaptation of Anacreon's text, insofar as it follows the original more closely, offers less amplification than Ronsard's, this does not prevent him from shaping the poem with elements of his own "invention."[16] Like Ronsard, Belleau adds many details in his opening stanza. Fascinated by the rose, which now has folds, Belleau also creates a delicate scene by calling Cupid "le mignon" [darling] and insisting on his tender innocence with "sa blanche main" [his white hand]. Belleau's language is rich in idiomatic French that contrasts with Ronsard's very frequent use of less natural diminutives: if, indeed, Belleau closely follows Ronsard's text, then Cupid's "main tendrette" (line 8) in Ronsard's poem becomes "sa blanche main" (line 6) in Belleau's. Faithful to Cupid's repeated cry of anguish in Greek, Belleau uses the expression "C'est fait de moy, / C'en est fait" (lines 9–10) [It is over for me], which is more familiar and less poetically stereotyped than Ronsard's "je suis perdu" (line 10) [I am done for]. More important, whereas Ronsard dilates his sources to the point of disturbing their elegant harmony and concision, Belleau makes a significant change that creatively reinforces this unity. Given the conceit in which the stinger is stung, Belleau prepares this ending by having Cupid evoke his wound with the language of love poetry and, thus, making him feel the very wound that he so often inflicts on others. Cupid speaks of himself as "Navré jusques au cœur" (line 11) [Wounded all the way to the heart], which, given that he was stung in his finger, can only remind us of the wounds his arrows make; two lines later he repeats that he is "navré." Finally, the association with love's wounds becomes irrefutable in line 22, where Venus describes Cupid's victims as "navrez."

Belleau's poem is, thus, quite different from Ronsard's, borrowing little from it apart from the idea of the swollen hand, not even the rhymes.[17] In fact, two different imitative techniques distinguish their respective treatment of sources. "D'Amour picqué d'une mouche à miel" can be said to be an example of faithful one-source imitation, for, while remaining close to its model, it competes with it by incorporating a few modifications that represent genuine innovations. Ronsard takes greater liberties with his "Le petit enfant Amour," embroidering at will, but then he is following two sources; his poem represents another form of humanist imitation, artfully combining two or more models to produce a new text. Since other sixteenth-century poets did not hesitate to present as their own works poems that translated their sources with much greater fidelity than Belleau's,[18] there is no reason why he could not have chosen to publish "D'Amour picqué d'une mouche à miel" as an epigram of his own invention. He probably would have done so if Ronsard had not preceded him in the imitation of Anacreon or if his adaptations of Anacreon, presented as his own poetry, had not run the risk of comparison with those of the head of the *brigade.*

It was not always necessary to choose between translation and imitation: there are instances in the works of both poets where a source text is adapted more than once, as a translation and as invention. For example, even before Estienne's edition had been published, Ronsard used the theme of the Anacreontic ode "L'Arondelle," that of love hatching little loves in his breast, in the last two tercets of his sonnet "Ces liens d'or, ceste bouche vermeille" (4: 10–11).[19] Ronsard next published what was basically a translation of the Anacreontic source in the second edition of his *Meslanges* (1555), a year before Belleau.[20] The more usual order, however, is to move from a translation to invention: Belleau first translated two similar Anacreontic odes as "Le Pourtrait de sa maistresse" and "Le Pourtrait de Bathylle," then, borrowing from both, composed "Le Pourtrait de sa Maistresse" (1565) for the *Première Journée de la bergerie.* These different adaptations were preceded by Ronsard's work on the same sources; Ronsard, however, begins by publishing not a translation but rather his own "Elegie a Janet" (1554).[21]

While the two French texts deriving from the same source show that Belleau's translation and his *Bergerie* poem handle Anacreon differently, both are influenced by Ronsard's elegy. Raymond has already pointed out the borrowings in certain lines of Belleau's translation, the "Pourtrait de Bathylle," from Ronsard's "Elegie a Janet."[22] However, in the

## Ronsard the Poet, Belleau the Translator

*Bergerie,* Ronsard's poem serves as a source not only of text but also of imitative technique; in a sense, Belleau imitates both Ronsard's text and Ronsard's imitation in "Le Pourtrait de sa maistresse," since he uses Anacreon as a point of departure for a more complete and sensual description of the charms of the female body and adds many new developments, much as we have seen in Ronsard's "Le petit Enfant Amour." Belleau evokes the same parts of the lady's body as Ronsard, proceeding traditionally, like him, from head to foot. Although the reflections to which they give rise are most often different (as in the case of Belleau's Petrarchan description of the eyes and his sensual lingering on the lady's breast), on occasion he still borrows from Ronsard. The description of the cheek in terms of roses, milk, and carnations, absent from the Greek original, is obviously indebted to Ronsard without being overly faithful; the use of a question "Sçais-tu, Peintre, qu'il te faut faire?" [Do you know, Painter, what you must do?] to give an instruction to the painter adds liveliness and variety by breaking the monotony of the imperatives that usually perform this function:

*Ronsard*
Apres au vif pein moi sa belle joüe
Du mesme taint d'une rose qui noüe
De sur du *laict,* ou du taint blanchissant
Du *lis* qui baise un *œillet* rougissant. (lines 81–84)

[After that, paint from life for me her lovely cheek
Of the same tint as a rose that swims
On milk, or of the paling tint
Of the lily that kisses a blushing carnation.]

*Belleau*
Sçais-tu, Peintre, qu'il te faut faire?
Il te faut mettre avec les *lis*
Des *oeillets* fraischement cueillis,

Et meslier le tout ensemble:
Ou bien comme la rose tremble
Nageant dessus le *lait* caillé. . . .(vol. 2, p. 115, lines 84–89)

[Do you know, Painter, what you must do?
You must put with the lilies
Freshly picked carnations
And blend them all together
Or just as the rose trembles
Swimming on clotted milk. . . .]

In another instance, Ronsard, carried away by the charms of the lady, seems unable to describe the lady's bosom, since he chastely claims he has never seen it. Belleau reproduces this language when about to evoke the lady's mouth:

*Ronsard*
 Je ne sçay plus, mon Janet, où j'en suis,
Je suis confus, & muet je ne puis,
Come j'ay fait, te declarer le reste
De ses beautés, qui ne m'est manifeste. . . . (lines 123–26)

[I no longer know, dear Janet, where I am,
I am confused, and mute, I cannot,
As I have done, declare to you the rest
Of her beauties, which are not visible to me. . . .]

*Belleau*
Mon dieu, mon Dieu, ie ne sçay plus
Où j'en suis, & quant au surplus,
Je voy, Peintre, qu'il me faut taire. . . .(vol. 2, p. 115, lines 93–95)

[My God, my God, I no longer know
Where I am, and as for the rest,
I see, Painter, that I must be silent. . . .]

183

However, instead of using Ronsard's expression "le reste," Belleau prefers to borrow from his two translations of the Anacreontic portraits, where one finds "au surplus" in "Pourtrait de sa maistresse" and "quant au surplus" in "Pourtrait de Bathylle." "Au surplus" is not Belleau's only reminiscence from these translations, for the portrait of his mistress in the *Bergerie* is literally framed with complete citations from the *Odes d'Anacreon*. The first stanzas are identical, and the endings inspired by the Pygmalion myth are nearly the same, except that Belleau makes his more dramatic with the repetition of "oste," suggesting painful rapture, and the apostrophe "Hà, mon Dieu":

> *Ode d'Anacreon*
> Il suffit, je la voy, c'est elle:
> Et possible est que la cruelle,
> Par la peinture que ie voy,
> Parlera doucement à moy. (vol. 1, p. 33, lines 43–46)

> [Enough, I see her, it is she:
> And it is possible that the cruel lady,
> Through the painting that I see,
> Will speak sweetly to me.]

> *Bergerie*
> Il suffit, Peintre, oste la main,
> Oste, ie la voy tout à plein.
> Hà, mon Dieu, ie la voy, c'est elle
> Et possible est que la cruelle
> Par la peinture que ie voy
> Parlera doucement à moy. (vol. 2, p. 117–18, lines 181–86)

> [Enough, Painter, remove your hand,
> Remove it, I see her completely.
> Oh, my God, I see her, it is she
> And it is possible that the cruel lady

Through the painting that I see
Will speak sweetly to me.]

The poem "Le Pourtrait de sa maistresse," itself an adaptation of Anacreon, is composed of earlier adaptations of Anacreon by Belleau, all of which are indebted to Ronsard's own versions. Belleau's reuse of parts of his translation in a poem employing a different imitative technique is significant. It shows his willingness to rework earlier texts and to compose essentially new poems from fragments of old ones. This foreshadows the work that will characterize the translations of his own poetry into Latin. At the same time, he has dared to present as his own invention a poem quite similar to one of Ronsard's, imitating and yet competing with him through modifications that reveal his own poetics.

In Belleau's poetry, competition with Ronsard on the same linguistic territory is a rare occurrence. The 1556 volume of the *Odes d'Anacreon* reserves a surprise, however, in that its last pages contain translations of three sonnets by Ronsard where, before the 1565 *Bergerie* collection and after the translations of Anacreon, Belleau works directly on Ronsard's text without a classical source as common origin. Here Ronsard is both source and model.

These translations are, of course, first and foremost an homage to Ronsard, as Laumonier notes in his presentation of the pieces.[23] More specifically, insofar as Latin was considered an immortal language that conferred eternal life on all that was written in it, Belleau's translations glorify and preserve Ronsard's poetry; in a sense, Belleau erects a monument to Ronsard. At the same time, however, translation provides him with the opportunity to modify and rewrite Ronsard's text, to impose his own choices. In this manner Belleau appropriates Ronsard's text and creates a new one, his own—which is, of course, precisely the goal of *imitatio*.

In general, Belleau's translations of "Amour, quiconque ait dit que le ciel fut ton pere" (Ronsard, 5: 45; see Appendix B), "Que laschement vous me trompez, mes yeulx" (Ronsard 5: 122; see Appendix C), and "Voiant les yeus de toi, Maitresse elüe" (Ronsard 5: 120) adopt as translation units the division of the sonnets into quatrains and tercets. While remaining relatively faithful to Ronsard's text, Belleau does not hesitate to retouch it here and there, however, adding words and even rearranging the order of lines so as to emphasize certain elements. Always sensitive to the general effect of a poem and perhaps with the structure of the epigram in mind, Belleau concentrates much of his reworking on unifying poems and rewriting their ends. Since Belleau's translations into Latin, a language known for its concision, are always longer than the French original, they also point to the use of amplification.

The Latin translation of "Amour, quiconque ait dit que le ciel fut ton pere" displays most of these characteristics. Tiny retouches abound and reinforce the already vivid images: Belleau adds that the lady was born wild: "te jetta / Tout à l'entour du coeur sa rage la plus fiere" (lines 7–8) [injected around your heart her fierce rage] is rendered by "rabiemque iam feroci / Immisit stomacho ferociorem" (lines 10–11) [and to your already fierce temper she added even fiercer rage]. Elsewhere, the complaint that nothing pleases Cupid more than "Pestes & totidem graves vibrare" (line 16) [to brandish as many serious afflictions] amplifies "Que tirer tout d'un coup mile mors de ta trousse" (line 11) [but drawing suddenly a thousand deaths from your quiver] by replacing "mile mors" with the more vivid "pestes" and insisting that these afflictions are as numerous as the cares with which Cupid lacerates our hearts. More importantly, though, Belleau introduces the powerful verb *vibrare* ("to brandish"), which evokes the rapid darting of snakes; it occurs in descriptions of violent battle scenes in the second half of the *Aeneid*, but Secundus also uses *vibrare* in his love poetry to evoke the dangers of a lady's eyes ("Basium 19," line 20).

One could suppose that translating a French poem that imitates Latin poetry back into Latin would result in a restoration of the borrowed Latin verses, especially since Belleau is clearly aware of these borrowings from Virgil and Catullus; he identifies them in his commentary on the second book of Ronsard's *Amours*.[24] Nevertheless, Belleau succeeds in varying on Virgil and Catullus mostly without reproducing them in his text, a more difficult task for him than for Ronsard. Whereas Catullus's "spinosas Erycina serens in pectore curas" [Venus sowing thorny cares in your breast] (*Carmina,* 64, line 72) does appear as the two words "Spinosis . . . curis" [with thorny cares], Belleau cleverly retouches and reinforces the Latin model with one word by insisting that the prickly cares are tenacious: "Spinosis tenacibusque curis . . ." (line 15) [with thorny and tenacious cares].

Belleau's greatest changes occur in his treatment of the second tercet of Ronsard's sonnet, which is expanded into the last six lines of his Latin translation. After keeping Ronsard's enumeration of the terrible woes that the unnatural lady inflicts on her lover, itself borrowed from numerous classical sources, Belleau gives the evocation even greater impact with a short, ironic summary: "Hae sunt delitiae tuae iocique" (line 17) [These are your delights and pastimes]. Instead of affirming rather flatly and prematurely, as Ronsard does, that the lady is not of celestial origin, Belleau prepares a more gentle transition by asking a rhetorical question: "Et tu natus es è sinu deorum / Coelesti, usqueadeo genus scelestum?" (lines 18–19) [And you were born from the womb of the heavenly gods, does the criminal race know no limits?]. Finally, Belleau retains from Ronsard's conceit the idea of opposing Venus's gentleness to the harshness of the lady whom she is supposed to have engendered. This contrast is reinforced in the French by Ronsard's use of words having the same radical in the last line, "douce" repeating "douceur." Belleau, however, chooses to make the idea more tangible by introducing a new image, that of honey, which he, in turn, artfully presents by means of the same device: "Si tam *melliflua* è parente natus, / Paulùm debueras habere *mellis*" (lines 21–22) [If you were born

187

from such a honey-dropping parent, you should have had a little honey].

The translation of "Que laschement vous me trompez, mes yeulx," in which the poet compares himself to Narcissus, languishing from an impossible love (see Appendix C), shows a similar preoccupation with Ronsard's use of his models. As with "Hae sunt delitiae tuae iocique," Belleau gives more structure to the poem by adding an intermediate conclusion, "O Dij quod genus istud est furoris!" (line 11) [O gods, what folly this is!], a subjective commentary by which the poet summarizes his own situation. However, some of Belleau's changes can, in fact, be likened to objective commentary on the poem's source. Laumonier remarks that the sonnet is a development of the tenth line of the preceding poem (124), where the poet exclaims "Un vray Narcisse en misere je suis";[25] Belleau seems aware of this connection, for he inserts the epithet "miser" when he translates "Faut il que . . . / Je brusle apres une image incertaine, / Qui pour ma mort m'accompaigne en toutz lieux?" (lines 5–8) as "Tabescamne ideo miser! sequacem / Imprudens iuvenis sequutus vmbram?" (lines 9–10). In addition, Belleau's translation sometimes reacts to the fact that Ronsard's first book of the *Amours* places great demands on the classical knowledge of the reader. Muret, in his commentary (1553) on this very poem, feels the need to explain that "l'amoureux Cephiside" designates Narcissus: "*L'amoureux Cephiside*] Narcisse, fils de Cephise, fleuve de Bœotie."[26] Belleau removes the erudite allusion, replacing "Cephiside" (line 12) with "Narcissus" (line 17).

The main theme of Ronsard's poem is the metamorphosis of Narcissus into a flower, evoked explicitly in the second tercet, for which Ovid's *Metamorphoses* was a source. Narcissus's transformation is described by the verb *amenuiser*, suggesting that he gradually pines, fades away, like wax that shrinks when exposed to heat:

> Et quoy, faut il que le vain de ma face,
>> De membre à membre *amenuiser* me face,
>> Comme une cire aux raiz de la chaleur? (lines 9–11)

## Marc Bizer

[Must my hollow countenance
  Make me shrink from limb to limb
  Like wax in the rays of the heat?]

Belleau is more accurate in his simile: instead of using the Latin equivalent of *amenuiser* to describe both Narcissus and the wax, he
differentiates between Narcissus, who fades away, and the wax, which
liquifies. However, the changes that Belleau makes in his translation can
perhaps best be appreciated by comparing them to Ronsard's source,
*Metamorphoses* (3: 487–90). Lines 13 and 14 of Belleau's poem contain
no fewer than four reminiscences of Ovid:

*Ovid*
Ut in tabescere *flavae*
igne levi *cerae* matutinaeque pruinae
sole tepente solent, sic *attenuatus* amore
*liquitur* et tecto paulatim carpitur igni.

[Just as yellow wax in a small flame and morning frost in the warm sun
melt, so weakened by love he becomes liquid and is gradually diminished
by a hidden fire.]

*Belleau*
Amans ut peream, simulque perdam
Quem mendax vacuis imago flammis
Membratim *extenuet*? propinquiore
*Flava liquitur* ut vapore *cera*!

[Loving in a way fatal to myself, but also deadly to the one whom the
deceitful likeness weakens limb by limb with empty flames? As yellow
wax is liquified by a fire too close!]

Ovid's simile shows strong evidence of *copia* and *variatio*. To the image
of the melting wax is added that of the morning frost, and Ovid empha-

sizes the idea of gentle but persistent heat by evoking it twice, a small flame in the first case and a warm sun in the second. After considerable delay, when Ovid finally introduces Narcissus in order to complete the simile, Narcissus is described as both weakened (*attenuatus*) and liquified (*liquitur*). His wasting away is then even further underlined by the verb *carpitur* [he is consumed], which is explained metaphorically by yet a third form of heat, *tecto igni*, Narcissus's hidden amorous fire. While not attempting such a stylistic tour de force, Belleau does retain the image by comparing Narcissus to melting wax and by using the same verb *liquitur* in that context. In addition, Belleau has taken care to create a system of associations within his poem so that the comparison of Narcissus to melting wax is made even more clear. Earlier, following Ronsard's "Je brusle apres une image incertaine" (line 7), Belleau had first underlined the Narcissus myth "Amavi, *proprio* perustus igne" (line 8) [I loved, consumed by a fire for *myself*], and then added his reference to the tenth line of the preceding poem: "Tabescamne ideo miser!" The Latin *tabesco*, while indeed meaning "to waste away," also frequently signifies "to melt," and it has a long association with wax in Latin poetry.[27] Then, immediately after "Flava liquitur ut vapore cera!" (line 15), the theme of fluidity becomes dominant as Narcissus weeps over the flowing waters, gradually merging with them. The emphasis is extreme here, since "liquitur" from the preceding verse is repeated by the related word "liquidam," which itself redundantly modifies "undam": "Sic flebat liquidam imminens in undam / Narcissus" [Thus wept Narcissus bent over the flowing waters]. The alliteration of the liquid "l" draws further attention to the theme of fluidity.

Belleau's reworking of Ronsard's poem amounts to a correction of the latter's imitation of Ovid. The changes Belleau incorporates in his Latin text seem to imply that Ronsard has strayed too far from his source precisely in those parts which should have been preserved, producing a poem that is too dispersed. Belleau not only reestablishes the original image of fluidity but also reinforces it by giving it a new textual framework. At the same time, Belleau's corrections show a distinct reverence for certain finds of the master, basically by modifying Ronsard's text through addition, while leaving the French original intact: "extenuet," already cited, is a good example of this technique, as is "membratim" (line 14), which literally translates Ronsard's "membre à membre" (line 10). Thus, responding to Ovid's text through Ronsard's by his own alliterative, semantic, and thematic means and, in particular, by insisting on the theme of liquefaction, Belleau has given Ronsard's sonnet greater unity. Finally, Belleau has shown considerably more sensitivity to figures of metamorphosis, which will later become prominent in one of his self-translations into Latin.

Four years later, Belleau again paid homage to Ronsard with his *Le Second Livre des Amours de P. de Ronsard, commenté par Remy Belleau de Nogent au Perche* (1560). Like the translations into Latin, this commentary was a way of consecrating Ronsard as poet laureate. Belleau was not the first to do this, nor was Ronsard the first French poet to be so honored;[28] seven years earlier, in the preface to his commentary on the first book of Ronsard's *Amours,* Muret had emphasized the novelty and, thus, the great honor of having one's works commented on if one were a vernacular author and still alive: "Ie pense qu'il ne m'est ja besoin de respondre à ceux, qui pourroient trouver estrange que ie me suis mis à commenter un livre François, & composé par un homme qui est encore en vie" [I think that there is no need for me to respond to those who might find it strange that I undertook to comment on a French book, and composed by a man who is still alive].

The role of commentator, while seemingly subordinate to that of the author commented upon, was nevertheless endowed with considerable prestige. The first book of Ronsard's *Amours* was such a success that it was reprinted along with Muret's commentary one year after it first appeared, and both Muret and Ronsard received royalties, contrary to the custom of the period.[29] Muret's portrait is printed in this edition, along with Ronsard's and Cassandra's. More specifically, as Gisèle Mathieu-Castellani points out, commentators considered themselves to be authors, "auctores" in the etymological sense, in that they were augmenting the original text with the light they were shedding on it.[30] Belleau's commentary on the second book of the *Amours* thus brought his status closer to Ronsard's.

The primary feature of Belleau's commentary is the paraphrase of significant portions of Ronsard's poetry. Marie-Madeleine Fontaine and François Lecercle, editors of the Droz edition of Belleau's commentary, note that this characteristic is troubling to the modern reader because of its very redundancy.[31] However, more than a mere prose copy of Ronsard's *Amours*, the parts of the commentary that paraphrase this poetry constitute a prose translation that actually competes with the author's verse: "la paraphrase permet d'instaurer une sorte de «rivalité stylistique». Elle prend, par moments, l'allure d'une véritable «mise en prose» du poème. Ainsi . . . l'exégète reprend une liste de comparaisons et allonge la liste des exemples" (p. xvii) [the paraphrase enables him to set up a sort of "stylistic rivalry." At certain times, it looks like a veritable "prose transposition" of the poem. Thus . . . the exegete reuses a list of comparisons and adds to the list of examples]. The history of the later editions of Belleau's commentary is significant in this regard, for as Fontaine and Lecercle show, the second (1567) and subsequent editions underwent drastic changes; furthermore, in all likelihood, they were made by Belleau in accordance with Ronsard's wishes.[32] It is precisely these competitive paraphrases, which incorporated elegant new finds, that were to suffer the most from the alterations introduced in 1567 and thereafter:[33]

> On a gommé des pages entières, les plus enthousiastes. . . . Des paraphrases lyriques, qui requièrent le lecteur (21ᵛ), des récits mythiques . . . une foule de petites remarques précieuses, comme le

## Marc Bizer

«coeur diamantin» de Marie (25ᵛ) . . . et surtout sur toutes ces «formes naturelles» dont Jamyn et Ronsard ont loué Belleau d'être «le peintre», enfin la notation même du plaisir, si intense chez Belleau (64ᵛ), sont devenus inconvenants. *Le Voyage de Tours*, véritable morceau de bravoure du commentaire, est le plus atteint: Clore ne tendra plus «ses rets au devant des ailes de Zephyre», les papillons ne prendront plus «leur viande de leur petit Mufle recoquillé», ni «les Avettes des cuisses», etc. (p. xxviii)

[Entire pages, the most enthusiastic ones, were erased. . . . Lyrical paraphrases, which address the reader, mythic tales, myriad precious little remarks like the "diamantine heart" of Marie, and especially about all those "natural forms," of which Jamyn and Ronsard had praised Belleau as "the painter," lastly, the noting of pleasure, so intense in Belleau's commentary, have become improper. The *Journey to Tours*, true tour de force of the commentary, is the most affected: Clore will no longer stretch her nets before Zephyr's wings, the butterflies will no longer take "their food with their little turned-up noses," nor "the bees with their thighs," etc.]

These expressions, not to be found in Ronsard's or any other poet's work, reflect Belleau's unique sensibility; in fact, Belleau's additions constitute attempts to define his own poetics with respect to Ronsard's. In paraphrasing Ronsard and transposing his poetry into prose, Belleau succeeds in creating a poetical prose that reflects this esthetic. This is not wholly without example in classical theory,[34] whose trace remains in Robert Estienne's French-Latin dictionary (1549): quoting Plautus, Estienne translates *contrefaire* [to imitate] by the Latin *commentari*, meaning "to think over, invent, compose."[35] *Commentari*, through its vernacular cognate *commenter,* also came to mean "write a commentary." Belleau's commentary on Ronsard, far from identifying itself with Ronsard's text, implements all of these meanings in order to affirm its author's own identity.

Not surprisingly, the fact that Belleau's commentary tends to become

193

an autonomous poetic text is in no way implied by its expressed *raison d'être*. Unlike Muret, who sought in his commentary to make the erudition of Ronsard's first book accessible to his readers, Belleau's purpose, as he states in his preface, is to show the role of imitation in the apparently "vulgaire" simple poetry of the second book. His aim is to counter the false impression that the second book is entirely of the author's invention, being the least derived from the Ancients:

> L'asseurance que j'ay que prendrez plaisir à recognoistre une infinité de belles & antiques imitations en ce qui a esté estimé le plus vulgaire & moins retiré des anciens me fera vous supplier, Monseigneur, de prendre ce petit labeur d'aussi bonne affection, que d'obéissante volonté je le vous presente.

> [The assurance I have that you will take pleasure in recognizing an infinity of beautiful and antique imitations in what has been considered the most common and least derived from the Ancients will bring me to beseech you, My lord, to accept this little work with as much good favor as the humble good will with which I offer it to you.]

One of Belleau's goals in using his own erudition to show the sources of Ronsard's poetry is to praise Ronsard's art of hiding them and to communicate this admiration to others. It is also to give legitimacy to this vernacular poetry by showing its prestigious antique origins, an important part of the duty of any proponent of Ronsard's poetry.[36] At the same time, however, one cannot help but wonder whether in the eyes of Ronsard's readers this commentary might not diminish Ronsard's authority by dismantling his poetry and revealing the source of the laureate's inspiration. Indeed, Belleau's commentary frequently designates Ronsard's poetry as a translation, either implicitly or explicitly:

> Ce sonnet est pris d'une Ode d'Anacreon (18$^v$) [This sonnet is taken from an Anacreontic ode]

194

Il y a presque un tel Sonet dedans Petrarque ($27^v$) [There is almost such a sonnet in Petrarch's work]

Tout est encore de Marulle . . . ($33^v$) [All is again from Marullus . . .]

Properce dit presque chose semblable ($47^v$) [Propertius says almost the same thing]

Tout est pris de Marulle ($80^v$) [All is taken from Marullus]

Ce sonnet est presque une traduction d'une Ode d'Anacreon ($14^v$) [This sonnet is almost a translation of an Anacreontic ode]

C'est une version de Marulle . . . ($38^r$) [It is a version of Marullus . . .]

C'est une traduction du mesme Marulle ($66^v$) [It is a translation of the same Marullus]

C'est la traduction de l'Ode de Saphon ($82^v$) [It is the translation of the Sapphic ode]

Given Belleau's expressed desire to reveal Ronsard's sources where one might think there were none, it is understandable that he marvels at Ronsard's ability to disguise his models: "Cette chanson est prise entierement de Marulle, mais si naïvement rendue en nostre langue, qu'on douteroit lequel des deus en a esté l'inventeur" ($48^v$) [This poem is entirely taken from Marullus, but so naturally rendered in our language, that one would hesitate to say which of the two invented it]. Even here, the expression "rendue en nostre langue," which carries a hint of translation, shows how close imitation and translation were in both theory and practice. Belleau is not unjust, though; he is careful to say when Ronsard's composition seems original: "Ce sonet est de l'invention de nostre auteur" ($23^v$) [This sonnet is of the invention of our author]; and "Tout est de son invention" ($33^r$) [All is of his invention]. He also speaks of Ronsard's imitations, although mainly in the context of the long poem "Le voiage de Tours," where the term "imitation" appears six times.

Admittedly, these citations take up little space in Belleau's considerable commentary and, more important, are more absolute in character than the majority of the remarks on Ronsard's borrowings. They do, however, have a certain impact because they are so numerous and because, as part of the notes on sources, they almost always conclude the passages of commentary. Since another aspect of the severe revision of the second edition was the elimination of the identification of sources, it is quite possible that Belleau's pleasure in revealing Ronsard's sources may have irritated the master who wanted the Italian, Greek, and Latin underpinnings of his new "naïve" poetry to remain hidden.[37]

Belleau's commentary bothered Ronsard both as a semi-autonomous, competing text and as an unveiling of the mechanisms of his art. If, on the one hand, Belleau's commentary represents in part an innovative prose translation of Ronsard's *Second Livre des Amours,* on the other hand it labels some of Ronsard's work as translation and, thus, reduces the distance separating the translator from the poet. These characteristics are in accordance with Belleau's status relative to Ronsard's at the time: Belleau was hardly a recognized poet, having published only a few of his *Petites Inventions* (which were first printed as part of Ronsard's *Bocages* and *Continuation des Amours*); he was known as the translator of the Odes of Anacreon, while Ronsard was the "Anacréon français."

Not long after Belleau's commentary on Ronsard's second book of the *Amours,* the first collection of his own poetry appeared, the *Première Journée de la Bergerie* (1565). The whole was greatly modified and enlarged in 1572, when Belleau added the *Seconde Journée.* One apparently minor change, noted by Eckhardt, reveals an evolution in Belleau's identity as a poet: a *chanson* of the *Première Journée* entitled "Douce, & belle bouchelette" is not presented in the same way in both editions.[38] In the 1565 edition, the prince-shepherd about to sing the song apologizes for the fact that it fits poorly into the collection as a whole since it is a translation from a foreign language: "Ce berger . . . les pria d'excuser la rudesse de sa voix, & la mauvaise lyaison de ce qu'il chanteroit, parce que ce n'estoit que la traduction d'un langage estranger . . ."[39] [This shepherd begged them to excuse the harshness of what he would sing, because it was just the translation from a foreign language . . .]. The "translation" is from the famous collection of *Basia* by the Dutch Neo-Latin poet Ioannes Secundus. However, as Eckhardt indicates, there is nothing terribly faithful about Belleau's translation, nothing that should keep even a scrupulous Renaissance poet from presenting it as imitation, i.e., as his own work.[40] This is precisely what happens in the second edition of the *Bergerie,* where the piece is no longer identified as a translation.[41] Such an important change in the manner of presentation illustrates Belleau's growing confidence in his status as an author.

This new assurance manifests itself also in Belleau's role as a translator, which did not end with the *Bergerie*: soon after its publication, Belleau chose to translate into Latin some of his own poetry, drawn precisely from the collection. The first edition of the *Bergerie* had included a cycle of thirteen sonnets imitating Secundus's *Basia*. In the second edition, this number grew to thirty-five. When Belleau published the third edition (1573) of his translation of the *Odes d'Anacreon*, one year after the complete *Bergerie,* he added the Latin translations of three of his *Baisers.* For the first time in Belleau's career, translating did not imply subordinating his status to that of Ronsard the poet, since he was now translating his own works. The act of translating some of his "Baisers" into Latin, instead of Ronsard's verse, implied that his poetry was worthy of immortality and that he himself was a poet laureate.

Moreover, the close relationship between Belleau's translations and Ronsard's works was not over, taking on even a physical dimension in the third edition of the *Odes d'Anacreon.* What happened, one might ask, to the translations of the three sonnets by Ronsard that had been originally appended to the Anacreontic poems in 1556? They remain, except that the first piece, "Amour, quiconque ait dit que le ciel fut ton pere" is replaced by another sonnet from the *Amours*, "Si mille œilletz, si mille lis j'embrasse" (Ronsard, 4: 32). However, perhaps constituting new evidence that Belleau was beginning to shake the Ronsardian yoke, these translations now follow Belleau's self-translations, "Mouches qui maçonnez . . . ," "Quand je presse en baisant," and "Ce begayant parler." Even more significantly, though, the translations from Ronsard are not formally separated in any way from the self-translations, nor are they identified any longer as originating from Ronsard. In the first (1556) edition of the Anacreontic translations, Ronsard's poems were preceded by the title "Traduction de quelques Sonetz de Pierre de Ronsard, par le mesme Belleau." In the third (1573) edition, the six Latin translations from Ronsard and Belleau are introduced with a very similar title, except that the mention "Pierre de Ronsard" has been removed and the target language specified: "Traduction de quelques sonnets françois en vers latins par le mesme Belleau."

The confusion in the attribution of authorship need not be considered as a deliberate attempt on Belleau's part formally to appropriate Ronsard's poetry for himself, for the printer's role in composing the texts is unknown to us. However, the typesetting of the 1573 edition of the translations of the *Odes d'Anacreon* had important consequences for all future editions of Belleau's Latin translations of French poetry. This arrangement of Belleau's translations was preserved not only in the fourth edition (1574) of the *Odes d'Anacreon* but also, most importantly, in the first edition of Belleau's *Oeuvres poétiques,* published one year after his death. Since this 1578 edition became the basis for all future editions, the outcome of this situation was that, in fact, all six pieces came to be considered translations from Belleau's own poetry.[42] Furthermore, given the prestige that translation into Latin conferred upon an author, the confusion in presentation that diminished the number of translations of Ronsard and added to the collection of the Belleau's translations of himself certainly benefited Belleau.

Marc Bizer

Belleau's three self-translations into Latin are in fact quite different with regard to the liberties they take with the French original. In all of them, however, he displays the same tendency to retouch and to enlarge the source, since the Latin poems are always longer than the French sonnets. Moving from the most to least faithful translation, one could say that "Quand ie presse en baisant . . ." follows its French source very carefully. "Ce begayant parler . . ." is most extraordinary for the technical virtuosity that Belleau demonstrates in the reworking of its beginning. The first quatrain in French is closely derived from a sonnet of the *Amours de Cassandre* by Ronsard (Ronsard, 4: 26).[43] Belleau's original French poem borrowed from Ronsard by forming the expression "Ce coral souspirant" out of "Ce beau coral" and "ce marbre qui souspire." The Latin poem retains only the enumerative structure of Ronsard's sonnet for the purposes of imitation, otherwise freeing itself completely. Specifically, the stuttering talk of the lady, only one in a long list of her enumerated charms, becomes the point of departure for a reworking of the referents of the poem itself, which gently mimic her speech defect. The use of diminutives and the extreme alliteration of the consonant "l" make the first few lines actually stutter:

*Ronsard*
Ce beau coral, ce marbre qui souspire,
Et ceste ébénne ornement d'un sourci,
Et cest albastre en vouste racourci,
Et ces zaphirs, ce jaspe, & ce porphyre . . . (lines 1–4)

[This lovely coral, this marble that sighs,
And this ebony, ornament of a brow,
And this alabaster shortened into a vault,
And these sapphires, this jasper, and this porphyry . . .]

*Belleau*
Ce begayant parler, ce sous-ris amoureux,
Cet oeil à demi-clos, ces blanchettes perlettes,

## Ronsard the Poet, Belleau the Translator

Ce coral souspirant, ces roses vermeillettes
Me font en vous baisant devenir langoureux.

(vol. 2, p. 281, lines 1–4)

[This stuttering speech, this amorous smile,
This half-closed eye, these white little pearls,
This sighing coral, these bright little red roses
Make me, while kissing you, langorous.]

*Latin translation of these lines by Belleau*
Blæsa illa mollicella verba, & blandula,
Risusque lenes languidique ocelluli
Tecum osculis dum luctor altercantibus,
(Elicere coelo sola quæ possent Iovem)
Papillulæque turgidæ, quæ lilium
Candore vincunt lacteo, labellaque
Minio, rosisque, & purpuræ certantia,
Comæque flavæ, eburneusque dentium
Æqualis ordo, macerant me perditè.

[Those lisping, ever so soft and charming words,
That gentle smile and those lowered eyes,
While we fight by exchanging kisses
(the only ones that could draw Jove from the heavens),
Those erect little nipples, that surpass the lily
With their milky whiteness, those lips
Competing with red, and roses, and purple,
Those golden locks, those even rows of
Ivory-white teeth torture me to perdition.]

Not only is the lady afflicted with a speech impediment but also the poet, for her beauty is such that it hinders the poet from expressing himself with his usual grace. Besides considerably lengthening the enumeration that reinforces the impression of ecstasy and disarray, by actually

Marc Bizer

mimicking the state of being tongue-tied, Belleau's rewriting constitutes
a clever variation on a poetic topos. Once again, Belleau has successfully
competed with Ronsard (himself following the example of Sappho,
Catullus, and Marullus), on whose sonnet "Ma langue s'engourdist" he
had earlier commented (44ʳ). He achieves this in all probability through
the imitation of the diminutives used by the Roman emperor Hadrian in
a famous Latin poem on a completely different subject, even to the
extent of borrowing the word "blandula" in the first line:

> Animula vagula, blandula,
> Hospes comesque corporis,
> Quae nunc abibis in loca,
> Pallidula, rigida, nudula,
> nec, ut soles, dabis iocos?[44]

> [Dear fleeting sweeting, little soul,
> My body's comrade and its guest,
> What region now must be thy goal,
> Poor little wan, numb, naked soul,
> Unable, as of old, to jest?]

Belleau also seems to have been influenced by a few lines from the *Ars
Amatoria* (Book 2, lines 159–60) where Ovid explains the importance of
seducing a lady with soft, eloquent language; however, his poem, with
its eloquent stuttering, sheds an ironic light on the Latin text:

> *Blanditias molles* auremque iuvantia *verba*
> Adfer, ut adventu laeta sit illa tuo.[45]

> [Bring sweet nothings, and words pleasing to the ear, so that she be
> glad of your arrival.]

By composing in Latin, Belleau escapes the intertextual influence

201

that Ronsard's authority exerted upon him in French. He enters a different world in which he is completely at home, that of the classical and Neo-Latin poets. Nevertheless, their formidable authority does not induce servile imitation in Belleau's work but, rather, inspires a creative mixing of sources reminiscent of Ronsard's own imitative technique.

The title "Ad apes," which Belleau gave to the Latin translation of his own "Mouches qui maçonnez . . . ," recalls inevitably an ode by Ronsard whose title it literally translates: "Aus Mouches a miel." However, it is Belleau's sonnet, and not its Latin version, that bears a close thematic resemblance to Ronsard's poem. More than a simple exercise in *variatio*, Belleau's Latin adaptation frees itself not only from Ronsard's example but also from its French original, as well as from the source of both: Secundus's "Basium 19" (see Appendix D).[46]

Ronsard had borrowed almost the entire structure of the "Basium 19" in his French adaptation[47]: the invitation extended from the poet to the bees to seek their food on the lips of his lady, the enumeration of the many flowers whose fragrance they disperse, and finally the warning not to sting her lips because of the lady's own formidable stinger. Belleau adopts this basic outline in his sonnet while highlighting new elements in order to produce a different general effect. Whereas Ronsard had condensed Secundus's lines "qui adhuc thyma cana, rosasque, / Et rorem vernae nectareum violae / Lingitis, aut florem late spirantis anethi?" (lines 1–3) into the epithet "Grand miracle de la nature" (line 2) applied to the bees, Belleau returns to a somewhat modified Secundian description in his first quatrain. He avoids Secundus's (lines 3–8) and Ronsard's long enumeration of flowers with their mythological origins (lines 9–21), preferring to vary the description of the lady's treasures by transforming a field of flowers into an idealized landscape: "Là trouverez un air embasmé de senteurs, / Un lac comblé de miel, une moisson d'odeurs" (lines 9–10). Belleau thus reestablishes the idea of the lips being a source of honey, yet only as one of their wonders, while Secundus concludes by virtually equating the two: they are "mellea

Marc Bizer

labra" (line 13). Finally, the lady is presented as a dangerous trap
("gardez-vous aussi des embuches cruelles," line 11) *per se* and not only
when provoked.

Faithful in its structure to Belleau's first reworking of Secundus's
"Basium 19" in French, his Latin version nevertheless gives the bees an
entirely new function: their portrait, expanded from Secundus's four
lines to six, cannot help but recall humanist poets because it is drawn
using technical language from Latin literary criticism. Whereas in the
French poem the bees are given no epithet, in Latin they are called
*doctae*. First applied in the context of poetry to Catullus, this term
underlined the aesthetic discernment of someone who wrote learned,
Hellenistic-style poetry.[48] In addition, instead of simply building a
honeycomb ("massonnez voûtes encirees"), the bees compose ("componere") cells that are carefully wrought ("arte laboratas"). *Florilegae*
does not merely replace Secundus's *mellilegae* in accordance with the
French source's greater emphasis on flowers and pollen than on honey;
it also refers to a topos because of its precise meaning in rhetorical
theory: the imitation of models in textual composition is often compared
to the collection of pollen and its transformation into honey by bees.
Specifically, *florilegae* evokes the imitative technique whereby the poet
composes a poem by putting together parts of several others, already
alluded to by *componere*, meaning "to assemble." Furthermore, several
Hellenistic anthologies of Greek poetry known in the Renaissance were
entitled *Florilegia*, such as Stobaeus's *Florilegium* whose poems Ronsard
and Belleau imitated, while anthologizing was itself a fundamental
activity of Renaissance humanists. Finally, like *componere cellas, fingitis
antra* translates *massonnez* while expressing yet another aspect of the
bees' craft: meaning "to mold," "to form," "to shape," and closely linked
to artistic creation, *fingitis* suggests that bees fashion wax caves not only
like sculptors[49] but also as writers shape verse.

Since *fingere* insists on the fruits of art as opposed to those of
nature,[50] it is not surprising that the theme of artifice and of creation is

203

much more present in the Latin. The work of the bees, described in much greater detail in Latin than in French, is also more elaborate, more refined: they mold caves with paneled ceilings—an architectural detail completely absent from the French sonnet. In addition, there is a clear reference to the work of the most famous artificer, Daedalus, in the word *Daedaleo*. Within this context, however, wax becomes a central image and a preoccupation of the poet. The Latin poem emphasizes its malleability and plasticity by means of the adjectives *laqueata* [with paneled ceilings] and, especially, *ducta* [drawn]. The alliteration of "l" in *laqueata* and *levi* emphasizes the idea of suppleness, foreshadowing the same alliteration that is applied to the flowing of honey in line twelve. Honey, symbol of the complete transformation of one material into another, recedes in importance behind wax, which can assume the most disparate forms without its substance being changed.

The portrait of the bees is concluded in line six with an explanation of their meaning for human artifice; *proditis*, a key word signifying "to show," "to reveal,"[51] expresses the idea that bees provide techniques ("artes") unknown to human ingenuity ("sollertia"[52]). However, because bees are traditionally associated with artistic imitation in Latin critical theory, we can infer that more than just giving us new skills, bees teach the act of borrowing itself, *imitatio*, without which poets would have to rely on their *naturel*.[53] The first six lines of the Latin can therefore be read as a debate on the best imitative technique to use in composing poetry. Wax suggests the transformation a source text can undergo through different adaptations, yet without becoming unrecognizable. If we may draw conclusions about Belleau's own imitative practice from this image, it would seem that he prefers close borrowing to a more removed adaptation that would totally transform the source. More generally, given the basic similarity between what bees and poets do, Belleau's contemplation of the activities of the bees amounts to a meditation on his work as a poet.

However, these reflections on poetic composition do not remain on an exclusively theoretical level, for they are carefully implemented in the poem, including in the discussion of imitation itself. At the outset, important classical texts on imitation are assembled through imitation to form a harmonious mosaic whose components are identifiable: the evocation of the bees borrows heavily from Virgil's fourth *Georgic*, completely devoted to them, but also from Macrobius (*Saturnalia*, 1: 5), Seneca (*Letters to Lucilius*, 84: 2–10), and Virgil (*Aeneid*, 1: 432–33). Further on, "Florum laeta seges" (line 11) echoes the beginning of the first *Georgic* (1: 1). The images of the idyll of the lady's lips (lines 10–14) are derived mainly from Virgil's fourth *Georgic*. Even the final evocation of the tortured poet ("imis penitus grassata medullis," line 18) does not mean that experience has come into the foreground; the fact that this expression probably comes from Ariadne's complaint in Catullus 64 ("[prius]quam cuncto concepit corpore flammam / funditus atque imis exarsit tota medullis" (lines 92–93) [until she had caught fire in her entire body and burned deeply in the core of her marrow] draws the Renaissance reader's attention more to the composition of a love poem than to the nature of that love. There is thus a movement in the Latin from a discussion of the theory of imitation in the first lines to its application to the composition of love poetry at the end.

Since Secundus's "Basium 19" is also largely indebted to the fourth *Georgic*, Belleau's "Ad apes" can be seen as an innovative reinterpretation and reworking of this source through the Neo-Latin poem's handling of it; this is reminiscent of Belleau's treatment of the Ovidian Narcissus myth in his Latin translation of Ronsard's "Que laschement vous me trompez mes yeulx." In this instance, however, the most relevant source passages are those that do not explicitly appear in Belleau's text: the evocation of the myths of Proteus and Orpheus. While Proteus is a central figure in Renaissance thought,[54] here suggesting, perhaps, the metamorphosis of the poet composing in more than one language, the background presence of Orpheus, the supreme figure of the poet and of his divine inspiration, further underlines the profoundly self-reflexive character of Belleau's Latin poem.

A veritable *Art of Poetry,* "Ad apes," like many *arts poétiques* of the Renaissance, applies the theory it develops and constitutes a striking example of its full realization. Thus, the tendency of the previous translations, including Belleau's commentary, to define his own poetics attains its most complete expression in this poem. Furthermore, given the considerable differences between "Ad apes" and "Mouches qui maçonnez . . . ," the Latin version shows that self-translation can be innovative recomposition.

For Belleau, translation was the activity in which the difficulties of writing in the shadow of the premier French poet most clearly come to the fore. Throughout Belleau's career, translation acted as a mask for poetry that competitively imitated Ronsard's work without seeming to do so. Belleau began his career by translating the poetry that Ronsard had already imitated and, most importantly, by changing the way Ronsard had adapted his source material. Belleau's translation of four sonnets from Ronsard's *Amours* and his commentary on the poems of the second book glorified and confirmed Ronsard as poet laureate, but at the same time modified Ronsard's text, using it to define a poetics unique to Belleau. Translation lost its character as an act both of open reverence and of mute emulation during Belleau's last years, when he transposed certain of his poems into Latin, making it an instrument of self-vindication. In publishing translations of his own work and substituting himself for Ronsard as source of text and authority, he learned to replace "his" with "my own" and to affirm, like Horace, "I have erected *my own* monument more lasting than bronze."

Marc Bizer

Appendix A

Εἰς ἔρωτα.

Ἔρως ποτ' ἐν ῥόδοισι
κοιμωμένην μέλιτταν
οὐκ εἶδεν, ἀλλ' ἐτρώθη·
τὸν δάκτυλον παταχθεὶς
τᾶς χειρὸς, ὠλόλυξε.
δραμὼν δὲ καὶ πετασθεὶς
πρὸς τὴν καλὴν Κυθήρην
'ὄλωλα, μῆτερ,' εἶπεν,
'ὄλωλα κἀποθνήσκω·
ὄφις μ' ἔτυψε μικρὸς
πτερωτός, ὅν καλοῦσιν
μέλιτταν οἱ γεωργοί.'
ἁ δ' εἶπεν· 'εἰ τὸ κέντρον
πονεῖ τὸ τᾶς μελίττας,
πόσον δοκεῖς πονοῦσιν,
Ἔρως, ὅσους σὺ βάλλεις;'

[Love once failed to notice a bee that was sleeping among the roses, and he was wounded: he was struck in the finger, and he howled. He ran and flew to beautiful Cythera and said, "I have been killed, mother, killed. I am dying. I was struck by the small winged snake that farmers call 'the bee'." She replied, "If the bee-sting is painful, what pain, Love, do you suppose all your victims suffer?"]

207

# Ronsard the Poet, Belleau the Translator

**Ronsard (vol. 7, Ode 20, p. 106)**
**"Le petit enfant Amour" (1555)**

Le petit enfant Amour
Cueilloit des fleurs, à l'entour
D'une ruche, où les avettes
4  Font leurs petites logettes.

Comme il les alloit cueillant,
Une avette, sommeillant'
Dans le fond d'une fleurette,
8  Lui piqua sa main tendrette.

Si tôt que piqué se vit,
Ah, je suis perdu (ce dit)
Et s'encourant vers sa mere
12  Lui montra sa plaie amere:

Ma mere, voiés ma main,
Ce disoit Amour tout plein
De pleurs, voiés quelle enflure
16  M'a fait une égratignure!

Alors Venus se sourit,
Et en le baisant le prit,
Puis sa main lui a soufflée,
20  Pour guarir sa plaie enflée.

Qui t'a, di moi, faus garçon,
Blessé de telle façon,
Sont-ce mes Graces riantes
24  De leurs aiguilles poignantes?

**Belleau (Gouverneur, p. 43)**
**"D'Amour picqué d'une mouche à miel" (1556)**

Amour nc voyoit pas enclose
Entre les replis de la rose
Une mouche à miel, qui soudain
En l'un de ses doigts le vint poindre:
Le mignon commence à se plaindre,
6  Voyant enfler sa blanche main.

Aussi tost à Venus la belle,
Fuyant, il volle à tire d'ælle:
«Mere, dist-il, c'est fait de moy,
C'en est fait, & faut qu'à ceste heure
Navré jusques au cœur ie meure,
12  Si secouru ne suis de toy.

Navré je suis en ceste sorte
D'un petit serpenteau, qui porte
Deux ailerons dessus le dos,
Aux champs une abeille on l'appelle:
Voyez donc ma playe cruelle,
18  Las! il m'a picqué jusqu'à l'os.»

«Mignon (dist Venus), si la pointe
D'une mouche à miel telle atteinte
Droit au cœur (comme tu dis) fait,
Combien sont navrez davantage
Ceux qui sont espoinds de ta rage,
24  Et qui sont blessez de ton trait?»

# Marc Bizer

*Ronsard*, "Le petit enfant Amour" (cont.)

Nenny, c'est un serpenteau,
Qui vole au printans nouveau
Avéque deux ailerettes
28  Cà & là sus les fleurettes.

Ah vraiment je le connois,
(Dit Venus): les villageois
De la montagne d'Hymette
32  Le surnomment une avette*.

Si donques un animal
Si petit fait tant de mal,
Quand son halesne époinçonne
36  La main de quelque personne,

Combien fais-tu de douleurs
Au pris de lui, dans les coeurs
De ceus contre qui tu gettes
40  Tes homicides sagettes?

*variant *Melissette*, from the Greek
*melissa* (bee)

[The little child Cupid
Was picking flowers, around
A hive, where bees have their
Little lodgings.

As he was picking them,
A bee, napping
Deep in a little flower,
Stung his tender little hand.

As soon as he saw he was stung,
Oh, I am done for (he said),

[Cupid did not see enclosed
Between the folds of a rose
A bee, which suddenly
Stung one of his fingers:
The darling begins to complain,
Seeing his white hand swell.

Immediately to Venus the lovely,
Fleeing, he flies straightaway;
"Mother, he said, it is all over for me,
It is all over, and now,
Wounded to heart, I must die,
If I do not receive your aid.

## Ronsard the Poet, Belleau the Translator

And hurrying to his mother
Showed her his smarting wound:

Mother, look at my hand,
Said Cupid all full
Of tears, see what swelling
A scratch has made!

So Venus smiled to herself,
And kissing him took him,
Then blew on his hand,
To cure his swollen wound.

Who, tell me, deceptive child,
Wounded you this way,
Was it my cheerful Graces
With their pricky needles?

No, it was a little serpent
That flies in the new Spring,
With two little wings
Here and there above the little flowers.

Oh, I know what it is,
(Said Venus): the villagers
From Mount Hymettus
Call it a bee.

If then an animal
So small does such harm
When his breath stings
The hand of someone,

How much pain do you inflict
By comparison with him, in the hearts
Of those against whom you fire
Your lethal little arrows?"]

Wounded I am this way
By a little serpent, which carries
Two wings on its back,
In the fields it is called a bee:
See then my smarting wound,
Alas! It stung me to the bone."

"Darling (said Venus), if the stinger
Of a bee such injury
Straight to the heart (as you say) makes,
How much more are wounded
Those who experience your rage
And who are stung with your arrow?"]

210

Marc Bizer

(Pseudo-)Theocritus, *Idyll* 19

ΚΗΡΙΟΚΛΕΠΤΗΣ

Τὸν κλέπταν ποτ' ἔρωτα κακὰ κέφτασε μέλισσα
Κήριον ἐκ σίμβλων συλεύμενον, ἄκρα δὲ χειρῶν
Δάκτυλα πάνθ' ὑπένυξεν. 'Ο δ' ἄλγεε, καὶ χέρ' ἐφύση
Καὶ τὰν γᾶν ἐπάταξε, καὶ ἄλατο. Τᾷ δ' 'Αφροδίτᾳ
Δεῖξεν τὰν ὀδύναν, καὶ μέμφετο ὅττι γε τυτθὸν
Θηρίον ἐντὶ μέλισσα, καὶ ἀλίκα τραύματα ποιεῖ.
Χ'ὰ μάτηρ γελάσασα, Τί δ' οὐκ ἴσον ἐσσὶ μελίσσαις.
Χ'ὼ τυτθὸς μὲν ἔης, Τὰ δὲ τραύματα ἀλίκα ποιεῖς; (pp. 146–47)

The Honey Thief

[A cruel bee once stung the thievish Love-god as he was stealing honey from the hives, and pricked all his finger-tips. And he was hurt and blew upon his hand, and stamped and danced. And to Aphrodite he showed the wound, and made complaint that so small a creature as a bee should deal so cruel a wound. And his mother answered laughing, "Are you not like the bees, that art so small, yet dealest wounds so cruel?"]

## Appendix B

| *Ronsard* (vol. 6, p. 45, lines 1–14) | Latin translation by *Belleau* |

Amour, quiconque ait dit que le ciel fut
    ton pere,
Et que Venus la douce en ses flancs te
    porta,
Il mentit lachement: une ourse en avorta
S'une ourse d'un tel fils se veut dire la
    mere.
Des chams Massyliens la plus cruelle fere
Entre ses lionneaus sus un roc t'alaitta,
Et, t'ouvrant ses tetins, par son lait te jetta
Tout à l'entour du cœur sa rage la plus
    fiere.
Rien ne te plaist, cruel, que sanglos & que
    pleurs,
Que dechirer nos cœurs d'épineuses
    douleurs,
Que tirer tout d'un coup mile mors de ta
    trousse.
Un si mechant que toi du ciel n'est point
    venu.
Si Venus t'eust conceu, tu eusses retenu
Quelque peu de douceur d'une mere si
    douce.

1 Quisquis te genitum parente coelo
  Et molli veneris sinu educatum
  Ausus dicere primus est Cupido,
4 Mentitus nimis impudenter ille est:
  Te sub rupe cava ferox abortu
  Vexata ante diem reliquit ursa,
  Si non inficietur* ursa talem:
8 Te Campo in Lybico feroce
    mamma
  Immistum catulis suis leoena
  Lactavit, rabiémque iam feroci
  Immisit stomacho ferociorem.
12 Nulla ô seve puer tibi voluptas
  Praeter vulnera, lachrymas, dolores,
  Praeterquam laniare corda nostra
  Spinosis tenacibusque curis,
16 Pestes & totidem graves vibrare,
  Hae sunt delitiae tuae iocique:
  Et tu natus es è sinu deorum
  Coelesti, usqueadeo genus
    scelestum?
20 Si verè Venere editus fuisses,
  Si tam melliflua è parente natus,
  Paulùm debueras habere mellis.

*inficietur=infitietur

# Marc Bizer

[Cupid, whoever said that heaven was
  your father,
And that sweet Venus carried you in her
  womb,
Lied cowardly: a she-bear miscarried
  you
If a she-bear will admit to being the
  mother of such a son.
The cruellest beast of the Massylian
  fields
Nursed you on a rock between her cubs
And, opening her teats to you, with her
  milk
Injected around your heart her fiercest
  rage.
Nothing gives you pleasure, o cruel boy,
But tearing apart our hearts with thorny
  anguish,
but drawing suddenly a thousand deaths
  from your quiver,
Someone as wicked as you hardly came
  from the sky.
If Venus had conceived you, you would
  have kept
However little sweetness from such a
  sweet mother.]

[Whoever dared to say that you were
  born of a celestial
Parent, and reared on the soft breast of
  Venus,
Cupid, he lied too shamelessly:
Horrified by the miscarriage, a fierce
  she-bear
Abandoned you prematurely under a
  hollow rock,
If a she-bear does not repudiate such a
  miscreation:
A leonine teat nursed you, alongside her
  Cubs, in the harsh Libyan desert,
And to your already fierce ill-temper
  She added even fiercer rage.
Nothing gives you pleasure, o cruel boy,
Except wounds, tears, pains,
Except when you lacerate our hearts
With thorny tenacious cares,
And brandish as many serious
  afflictions,
These are your delights and pastimes:
And you were born from the womb of
The heavenly gods, does the criminal
  race know no limits?
If you were truly the offspring of Venus,
If you were born from such a honey-
  dripping parent,
You should have had a little honey.]

213

# Appendix C

| *Ronsard* (Laum. 4, p. 123) | *Latin translation by Belleau* |
|---|---|
| Que laschement vous me trompez, mes yeulx, | Quam me decipitis malignè ocelli, |
| Enamourez d'une figure vaine: | Fallacis memores figurae ocelli! |
| O nouveaulté d'une cruelle peine, | Heu nimisque ferox, ferumque fatum |
| O fier destin, ô malice des cieulx. | Voto supplice nescium moveri, |
| Fault il que moy de moymesme envieux, | 5 Astrorum scelus heu nimis cruentum! |
| Pour aymer trop les eaux d'une fontaine, | Si fontis leviter fluentis undas |
| Je brusle apres une image incertaine, | Fallaci nimis ore fontis undas |
| Qui pour ma mort m'accompaigne en toutz lieux? | Amavi, proprio perustus igne, Tabescamne ideo miser! sequacem |
| Et quoy, fault il que le vain de ma face, | 10 Imprudens iuvenis sequutus umbram? |
| De membre à membre amenuiser me face, | O Dij quod genus istud est furoris! |
| Comme une cire aux raiz de la chaleur? | Amans ut peream, simulque perdam Quem mendax vacuis imago flammis |
| Ainsi pleuroyt l'amoureux Cephiside, | Membratim extenuet? propinquiore |
| Quand il sentit dessus le bord humide, | 15 Flava liquitur ut vapore cera! |
| De son beau sang naistre une belle fleur. | Sic flebat liquidam imminens in undam Narcissus, subitum repentè florem Cum vidit, moriente se, renasci. |

## Marc Bizer

[How cowardly you deceive me, my
    eyes,
Enamoured of a vain face.
Oh new cruel anguish,
Oh proud destiny, oh cruelty of the
    heavens.
Must I, desirous of myself,
For having loved the waters of a
    fountain too much,
Burn for an unstable image,
Which for my death accompanies me in
    every place?
Must the emptiness of my face
Make me shrink from limb to limb
Like wax in the rays of heat?
Thus wept the amorous Cephisides,
When he felt on the humid bank
From his lovely blood a lovely flower
    being born.]

[How cruelly you fool me, eyes,
Eyes that remember a deceptive face!
Alas too fierce, too wild fate
Incapable of being moved by the wish of
    a supplicant,
Alas too monstrous crime of the bloody
    stars
If I have loved, consumed by a fire for
    myself,
The waters of the gently flowing
    fountain,
The waters of the fountain with a too
    deceptive face,
For this, wretched, shall I waste away!
    For having
Foolishly followed the pursuing shadow
    of a youth?
O gods, what folly this is!
Loving in a way fatal to myself, but also
    deadly to
The one whom the deceitful likeness
    weakens
Limb by limb? As yellow wax
Is liquified by a fire too close!
Thus wept Narcissus bent over the
    flowing waters,
When, dying, he suddenly saw a flower
Unexpectedly spring up again ]

# Ronsard the Poet, Belleau the Translator

# Appendix D

**Ioannes Secundus**
*Basium* 19

Mellilegae volucres, qui adhuc thyma cana,
    rosasque,
Et rorem vernae nectareum violae
Lingitis, aut florem late spirantis anethi?
Omnes ad dominae labra venite meae.
Illa rosas spirant omnes, thymaque omnia
    sola,
Et succum vernae nectareum violae.
Inde procul dulces aureae funduntur anethi;
Narcissi veris illa madent lacrimis;
Oebaliique madent iuvenis fragrante cruore;
Qualis uterque liquor, cum cecidisset, erat,
Nectareque aetherio medicatus, et aëre
    puro,
Impleret foetus versicolore solum.
Sed me, jure meo libantem mellea labra,
Ingratae socium ne prohibete favis.
Non etiam totas avidae distendite cellas,
Arescant dominae ne semel ora meae
Basiaque impressans siccis sitienta labris,
Garrulus indicii triste feram pretium.
Heu, non et stimulis compungite molle
    labellum:
Ex oculis stimulos vibrat et illa pares.
Credite, non ullum patietur vulnus inultum:
Leniter innocuae mella legatis apes.

[Honey sipping winged creatures, do you
    still lick the white thyme, roses,
And the dew of nectar of the Spring violet,
Or the flower of Dill giving off its
widespread fragrance?
Come all to the lips of my lady.
They alone give off the fragrance of all
    roses, of all thyme,
And the essence of the nectar of the Spring
    violet;
From there the sweet breeezes of Dill pour
    forth;
They are moist with the true tears of
    Narcissus;
They are moist with the fragrant blood of
    Hyacinthus;
Both humors, when they had fallen
Mixed with heavenly nectar and pure ether,
Impregnated the earth with colorful fruit.
However, since I have the right to sip the
    honeyed lips,
Do not keep your partner, ingrates, from
    the honeycombs.
Don't overload all of your cells, either,
    greedy bees,
Lest the mouth of my lady go dry;
For, pressing thirsty kisses on dry lips,
Indiscrete, I would have to pay dearly for
    the revelation.
Alas, don't sting the soft lip with your
    stingers:
Her eyes brandish stingers the equal of
    yours.
Believe me, she will never let a wound go
    unavenged:
Gently, bees, without hurting, pick your
    honey.]

# Marc Bizer

**Ronsard, Aus Mouches a Miel**
**[2: 55: Ode 20] (1550)**

*Bergerie* (1565)

Où allez vous files du ciel
Grand miracle de la nature,
Où allés vous mouches à miel
Chercher aus champs vostre pasture?
Si vous voulés cueillir les fleurs
D'odeur diverse, & de couleurs,
7   Ne volez plus à l'avanture.

Autour de sa bouche alenée
De mes baisers tant bien donnés,
Vous trouverés la rose née,
Et les oeillets environnés
Des florettes ensanglantées
D'Hyacinthe, & d'Ajax, plantées
14   Autour des rommarins là nés.

Les marjolenes i fleurissent
L'arôme est continuel,
Et les lauriers qui ne perissent
Pour l'iver tant soit-il cruel,
L'anis, le chevrefueil qui porte
La manne qui vous reconforte,
21   I verdoie perpetuel.

Mais je vous pri gardez vous bien,
Gardez vous qu'on ne l'eguillonne,
Vous apprendriés bien tost combien
Sa pointure est trop plus felonne,
Et de ses fleurs ne vous soulez
Sans m'en garder, si ne voulez
28   Que mon ame ne m'abandonne.

Mouches qui massonnez les voûtes
  encirees
De vos palais dorez, & qui dés le matin
Volez de mont en mont pour effleurer le
  thyn,
Et suçoter des fleurs les odeurs savourees:
Dressez vos ailerons sur les levres sucrees
De ma belle maistresse, & baisant son tetin
Sur sa bouche pillez le plus riche butin
Que vous chargeastes onc sur vos ailes
  dorees.
Là trouverez un air embasmé de senteurs,
Un lac comblé de miel, une moisson
  d'odeurs:
Mais gardez-vous aussi des embuches
  cruelles.
Car de sa bouche il sort un brasier allumé,
Et de souspirs ardens un escadron armé,
Et pource gardez-vous d'y brusler vos
  ailes.

# Ronsard the Poet, Belleau the Translator

**Belleau, Ad Apes, Latin translation of his Mouches qui massonnez . . . (1573?)**

1 Arte laboratas doctae componere cellas
Florilegae volucres, doctae fragrantia mella
Stipare, & flores summos libare peritae,
Cerea Daedaleo sub fornice fingitis antra,
5 Rara favis, laqueata, levi discrimine ducta,
Quasque humana negat solertia, proditis artes,
Si tamen ignoratis ubi bene fundat odores
Terra suos, teneras quibus aut in montibus herbas
Quisve locus claudat divinos nectaris amnes
10 Labra meae Dominae petite, hic confusa virescit
Florum laeta seges, Casiaeque, Crocique, Thymique
Hinc mellis currunt latices, hinc manat odorum
Hesperidum quicquid vobis violaria fundunt,
Quicquid odoriferi Pestana rosaria Veris.
15 Cautius at, moneo, roseis confidite labris:
Nam flamma ut cineri, labris supposta, periclum est
Ustulet ut pennas, ipsam quae absumeret Aetnam
Ne dum vos, imis penitus grassata medullis

[Expert in the art of composing well-wrought cells,
Flower-sipping winged creatures, knowledgeable in
Loading with fragrant honey, experienced in tasting flowers on high,
You fashion wax caverns under a Dedalian vault,
With rare honeycombs, paneled ceilings, drawn with fine dividers,
The arts refused to human ingenuity, you provide.
If however you ignore where the Earth pours forth
Its fragrances, or on which mountains its tender herbs
Or which place confines divine rivers of nectar,
Seek the lips of my Lady, there grow green
The rich fields of flowers of every sort, cinnamon and crocus and thyme,
From there flows liquid honey, from there streams
All that the violet gardens of the Hesperides,
All that the rose gardens of Paestum pour forth for you in fragrant Spring.
I warn you though: trust her rosy lips with great caution.
For like a flame hidden under ash, there is the danger
That you will burn your wings, a flame that would consume Aetna herself,
And so yourselves all the more easily, raging deep in the core of my marrow.]

218

# Marc Bizer

## Notes

1. By using the word "seduction" I am alluding specifically to the famous poem "Ad lectorem" in Du Bellay's *Poemata*, where the Latin language is compared to a mistress and French to a spouse; erotic pleasure is obviously associated with Latin. I. D. McFarlane remarks wittily, ". . . only Ronsard of these poets remained faithful to the programme of the *Deffense* and to his own decision to forsake Latin pastures; all the others took out an insurance policy with posterity in Latin poetry"; see I. D. McFarlane, *Renaissance France 1470–1589* (London: E. Benn; New York: Barnes and Noble, 1974), p. 262.]

2. It would be anachronistic, of course, to assume that the present-day subordination of translators to authors automatically applies to the Renaissance, when translators enjoyed great prestige for the important role they were playing in the transmission of ancient culture; furthermore, imitative authors often "translated" or plagiarized when adapting ancient texts into their native tongues. This hierarchy would only gradually become established from 1540 onward as a result of the quarrel between imitators and translators; for further information, see Luce Guillerm, *Sujet et l'écriture et traduction autour de 1540* (Paris: Aux Amateurs de Livres, 1988). Nevertheless, this new system of values forms the backdrop for Belleau's works, since it was clearly adopted by the spokesperson for the Pléiade, Joachim Du Bellay, in *La Deffence et illustration de la langue françoyse* (1549). Du Bellay specifically condemns poetic translations in the manifesto as follows: "Celuy donques qui voudra faire œuvre digne de prix en son vulgaire, laisse ce labeur de traduire, principalement les poëtes, à ceux qui de chose laborieuse et peu profitable, j'ose dire encor' inutile, voyre pernicieuse à l'acroissement de leur Langue, emportent à bon droict plus de molestie que de gloyre" (I, vi); see Joachim Du Bellay, *La Deffence et illustration de la langue françoyse,* ed. Henri Chamard (Paris: Librairie Nizet, 1970), pp. 41–42.

3. *Inventio* is the first of the three parts of rhetoric traditionally associated with poetic composition (*inventio, dispositio, elocutio*); it involves choosing subject matter for a work from pre-established stocks of topics and in no way implies "creation," which would be historically incorrect.

4. Unless otherwise indicated, all citations from Belleau's works are taken from Gouverneur's 1867 edition, which was based on the first edition of Belleau's complete works (1578): *Oeuvres complètes de Rémy Belleau,* ed. A. Gouverneur (Nogent-le-Rotrou: A. Gouverneur, 1867). Ronsard's poems are cited from Laumonier's edition: Pierre de

# Ronsard the Poet, Belleau the Translator

Ronsard, *Oeuvres complètes*, ed. P. Laumonier, I. Silver, and R. Lebègue, 20 vols. (Paris: SATF, 1924–75) (cited hereafter as Ronsard). All translations except those from the Greek are my own.

5. This foreword, replacing the dedication to Belleau's patron Monseigneur Chretophle de Choiseul, Abbé de Mureaux in the 1556 edition, immediately precedes Ronsard's preface. The second edition (1572) is lost.

6. It is here that Ronsard ushers in Belleau as a member of the Pléiade: "[la France] te concevant, Belleau, qui viens en la Brigade des bons, / Pour accomplir la septieme Pleiade" [France, conceiving you, Belleau, who are joining the Brigade of the Good, to complete the seventh Pleiades].

7. See Henri Chamard, *Histoire de la Pléiade*, 4 vols. (Paris: Didier, 1939–63), 2: 56–58, and Pierre de Nolhac, *Ronsard et l'humanisme* (Paris: Honoré Champion, 1921, 1966), pp. 108–13, for the history of the discovery of Anacreontic poetry.

8. See *Anacréon et les poèmes anacréontiques avec les traductions et imitations des poètes du XVI<sup>e</sup> siècle*, ed. A. Delboulle (Le Havre: Lemale et Cie, 1891).

9. "Le rapprochement nous montre Belleau, traducteur d'Anacréon, sous la dépendance absolue de Ronsard" [the comparison shows us Belleau, translator of Anacreon, completely dependent upon Ronsard]; see Alexandre (Sandor) Eckhardt, *Rémy Belleau, sa vie, sa «Bergerie»* (Budapest: Nemeth, 1917), p. 34.

10. "Les mots et les rimes de Ronsard peuplent la mémoire de Belleau et glissent quelquefois sous sa plume" [Ronsard's words and rimes populate Belleau's memory and sometimes slip out from under his pen]; see Marcel Raymond, *L'Influence de Ronsard sur la poésie française*, 2 vols. (Paris: Henri Champion, 1927), 1: 172.

11. "Ronsard n'avait laissé à personne le mérite de le devancer et l'on sait *par quelles exquises paraphrases* il venait de précéder son disciple [Belleau]" [Ronsard had left to no one the glory of going before him and we know by *what exquisite paraphrases* he had just preceded his disciple]; see Nolhac, *Ronsard et l'humanisme*, p. 110 (my italics; henceforth all italics in citations have been added by me for emphasis).

# Marc Bizer

12. "[Ronsard] a usé de toutes les variétés de l'imitation, depuis la simple traduction jusqu'au long développement" [Ronsard used all of the types of imitation, from simple translation to the long development]; see Paul Laumonier, *Ronsard, poète lyrique: étude historique littéraire* (Paris: Hachette, 1923), p. 606.

13. The text and translation are from the Loeb edition: *Greek Lyric*, ed. and trans. D. A. Campbell, 4 vols. (Cambridge: Harvard University Press; London: W. Heinemann 1982–92), 2: 206.

14. *Theocritus*, ed. A. S. F. Gow with translation and commentary, 2 vols. (Cambridge: Cambridge University Press, 1952), 1: 146–47.

15. Chamard notes that the "montaigne d'Hymette" is famous for its honey (2: 64); it recurs in Ronsard's works as part of the honey *leitmotiv* and, thus, contributes to the establishment of this image as a symbol of his poetics.

16. In the sense of the rhetorical term *inventio*; see n. 3 above.

17. It is Eckhardt who first noticed Belleau's borrowings from Ronsard in his translations and imitations, demonstrating in one instance that "Belleau traduit en reprenant les rimes et les tournures de Ronsard" (p. 165) [Belleau translates while reusing Ronsard's rhymes and expressions] and in another that "On peut relever . . . un grand nombre de vers et de rhymes identiques chez les deux poètes. Ronsard est toujours antérieur à Belleau; l'influence réciproque est impossible" (p. 166) [One can point out the great number of identical lines and rhymes in both poets' works. Ronsard is always before Belleau; reciprocal influence is impossible].

18. See the remarks of Hugues Salel who retorted that if one took away the "larrecin" (theft) in the works of so-called imitative poets, only a blank page would be left; see Bernard Weinberg, ed., *Critical Prefaces of the French Renaissance* (Evanston, Ill.: Northwestern University Press, 1950), p. 128. See also n. 2 above.

19. Delboulle, *Anacréon et les poèmes anacréontiques*, pp. 106–07; Ronsard, 6: 199.

20. He declared it was taken from Anacreon: "prise d'Anacreon"; see Ronsard, 6: 199–201.

# Ronsard the Poet, Belleau the Translator

21. These poems are too long to quote here in their entirety; appropriate excerpts will be given when necessary; see Ronsard, 6: 152.

22. Raymond, *L'Influence de Ronsard*, 1: 188–90.

23. "Un nouveau témoignage de l'amitié de Belleau pour Ronsard" [new proof of Belleau's affection for Ronsard] (Ronsard, 7: 326). Belleau was not the only person to glorify Ronsard's works by translating them into Latin; see Malcolm C. Smith, "Latin Translations of Ronsard," *Acta Conventus Neo-Latini Guelpherbytani: Proceedings of the Sixth International Congress of Neo-Latin Studies: Wolfenbüttel 12 August to 16 August 1985*, ed. Stella P. Revard, Fidel Rädle, and Mario A. Di Cesare (Binghamton: Center for Medieval & Early Renaissance Studies, 1988), pp. 331–37.

24. Belleau also cites Homer and Theocritus as Greek sources; see Rémy Belleau, *Commentaire au second livre des Amours de Ronsard,* ed. Marie-Madeleine Fontaine and François Lecercle (Geneva: Droz, 1986), Appendix 3, pp. 72–73. This commentary appears in the 1578 edition, but appeared in 1560 as part of Muret's commentary on the first book of the *Amours*. The editors note that, in this edition, "Ronsard a redonné à Belleau toute une série de commentaires dont il était vraisemblablement l'auteur en 1560" (p. xxxiii) [Ronsard gave back to Belleau a whole series of commentaries of which he was probably the author in 1560].

25. "Ce sonnet est comme une explication du vers 10 du précédent" [This sonnet is like an explication of line 10 of the preceding one]; Ronsard 4: 122.

26. Marc-Antoine de Muret, *Commentaires au premier livre des Amours de Ronsard,* ed. Jacques Chomarat, Marie-Madeleine Fragonard and Gisèle Mathieu-Castellani (Geneva: Droz, 1985), p. 81.

27. For example, in his *Ars Amatoria* (2: 89) Ovid evokes the wax wings of Icarus that melt when exposed to the sun, "*Tabuerant* cerae" ["The wax wings had melted"]. Lucretius compares falling rain to wax melting on a fire: ". . . quasi igni cera super calido *tabescens* multa liquescat" (*De natura rerum*, 6: 516–17) ["as if a great quantity of wax were to melt on a hot fire"].

## Marc Bizer

28. See the introduction to Rémy Belleau, *Commentaire au second livre*, pp. xv–xxvi. Du Bellay was the first Pléiade poet whose works were the object of a commentary, that of Jean Proust (1549).

29. Thirty écus were given, one-third to the poet and two-thirds to the commentator. This disparity is explained by the fact that Ronsard was being paid for the few poems that he had added to this second edition. See the remarks of Mathieu-Castellani in Muret, *Commentaires au premier livre*, p. vii.

30. "On ne saurait oublier que le commentateur entend être considéré comme auteur à part entière, *auctor* augmentant en effet la production de l'éclairage que sa lecture lui confère, s'autorisant lui-même, en outre, de cette autorité qu'il apporte, par ses gloses, à l'oeuvre-objet" (Belleau, *Commentaire*, p. x) [One must not forget that the commentator expects to be considered an author in every respect, insofar as he is an *auctor* augmenting the production of illumination that his reading confers on the text, furthermore authorizing himself, with this authority that he brings, by means of his glosses, to the work-object].

31. "Cette importance de la paraphrase est, du reste, déroutante pour le lecteur moderne: elle confère au discours de Belleau une allure complètement redondante" (*Commentaire au second livre*, p. xvi) [The extent of the paraphrase is, moreover, troubling for the modern reader: it makes Belleau's discourse seem completely redundant].

32. I thank Maurice Verdier for referring me to his review article in which he rejects Fontaine's and Lecercle's hypothesis (*Commentaire au second livre*, pp. xxx–xxxi) that Ronsard's secretary, Amadis Jamyn, was responsible for the changes, showing convincingly that Belleau himself made them; *Bulletin de la Société des Amis de Montaigne*, VII[e] série, 5–6 (July–December 1986), pp. 103–06.

33. "Dès 1567 de longs développements sont supprimés—et ce sont même les principales altérations subies par le commentaire" (*Commentaire au second livre*, p. xvi).

34. Quintilian links translation, paraphrase, and imitation together in a striking passage on education from the tenth book of his *Institutiones* (X, 5, 2–5).

35. Robert Estienne, *Dictionnaire Francoislatin, AUTREMENT DICT Les mots Francois, avec les manieres d'user d'iceulx, tournez en latin* (Paris: Robert Estienne, 1549). See

223

also Robert Estienne, *Dictionarium Latinogallicum, iam indè post multas editones plurimum adauctam* (Paris: Carolus Stephanus, 1561).

36. "Les commentateurs de Ronsard, promus au rang d'interprètes compétents, se donnent pour objet de défendre et illustrer la poésie ronsardienne, d'autoriser son discours" [The objective of Ronsard's commentators, promoted to the status of competent interpreters, is to defend and illustrate Ronsard's poetry, to authorize his discourse]; see Mathieu-Castellani in Muret, *Commentaires au premier livre*, p. ix. Mathieu-Castellani adds in a note: "Loin de dévaloriser un texte, la production de ses sources est perçue comme le moyen de rendre à la poésie vulgaire son importance, mal vue du lecteur ignorant" [Far from devaluing a text, the unveiling of his sources is seen as the way to restore to vernacular poetry its importance, held in low esteem by the ignorant reader].

37. "Beaucoup de références à des auteurs anciens ou modernes sont supprimées, d'autres, plus rarement, ajoutées" (Belleau, *Commentaire au second livre*, p. xxviii) [Many references to ancient or contemporary authors are eliminated, others, more rarely, added].

38. Eckhardt, *Rémy Belleau*, 160–62.

39. Rémy Belleau, *La Bergerie* (1565), ed. Doris Delacourcelle (Geneva: Droz, 1954), p. 95.

40. Eckhardt, *Rémy Belleau*, p. 162: "La traduction, on le voit, n'est pas trop fidèle; le poète développe l'original, le quitte de temps à autre quand il se rappelle d'autres lieux communs, puis revient au poète latin" [The translation, one notes, is not too faithful; the poet develops the original, leaves it from time to time when he remembers other commonplaces, then returns to the Latin poet].

41. Ronsard did the same with "L'Arondelle" (see page 181 *supra*): its title in the 1555 edition of the *Meslanges* is "L'arondelle, à Jan Brinon, prise d'Anacreon," which thereafter becomes simply "Ode."

42. This includes the author of the present article. A. Gouverneur, the last editor of Belleau's works to include the Latin translations (*Oeuvres complètes*, 1867), was certainly of the opinion that the poems are self-translations, for he explains in a note at the bottom of the first page of the translations (t. 1, p. 159) that the original texts are all to be found

Marc Bizer

in the *Deuxième Journée de la Bergerie*: "Le texte de ces divers sonnets se trouve dans la II[e] Journée de la Bergerie (t. 2, p. 280 et suiv.)." Belleau's Latin translations finally disappeared from his complete works with the publication of Marty-Laveaux's edition in 1878.

Paul Laumonier was not fooled, however, since he includes Belleau's Latin translations in his edition of Ronsard's works (Ronsard, 7: 306–08). It was Maurice F. Verdier, whom this presentation had long ceased to mystify (if it had ever), who kindly set me on the right track. I am indebted to him for all of my remarks concerning the contents of the different editions of the *Odes d'Anacreon.*

43. Interestingly, in the different editions of the *Amours* between 1560 and 1587, the poet addresses Belleau: line 11 reads "Sinon, Belleau, leur beauté que j'honore" instead of "Sinon le beau de leur beau que j'adore" [Except, Belleau, their beauty that I honor].

44. Text and translation: *Minor Latin Poets*, trans. J. W. Duff and A. M. Duff (Cambridge: Harvard University Press, 1934, 1968), pp. 444–45. For another interpretation of this poem, where the line "Pallidula, rigida, nudula" is seen as modifying *loca* instead of *animula*, see Henry Bardon, *La Littérature latine inconnue*, 2 vols. (Paris: Klincksieck, 1952–53), 2: 233–34.

45. Text: Ovid, *The Art of Love and Other Poems,* trans. J. H. Mozley (Cambridge: Harvard University Press, 1957), p. 76.

46. Ioannes Nicolai Secundus, *Basia*, ed. Georg Ellinger, in *Literaturdenkmäler des XV. und XVI. Jahrhunderts*, ed. Max Hermann (Berlin: Weidmansche Buchhändlung, 1899), pp. 15–16.

47. Laumonier notes that, in their French poems, Ronsard paraphrases Secundus while Belleau imitates him; he does not specify, however, what he means by "imitation" and "paraphrase" (Ronsard, 2: 55).

48. See Kenneth Quinn, *The Catullan Revolution* (Melbourne: Melbourne University Press, 1959), p. 105, n. 5: "The epithet *doctus*, by the way, really meant 'possessing good taste'." In a famous line of his *Ars poetica*, Horace insisted on learning as being the condition *sine qua non* of good writing: "Scribendi recte sapere est et principium et fons" (line 309). Robert Estienne, in his *Dictionnarium Latinogallicum*, defines *doctus* as

225

# Ronsard the Poet, Belleau the Translator

"enseigné," "endoctriné"; someone who is "endoctriné" has *doctrina* (learning).

49. Robert Estienne gives as the basic meaning of *fingere* "faire quelque chose de terre a potier, La faconer & luy bailler son tour" [to make something from clay, mold it and give it its shape].

50. See the definition of Robert Estienne in his *Thesaurus Linguae Latinae*, 4 vols. (Basileae: E. & J. R. Thurnisiorum, 1740): "Componere, formare, proprie de figulo dicitur, qui vasa format ex luto. Inde generale fit vocabulum ad caetera quae ingenio, manuque hominis artificiose formantur" [To compose, to form, is properly said of a potter, who forms vases from clay. Whence it becomes a general word applied to the other things that are formed with craft by the ingenuity and hand of man].

51. *Thesaurus Linguae Latinae*: "ostendere," "patefacere." This is its meaning in a line of Ovid's *Remedia Amoris* (line 11), cited in the *Thesaurus*: "artes suas prodere." In other contexts, *prodere* suggests the handing down of a tradition and, even, writing for posterity as Robert Estienne illustrates: "prodere, absolute, pro scribere & componere, quod posteri legant, quasi Dare posteris" [*Prodere* (to deliver, to transmit), in place of to write and to compose, for posterity to read, as if to give to posterity].

52. *Dictionarium latinogallicum*: "vivacité & subtilité d'esprit," "ingeniosité" [vivacity and subtility of mind, ingenuity]. *Thesaurus*: "in omni re prudentia & industria, perspicacitas & ingeniorum acumen" [In all things prudence and industry, perspicacity and sharpness of mind].

53. Cf. the title of book 2, chapter 3: "Que le naturel n'est suffisant à celuy qui en Poësie veult faire oeuvre digne de l'immortalité" (*Deffense,* 103) [That natural talent is not sufficient for him who in Poetry wishes to compose a work worthy of immortality].

54. See Thomas Greene, "The Flexibility of the Self in Renaissance Literature," *The Disciplines of Criticism*, ed. Peter Demetz, Thomas Greene, and Lowry Nelson, Jr. (New Haven: Yale University Press, 1968), pp. 241–64.

# Fischart's Rabelais

## Florence M. Weinberg

Johann Fischart, Strassburgher, published his translation of *Gargantua* in 1575, twenty-two years after Rabelais's death. His additions to the text, by 1582 amounting to two-thirds more material, his proximity to France, and his access to much reforming religious controversy all promise profound contemporary insights into the meaning of the original. This study will investigate some of Fischart's contributions to the art of translation *per se*, and to translation as a tool to inform and reform the public. Fischart's title page, as it evolved from 1575 to 1582 and 1590, will provide an exemplary microcosm of his method. The focus of the study will then shift to his introduction, containing the *apologia* for his choice of Rabelais as a text to translate, and then it will highlight a number of selected texts where unmistakably Evangelical passages in the original, from Rabelais's *Prologue* as well as from the body of *Gargantua*, are rendered into Fischart's unique idiom. Proceeding inductively from Fischart's texts, then, this study will illustrate his understanding of his craft and our understanding of his place among the stream of reformers and humanist translators, in the continuum of medieval, Renaissance, and baroque translators.

While Luther and his generation saw translation primarily as a means to make plain to the community of readers the *only truthful* meaning of the Bible, they discovered—as an unintended by-product of the humanist determination to establish the true original text while rendering it into the vernacular—laws common to the vulgar tongues and to the three sacred idioms. These discoveries affected the way in which the vulgar tongues were conceived and, hence, written. Claims to a more-or-less "scientific" codification of the philological data the humanists discovered would, of course, wait until the nineteenth century, but many of the practical results of humanistic study of the ancient languages can be seen in a sudden leap in the subtlety and sophistication of the "vulgar" idioms during the sixteenth century. The translator considered his task as an outward and didactic one: translation is a means of improving the current written and spoken language of the community. There is no doubt that Fischart followed in Luther's footsteps: his translation was a didactic device meant to serve the public and widen its horizons, teach it new vocabulary, and bring before it new ideas, new situations. It also had pretensions at teaching morality by placing good examples before the public or, conversely, *via negativa*, showing how bad examples meet a deservedly horrible fate.

The results of Fischart's efforts in translating *Gargantua* approximate what Du Bellay recommended in *La Deffense et illustration de la langue françoise*, namely, to embellish the language by creating neologisms based on Greek, Latin, Italian, and even words adopted from dialects. Fischart took up an enormous challenge: Rabelais created hundreds, perhaps even thousands, of new words, some of which have become everyday terms, among them "progrès" and "crépuscule." In order to translate Rabelais's neologisms, Fischart, with an even more primitive idiom at his disposal, had to invent words as well, something he accomplished with great verve and talent. He adapted Rabelais's Latinate and Greek inventions; he exploited the language of the common people; he invented "portmanteau" words. The title he finally adopted for his version of *Gargantua* is just such a neologism: *Geschichtklitterung*, an ink-spattered history; messy (blotted) stories. As with Rabelais's creations, many of Fischart's have enriched the German language, and he therefore ranks with Luther as a founder of modern German.

Fischart's didactic purpose explains why he chose to translate one of the most learned of humanists whose text is among the most challenging to render into another language; it would explain his willingness to struggle with Rabelais's French neologisms and lists. It would even justify his delight in Rabelais's crudity as well as the addition of his own scatological language, since that would engage the interest of the relatively uneducated reader in need of enlightenment. Fischart thus, while addressing his peers, reached down to the lowest level in order to raise it to his own, providing plenty of belly laughs along the way.

Didacticism during the sixteenth century in Germany assumed many forms: Friedrich Dedekind and Kaspar Scheidt's *Grobianus* attempted to shock its readers into good behavior through grossly negative example. Translations of ancient texts into the vernacular became increasingly popular as the reading public vastly increased. Humanist educators saw a need to convey ancient learning in capsule form to those same readers for ready retrieval; hence the creation of dictionaries and compendia of all sorts: Valeriano Bolzanii's *Hieroglyphica* presented collected symbols of many types under the fashionable rubric of "hieroglyphics," recently popularized by Horapollo; Erasmus published his *Adages* and *Apophthegms*; and Ravisius Textor and Estienne published their dictionaries. Both Rabelais and Shakespeare took full advantage of such compendia; Fischart did likewise, for, in addition to appealing to the crude and barely literate with his scatological jokes, he also catered to the learned reader of compendia: he incorporated the crudity into his own disorderly compendium of synonyms with which he stuffed Rabelais's text. His procedure is typified in his successive "translations" of Rabelais's title page.

In 1542, four editions of Rabelais's *Gargantua* were published in Lyon. The title page of F. Juste's version reads: *La Vie treshorrificque du grand Gargantua, pere de Pantagruel . . . [The Very Horrific Life of the Great Gargantua, Father of Pantagruel . . .]*; P. de Tour's: *Grands Annales tresveritables des Gestes merveilleux du grand Gargantua et Pantagruel son filz, Roy des Dipsodes [Great and Entirely True Annals of the Marvelous Deeds of the Great Gargantua and of Pantagruel his*

Florence M. Weinberg

*Son, King of the Dipsodes*]; Etienne Dolet's version is titled: *La Plaisante et joyeuse histoyre du grand geant Gargantua, et Pantagruel son filz, Roy des Dipsodes* [*The Pleasant and Joyous History of the Great Giant Gargantua, and of Pantagruel His Son, King of the Dipsodes*]; and the *Grands Annales ou croniques Tresveritables des gestes merveilleux du grand Gargantua et Pantagruel son filz.* Later editions adopt one or another of these titles, using "Treshorrifique," "Plaisante et joyeuse," or a combination thereof. Fischart's first translation enlarges, to some extent, on the original title, but remains a "translation" in the accepted sense:

> *Affenteurlich und Ungeheurliche Geschichtschrift vom Leben/rhaten und Thaten der for langen weilen Vollenwolbeschraiten Helden und Herrn Grandgusier / Gargantoa / und Pantagruel / Königen inn Utopien und Ninenreich.* Etwan von M. Francisco Rabelais Französisch entworfen: Nun aber überschrecklich lustig auf den Teutschen Meridian visirt / und ungefärlich obenhin / wie man den Grindigen lausst / vertirt durch Huldrich Ellposcleron Reznem. Si premas erumpit: Si laxes effugit. Anno 1575.[1]

> [*Apeventurous and Monstrous History of the Life/Counsels and Deeds of the Long Ago Fully and Properly Boasted Heroes and Lords Grandgusier, Gargantoa and Pantagruel, Kings in Utopia and Nowherempire.* Designed in French at some time or other by M. Francisco Rabelais; now however metaterribly and hilariously turned towards the German meridian, and safely from above, as one delouses the lousy, turned about by Huldrich Ellposcleron Reznem. "If you squeeze it, it bursts forth; if you relax, it flees." 1575.]

Fischart displays his humanistic training in the rendering of his name. Since a mere Latin "Johannes Piscator" would be too prosaic, he translates "Johann" into the Old German version, Huldrich; his last name into Greek: *Ellopos* = fish; *scleron* (*-os*) = hard, to make up Fisch-hart.

230

## Fischart's Rabelais

Fischart's 1582 edition enlarges upon the first, beginning *Affentheur-lich Naupengeheurliche Geschichtklitterung* [Ape-venturous, Monstrously Whimsical Storyscribble], and substitutes a neologism for *Geschicht-schrift*, adding *naupengeheurlich* [whimsically-difficult], and dropping the less exotic *Ungeheurliche*. The title continues, dropping "vom Leben," adding, "vor kurtzen langen weilen" [a short long time ago]. Fischart plays also on *Kurzweil* (entertainment, fun) and *Langeweile* (boredom) to add still further connotations to the title. Fischart has thought of a series of comic place names to expand the list: *Utopien / Jederwelt und Nienenreich / Soldan der Neuen Kannarien und Oudyssen Inseln: auch Grossfürsten im Nubel Nibel Nebelland / Erbvögt auf Nichilburg / und Niderherren zu Nullibingen / Nullenstein und Niergen-heym* [Utopia / Anyworld and Nowherempire / Sultan of the New Canaries and Odyssey Islands: also Grand Princes in Newbel Mist and Fogland / Hereditary Governor of Nihilburg and Underlord of Nullilby, Nulston and Nowherehome]. His commentary on his own translation is likewise expanded. He adds:

> inn unser Mutterlallen über oder drunder gesetzt. Auch zu disem Truck wider auff den Amposs gebracht / und dermassen Panta-gruelisch verposselt / verschmidt und verdängellt / dass nichts ohn ein Eisen Nisi dran mangelt. . . . Si laxes erepit; (Zu luck entkriechts) Si premas erumpit; (Ein Truck entziechts). Im Fischen Gilts Mischen. Getruckt zur Grensing im Gänsserich, 1582.

> [more or less translated into our motherbabble. Also for this printing placed on the anvil once more, and there so Pantagruelically buffooned, smithied and hammered that nothing except the iron is missing. . . . "Hold it too loose and it slithers away; squeeze it and it bursts forth." If you fish, it's proper to mix the catch. Printed at Grensing (Bordertown?) in Ganderland, 1582.]

Florence M. Weinberg

The last edition of 1590 adds still more: the heroes are now "vor kurtzen langen unnd je weilen Vollenwol-beschreiten Helden" [A Short Long Time Ago and Any Time Fully and Properly Boasted Heroes]. "Grandgusier" has become "Grandgoschier," "Gargantoa" transformed into a more onomatopoeic "Gorgellantua"; Pantagruel has gained several adjectives: "und des des [sic] Eiteldurstlichen Durchdurstlechtigen Fürsten Pantagruel" [and the Simplethirsty, Thoroughlythirstpanting Prince Pantagruel]. The placenames have likewise been embroidered upon to add Nullatenenten, Fäumlappen, Dipsoder, Dürstling and Finster-stall [Nullhold, Foamlapland, Dipsoder, Thirstling, and Darkstable]. The comment on his translation likewise continues to evolve: "Auff den Amposs gebracht, und dermassen mit Pantadurstigen Mythologien oder Geheimnus deutung verposselt, verschmidt und verdängelt dass nichts ohn das Eisen Nisi dran mangelt" [Placed on the anvil and there buf-fooned, smithied, and hammered with such panthirsty mythologies or pleasant secrets that nothing except the iron is missing]. The remainder is left as it stands, except for the date.

Fischart's method is clear: he begins with a nearly literal translation and a minimum of his own *inventio*. With each succeeding edition, he embroiders upon his own accretions until the final version seems to have little to do with the starting point. Yet, if one examines the mood of Rabelais's original, it would appear that the accretions do not stray too far from it, but instead amplify it like musical variations on a theme. In a sense, the additions make clear what Fischart thought he saw in Rabelais; what he believed the text to say, in essence. The intended musical effects of Fischart's prose (also seen in Rabelais) could well become the focus of a study in comparative literature, although it lies beyond the scope of the present work.

Fischart translates all of *Gargantua* as literally as he can manage, but he feels no compunction at adding his own material, even in the first version. Most of the significant interpolations and additions occur in the first few chapters. As we have seen in his treatment of the title page, so also he expands the dedicatory poem, "Aux lecteurs," from ten lines to thirty-six, in which he exploits Rabelais's intertextual allusions to Aristotle, Hippocrates, and Democritus, actually creating his own poem on the same themes, rather than translating the original.

In the introduction that precedes his continued translation of Rabelais, Fischart states his purpose, makes excuses for the apparently shocking passages, and develops certain themes present in his expanded liminary poem. Instead of dedicating his introduction "Aux lecteurs," as Rabelais had done, he expands Rabelais's dedication while simultaneously imitating his model's salutation at the beginning of the Prologue ("Beuveurs très illustres, et vous, véroléz très précieux" [Most illustrious topers, and you, most precious poxy ones]): "An alle Klugkröpffige Nebelverkappte NebelNebuloner, Witzersauffte Gurgelhandthirer [in earlier editions, Gargantuisten] und ungepalirte Sinnversauerte Windmüllerische Dürstaller oder Pantagruelisten."[2] This could be roughly translated as "To all self-willed, fog-muffled, fogbound-and-nebulous ones, drownedwitted, throatmanipulating (Gargantuan) and unpolished, rusty (sour)-minded, windmillerish (windbagish) Allathirsters or Pantagruelists." After his dedication, Fischart continues with an apostrophe that insults his readers (or hearers)[3] roundly with "fond abuse" intended to provoke laughter and, hence, free them from the fog of everyday concerns.

Having thus caught the reader's attention, Fischart proceeds to teach through a Ciceronian triad of negative examples. First he portrays the practice of the ancient Spartans, who taught their children not to drink to excess by presenting to them the spectacle of disgustingly drunken servants in the public square, who "rasen, balgen, walgen, schelten, gaucheln, fallen, schallen, burzeln, schrien, gölern, prellen, wüten, sincken, hincken, speien und unflätig . . . sein" [rave, fight, pummel, scold, stagger, fall, clang, tumble, shriek, bellow, toss, rage, sink, limp, spit, and act obscenely], in a list that grew with every successive edition and that is very reminiscent of Rabelais's technique, for example, in describing Diogenes's treatment of his tub in the Prologue to the *Tiers Livre*.[4] Fischart's second negative example describes how a prince once prevented a ridiculous fashion in men's clothing from becoming popular by dressing the hangman in them and posting him on the heavily used castle bridge. In the third example, parents who wish to prove to their children that crime does not pay take them to hear the last speech of those about to be hanged. Like both ancients and moderns who have taught good behavior through comic example, he will show "ein verwirrtes ungestaltes Muster der heut verwirrten ungestalten Welt" [a confused and formless model of today's confused and formless world] that will lead away from folly. Is he in danger of being considered as dirty as the world he describes? Fischart continues more graphically: is a mirror dirtied by what it reflects?[5] The dirty or "dark" mirror image at once recalls St. Paul's line from 1 Corinthians 13: 12: "For now we see as in a mirror, darkly, but then face to face." That Fischart does not in any way develop the allusion seems typical of a new sensitivity among non-Catholic authors and translators: they refuse to mix the sacred and the profane. This tendency will be illustrated later, in Fischart's renderings of Rabelais's more evangelical passages.

There follows a plethora of *exempla*, then a list of authors, both ancient and modern, who are considered wise despite their sometimes shocking presentation. All nations have some sort of carnival, where "fools" are given license and freedom to satirize the "wise." Rabelais was just such a fool, who, although no saint, was also no "Gottloser Atheos unnd Epicurer" [Godless atheist and Epicurean].[6] He was a physician respected by kings and humanist poets and, most of all, by Marguerite de Navarre. Francis I's sister apparently remains an authority to Fischart, who undoubtedly knew that she had provided a refuge in Pau and Nérac for reformers who were threatened by persecution from the

## Fischart's Rabelais

Sorbonne or, after the Affaire des Placards, by her own brother. Among the refugees were Jean Calvin and Clément Marot. Fischart inserts his translation of Ronsard's "Epitaphe de François Rabelais," which first appeared in 1554, as part of his praise of Rabelais. Again following the pattern established already on the title page, Fischart retains the tenor of Ronsard's ode but adds new material and embroiders on existing themes. In Ronsard's original, Rabelais appears as a hopeless alcoholic, swilling wine as a pig does milk and tumbling drunkenly among the slops and tankards on the tavern floor:

> La fosse de sa grande gueule
> Eust plus beu de vin toute seule
> (L'epuisant du nez en deus cous)
> Qu'un porc ne hume de lait doux,
> . . . . . . . . . . . . . . .
> Car alteré, sans nul sejour
> Le gallant boivoit nuit & jour
> . . . . . . . . . . . . .
> Et se couchoit tout plat à bas
> Sur la jonchée, entre les taces:
> Et parmi des escuelles grasses
> Sans nulle honte se touillant,
> Alloit dans le vin barbouillant
> Comme une grenouille en sa fange:
> Puis ivre chantoit la louange
> De son ami le bon Bacus. (lines 9–31)[7]

> [The pit of his great gullet
> Could have drunk more wine all alone
> (Emptying it in two tosses of the nose)
> Than a hog can swill of sweet milk,
> . . . . . . . . . . . . . . .
> For, athirst without pause
> The gallant drank day and night
> . . . . . . . . . . . . . . .

And he lay flat out, low down
On the floor, among the cups:
And among the greasy platters,
tumbling without shame;
He went splashing in the spilled wine
Like a frog in its mud
Then drunkenly sang the praises
of his friend the good Bacchus.]

Since sixteenth-century readers readily made the connection between wine and *spirit(s)* (as English, German, and French speakers still do), it appears clear that this "vilification" of the eminent doctor, whose life, we believe, was a relatively moderate and sober one, refers to the life of the spirit. Whether Ronsard meant poetic inspiration or wisdom remains moot. Fischart, at any rate, understood both, since he uses Ronsard's poem as one more exemplum to show that wise poets can write apparently shocking material without themselves being soiled, and that carnivalesque fools are necessary to call conventional "wisdom" into question. Fischart's interpolations underscore this reading. Rabelais's poetic "wine" comes from all available sources:

Er trank Jüdischen Wein allein
Der nicht getauffet was,
Und den Lateinischen Wetzstein,
den mitteln auss dem Fass. (lines 29–32)

[He drank Jewish wine alone
That was unbaptised
And Latin Wetzstein,
From the middle of the barrel.]

He drank neither scum nor dregs, which, for Rabelais, would be scholastic commentaries on original sources, but, instead, undiluted Jewish wine

## Fischart's Rabelais

("nicht getauffet" can mean not watered as well as unbaptized) and Roman Wetzstein, a highly prized wine from the island of Cos. He drinks the *middle* of the barrel, in other words, the essence untainted by the wood or by the ladles of previous topers. His inspiration here comes from ancient Jewish and ancient Greek wisdom—the sources of humanistic Bible study and humanistic learning. In addition, Fischart knows the rather obscure fact that Cos was not only the native island of Hippocrates but also the home of a cult dedicated to Aesclepius and, thus, the source of all medical lore. In this way, Fischart pays tribute to Rabelais the physician.

Fischart's closing lines constitute an important addition to the original poem. He tells the reader that, since wine is a preservative, Rabelais's body cannot decay and, since the spirit is immortal, his renown (*Nam*) lives on as well. Wine (spirit) was his baptismal liquid (*Weih*) and his embalming agent (*Balsam*), a source of eternal life and/or health both for him and for those who visit his grave (read his book). The balsam still appears (or glows) here, Fischart tells us; its healing power is still effective, so much so that the visitor—the reader—will become intoxicated (inspired) by the fumes arising from the "grave." Fischart ends his interpolation by inviting the reader to "do right by" Rabelais and offer him spirit for spirit, perhaps signifying that, in turn, the reader should become inspired, create something, and dedicate it to Rabelais along with a "gsaltzen Ränfftlin Brot," a salty crust that would insure that further drinking (imbibing the spirit) would continue to inspire works that would, in turn, inspire "topers" in an eternal chain of cause and effect. Rabelais would prefer this, Fischart tells the reader, rather than prayer, since that belongs to God. Fischart correctly reflects Rabelais's dislike of hagiography, which he, like the Protestants who followed him, viewed as a sort of idolatry or polytheism. Fischart has obviously understood and exploited Rabelais's (and Ronsard's) play with the connotations of the wine. His poem remains entirely on a secular level, however. Nothing that he refers to need carry any connotation other than that the wine can inspire literary creativity, or greater understanding by the reader. Already, in the preliminary material, Fischart is setting a pattern that will be seen in the body of *Gargantua*: he eliminates any hint of an evangelical message.

Fischart's prose continues, relating Rabelais to Hippocrates, who taught, in the sixth book of *Epidemics*, that a doctor should heal the body through medicine, the spirit through laughter, since many ills come to the body through the mind. Fischart's examples multiply with his editions: he comments on joyful and, therefore, healthful activities other than reading, such as sex and music. He ends with a comment on his translation:

> Derwegen da man jn je wolt Teutsch haben, hab ich jhn eben so mehr inn Teutsch wellen verkleiden alss dass ich einen ungeschickteren Schneider müst druber leiden: Doch bin ich an die Wort und Ordnung ungebunden gewesen: unnd mich benügt, wann ich den verstand erfolget: auch hab ich jhn etwan, wann er auss der Küheweyd gangen, castriert, und billich vertiert, das ist, umbgewand. (pp. 19–20)

> [Because the reader has always wanted him (Rabelais) in German, I have all the more desired to reclothe him in German rather than allow him to suffer from a less skilled tailor (hack): However, I have not been bound by the word and the order, but have been satisfied to follow the meaning: also I have occasionally, when he wandered outside the cow-path, castrated him, and fairly reversed him, that is, turned him around.]

Fischart appears to recognize that German "clothing" might fit Rabelais rather poorly; in any case, he modestly calls himself a (relatively) unskilled tailor, who labors painfully over the task of changing one suit of clothes for another. The metaphor implies that the essence, the man within the clothing, will remain the same, while only the outer covering will be altered, more or less skillfully. Fischart does not recognize initially that a change in language will change anything in depth in Rabelais's text. However, he acknowledges that he has not kept strictly to the letter and the order of the original, being satisfied to follow the "verstand," the message. At this point, Fischart adds a remark that shocks the modern reader: when Rabelais wanders too far off the cow-path, Fischart castrates him, "und billich vertiert," that is, "fairly and equitably" turns him around. *Vertieren*, a Latinate word, is elsewhere used simply to signify "translate." Here, however, it takes on multiple meaning. As a composite of *Tier* and *ver-*, it would mean "to bestialize"; literally, as a derivative of Latin, it would mean "to turn (around)," as Fischart then repeats. Fischart is doubtlessly led by association with "cow-path" to think of the bestial connotations of the word, although these reflect upon his handling of Rabelais in a negative way that he may not have foreseen. It appears, rather, that Fischart is reassuring the "conservative side" of the community—in particular, the rabidly Lutheran wing—that he is trying to entertain and enlighten through this offering, that he has not translated anything too far from good taste (off the beaten track). The unintentional irony of his statement is that, for the purist, his interpolations as well as his omissions do "bestialize and castrate" the original.

Fischart now turns to Rabelais's own Prologue, which he entitles "Ein und Vorritt," with his usual flair for puns. *Vorwort* [Foreword] is here combined with *vorreiten*, "to ride or strut before, to teach how to ride"; *einreiten* is of course implied also, "to ride into, to train (i.e., 'break') a horse, to accustom to." Fischart is "launching into" his rendition of *Gargantua*, strutting his stuff, teaching, and accustoming the reader to the Rabelaisian/Fischartian style.[8]

Once one disentangles the two initial pages, one discovers that

Florence M. Weinberg

Fischart did, indeed, translate the first few lines of Rabelais's Prologue. Fischart's version shows innovation, even where he is translating closely—and he does add a good deal more material. He makes a minor error due to his ignorance of a scribal abbreviation, but his ingenious innovation is typified in his addition to Alcibiades's comparison. According to Rabelais, Alcibiades, in the *Symposium*, compared Socrates to Silenus, ugly and ridiculous on the outside but filled with divine wisdom. Fischart adds "Silenis oder Seullänen." His neologism *Seullänen* combines *Saue* and *Seule* ("pillar" or "little sows") with *Lehne* ("support/ prop" or "wild sow"); "-änen" also recalls "ähnlich," similar, as well as an allusion, to *ahnen*, to have forbodings or to intuit. *Der Ahn* is also the forbear. Hence, in one "portmanteau" word he tells us that our forbear, the intuitive Socrates, was like a Silenus or (like) little sows, like a sow-prop, like a prop-sow, like little sows + a wild sow, like a pillar and a support.

Rabelais compares Socrates not only to Silenus but also to the small, hollow, statuettes of the god that he understands to be boxes. He describes these Sileni briefly:

> Silenes estoyent jadis petites boites, telles que voyons de present es bouticques des apothecaires, pinctes au dessus de figures joyeuses et frivoles, comme de harpies, satyres, oysons bridez, lievres cornuz, canes bastées, boucqs volans, cerfz limonniers et aultres telles pinctures contrefaictes à plaisir pour exciter le monde à rire (quel fut Silene, maistre du bon Bacchus); mais au dedans l'on reservoit les fines drogues comme baulme, ambre gris, amomon, musc, zivette, pierreries et aultres choses precieuses. Tel disoit estre Socrates. (pp. 9–10)

> [Sileni were once little boxes, such as you now see them in apothecary shops, painted outside with joyous and frivolous figures, like harpies, satyrs, bridled geese, horned rabbits, saddled dogs, flying goats, harnessed stags and other such paintings made up at will to cause everyone to laugh (such was Silenus, good Bacchus' master);

240

# Fischart's Rabelais

but inside were preserved fine drugs like balm, ambergris, car-
damum, musk, civet, jewels and other precious items. Just so, he
said, was Socrates.]

Fischart's description continues for three lengthy paragraphs that become
longer with each successive edition, ending as approximately sixty-nine
lines. Fischart's additions depart radically from Rabelais's mood and
allow him to introduce anti-Catholic propaganda that is simultaneously
self-advertisement:

> Sileni, solt jr mich verstehn, waren etwann die wundergestalte
> Grillische, Grubengrotteschische, fantästische krüg läden, büchsen
> und häfen, wie wir sie heut in den Apotecken stehen sehen, von
> aussen bemalet mit lächerlichen, gecklichen, ja offt erschrecklichen
> Häw unnd Grasteuffeln, wie sie auss Pandore büchs fligen, unnd der
> *Grillen* Römischen Mül stiben, gesellen die im hafen schlecken, und
> haben die Kertz im hindern stecken, wie sie Dantes inn der
> fegfeurigen Höllen beschreibet, Jott unnd Michelangel im Jungsten
> gericht malen, Olaische Mittnächtige Meerwunder, wie sie einem zu
> mitternacht inn der Fronfasten, wann man zu vil Bonen isst . . .
> fürkommen. (pp. 22–23)

> [Sileni, understand me well, were once upon a time the wonderfully
> shaped, cricketish, gravecryptic, fantastic jars, chests, boxes, and pots
> like those we see today standing in apothecary shops, painted outside
> with laughable, grotesque, yes, often frightening hay and grasshop-
> pers, like the ones that flew out of Pandora's box and that scattered
> from the Roman *Cricket* Mill, creatures that slink into pots, and that
> have candles stuck in their backsides, as Dante describes them in his
> Purgatorish Hell, as Giotto and Michelangelo paint them in the Last
> Judgment, oily sea monsters of the dark of night, as they appear at
> midnight, during Lent, when one has eaten too many beans.]

Florence M. Weinberg

Fischart frequently seizes the opportunity to point to himself, drawing attention to his cleverness as narrator/translator. Only on rare occasions does Rabelais distract the reader from the text; he keeps himself at a tactful distance. Fischart's reference to the horrors from Pandora's box, including grasshoppers (literally, grass devils) that also fly copiously from the "Roman Cricket Mill," recalls his own invective-filled pamphlets, one of which is mentioned by name among other freakish apparitions, "der Gorgonisch Römisch Medusenkopff" [The Gorgonic Roman Medusahead]. Fischart indulges here in gratuitous vilification of Roman Catholicism, which he identifies with the mythic origin of all evil, Pandora's box. He has taken a long step further than Rabelais, whose passage is free of any intent to criticize. Even where Rabelais does criticize, as in the monks' failed defense of the abbey close against Pichrochole's hordes, his criticisms of the Church are still moderate and still aimed at a purgation of ills from within.

Fischart's imagination is stimulated by Rabelais's list of grotesques; for his very partisan mind, the most grotesque of all is "Roman." This horror leads him to other nightmares, those painted by "Roman" artists Giotto and Michelangelo, not to mention Hieronymus Bosch and Matthias Gruenewald, whose great Isenheimer Altar painting of the Temptation of St. Anthony he might have seen in the immediate neighborhood of Strassburg. These are the nightmares one might have after eating too many beans: Ovidian monstrosities and wine-guzzling Grillos—here Fischart associates *Grillen* (Grille means a cricket, whim, fancy, or caprice) with Odysseus's sailor, Grillo, who, having been transformed into a pig by Circe, chose to remain in porcine shape. After his lengthy interpolation, Fischart, as it were, heaves a satisfied sigh, "Ecce, das sint die Rechte Sulenen und Lenseulen und Eselen darauff Silenus reutet" [Behold, these are the proper sowprops and propsows and asses on which Silenus rides]. Here, Fischart takes up again his play with *Silenus*, with its connotation of sow (Su), prop or sow (Lehne), as well as little sow (Seule). In 1582 he adds the end of the line "und Eselen

242

darauff Silenus reutet." In a near-anagram, he transforms the sows into traditional Silenic donkeys (Sulene-Eselen), substituting for the normal spelling of "reiten," "reuten," an alternative that also means "to root," thus carrying forward the piggish theme of the entire development.

Whereas Fischart is quick to interpolate anti-Catholic gibes, he suppresses Rabelais's reference to spiritual matters. The original text recommends that the reader pay close attention to Rabelais's book, like the man opening a bottle of wine or the dog cracking the marrow bone. The translation remains fairly close to Rabelais, though there is a significant difference at the crucial passage. Rabelais recommends:

> Puis, par curieuse leczon et meditation frequente, rompre l'os et sugcer la sustantificque mouelle—c'est à dire, ce que j'entends par ces symboles Pythagoricques—avecques espoir certain d'estre faictz escors et preux à ladicte lecture. Car en icelle bien aultre goust trouverez et doctrine plus absconce, que vous revelera de tresaultz sacremens et mysteres horrificques, tant en ce que concerne nostre religion que aussi l'estat politicq et vie oeconomicque. (p. 14)

> [Then, by studious reading and frequent meditation, break the bone and suck out the essential marrow—that is to say, what I understand by these Pythagorean symbols—with the certain hope of becoming both wiser and more courageous through the said reading. For in it you will find quite another flavor and a more recondite doctrine, that will reveal to you very high sacraments and horrific mysteries, both concerning our religion as well as our public and private life.]

Fischart translates:

> Derwegen ersprecht das beyn fleissig durch genaw sorgfeltiges lesen, unnd stätem unauffhörlichem nachsinnen, und sauget darauss dz substantzialisch wesenlich Marck. . . . Schlappert nit auff chorherrisch die Wort in euch, wie der Hund die Sup, sonder kauet und widerkauet sie wie die Küh, distilliert sie durch neun balcken, so

243

## Florence M. Weinberg

findet jr die Bon, das ist, findet was ich durch diese Pitagorische
unsimpele simbolen, unnd geheime losungen gesuchet hab: inn
gewisser hoffnung dadurch euch gantz trucken auss dem bad
aussgezwangen und abgeriben heimzuffertigen. (p. 29)

[Therefore address the bone diligently through careful enough
reading, and continuous and incessant contemplation, and suck there-
from the substantial, essential marrow. . . . Do not rattle off the
words church-choirishly as dogs lap up soup, but chew and re-chew
them like cows, distill them through nine beams and thus find the
bean, that is, find what I have sought (to convey) through these
Pythagorean unsimple symbols and secret magic formulae, in the
certain hope that through them you will pluck yourselves quite dry
out of the bath, and, well towelled, will get yourselves home.]

The reader is exhorted to read carefully and contemplate deeply; Fischart
brings in another animal besides the dog—one not normally connected
with deep thinking—as a metaphor for long deliberation: the cud-
chewing cow. Besides the cow, he introduces the metaphor of distillery;
we are to distill his message (distantly echoing Rabelais's) through nine
beams in order to find the "bean," what he meant by the "Pythagorean
unsimple symbols." He hopes that thereby we can pluck ourselves from
the bath, dry off, rub ourselves vigorously, and wend our way home.
There is no mention of religion, high sacraments, and horrific mysteries.

Fischart enlarges Rabelais's assertion that he "merely" wrote his
book while eating and drinking, and he expands the exclamation,
"L'Odeur du vin, ô combien plus est friant, riant, priant, plus céleste et
délicieux que d'huile" [The odor of wine, O how much more inviting,
laughing, praying, more celestial and delicious than that of oil!] to three
pages in which he accumulates examples of poets who drank heavily and
who yet (or perhaps consequently) are considered great artists, as opposed to those who drink water or smell of the oil of study lamps, who
are trivial. Caspar Scheidt figures among the modern positive examples,
who invokes Bacchus:

## Fischart's Rabelais

Ich muss mich vor eyn wenig kröpffen, Dass ich ein guten Trunck
mög schöpffen: Hör Bache mit dem grossen Bauch, Lang mir dorther
den vollen schlauch, Eyn gute Pratwurst auss dem sack, Dass mir ein
Küler trunck darauff schmack. . . . Hehem, das heist eyn guter
tranck, Jetz bin ich gsund, vor war ich kranck. (pp. 30–31)

[I must stuff myself a little, so I can raise a good thirst: Hear, O
Bacchus with the great belly, pass over to me the full (wine) skin,
a good bratwurst out of the sack, so that a cool drink will taste the
better afterwards. . . . Ahem! That's what I call a good swig! Now
I am well; before, I was sick.]

Here are no metaphorical second intentions, no veiled allusions to possibly heavenly or spiritual inspiration, but instead the hearty atmosphere
of a sixteenth-century Weinstube; an appetizing allusion to Bratwurst and
cool wine.

As Fischart proceeds to identify healthy poets with wine-bibbers, he
comes across a promising set of puns, which he manipulates with genius,
deriving poet from *potus, potae*: "Will ich sie lassen die bodenloss
Göttin Potinam walten, sintemal Poeten von *Potus, Potae, il boit*, and
Pott kommet." The English speaker must bear in mind that in Allemanic
dialect there is hardly any distinction in pronunciation between *p* and *b*;
hence "il boit" would have been pronounced approximately "il poët."
Fischart continues the development later:

O ihr Polulente Poeten, potirt der pott und bütten, unnd potionirt
euch potantlich mit potitioniren, compotiren unnd expotiren, dann
potiren und appotiren kompt von petiren und appetiren, unnd pringt
potate poesei, dieweil potantes sint potentes. Unnd Potentaten sint
Potantes. (pp. 31–32)

In a mere two sentences, Fischart connects all the Latin words he can
recall that have to do with drinking and contain the root "pot," with

245

Florence M. Weinberg

Allemanic and French words of the same category: "I will let the bottomless goddess Potina [the Roman goddess who presided over children's drinking] rule them, since *poet* comes from *potus, potae, il boit* and *pot*," and "O you drinking poets, quaff the pot and vats and pledge yourselves draughtily with repeated tippling, symposia and quaffings, because drinking and intoxication come from seeking and appetite, and produce potable poetry, since drinkers are potent, and potentates are topers."[9] He promises the readers good entertainment from *Rabiles res Mirabiles* and concludes this enlargement of Rabelais's prologue by the words: "*Subscripsit.* Inn Freuden Gedenck Mein" ["joyfully think of me," or "think of me when you are joyful"]. The initials IFGM are, of course, those of Iohann Fischart Genannt Mentzer.

A few further selections from *Gargantua* should suffice to establish a pattern to illustrate Fischart's treatment of Rabelaisian passages that have a spiritual reference, or a downright religious message.

One of the most memorable of the explicitly religious passages occurs shortly after the Pichrocoline War begins. Grandgousier is informed of his neighbor's aggression, and he laments at length:

"Holos! holos! (dist Grandgousier), qu'est cecy, bonnes gens? . . . Picrochole, mon amy ancien . . . me vient il assaillir? . . . Ho! ho! ho! ho! ho! Mon Dieu, mon Saulveur, ayde moy, inspire moy conseille moy à ce qu'est de faire! . . . Qu'il me ayt doncques en ce poinct oultraigé, ce ne peut estre que par l'esprit maling. Bon Dieu, tu congnoys mon couraige. . . . Si par cas il estoyt devenu furieux . . . donne moy et pouvoir et sçavoir le rendre au jouc de ton sainct vouloir par bonne discipline." (pp. 177–78)

["Alas! alas!" cried Grandousier, "What is this, good people? . . . Picrochole, my life-long friend . . . is he coming to attack me? . . . Oh! oh! oh! oh! oh! my God, my Savior, help me, inspire me, counsel me in what must be done! . . . That he has thus outraged me to such a point can only come through the Evil Spirit. Good God, thou knowest my heart. . . . If perhaps he has become mad . . . give me the strength and wisdom to return him to the yoke of thy holy will by good discipline."]

Fischart translates:

Och, och, wie geschicht mir? . . . Soll Picrochol mein alter Freund . . . mich also feindlich besuchen? . . . Ho, ho, ho, ho, Mein Got helf mir . . . es muss vom bösen Geist herkommen dass er mich also betrübet. O du liebe Billigkeit, kenst mein hertz; wie wann er vieleicht wer unsinnig worden und er mir jetzund darumb in die hand gerhit, auff dass ich ihn wider zu recht prechte? (p. 306, lines 12–16)

[Alas, alas, what is happening to me? What is this, good (pious) people? . . . Shall Picrochol, my old friend . . . attack me like an enemy? . . . Oh, oh, oh, oh, my God, help me . . . it must be from the Evil Spirit that he grieves me thus. O thou beloved Justice, thou knowest my heart; perhaps he has become mad, and now therefore has fallen into my hands, so that I could bring him back to rights?]

Fischart fails to translate "Mon Saulveur, . . . inspire moy . . . à ce qu'est de faire" [My Savior, . . . inspire me . . . in what must be done!] and he substitutes "O thou beloved Justice" for "Bon Dieu." For "give me the strength and wisdom to return him to the yoke of thy holy will by good discipline" he substitutes "[he] has fallen into my hands, so that I could bring him back to rights." A certain religious tone remains in Fischart's version, but all references to Christ (the Savior) are dropped, and mentions of God by name are cut back to one.

In Grandgousier's letter to his son, in which the father calls the son to help in this time of emergency, Picrochole's state of mind and soul are described: "J'ay congneu que Dieu éternel l'a laissé au gouvernail de son franc arbitre et propre sens, qui ne peult estre que meschant sy par grâce divine n'est continuellement guydé" (p. 181) ["I know that the eternal God had left him to the rudder of his own free will and intelligence, which can only be evil if it is not continually guided by divine grace"]. Fischart's version turns the original letter, an urgent and eloquent plea for Gargantua's help, into a parody of inflated bureaucratic prose. His translation of the above passage runs: "Perhaps, in order to punish him, God has tightened his rein so that we, irritated by his outrage, can drive him in according to his just desert, punish him and bring him before the bar."[10] Fischart, alert to the hornet's nests of controversy that could be stirred up by the mention of free will and divine grace, drops the references altogether (although he does mention God), and exchanges rudder for rein, moral for civil law.

When Grandgousier's ambassador to Picrochole, Ulrich Gallet, returns after failing to make peace with the aggressive neighbor, he finds the old giant "on his knees, bareheaded, bowed down in a little nook of his study, praying to God that he deign to moderate Picrochole's fury and bring him to reason, without proceeding against him by force" (p. 187). Fischart omits the entire passage. Gallet gives his judgment about Picrochole: "There is no order in him; the man is completely out of his mind and forsaken by God" (p. 187). Here Fischart substitutes: "The poor man needs St. Lienhart with the big chains and the Angel Michael with Lucifer's heavy shackles" (p. 319, lines 24–26). The evangelical original is either omitted or, in this passage, distorted by what Rabelais would consider saint-worship, something that both he and Erasmus condemned.

Evidence of a sea change in religious attitudes accumulates with every passage dealing with faith and pious practices. Gargantua's new humanist education stresses Bible study and individual prayer, since Rabelais attempts to correct the Church's monopoly on prayer, its fossilized rituals, its refusal to allow the faithful to read and interpret the Bible for itself. Accordingly, Gargantua hears a biblical passage read to him as he is being rubbed down in the morning. Afterwards, "Selon le propos et argument de ceste leczon souventesfoys se adonnoit à reverer,

248

adorer, prier et supplier le bon Dieu, duquel la lecture monstroit la majesté et jugements merveilleux" (p. 145) [According to the subject matter and the argument of this lesson, he often set himself to venerate, adore, pray to, and supplicate the bountiful God, whose majesty and marvellous judgments were shown by the reading]. Fischart translates: "And according to the content of such a lesson, he set himself to calling upon and supplicating God, since such reading produces mighty right and zealous prayers, like those we see in the Venetian Mary-Psalter."[11] Fischart here violates the original text, since Rabelais never mentions the Virgin Mary, except when she is invoked by characters who are emphatically not to be imitated (like Panurge during the Storm at Sea in the *Quart Livre*).

Fischart's treatment of Frère Jean is a mixture of forced acquiescence to a heroic character in the work he is translating and violent distaste that expresses itself in mini-diatribes against monks and Catholic practices in general. A single example should suffice to illustrate. After Jean/Jan has successfully defended the abbey-close from the invading hordes, Fischart adds a paragraph in ironic—even sarcastic—praise of the hero:

> Hei der solt Abt zu Fulda werden, der könt mit den Bischofflichen von Hildesheim auff dem Tag umb die session herumb huddeln: Ja er solt Bischoff zu Cölln werden, der köndt den Grafen von Bergen inn ein Eisenkorb setzen, und ihn zur Sommerzeit mit Honig beschmiren dass ihn die Mucken zu tod stechen. Also muss man das Geistlich gut schützen. (p. 304, lines 17–25)

> [Hey, he should become abbot of Fulda; he could bungle around the Session with the Bishops and the Hildesheim Congress. Indeed, he should become Bishop of Cologne, he could set the count of Bergen in an iron basket, and in summertime smear him with honey so the gnats can bite him to death. This is how spiritual matters must be well protected.]

Fischart refers to three Roman Catholic strongholds: the prosperous abbey of Fulda in Hesse-Nassau, to Hildesheim, and Cologne. Bishops in session do not preside, it would seem, they "herumb huddeln"—botch or bungle around. Jan's greatest achievement as Bishop of Cologne would be to torture to death a Zwingliite count, by hanging him in a cage from the church tower (a torture practiced elsewhere at the time as well, e.g., in Konstanz). Fischart has forgotten, for the moment, that he is speaking of one who is a defender of the faith and who, for Rabelais, symbolizes the simple, rough-and-ready nature of early (primitive) Christianity. His Lutheran loathing of all that is redolent of monkery leads him to attack his own hero, with the result that the character, as he presents him, is woefully incoherent.

Fischart also cannot find it in his heart to admire Thélème, still reeking to him of monasticism. He omits much of the description of the clothing of the inhabitants, hastening over and even mistranslating some passages that describe the architecture. In 1582, he contributes a poem on the library of Thélème that repeats commonplaces on books as preservers of culture and the arts, explaining how to treat books (not to read them with greasy fingers after eating, nor to wet the fingers with saliva while turning pages, for example).

One passage dealing with religious practices wins Fischart's unconditional approval and is translated at length, with interpolations that enhance the original rather than undercutting it: chapter 43 censures pilgrimages as well as the superstitious belief that saints who are associated with curing certain diseases also cause them. Fischart allows the chapter to stand "unedited," probably because Luther condemned pilgrimages in many of his statements.[12]

As most of Fischart's critics have noted, the author mainly contributes semantic word-play to Rabelais's text. He is far less daring than his model in his promises: Fischart never claims that he is delivering divine wisdom; he merely intends to wash his readers clean. He tones down all of Rabelais's references to sacred matters, clearly indicating his place on the Lutheran side by his repeated attacks on Roman Catholicism and by his choice of biblical allusions to the Old Testament.

Some of the most important expansions appear to be those exploiting the connection of wine with spirit. Rabelais's allusions to spirit, in my opinion, imply both wisdom and divine guidance by the *holy* spirit. Fischart undoubtedly understood Rabelais's ambiguities, but he typically limits the allusions to one type of spirit; poetic inspiration. The *Weinrausch, furor* or ecstasy, hence, has little to do with whisperings of divine wisdom, but more to do with whisperings to Fischart by the Muse of promising word-plays.

Translations made in the Renaissance seem to fall into two categories: "sacred" texts and "other." Sacred texts, of course, included the Bible, to be translated with perfect accuracy: "not a jot nor a tittle" is to be added or subtracted. Almost as sacred to the humanist scholars were the texts of Classical Antiquity, also to be rendered as precisely as possible. The most rigid of these early philologists and textual exegetes were the Calvinists at Geneva and their disciples, who worked almost exclusively on the Bible. The second category of translations, "other," included all sorts of secular texts written by contemporaries for the entertainment of the reader, such as poetry, chapbooks, and other works of fiction, such as the books of Pantagruel. Fischart provides evidence that there was as yet no sense of such authors' "rights" to the text they had created as "personal property," but that the translator could re-mold the original in any way, except that he was bound (more or less) to retain the essential meaning (*Verstand*). At the same time, these profane, "other," texts were not deemed worthy to contain sacred passages, since the sacred and profane must not be mixed. This distinction began to be observed by reformers after Rabelais, and it may well be a mark of the evolving Protestant consciousness, in which the messages of the Old Testament, such as the Ten Commandments, play an important role. For instance, the prohibition "Thou shalt not take the name of the Lord thy God in vain" was probably understood to apply not only to oaths, but also to "vain" contexts such as popular literature. Traditionally, Roman Catholics had never seen anything wrong with mingling sacred and profane things (since the world is full of such mixtures), and this attitude is shown in the obscene texts of early sixteenth-century Franciscan sermons.[13] Fischart "cleans up" Rabelais by omitting the religious references—proving that he believes that Rabelais has a religious message, one that is too sacred to be allowed to remain in a comical, bawdy, farcical context.

The second great translator of Rabelais, Sir Thomas Urquhart, published the first two books of *Pantagruel* exactly one hundred years after Rabelais's death. With him, the copious interpolations disappear: he did his conscientious best to render Rabelais word-for-word. His desire for precision sometimes led him astray. He relied heavily on Cotgrave's *Dictionary*, and—for the sake of accuracy—he sometimes used Cotgrave's commentaries for equivalents (such as "the reddish-long-billed-stork-like-scrank-legged-sea-fowles" for *flamans*). Urquhart's choice of vocabulary occasionally reflects his Scots origins (e.g., dounby, the doup of an egg, bannock, and Laird); he sometimes failed to resist the temptation to add to Rabelais's exuberant lists. According to a recent study, Urquhart also carefully read Fischart himself and sometimes preferred Fischart's accretions to the original text, although the passages or translations from Fischart are never long enough to disturb the flow of the Rabelaisian narrative.[14] However, Urquhart, in contrast to Fischart, presented a sober, faithful, and modest rendition of the original. One might theorize that the late eighteenth-century idea of translation, which continues to the present day, might have its origins in early biblical translation and exegesis and in humanist translation of the classics. The original, even though it be mere "entertainment," was viewed as a kind of sacred text, not to be tampered with; it should be rendered so closely into the target language that sometimes the result is like a "half-way house" between source and target languages. In contrast, Fischart shows a good deal of healthy egotism in his handling of Rabelais. While he believes in Rabelais's genius, and gives evidence that he greatly admires the French author (as the pun *Rabiles res Mirabiles* would indicate), he also feels no compunction at dropping passages that he thinks lead outside the "cow-path" of a text safe for his readership and for himself: he takes no risk of being persecuted, not even "jusques au feu exclusivement" [up to, but not including, the pyre] by the rabidly Lutheran clergy of Strassburg. Conversely, he joyfully stuffs the Rabelaisian original as full as a sausage skin with his own additions: lists, anecdotes, and exempla drawn from Antiquity, as well as his sometimes ingenious verbal games.

In his display of humanism, he outdoes Rabelais in sheer *copia*, redundancies which were very much to the taste of the period and through which a humanist could display his learning. In Fischart's case, such exercises as his variations on *poto* actually smell of the oil of the scholar's study lamp. Ironically, they remind us of Fischart's category of trivial poets; they are redolent of copy-book exercises done in the Gymnasium under Johannes Sturm's discipline.

Fischart's is a baroque procedure, a constant *Häufung*, a heaping up of *ornatus* continued from one edition to another (although additions in the last edition are minimal). It is tempting to say that Fischart exemplifies the evolution of a late Renaissance to a Baroque translator, but the thought that other, later, translators were less daring, exuberant, and high-handed with the author's work gives us pause. Fischart *appropriates* the original text and makes it his own. If one examines Rabelais, supposedly an early Renaissance figure, in the light of recent definitions of the Baroque, one sees that he, too, fit the definition well, since he covered the vast distance between religious sentiment and crassest physicality, between beauty and the grotesque, egocentricity and the impersonal or universal, the momentary and the eternal.[15] Fischart,

253

temperamentally and temporally suited to deal with these same concerns, takes up Rabelais and carries his "baroque" tendencies to the impossible extreme. Because he does "take over" the text, his translation typifies many original baroque works: it is intricate, ingenious, and, above all, provides limitless *Häufung* and *inventio*.

Fischart, a master punster and wordspinner himself, was attracted to Rabelais by his word-plays. In Rabelais, there is no experimentation with nonsense syllables like Lewis Caroll's "'Twas brillig and the slithy toves . . ."; every word counts. Except in the lawsuit between Baisecul and Humevesne, meant to confound the reader just as the lawyers and judges were confounded, and in the *Fanfreluches antidotés* at the beginning of *Gargantua*, a deliberate riddle (although meant to convey meaning to certain initiates), there are few if any words or passages in Rabelais that do not communicate, however ambiguously.[16] The joy of word creation for a Renaissance man was the joy of combining real, pre-existing word parts (drawn from foreign languages, frequently) to form a new whole that conveyed an immediate meaning. Fischart follows Rabelais's lead. His *copia* remains meaningful on the most literal level. His translation fascinates in that very many of his neologisms have two, three, four, or more further resonances, all of which enhance his meaning and further the comic atmosphere. Fischart would be virtually untranslatable back into any other language, not because he writes nonsense, but because each pun has too many connotations.

Fischart does not, in fact, provide the hoped-for insights into Rabelais's deep meanings as understood by his contemporaries. Rather, he demonstrates by his omissions that he was aware of the older author's religious opinions, but he prefers not to translate such passages out of prudence and a conviction that Rabelais's mix of sacred and profane is "improper" and maybe even blasphemous. His additions have no profound philosophical, sociological, or political meaning, but they do present pleasant, clever, associative, and often rewarding word-games for

# Fischart's Rabelais

the reader-interpreter. They also provide a vital record of a stage in the development of "Protestant" translation, as well as of the European baroque.

## Notes

1. The editions used for this work are: François Rabelais, *Gargantua: première éd. crit. faite sur l'Editio Princeps*, ed. Ruth Calder and Michael A. Screech (Geneva: Droz, 1970); Johann Fischart, *Geschichtklitterung (Gargantua): synoptischer Abdruck der Bearbeitungen von 1575, 1582 und 1590*, ed. Hildegard Schnabel (Halle: M. Niemeyer, 1969); and Fischart, *Geschichtklitterung (Gargantua); Text der Ausgabe letzter Hand von 1590*, ed. Ute Nyssen and Hugo Sommerhalder (Düsseldorf: Rauch, 1963–64). Page and line numbers, where deemed necessary, will appear in parentheses after quotations. Unless there is a need to distinguish among Fischart's three editions, I will quote from the Nyssen/Sommerhalder edition.

2. Klugkröpffige, a composite of *klug* (wise) and *kröpffig*, from *Kropf* (craw, maw), means self-willed or obstinate, with a simultaneous play on "sich Kröpfen," to eat and drink one's fill. There is also an allusion to "köppfig," (-headed), evoking the connotation "wise-headed." In one unit, Fischart has combined three elements: the (1) wise man who (2) goes his own way and who (3) eats and drinks his fill (either of literal food and drink, or of the author's words). "Nebelverkappte" can mean muffled, disguised, or even rendered invisible in fog, since the Nebelkappe in Germanic heroic epics is a magic device that causes its wearer to disappear—a device that has its origin in Homer. "NebelNebuloner" is doubtless a citizen of the kingdom mentioned on the title page: "Nu bel NibelNebelland."

3. Fischart appears to be addressing a listening as well as a reading audience, as he makes an effort to gain its rapt attention: "orenfeste, orenfeisste, allerbefeistete, ährenhaffte und hafftären, orenhafen, unnd hafenoren oder hasenasinorige insondere liebe Herrn, gönner und freund. E. Keinnad unnd dunst sollen wissen" [strong eared, fat-eared, completely fattened up, honorable (*ehrenhaft* and simultaneously corn-eared) and (corn-honorable, ear-potted and pot-eared or rabbit-and-ass-eared), especially beloved Sirs, patrons and friends; your Nothingness and Fog should know].

# Florence M. Weinberg

4. "Diogènes . . . le tournoit, viroit, brouilloit, garbouilloit, hersoit, renversoit, nettoit, grattoit, flattoit, barattoit" [Diogenes . . . twirled it, whirled it, scrambled it, bungled it, frisked it, jumbled it, tumbled it, flattered it, scratched it]—and so on for eleven more lines. Both authors' lists contain words that do not fit logically but are called into being by pure sound association.

5. With these words on the mirror, Fischart presents an interesting reflection on the author vis-à-vis the world. He excuses both Rabelais and himself, for the dirt, if any there be, is to be found in the world rather than in the mind of the author and his translator. The moral opprobrium is, thus, cleverly directed back, reflected back, upon the source: the world.

6. Fischart's defense indicates that he knew of serious attacks, like the monk Puy-Herbault's, that had been made against Rabelais as an atheist and Epicurean by readers who did not agree with his evangelical message, and that he knew that Rabelais's reputation as a "godless drunkard" was widespread.

7. For the full poem, see Pierre de Ronsard, *Oeuvres complètes*, ed. P. Laumonier (Paris: Hachette, 1914–74), vol. 6, *Bocage de 1554*; *Meslanges de 1555*, pp. 20–24.

8. The reader should be aware that my re-translations and explanations often cover only a part of the possibilities offered by Fischart's text. A truly exhaustive explication would become too tedious and would make a coherent account of Fischart's procedure virtually impossible.

9. Some, but probably not all, the Latin words (ab)used in this passage are: *appotus* (intoxicated), *compotatio* (symposium, drinking-bout), *expoto* (to quaff), *potatio* (a drinking-bout), *potator* (a tippler), *potatorius* (pert. to drinking), *potatus* (draught), *potax* (toper), *potio* (a drink), *potio* (verb: put in the power of), *potito* (to drink heavily), *poto* (verb: to drink), *potor* (a tippler), and *potulentes* (drinking).

10. "Villeicht Gott ihm zur straff den Zaum nun etwas verhenget, auf dass wir durch seinen frevel erregt, ihne nach gebür eintreiben, züchtigen und . . . zum barren pringen" (p. 309, lines 30–32).

11. Ed. Schnabel, p. 273 and note: "Und nach dem einhalt solcher lection schickt er sich Gott anzurufen und zubitten: Dan solches lesen mächtige richtige und eiferige gebett

stellet, wie an dem Venedischen Marienpsalter zusehen."

12. "It is indeed certain that such pilgrimages, lacking [the authority of] God's word, are not commanded, and are also not needful, since we can live much better and can abandon them entirely without sin or danger. Why then does a man leave his own preacher at home, God's word, his wife and child, etc., which are needful and commanded, to run after needless, uncertain, harmful will-o-the-wisps of the Devil?" From "Artikel, so da hätten sollen aufs concilium zu Mantua, oder es würde sein, überantwortet werden," 1538, in Martin Luther, *Werke*, 4th ed. (Leipzig: Eger & Sievers, 1924), 1: 49. Similar statements are to be found in "Vermahnung an die Geistlichen, versammelt auf dem Reichstag zu Augsburg," 1530, and "Auslegung des ersten Gebotes."

13. Etienne Gilson, "Rabelais franciscain," in *Les Idées et les lettres*, 2nd ed. (Paris: Vrin, 1955), and Alban J. Krailsheimer, *Rabelais and the Franciscans* (Oxford: Clarendon Press, 1963), both make this point.

14. See Enny E. Kraaijveld, "Les premiers traducteurs de Garantua: Urquhart lecteur de Fischart," *Etudes Rabelaisiennes* 25 (1991): 125–30.

15. See Lowrie Nelson's article, "Baroque," in *The Princeton Encyclopedia of Poetry and Poetics*, ed. Alex Preminger, F. J. Warnke, and O. B. Hardison (Princeton: Princeton University Press, 1965), pp. 66–68.

16. Kurt Weinberg remarks (private communication) that the great Renaissance word-builders (Luther, Rabelais, Fischart et al.) were pioneers in the development of the vernaculars as sophisticated linguistic systems (a function they had begun usurping from Latin). In their enthusiasm and exuberance, the possibilities of linguistic play seemed endless. By contrast, Lewis Caroll's creation of nonsense words such as *jabberwocky* is symptomatic of the end of the development in which all language is recognized as limiting, even as a "prison house," through which reality cannot, in fact, be accurately expressed.

# "La grécité de notre idiome": Correctio, Translatio, and Interpretatio in the Theoretical Writings of Henri Estienne

## Kenneth Lloyd-Jones

*Entre les beaux & grands avantages que Dieu
a donnez aux hommes pardessus tous les autres
animaux, cestuy-ci estant un, qu'ils peuvent s'entrexposer
leurs conceptions par le moyen du langage. . . .*
(H. Estienne, *Project . . .* , 1579)

When the Abbé Espagnolle published his *Vrai Dictionnaire étymologique* at the end of the nineteenth century, he argued the case for what he called "la grécité de notre idiome" [the "Greekness" of our language] in a way that could only have gratified a number of his Renaissance predecessors, eager as they had been, in their turn, to dignify French with Hellenic rather than Roman ancestors:

> Il est . . . deux vérités philologiques qui scandalisent encore, mais qui finiront bien par se faire accepter: l'une, que le système qui veut que les langues dites néo-latines soient une évolution du latin est vain et incohérent, contredit à la fois par l'histoire bien lue et par la philologie bien entendue; l'autre, que le fond commun des langues dites néo-latines est grec.[1]

> [There are . . . two philological truths which continue to scandalize, but which will surely end up by being accepted. The first is that the system which insists that the so-called neo-Latin languages have evolved from Latin has neither substance nor coherence, and is simultaneously contradicted by history, properly read, and by philology, properly understood. The second is that the common heritage of the so-called neo-Latin languages is Greek.[2]]

259

Espagnolle goes on to specify that he is referring not to Hellenistic Greek but to that primitive Greek subsisting in the oldest dialects (Doric and Aeolian) and thought to have been spoken by the aboriginal Aegeans, the Pelasgians: French is, thus, not the child of either "Hellenic" or Latin, but their brother, separated at birth, whose features have been modified by isolation, "mais resté foncièrement grec ou pélasgique comme eux" (p. xxiv) [but having remained, like them, profoundly Greek or Pelasgic]. Like his Philhellenic predecessors, Espagnolle considers that the demonstration of a special relationship between French and Greek involves more than the rectification of linguistic theory, for important questions of cultural pedigree and the national sense of honor and identity are at stake. An otherwise sceptical reviewer of one of Espagnolle's multitudinous volumes proudly remarks that, following the Pelasgian migrations (some of which had indeed reached as far as Marseilles), "tous leurs dialectes resplendissent dans Homère et se perpétuent dans les patois français, surtout pyrénéens, mais aussi dans celui de l'Ile de France, devenu langue scientifique universelle"[3] [Homer is resplendent with all of their dialects, which live on in the various French *patois,* especially those of the Pyrenees, but also in the *patois* of the Ile de France, which has become the universal language of learning]. There is an unmistakable wistfulness in his closing observation that, even though he is not convinced by Espagnolle's arguments, he would dearly love them to have been true: "Nous dirons même . . . que nous préférerions que le français fût tiré ostensiblement du grec, instrument plus ductile de la pensée que le latin" (p. 213) [We will even say . . . that we would prefer that French were demonstrably derived from Greek, a more pliable instrument for our thought than Latin].

Given the common Indo-European origins of both the Greek and the Latin components of our linguistic heritage, and the advanced state of philological science by the end of the last century, we may safely consign Espagnolle's theories to the domain of the amiably eccentric. If they

Kenneth Lloyd-Jones

have been adduced here, it is to illustrate the tenaciously long-lived character of much of French Renaissance thinking about Greek, and its place in the evolving sense of the distinctive values of French style and thought. This relationship was often conceived in terms of differentiation from the impact of Latin,[4] much as French was defining itself against Italian during the same period.[5] Indeed, it seems plausible to suggest that some part of the extraordinary prestige enjoyed by Greek at this time stems directly from the fact that, unlike Latin, it was untainted by the historical link to Italian.[6] But if Greek was somehow "purer," through being older than Latin, it was also, in the eyes of many, more "modern"—i.e., more like French—than Latin. This notion was justified by the presence in Greek (as in French, but not as in Classical Latin) of such features as, for example, both a perfect and a preterite (aorist) tense; the capacity to construct dependent clauses with ὅτι (cf. French *que*), where Latin uses accusative subject and infinitive; an optative (seen as equivalent to the conditional); definite articles, and (with the use of τις) an equivalent to the indefinite article (cf. Latin *quidam*); and the ability to construct progressive tenses, with the verb *to be* and present participles (although this construction, never as systematic as in Italian or Spanish, had virtually disappeared from French by the sixteenth century).

For the generation of humanists brought up on Budé's celebration of Greek as "uberior Latina, ad sensusque animi exprimendos & felicior & significantior"[7] [more copious than Latin, and more felicitous and more telling for the expression of meanings], and urged on by Gargantua's praise of "[la langue] grecque, sans laquelle c'est honte qu'une personne se die sçavant"[8] [Greek, without which it is shameful for anyone to call himself learned], there was indeed the sense of a special relationship between Greek and French. And, in the consideration of all that this implied, Humanist reflection on translation was to be of major consequence.

## The Theoretical Writings of Henri Estienne

During the generation that succeeded the great pioneering work of Budé,[9] humanist Greek activity in France can be broadly said to comprise five major emphases: *pedagogical,*[10] *literary,*[11] *historico-cultural,*[12] *philosophical,*[13] and *philological.* This chapter will concentrate on the most important representative of the last category, Henri Estienne (ca. 1531–98).[14]

One of the greatest scholar-printers of the French Renaissance and the most distinguished Hellenist of his generation, Henri Estienne's importance in the history of humanist translation is as much that of theoretician as of practitioner. His theory of translation will be discussed here with particular, but not exclusive, reference to Greek, since it is not always possible to isolate his thoughts in this area from his views on the French language's relationship to Latin, and even to other vernaculars. For him, there is no distinction to be drawn between the functions of philologist, translator, textual editor, or even printer. Each is engaged in the same activity, one that is marked by its intellectual, social, and moral dimensions: each is charged with the reception, verification, and transmission, in a renewed form for which he is ethically responsible, of texts of universal worth. In his *Artis Typographicae Querimonia,* published in 1569 to celebrate the one hundredth anniversary of printing in France,[15] his preface, addressed "lectori bonis literis bene cupienti"[16] [to the reader truly desirous of good literature], discusses printers—but printers like himself, combining in equal parts the functions mentioned above. In stressing the requirement of scholarship for the fulfillment of their mission, his choice of words is revealing: "fungentes munere *Correctorum*" (p. 140) [carrying out their duty as *editors and critics*]. The word *corrector* does of course mean "corrector," and in sixteenth-century usage certainly had the sense of "proof-reader"; however, we know Estienne to have been enough of a Ciceronian to be sure that he also has in mind here the compound Classical Latin idea of (political or social)

262

reformer, (literary) critic, and (moral) censor. The overtones of intellectual acuity and moral accountability are clear. Uneducated "correctors"
are a social danger: "Quid enim, obsecro, aliud est, hanc in illos
Scriptores potestatem eius modi hominibus permittere, quam gladios
furiosis in manus tradere?" (p. 140) [For what else is it, I ask you, to
grant such power over those (great) writers to men of this kind, if not to
deliver swords into the hands of the insane?]. He angrily tells of one
Latin "expert" who, each time he found the words *proci* or *exanimare*
[suitors (also, noblemen): to terrify, to be out of breath], changed them
to *porci* and *examinare* [pigs: to weigh, to consider], thereby making
irreparable nonsense of various texts by Cicero and Horace (p. 140). As
for Greek, the situation is even worse, but modesty forbids that Estienne
discuss it here, since he knows full well the values he brings to his own
work, "est enim, Dei beneficio, cur invidear ab ὁμοτέχνοις, potius quam
cur invideam" (p. 142) [for the fact is, with God's favor, that I am more
to be envied by my fellow-craftsmen, than I have cause to envy them].
The theoretical underpinnings of his approach to the question are made
clear in his concluding praise of the craft of *correctio:*

> Haec fugat a Scriptis tenebras, lucemque reducit:
> Una haec cum mendis aspera bella gerit. (p. 147)

> [It is what banishes ignorance and obscurity from what has been
> written, and restores the light: it alone wages bitter warfare against
> inaccuracies.]

Without faith in the edition, or the translation, we can have no faith in
the original, and—if ever, as he adds with a touch of asperity, we are to
cease being subjected to bulls that fly, or dolphins that run like wild
boars—the work of the *corrector* must remain of the highest social and
cultural importance.

Estienne's adherence to this ideal of *correctio* as a function of *translatio* characterizes his entire approach to the question at hand. His edition of Valla's fifteenth-century Latin translation of Herodotus is specifically flagged as "having been revised by Henri Estienne,"[17] and contains on its title page a couplet that reaffirms his view of his role:

> Herodoti Latium possederat hactenus umbram,
> Nunc Latium corpus possidet Herodoti.

> [Hitherto, the Latin world had possessed the shadow of Herodotus, but now the Latin world possesses his substance.]

A further couplet inside the volume reinforces the point:

> *Eiusdem, in Herodoti interpretationem a se recognitam*
> Qui verax propria, mendax interprete lingua
> Ante fui, verum nunc in utraque loquor. (fol. iᵛ)

> [*By the same, on the translation of Herodotus revised by him*: I who, truthful in my own language, was formerly a liar in my translated tongue, now speak the truth in both languages.]

Estienne cites a number of mistranslations in which, for example, the word ἱερόν ("temple") turns up as a hitherto unknown Mount Hirum, or the relative pronoun οἵτινες emerges as a new tribe, the Hoetines, and remarks that such horrors would provoke laughter, but for the fact that they translate "eloquentiam summam in meram infantiam" (fol. iiʳ) [supreme eloquence into undiluted infantile babble]. We may be sure that he is fully aware of the etymology of the word *infans*: the one without speech. The perpetrators of such blunders are literally to be wished off the face of the earth: "O quam opportune in Deucalionea tempora incidisset huius modi interpretes: quam strenuus humani generis reparator, sine lapidum iactatione, fuisset" (fol. iiʳ) [How fitting, if translators of this kind were to have been around in the time of Deucalion: what

Kenneth Lloyd-Jones

energy the restorer of the human race would have brought to not casting a single stone!].

There is nothing abstract in Estienne's reflection on the nature of language and linguistic relationships. If, in his younger days, he had devoted his professional energies to classical languages and literature, he writes to Henry III in 1579, it was for those same reasons that now inspire him to argue for "la Precellence du langage François" [the pre-eminence of the French language], "ne pouvant raisonnablement denier à celle qui m'est naturelle, autant de bien que j'en avois faict à ces es-trangeres"[18] [since I could not reasonably deny to my native language as much good as I had done to those foreigners]. Linguistic eminence is inseparable from national prestige, just as the capacity for eloquence is inseparable from personal distinction, and a translated quatrain from Euripides serves to make the point. The original (which Estienne does not quote) reads as follows:

λόγος γὰρ ἔκ τ' ἀδοξούντων ἰὼν
κἀκ τῶν δοκούντων αὐτὸς οὐ ταὐτὸν σθένει.
(*Hecuba*, lines 294–95)

[for speech coming from those held in no esteem does not have the same power as that of those who are revered.]

Estienne offers the following translation:

L'homme d'autorité, l'homme qui n'en a point,
Venans à haranguer touchant un mesme poinct,
Encore que tous deux tiennent mesme langage,
Celuy de l'un sera pezé davantage. (fol. 3ʳ)

[When the man of authority and the man with none come to argue the same point, even if both speak the same language, the language of the former will be the more greatly heeded.]

265

The forthright message of the translation, intended to convince the king of the need to be eloquent in his efforts to stem the rising tides of civil war and religious fratricide, is further reinforced by a translation of some lines from Virgil (which once again Estienne does not actually provide):

> ac veluti magno in populo cum saepe coorta est
> seditio saevitque animis ignobile vulgus,
> iamque faces et saxa volant, furor arma ministrat;
> tum, pietate gravem ac meritis si forte virum quem
> conspexere, silent arrectisque auribus astant;
> ille regit dictis animos et pectora mulcet. (*Aeneid,* 1:152–57)

> [just as often in a large crowd, when insurrection has broken out and the low-born people rage with many passions, and already flaming torches and rocks are flying, frenzy supplies the arms; then, if by chance they have caught sight of a man respected for his piety and his good deeds, they fall silent and stand with their ears cocked; such a man governs their minds with his words, and soothes their hearts.]

The rendering from the Latin is offered as confirmation of the Greek dramatist's point, and Estienne prefaces it with the assertion that he has translated as closely as possible:

> Voicy qu'il dit (autant que j'ay pu exprimer la nayfveté de son langage Latin):
>> Comme en une grand' ville, abondamment peuplée,
>> Qui par sedition vient à estre troublée
>> Quand tout le menu peuple à toute cruauté
>> D'un courage mutin est soudain incité,
>> Desja volent en l'air & pierres & flambeaux,
>> La fureur pour s'armer trouve moyens nouveaux:
>> Alors se presentant à eux un personnage,
>> Tant pour sa pieté respecté davantage,
>> Qu'außi pour ses bienfaicts, on les voit s'arrester,

266

# Kenneth Lloyd-Jones

Et l'oreille attentive à ses propos prester.
Luy gouverne leurs cueurs, luy appaise leur ire,
Par les raisons qu'il sçait en un tel cas deduire. (fol.4ʳ–4ᵛ)

[Here is what he says (as closely as I can express the naturalness of his Latin): When, in a large and abundantly populated city, troubled by sedition when the common people are suddenly incited by rebellious courage to commit acts of complete cruelty, and stones and flaming torches are already flying through the air, Fury finds new means to arm herself: then, when a personality presents himself to them, who is all the more respected for his piety since he is also respected for his good deeds, you see them halt, and lend a careful ear to his words. This man rules their hearts, this man soothes their wrath, through the reasoning that he can, in such circumstances, call forth.]

A comparison of these translations with their originals, whose subject is the efficacity of eloquence, and which are therefore of special interest to the translator, reveals a good deal about Estienne's priorities and methods. A scant two lines of Greek become four in French, partly as a result of the natural density of the original, which can rely on such linguistic features as case endings, the conventions of poetic contractions, and the use of substantivized participles to give it its epigrammatic tone. But, clearly, other factors are at play: in his decision to preserve verse-form over prose,[19] his translation of the broadly referential Greek plurals by the specific and personal French singular, his use of the regular *cola* of the opening line, the shift of grammatical subject from λόγος to "l'homme d'autorité," and, particularly, in his election to change the main verb (negative in Greek) into the closing affirmative, Estienne reveals his sensitivity to the rhetorical thrust of the translation, as well as to the semantic content of his original. Political urgency, rather than literary embellishment, governs his choice of formal arrangement, but the plain, lapidary character of the original is preserved and its affectivity enhanced.

In his Latin translation also, the number of French lines is double that of the original (an intentional formal decision, perhaps, since hexameters are put into alexandrines), but there is relatively little resort to redundancy. The "nayfveté" of the original is indeed preserved, as are both the balance of the *cum* . . . *tum* construction, and the climactic structure, in which two long clauses conclude in a single, aphoristic proposition. The thought-order of the original ending is, however, reversed in the translation. The Latin emphasizes the man (*ille*), as indeed does the French (the repetition of *celuy*). But whereas the original stresses his acts (*regit* . . . *mulcet*), the translation grants an entire line to the quality of character at issue (*dictis* rendered as "Par les raisons qu'il sçait en un tel cas deduire"), in a clear attempt to accentuate further the rhetorical point: the explicit Latin reference to the man Aeneas becomes, in French, an allusive evocation of his qualities, in order to stress the need for another man, the royal reader, to be eloquent. Estienne is not a creative artist, seeking to impose his own vision on the Greek or Latin originals, but a patriot, urgently endeavoring to have the king wield his authority in a situation of ongoing national catastrophe—the Wars of Religion. It would be paradoxically easy, in such a situation, for eloquence to get in the way of eloquence, but Estienne's translative choices make sure that his versions have their own persuasiveness.[20]

If the country needs an eloquent ruler, however, that ruler must have access to an equally cogent and compelling medium. National honor requires that all doubt be removed from those who query "si nostre langage est aussi capable de ceste vertu de bien dire que l'un ou l'autre de ceux qui luy veulent faire concurrence, & se rendre ses competiteurs" (fol. 5ᵛ) [whether our language is as capable of this virtue of eloquence as either one of those which seek to rival with it and be its competitors]. But the issue of the intrinsic quality of a language transcends the national need to show that French is superior to Italian and Spanish. It concerns the nature of language itself, which is why those engaged in the labor of inter-lingual transfer have such a burden of responsibility, as the liminary "*Au Lecteur, qui se voudra rendre neutre*" [*To the Reader, who is good enough not to take sides*] makes explicit:

> Entre les beaux & grands avantages que Dieu a donnez aux hommes pardessus tous les autres animaux, cestuy-ci estant un, qu'ils peuvent s'entrexposer leurs conceptions par le moyen du langage, il est certain que ceux qui sçavent mieux faire cela, n'ont seulement cest avantage general, ains sont außi avantagez pardessus les autres hommes. Mais d'autant que le langage est comme l'instrument duquel ils usent, & qu'un bon ouvrier fait d'autant meilleur ouvrage qu'il ha meilleur instrument, il importe beaucoup, pour parvenir à ceste excellence, d'user d'un langage accompli en toutes sortes. (fol. 8ʳ)

> [Among the many and beautiful advantages that God has granted humankind over the other animals, there is this one—that they can expound their ideas to one another through the medium of language. It is certain that those who know best how to do this have not only this general advantage, but also have advantages over all other men. But, to the extent that their language is like the tool they use, and that a good craftsman does all the better work for having a better tool, it is extremely important, in order to attain this excellence, to use a language which is fully developed in every respect.]

Estienne's efforts are thus constantly geared to validating the superiority of the French language over the competing vernaculars, based on its special relationship with Greek, itself superior to Latin for the reasons we have seen. His most exuberantly satirical defense of French against the all-pervading Italianism he found at court contains a number of important passages in this regard. The *Deux Dialogues du nouveau langage françois,*[21] in which, as P. M. Smith rightly observes, Estienne "fait entrer la philologie dans la littérature" (p. 18) [brings philology into literature] does indeed reveal some of the scientific weaknesses of Estienne's linguistics. As Smith remarks, "le philologue se double d'un patriote" (p. 19) [the philologist goes hand in hand with a patriot], and while this leads him to have a healthy respect for the older forms of French syntax and morphology and a special affection for proverbial or folkloric French, it also leads him to view significant borrowing from contemporary vernaculars as a sign of national debility, and to consider linguistic change as a process of corruption, rather than evolution. Nevertheless, the *Deux Dialogues* contain passages that help us further refine Estienne's understanding of both the philosophical and linguistic dimensions of translation, and this is particularly true with what might be termed the translation of linguistic registers—first intra-lingually, then inter-lingually, between contemporary vernaculars, and last between French and its classical ancestors.

The two major participants in the dialogues are named "Jan Franchet, Dict Philausone, gentilhomme courtisanopolitois" (p. 35) [Jack Frenchy, called Phil-Italy, a courtieropolitan gentleman] and "Celtophile" [i.e., one who loves what dates from pre-Roman France]. A brief extract from Philausone's *Prologue* will show what his problem is:

> Messieurs, il n'y a pas long temps qu'ayant quelque martel en teste (ce qui m'advient souvent pendant que je fay ma stanse en la cour), et, à cause de ce, estant sorti apres le past pour aller un peu spaceger, je trouvay par la strade un mien amy nommé Celtophile. Or, voyant qu'il se monstret estre tout sbigotit de mon langage . . . je me mis à ragionner avec luy touchant iceluy en le soustenant le mieux qu'il m'estet possible. Et voyant que nonobstant tout ce que je luy pouves alleguer, ce langage italianizé luy semblet fort strane, voire avoir de la gofferie et balorderie, je pris beaucoup de fatique pour luy caver cela de la fantaisie. (pp. 35–37)

> [Gentlemen, not long ago, having a hammering in my head [*Italianism*] (which happens to me often when I reside [It: *stanza*] at Court), and on that account having gone out after the repast [It: *pasto*] for a stroll [It: *(s)passegiare*], in the street [It: *strada*] I came

270

across a friend of mine called Celtophile. Now, seeing that he
showed himself to be entirely amazed [It: *sbigottito*] at my speech
. . . I began to reason [It: *ragionare*] with him about it, defending it
to the best of my ability. And seeing that, in spite of everything I
could adduce for him, this Italianized language seemed most strange
[It: *strano*] to him, and even to contain coarseness and stupidity [It:
*gofferia, balordo*], I took great pains [It: *fatica*] to dislodge [It:
*scavare*] this from his imagination.][22]

While we have here an amusing assumption of the reader's *lack* of
need of translation for the text to have its effect, the issue is seen to
have more serious dimensions when the question of the translation of
appropriate register is raised. When Philausone later offers for discussion
the phrase, "Cela sera pour me faire entrer au paradis de mes desirs . . ."
[That would put me in paradise, as far as my wishes go . . .], Celtophile
replies, "Je trouve que parler ainsi, c'est profaner le mot 'paradis'" (p.
334) [I find that talk of that kind profanes the word 'paradise']. What
would he make of a stable in which horses had straw in abundance, and
of which it was said "C'est le paradis des chevaux" [It's paradise for the
horses]? Celtophile answers that he would see therein a "double profana-
tion," since it also implicitly denies the inferiority of horses to human
beings, created in the image of God (p. 335). This of course raises the
complex issue of the shifts undergone by figurative usage between transmission and reception, and it is interesting to note that Estienne's understanding of the question lies more in the domain of what amounts to
natural law than that of linguistic considerations:

> Pour le moins faudroit-il qu'on nous confessast que c'est contre
> raison et contre le sens naturel d'attribuer de la divinité au jeu et aux
> danses comme font ceux qui disent: "Il joue divinement bien," "Il
> danse divinement bien" . . . , "Il sçait mentir divinement bien". . . .
> Pourquoy dira-on ici "divinement" bien plustost que "diabolique-
> ment" bien? (pp. 337–38)

## The Theoretical Writings of Henri Estienne

[At the least, it should be granted us that it goes against reason and against common sense to attribute divinity to gambling and dancing, as those do who say, "He plays divinely well, he dances divinely well . . . , he knows how to lie divinely well." . . . Why would we say "divinely well" here, rather than "diabolically well"?]

The problem of interpretive values within the same language becomes even more acute when we move to inter-lingual translation. As Celtophile points out, "Il n'est pas vrai" [It is not true] carries a different semantic content from "Non è vero?" [Don't you think so? (as in "n'est-ce pas?")]: "Ne sçavez-vous pas qu'on estime *Il n'est pas vray*, et *Vous avez menti*, estre cousins germains?" (p. 369) [Don't you know that people consider "That's not true" and "You have lied" to be first cousins?]. Philausone agrees, and recalls having been so amazed as to doubt their masculinity when he first heard Italians accept such a phrase as "Non è vero[?]" without reaching for their swords. This elicits from Celtophile a response that illustrates Estienne's deep understanding of the interpretive dilemma inherent in all forms of translation, with its multifold social and cultural ramifications: "Voyla que c'est, vous jugiez de vostre cueur l'autruy" (p. 370) [That's what happens; you were gauging someone else by the measure of your own heart]. All perception involves translation.[23]

If such interpretive problems arise between speakers of the same tongue, and even more so between speakers of languages that are nonetheless highly proximate, how much thornier are the problems involving shifts between Greek and/or Latin and our modern vernaculars, separated not only by time but by vastly different social structures and philosophical assumptions. Pondering the implications of the figurative use of the word *Fortune,* as in "La Fortune luy rit" (p. 339) [Fortune smiles upon him], Philausone observes:

Et aucuns (je ne sçay si c'est pour opposer la philosophie stoique à

272

## Kenneth Lloyd-Jones

la religion christianique) font sonner fort haut, et à tout propos *fatal* et *fatalité,* et *fatalement,* et une *fatale destinée.* (p. 339)

[And some (I don't know whether in order to contrast stoicism with Christianity) pronounce out loud, and on any pretext, words like *fateful, fatality, fatefully/inevitably* and a *fateful destiny.*]

Following a disussion of the concept in the works of Pliny, Plato, and Juvenal, Celtophile raises the status of the question in Herodotus:[24]

Et quant à Herodote . . . il faut que ceux qui l'ont bien et diligemment leu, confessent maugré leurs dents qu'il y a différence de sa tych$\eta$ et de celle des autres, veu qu'il joint theia avec tych$\eta$.[25] Ce qui m'a faict penser quelquesfois à ce que dit la populasse tant ailleurs qu'à Paris: "C'est Fortune, Dieu le veult." (p. 343)

[And as for Herodotus . . . those who have read him carefully and diligently must admit, in spite of themselves, that there is a difference between his "tyche" [Gr: Fortune] and that of others, given that he allies the word "theia" [Gr: goddess] to "tyche." This makes me sometimes think of what the common folk say, as much in Paris as anywhere else: "It's Luck, God wills it."]

Beneath this seemingly anodyne exchange, we cannot fail to hear echoes of the polemic over the impossibility of innocent translation conducted between Erasmus and Dolet half a century earlier, on the subject of Ciceronian imitation.[26] We are once again confronted with "the chastening awareness that translation takes place in the interpretive activity of our thought,"[27] a fact whose intractability fifty years of religious schism had done nothing to lessen. To translate is to interpret, and to interpret is always to risk entanglement with the current orthodoxy. As he muses on the doctrinal consequences of "translating," even figuratively, our concept of the force that governs the passage of events by a

273

word like τύχη, Celtophile's conclusion takes on dramatic overtones in a society bloodily divided over the question of free will and predestination: "il y a bien grande différence entre parler et escrire courtisanement, ou poetiquement, et parler ou escrire chrestiennement" (p. 344) [there is truly a big difference between speaking and writing like a courtier, or like a poet, and speaking and writing like a Christian].

It must, however, be stressed that Estienne is neither doctrinaire nor partisan in his religious positions: while there can be no doubt of his Huguenot convictions—he had left Paris for Geneva in 1550—there is sufficient evidence of his problems with Calvin's city government,[28] and of his many return trips to Paris (particularly to try to be of help to Henry III) to free him from any accusation of dogmatism. As in the earlier case of his call for royal eloquence, here also his primary interest is philological, as someone whose business involves the complexities inherent in all acts of linguistic transfer. Τύχη and *fortuna* are concepts that call into question the links between cause and effect and posit an element of randomness in the force that secures outcomes. The problem inherent in the effort to accommodate such concepts to the teleology that is basic to Christianity, while a challenge to faith and dogma for the theologian, is essentially a linguistic issue for Estienne. Celtophile has clearly understood the ideological problem implicit in his discussion of τύχη:

> on voit quelques uns de ceux mesmement qui sont gens de biens, et qui sentent de la providence de Dieu comme bons chrestiens en doivent sentir, ne se pouvoir garder aucunesfois d'user ainsi de ce mot Fortune, comme si c'estoit une dame à laquelle ils attribuassent quelque chose. (p. 343)

> [you sometimes see even those who are good people, and who feel about God's providence as good Christians must feel about it, but who are unable to stop themselves on occasion from using this word

*Fortune* in that manner, as if it were a lady to whom they might attribute something.]

Celtophile does not hesitate to condemn such people for their "fausses et blasphemes imaginations" [erroneous and blasphemous imaginings]—but what is crucial to note here is his (and Estienne's) remedy. Far from referring such errant souls to the teachings of the Church, the Bible, or patristic authority, the solution is to be found in the writings of the pagan writers themelves:

> Et toutesfois comme j'ay renvoyé à Platon ceux qui font de fausses et blasphemes imaginations soubs le nom de Nature, aussi voudrois-je renvoyer à Juvenal ceux qui font le mesme soubs le nom de Fortune. Car il vaut bien mieux que les profanes mesmement soyent ceux qui facent le proces à ces profanateurs, c'est-à-dire, à ceux qui parlent ainsi profanement. (p. 343)

> [But just as I referred to Plato those who hold to such erroneous and blasphemous imaginings on the subject of Nature, so I would like to refer to Juvenal those who do the same thing on the subject of Fortune. For it is far better that it be the profane themselves who prosecute the case against these profaners, that is to say against those who speak profanely in this manner.]

We may well wonder, however, whether the text of Juvenal summoned forth to help bring the idea of $\tau\acute{u}\chi\eta$ into the realm of orthodoxy was ever likely to succeed:

> Nullum numen abest si sit prudentia: sed te
> Nos facimus Fortuna deam, caeloque locamus.[29]

> [No (divine) power is absent if (human) prudence is present: but we are the ones, oh Fortune, who make a goddess of you and situate you in the heavens.]

The assertion that it is human terminology, rather than natural Truth, that confers existence on divine power must have been as disconcerting to Genevan Calvinist as to Catholic post-Tridentine orthodoxy! Nothing could better illustrate the philological, rather than theological, nature of Estienne's concern than this contention that the best voice to speak for classical antiquity is the voice of classical antiquity itself. His position, mild enough in appearance, calls for something with immensely far-reaching potential in the context of his time—the replacement of the Church's interpretive authority by the scholar's translative authority. The issue is ever-present in much of Renaissance debate over language: the ancient necessity to distinguish between theology and philosophy (between belief and knowledge), the former calling for faith, which is ineffable because it deals with the transcendental, the latter for the use of reasoned discourse to attain what we affirm to be true. The translation of concepts having no equivalent in the target language, and thus in the orthodoxy of the target society, is not only a threat to the upholders of dogma but also a challenge, first to the interpretive, and then to the linguistic skills of the translator, whatever form the "translation" takes. It is not a problem generated by our failure to agree on what is true, but one that is inherent to the nature of language itself, independently of the subject matter. Indeed (and this is another of the far-reaching consequences of Estienne's position), just as there is no innocent translation, there is no privileged material (no "universal verity")—not even the most apparently unassailable of revealed truths, even those enjoying the status of dogma, can withstand the consequences of their metamorphosis into language.

This is true whether we speak of such weighty matters as the nature of Providence or of infinitely more mundane issues, as Estienne's *De latinitate falso suspecta* . . . makes clear.[30] He believes that the study of etymology will show that the principles governing the shifts from Greek to Latin are the same as those between Latin to French. (It must be

allowed that there is more than a little inconsistency in Estienne's positions on linguistic evolution: on occasion, the patriot rules the philologist.)[31] Discussing Latin "borrowings" from Greek, he writes, not without a substantial measure of wishful thinking:

> Quod enim Latini quondam in Graecae linguae usurpatione fecerunt,
> ut nonnullarum vocum quibus prisca Graecia usa fuisset, memoriam
> prope intermortuam renovarent (veluti quum *Porcum* dixerunt, ex
> vetusta graecorum voce πό ρκο ς; quum *Leporem* ex antiquo illorum
> vocabulo λέπο[ρ]ις nominarunt: . . . quum denique *Graecum* dixerunt,
> sicut antiqua Graecia Γραικόν vocaverunt, qui postea "Ελλην fuit
> nominatus. (pp. 2–3)

> [Because, in fact, the Latins formerly assumed possession of the
> Greek language, just as primitive Greece had used words from other
> languages, they revived a virtually semi-conscious memory: as when
> they said *porcum* (pig), from the ancient Greek word πό ρκο ς, or when
> they said *leporem* (hare) from their old noun λέπο[ρ]ις; . . . when,
> finally, they said *Graecum* (Greek), just as in ancient Greece they
> said Γραικόν, which was later said "Ελλην.]

Unfortunately for Estienne, his etymologies are on the shaky side, since
his chief sources seem to be not Hellenistic writers but Varro and
Plutarch.[32] Πό ρκο ς is indeed attested (Liddell-Scott, p. 1450), but only as
a transliteration of the Latin *porcus* (Plutarch, *Publicola,* 11). Its primary
meaning is a kind of "fish-trap," which may be behind the type of fish
(*porkos*) noted by A. Ernout and A. Meillet, whose remarks show the ill-
founded nature of Estienne's wished-for etymology:[33]

> Les textes de Varron sur lesquels on fonde l'existence d'un πό ρκο ς
> grec sont obscurs ou corrompus . . . le mot avec ce sens ne figure
> que chez Plutarque, où il est donné expressément comme un mot
> latin.

## The Theoretical Writings of Henri Estienne

[The texts of Varro which serve to justify the existence of a Greek πό ρκο ς are obscure or corrupt . . . (in the sense of "pig") the word is found only in Plutarch, where it is specifically given as a Latin word.]

Λέπο ρ ις is, however, a word for "hare" in Aeolian (Liddell-Scott, p. 1039), and Γραικό ς is in fact the "local name for a tribe in West Greece, applied by the Italians to the Greeks in general" (p. 358).

Such "lexical" etymology is then extended to what we might term "interpretive" etymology: a further discussion later in the book centers on similar issues arising out of the relationship between French *bouche* and Latin *os* [mouth]. The metaphorical possibilities of the Latin, as exemplified in expressions such as *os portus* or *os fluminis,* suffice to justify not only lexical but also figurative translation into French: "la bouche du port" and "la bouche d'une riviere" (pp. 58–59) [the harbor mouth, the mouth of the river]. Indeed, Estienne goes so far as to intimate a case for figurative translation itself as a means of enrichment for the target language, even when the norms of the latter are apparently defied: "Necnon ut *ulceris os* dictum fuit a Virgilio, sic *La bouche d'un ulcere,* minime insolens in nostro sermone fuerit" (p. 59) [Besides, since *ulceris os* was said by Virgil, *la bouche d'un ulcere* [the mouth of an ulcer] would not be in the least outlandish in our own language].

But ultimately the translative problem is conceptual rather than lexical, as Estienne reminds us in one of his earliest publications, his *Ciceronianum Lexicon Graecolatinum, id est, Lexicon ex variis Graecorum sciptorum locis a Cicerone interpretatis collectum* . . . (Paris: H. Estienne, 1557) [*A Ciceronian Graeco-Latin Lexicon, i.e., A Lexicon Assembled from the Various Passages of the Greek Writers Translated by Cicero* . . .]. Here, once again, the format and primary function bespeak an essentially pragmatic, philological purpose, but the underlying assumptions tell us a great deal about his view of translation. To the extent that much of the Renaissance understanding of Greek philosophy comes through Cicero's discussions of it, Estienne argues, it is essential to grasp Cicero's own understanding of the terms in use, and we know well how Cicero himself struggled with the translative problems inherent in bringing Greek philosophy to the Roman world. Other than the *De officiis,* of course, the theoretical text Estienne has in mind is doubtless the *De optimo genere oratorum* [*On the Best Kind of Orators*], one that modern analysts of Classical rhetoric have tended to judge harshly because of its inferiority to texts such as the *Orator.*[34] It is, however, a treatise that well repays study by students of Renaissance translation, since it enhances our understanding of the links between rhetoric and translation: Cicero argues that since eloquence is a distinct good, and since the best was to be found in Athens (above all in the oratory of Demosthenes), then Rome needs translations of Greek eloquence. He thus presents the text as a preface to his translation of two Greek speeches (a translation no longer extant, if indeed it was ever done), and its interest for Humanists like Estienne lies in the fact that it contains a number of Cicero's most straightforward declarations of his own principles as a translator. It is not the place to discuss these principles in detail here, but it is worth reminding ourselves of Cicero's primary statement of purpose and method:[35]

> Converti . . . ex Atticis duorum eloquentissimorum nobilissimas orationes inter seque contraria, Aeschinis et Demosthenis; nec converti ut interpres, sed ut orator, sententiis isdem et earum formis tamquam figuris, verbis ad nostram consuetudinem aptis. In quibus non vorbum pro vcrbo nccc33c habui ιcddeιe, sed genus omne verborum vimque servavi. Non enim ea me adnumerare lectori putavi oportere, sed tamquam appendere. Hic labor meus hoc assequetur, ut nostri homines quid ab illis exigant, qui se Atticos volunt, et ad quam eos quasi formulam dicendi revocent, intellegant. (*De opt. gen. orat.,* 14–15)

## The Theoretical Writings of Henri Estienne

[I have translated . . . the most noble speeches against each other by the two most eloquent Attic [orators], Aeschines and Demosthenes. And I have translated them not as an interpreter, but as an orator, with their ideas—and their forms as well as their figures [of speech]—made suitable to the usages of our own language. In this regard, I have not held it necessary to render word for word, but I have conserved the general character of the words and their [expressive] force. In point of fact, I have not thought it my job to dole them out one by one to the reader, but rather to provide him with equivalent weight. It will follow from my efforts that our people might know what to require from those who fancy themselves as practitioners of the Greek mode, and to what principle of style, as it were, to hold them accountable.]

This claim for translation not only as an effort to attain like effect but also as a means of both securing the enhancement of the target language *and* as a means of deeper penetration into the source language, was to provide much of the inspiration for Renaissance translation theory.

Consequently, Estienne's concern, as we read Cicero's writings on Greek philosophy, is that we be sensitive to the registers of both the source and the target languages. Once again, we are made to understand that to rely on translation is to rely on interpretation: metaphysical concepts undergo alteration in the course of verbalization, and this is necessarily even more the case when the initial verbalization is then itself subject to translation. The concerns of his times, in which Christians must grapple not only with sundered unity but also with a new awareness of Classical thought viewed by many as posing major problems for orthodoxy, are reflected in some of the Greek words he glosses: Estienne uses translation into Latin to ensure that we do not bring anachronistic assumptions to our grasp of Classical philosophy. Few words, for example, have as much Christian resonance as a word like Σωτήρ, always used in New Testament Greek to mean "the Savior"; Estienne carefully translates it as "qui salutem dedit" (p. 158) [who

280

brought good health], clearly relying on the reader's (Ciceronian) awareness that *salus* is not to be understood here as Church Latin "salvation"
(cf. French "salut"). Τύχη is here also specified as meaning "Fortuna" (p.
141), with the personified Latin deity meant to preclude any assimilation
with the Christian understanding of divine providence. Similarly, κόσμος
is translated as "mundus" [usually *world,* although sometimes *mankind,*
by synecdoche] (p. 34), to clarify that the reference is specifically to a
physical universe rather than an ethical or divine concept (such as the
word can assume in Classical Greek), or the common meaning of
"humankind in general" that it assumes in the New Testament.[36]

But Estienne's assumption that the reader can be relied on not to
impose Christian readings onto the *Latin* translations is clearly only as
safe as the subject matter is familiar. When the topic is novel or unfamiliar, translation must yield to explanation. We find, for example,
unmistakable signs of Estienne's interest in the critical analysis of Stoicism in his manner of handling a key term like πάθος, which (following
Cicero) he precisely glosses as "Morbus, quicunque est motus in animo
turbus" (p. 169) [Distress, whatever constitutes a disordered impulse in
the mind]. Estienne's intention is clear: since πάθος in Classical Greek
can also mean "anything that befalls one, an incident, accident, . . . one's
experience, . . . any passive state" and even "pathos" as we understand
the word today,[37] it is important to specify the Stoic sense of the term.
Hence its translation as *morbus.* But this translation must then be defined
in its turn, since *morbus* itself has as its primary connotation in Classical
Latin that of a physical disorder: "disease, illness, sickness."[38] Thus, to
bring out the contextually essential psychological (rather than
physiological) dimensions of the concept, Estienne uses a technical
adjective such as *turbus,* which is not generally attested in Classical
Latin, where one is more likely to find *turbidus,* but certainly found in
Late Latin and medieval medical usage. Finally, a similarly detailed
attention is brought to the differentiation between the Stoic sense of

πάθο ς and the closely related πάθη, a more neutral word tending to mean "the condition in which one finds oneself" and, thus, less scientifically precise for the purposes of the psychological considerations basic to Stoicism. The assumptions made by Estienne with regard to how far he can trust his readers' grasp of the Latin translations of such essential concepts in Greek philosophy are not only fascinating in themselves but also provide us with further insight into his sense both of linguistic relationships and of his mission as a humanist philologist. The *corrector* mediates the tension between *translatio* as a gesture of carrying meaning over into the target language, and *interpretatio* as an attempt to preserve the integrity of the source from the depletions inherent in all efforts at replication.

As noted at the outset, Estienne's importance in the field of humanist translation is essentially that of a theoretician. He obviously has heartfelt enthusiam for his mentor Budé's view of

> la [langue] grecque, laquelle est la plus ample & la plus copieuse & abundante en termes & vocables, de toutes langues dont nous aions congnoissance, & en laquelle seule langue, eloquence, qui par les anciens a esté appellée royne des hommes & des sciences, peut pleinement & amplement monstrer & exhiber sa grande puissance & soy estendre de toutes parts.[39]

> [Greek, which is the most ample, the most copious and the most abundant in figures of speech and vocabulary of all the languages we know of, and in which alone, eloquence, which was called by the Ancients the Queen of humankind and of knowledge, can fully and amply show and reveal its great power, and extend itself throughout the world.]

Couched as it is in terms taken from the standard terminology of rhetoric, such a definition (not untypical in itself of what we find among other Hellenizing Humanists of the time) must have seemed entirely natural to Estienne. It surely nourished his sense of that special relationship between Greek and French which led him to affirm more than once that "multo maiorem Gallica lingua cum Graeca habet affinitatem quam Latina"[40] [the French language has much greater affinity with Greek than with Latin]. The number of texts he actually translated is relatively small, and apart from brief excerpts chosen for the sake of example, these are done into Latin, not French. Given what we have seen of his activities as *corrector,* this should not surprise us. There can be no doubt of his sensitivity to the importance of both source and target languages in the translative process, or of his approval of Cicero's ideal of the translator as an *orator:* it is clear, however, that he sees himself far more as the *interpres* whose role it is to ensure that the values of the original are accurately conveyed. It will now be helpful to focus more closely on Estienne's view of the relationship between Greek (and to a certain degree Latin) and French, in order to bring out more fully a number of specific aspects of his theory of translation.

Promotion of Greek is not only a matter of philological duty and patriotic pride for Estienne but also a deeply felt act of filial piety, as may be seen on the title-page of his monumental *Thesaurus Grecae Linguae,* where he speaks of himself as "paternae in Thesauro Latino diligentiae aemulus"[41] [a zealous imitator of my father's conscientiousness in the *Thesaurus Latinus*].[42] Much of his professional energy was to go into the editing of Greek texts and the publishing of philogical, pedagogical, and polemical works dedicated to improving the level of Greek learning in France.[43] His *De abusu linguae grecae* [*On the Mistreatment of the Greek Language*] is a reasoned catalog of the mistakes he has noted, not so much in contemporary usage as in Latin borrowings ("mistranslations," by his lights) from Greek.[44] These range from lexical matters such as "wrong" number, for example (making Greek neuter plurals into Latin feminine singulars: τὰ ῥητορικά > *rhetorica*, τὰ διαλεκτικά > *dialectica*[45]), to the type of more serious problem seen earlier:

> Iam vero quemadmodum *hypocrita*, ὑποκριτής, alium usum in Evangelis habet scriptis quam eum qui passim apud scriptores Graecos invenitur . . . ita etiam *parabola*, παραβολή. (pp. 106–07)

> [Just as, indeed, *hypocrita* (=hypocrite), ὑποκριτής (=actor), has a different sense in the Gospels from the one found throughout the Greek writers . . . so also the word *parabola* (=parable), παραβολή (=simile, proverb).]

But in the matter of the relationship between the national language and Greek, it is less the threat to religious orthodoxy than the exploration of the bond between them, and of his role in the consolidation of this bond, that interests Estienne. This can lead him from what we must judge today as well-intentioned inaccuracy to a number of further insights into the nature of translation. In his *Hypomneses de Gall. Lingua*,[46] where he argues for such phonetic impossibilities as the presence of a directly causal connection between French diphthongs such as *eu* and *oi*, and εὖ and οἶ (pp. 45–47),[47] he also utilizes translation from Greek as a means of validating the vernacular. It is a source of some satisfaction for him, for example, to note that French, like Greek, can use substantivized infinitives:

> Dicitur enim *Son boire & son manger*, ut, *On luy fournit son boire & son manger*; hic quoque infinitivus vice nominum fundentibus, more Graeco. Ita enim dicunt τὸ πιεῖν καὶ τὸ φαγεῖν. (p. 68)

> [(French has) "He is provided with his *boire* and his *manger*." Here too we use the infinitive like nouns, in the Greek manner, for they also say "to drink" and "to eat."]

Estienne would no doubt have found comfort in the embarrassment
bound to accompany such attempts to translate his text into a language
whose grammatical categories do not sit well with either source or
target!

More than any other of his publications, however, it is his *Traicté de
la conformité du langage françois avec le Grec* which accords the fullest
treatment to the topic.[48] It is here that he demonstrates most extensively
his sense of the phenomenon of language and of linguistic relationships,
and their consequences for our efforts to transfer meaning. His purpose
is stated plainly at the start: he intends to prove,

> monstrans à l'oeil combien le langage François est voisin du Grec
> . . . afin que par ceste comparaison, chascun voye combien le Latin,
> l'Italien, l'Espagnol, sont esloignez du Grec, duquel le nostre est
> prochain voisin. . . . La langue Grecque est la roine des langues, &
> . . . si la perfection se doibt cercher en aucune, c'est en ceste la
> qu'elle se trouvera . . . la langue Françoise, pour approcher plus pres
> de celle qui a acquis la perfection, doibt estre estimee excellente
> pardessus les autres. (*fols. 4ᵛ–5ʳ)

> [before your very eyes, how close French is to Greek . . . so that, by
> this comparison, everyone might see how much Latin, Italian, and
> Spanish are distant from Greek, whose close neighbor our own
> language is. . . . The Greek language is the queen of languages, and
> . . . if perfection is to be sought in any, it is in Greek that it will be
> found. . . . French, since it comes closer to the language that has
> attained perfection, must (then) be considered to be pre-eminent
> above those others.]

We might perhaps be tempted to smile at the naive circularity of
Estienne's syllogism or, later in the book, at his argument that the
perfection of Greek lies in the fact that it lends to all other tongues but
borrows from none (*fol. 5ᵛ), given his acknowledged awareness of the

processes of linguistic development. As always, however, we must beware the risk of anachronistic judgment, which might lead us to dismiss as mere inconsistency what, within the framework of polemic eloquence, was doubtless meant to be seen as a legitimate tactic in the effort to be persuasive. Since linguistic transfer involves the Ciceronian distinction between *interpres* and *orator,* the issue turns once again on rhetorical values. The rhetorical basis of what is taken to constitute a language's intrinsic qualities is fully revealed in Estienne's contention, as he champions Greek, that linguistic perfection lies in ease of pronunciation, gratification to the ear, and a lexicon that is "copieux, & abondant en mots de toutes sortes" (*fol. 5ʳ) [copious and abundant in words of every kind]. The echoes of Cicero's requirements for the best type of speaking are unmistakable: "Docere debitum est, delectare honorarium, permovere necessarium" (*De opt. gen. orat.,* 3) [To edify is a duty; to delight is to bestow a gift; to move is a necessity]. In the light of what we have seen earlier, it clearly follows that, for Estienne, translation specifically involves the representation of the rhetorical resources of the source language through the exploitation of their equivalents in the target language.

Thus, the co-existence of the partitive genitive in both French and Greek, for example, makes of the ease of replicability a mechanism for not only verifying the accuracy of a given translation but also establishing an authentic reading of the source text:

> Nous disons, Manger du pain, Manger le pain: & quelquesfois sans ces particules Du & Le, Manger pain. . . . Lesquelles façons de parler ne peuvent estre discernees par les Latins, qui disent indifferement *panem edere*: mais les Grecs les dicernent tresbien, usans de ces trois manieres correspondantes aux trois nostres, φαγεῖν τῷ ἄρτου, φαγεῖν τὸν ἄρτον, φαγεῖν ἄρτον. (p. 3)

> [We say "to eat some bread, to eat the bread," and sometimes

without these articles, "to eat bread." . . . These ways of speaking cannot be differentiated by the Latins, who say indiscriminately *panem edere;* but the Greeks differentiate between them perfectly well, using (these) three forms which correspond to our three.]

This "co-incidence of translation" then enables Estienne the advocate of the vernacular to become Estienne the *corrector.* Turning to Thucydides, he goes on:

> Au moyen de quoi, ce que Thucydide dit au commencement de son livre 5, καὶ διελὼν τοῦ παλαιοῦ τείχους, le Latin ne sçauroit traduire mot à mot, & sans rien adjouster: mais si fera bien le François, quand il dira, Et ayant retrenché de la vieille muraille. . . . Et toutesfois ni Laurent Valla, ni Messire Claude de Seyssel n'ont pris garde à cest usage du Genitif: car ils ont traduict ce passage comme si Thucydide eust dit, διελὼν τὸ παλαιὸν τείχος: combien que cela mesme qui suit, les deust avoir advertis, κατὰ τὸ διῃρημένον τοῦ παλαιοῦ τείχους.[49]

> [Because of this, what Thucydides says at the start of his Book V, "and having breached (some part) of the ancient fortification," could not be rendered word by word in Latin, and without adding something. But French will do it perfectly well. . . . And even so, neither Lorenzo Valla nor Master Claude de Seyssel paid attention to this use of the genitive, for they translated as if Thucydides had said, "having breached the ancient fortification," even though the very next thing should have alerted them: "(and rushed in with him) at the breach in the ancient fortification."]

This is not strictly fair to the translators mentioned, of course, since Valla was working from Greek to Latin (which, as Estienne concedes, does not have a partitive genitive of this kind), and Seyssel was engaged in putting Valla's Latin into French and was, thus, probably unconcerned by its presence in the original. Nevertheless, Estienne's observation is significant in that it shows how such recourse to philological translation can allow the emendation of earlier renderings. It is not merely a question of avoiding what Estienne considers his predecessors' habit of frequently giving their readers "des qui pro quo d'apothiquaire" [the mumbo-jumbo of apothecaries], but of holding translators to account for the trustworthiness of what they tell us about the past.

There are, of course, moments when both his enthusiasm for Greek and, in consequence, the uncritical application of some of his theoretical positions leads Estienne into an area that ranges from the eccentric to the outlandish.[50] In his *Observation XI* on Greek and French nouns, for example, he is pleased to note:

> au lieu que les Latins ont transposé les lettres de quelques noms propres Grecs, nous les avons retenus au mesme ordre. Exemple, les Grecs disent ʼΑλέξανδρος, les Latins *Alexander,* nous Alexandre. (p. 22)

> [whereas the Latins have transposed the letters in some Greek proper nouns, we have kept them in the same order. For example: the Greeks say ʼΑλέξανδρος, the Latins *Alexander,* the French "Alexandre."]

While we might excuse his failure to realize that French nouns derive essentially from the Latin accusative forms into which the other oblique cases had mostly collapsed in Gallo-Roman, thus making *Alexandre* inescapably the progeny of *Alexandrum,* we may well judge that on occasion he goes too far. When, on the same page, he announces "Quand aux terminaisons de quelques noms propres, nous nous accordons aussi fort bien avec les Grecs: disons Simon, Ciceron, ainsi qu'eux disent Σίμων, Κικέρων: & non pas Simo, Cicero, comme les Latins" [As for the endings of certain proper nouns, we are also in complete harmony with the Greeks: we say *Simon, Cicéron,* just as they say Σίμων, Κικέρων: and

Kenneth Lloyd-Jones

not *Simo, Cicero,* like the Latins], Estienne comes dangerously close to arguing that the Greeks knew Latin better than the Romans. Such an extremely ahistorical perspective, positing the value of French on the rendering of a Greek form itself no more than a back-formation from Latin, clearly jeopardizes the ideal of philological probity he strives for elsewhere.

Less problematic, and ultimately more in keeping with the rest of his interpretive theory, is his comparison of Greek and French past tenses, in which the recourse to translation allows the exploration of more genuinely philological concerns. With regard to the imperfect, for instance, he notes that

> nous disons, Ainsi qu'il mouroit, ou Comme il mouroit, survint un sien ami, à grand peine les Latins diront ils *Quum ipse moriebat, amicus eius supervenit,* au lieu de *Quum moreretur:* mais les Grecs diront ils comme nous, . . . ὡς δὲ αὐτὸς ἀπέθνησκεν, ἐπέστη ὁ φίλος αὐτοῦ, ou ἐπεὶ δὲ αὐτὸς ἀπέθνησκεν. (p 60)

> [. . . we say, "While he was dying," or "As he was dying, a friend of his arrived," (whereas) the Latins will (use the imperfect indicative [only]) with great awkwardness, rather than (the imperfect subjunctive). But the Greeks will say (it) as we do, "While he was dying," or "As he was dying."]

Here, the translation of the French into a consciously infelicitous Latin serves—independently of the patriotic points scored—to highlight a perfectly valid consideration of the three different languages' approach to the temporal aspect of the subjunctive mood.

Similarly, some lines from the *Iliad* provide Estienne with the opportunity to explore, through the means of both conventional translation and back-translation (i.e., into an invented version of the source language), issues of some complexity in the domain of comparative philo-

289

logy. Mulling over the relationship between French and Greek use of the perfect forms, he writes:

> Je commenceray par un exemple pris du pere de tous les poetes: lequel exemple contient des motz dorez, ou plustost une sentence doree: & est au premier livre de l'Iliad:
>
> Ο κε θεοῖς ἐπιπείθηται, μάλα τ᾽ ἔκλυον αὐτοῦ.[51]
>
> Lequel vers merite mieux d'estre en la bouche d'un Chrestien que d'un Payen, en changeant seulement les Nom & Verbe pluriels en singuliers, & disant,
>
> Ο κε θεῷ ἐπιπείθηται, μάλα τ᾽ ἔκλυεν αὐτοῦ.
>
> C'est à dire,
>
> *Qui porte à Dieu obeissance entiere,*
> *Est exaucee par luy en sa priere.*
>
> Mais pour le traduire simplement, & en gardant les mesmes temps, il faudroit dire, Quiconque obéit à Dieu, il l'a aussi tost exaucé. Ou par le pluriel, (pour estre plus intelligible) Celuy qui obéit aux dieux, ils l'ont aussi tost exaucé: ou (avec le Pleonasme du Pronom) ils vous l'ont aussi tost exaucé. (pp. 64–65)

[I shall begin with an example taken from the father of all poets, an example that contains some golden words, or rather a golden precept, from Book One of *The Iliad:* "He who obeys the gods, him do they particularly set free." This line deserves more to be on the lips of a Christian than a pagan, if we change the plural noun and verb into the singular, and say, "He who obeys God, him does He particularly set free," in other words:

*Whosoever obeys God with all dedication,*
*To him then God grants his entire supplication.*

But to translate it simply, keeping the same tenses, we would have to say, "He who obeys God, his prayer has He straightaway granted." Or with the plural (to be more understandable), "He who obeys the gods, his prayer have they straightaway granted." Or (with the pleonastic pronoun), "his prayer have they straightaway granted, don't you see."[52]]

Kenneth Lloyd-Jones

The issues raised in this paragraph are both numerous and far reaching. In addition to the omnipresent question of the tension between Christian and pagan registers, Estienne, ever faithful to his concern for the rhetorical features of translation, offers no less than four versions of his source text. It is as if the complexity of translation has been broken down into a number of components, some of which focus more on *translatio,* others more on *interpretatio.* The first, into a French rhymed couplet, serves to convey the original in a formalist manner, in which the order of both words and ideas, itself affected by the demands of Greek scansion, is altered as a function of the requirements of French versification; it may thus be seen as chiefly addressed to a literary readership, concerned with esthetic or stylistic matters. The second, interestingly marked as "simple," conveys the thought of the source text in such a manner as to present no danger to orthodoxy, but this is immediately corrected by the third version, intended "to be more understandable." Since the principal difference between these last two lies in the suppression of the element of compatibility with Christianity, in favor of a more accurate linguistic version of the source, Estienne's notion of "more understandable" here is obviously more philological than philosophical. Unlike the second version, the third version is, thus, more comprehensible to the student of Greek who is using the translation as a means of verifying the original. Finally, the fourth version, with its "pleonastic pronoun," is frankly popular in tone. Classical rhetorical theory assigned the ethical dative to the third stylistic category, that of *oratio extenuata* or *tenuis*[53] [the "simple" or "plain" style], and we may thus suppose the intended readership here to be at the other extremity from that of the first translation. As noted earlier, Estienne has a special fondness for popular, older, and more authentically French vocabulary and forms of expression, those he considers as "smelling of the market place" [sentans Place Maubert[54]], and there is an echo of this aspect of his interests in the fourth version.

## The Theoretical Writings of Henri Estienne

It is readily conceded that Estienne's primary purpose in this passage is linguistic: to explore the importance of aspect rather than tense as a means of defining temporal relationships in Greek. Nevertheless, his recourse to such a variety of renderings clearly undermines any conception of translation as a monolithic undertaking, and offers further evidence of his sense that in spite of superficial likenesses (so superficial, indeed, that they cannot be expressed in a single, definitive form), deep structure may not, in the end, be transferable.

Similarly, in spite of his oft-repeated (and no doubt intentionally polemic) assertion that French is distinguished because of its resemblances to Greek, a final example, also taken from Homer (*Iliad*, 4:452–55), reminds us that it is ultimately the dissimilarities between different linguistic structures that form the crux of what is problematic about translation. As he writes,

> Autre exemple pris du livre 4 du mesme poeme,
> ὡς δ᾽ ὅτε χείμαρροι ποταμοὶ κατ᾽ ὄρεσθι ῥέοντες
> ἐς μισγάγκειαν συμβάλλετον ὄβριμον ὕδωρ
> κρουνῶν ἐκ μεγάλων κοίλης ἔντοσθε χαράδρης,
> τῶν δέ τε τηλόσε δοῦπον ἐν οὔρεσιν ἔκλυε ποιμήν. . . .
> Ainsi dirions-nous, Comme quand il y a des torrents qui tombans à val d'une montaigne viennent à s'engorger dedans le creux d'une vallee, le pasteur qui est bien loing en a incontinent ouy le son, ou, aura aussi tost ouy. Car j'enten que ce Preterit a ouy se prenne icy ne plus ne moins que quand nous disons, Le moindre bruit qu'on face pendant que je dors, je l'ay incontinent ouy, ou, Je l'auray aussi tost ouy. Au lieu de dire par le Present, Je l'oy incontinent: C'est à dire, J'ay coustume de l'ouir incontinent. Comme aussi en cest exemple . . . Si une souri seulement fait bruit, je suis incontinent esveillé: ce Preterit Je suis esveillé, se prend pour Je m'esveille: & Je m'esveille, se prend pour J'ay accoustumé de m'esveiller. (pp. 65–66)

# Kenneth Lloyd-Jones

[Another example taken from Book Four of the same poem: "As when winter-flowing rivers, rushing down from the mountains, throw both together their mighty waters into a hollow valley, out of their great springs deep in the cleft gully, and the shepherd could hear their noise far away in the mountains. . . ." We would say it like this: "As when there are torrents which, falling downward from a mountain, come into full flood in the hollow of a valley, the shepherd who is quite far has immediately heard the noise," or "will immediately have heard." For I understand that this preterite "has heard" should be taken here for no more or no less than (our usage) when we say, "The slightest noise that anyone might make while I sleep, I have immediately heard it," or "I will have immediately heard it," rather than saying in the present, "I hear it immediately," which is to say, "I habitually hear it immediately." As also in this example . . . "If a mouse makes the slightest noise, I have become rightaway vigilant/alert/awake." This preterite . . . can [however] mean "I am rightaway vigilant," and "I am rightaway vigilant" can mean "I am habitually vigilant."][55]

Here, Estienne's translation—surprisingly, in one sense—borders on paraphrase. Knowing his delight in philological precision, we might have expected him to render more exactly the compound adjectival thrust of χείμαρροι and, particularly, to have wanted to demonstrate his sensitivity to the dual form of the verb συμβάλλετον, yet neither of these important elements is reflected in his translation. The fact is, of course, that Estienne's interests lie elsewhere; linguistic structures are, in the end, important because they express human truths. The immediate focus of his reflection is the Greek verb-form ἔκλυε, and attendant niceties of grammar. But, in spite of some confusion over aspect versus tense, with a consequent fall-back to a slightly doctored piece of French to substantiate his point, the basic concern is both clear and compelling. Mice and mountain streams are part of the common fund of human experience and, as such, they might speak of what unites us. The differences in our various ways of expressing this experience can all too often, however, set us apart. Whether we hear it as the squeak of a mouse or as a distant torrent cascading into the valley, the discourse of other times and other places can indeed be disquieting, and all the more so when we endeavor to accommodate its unfamiliar voice to our own. What we have seen of Estienne's understanding of the interpretive entanglements that beset the translator shows how fully he sensed the divisive potential of it all. But his frequentation of Greek thought, inalienably shaped by its particular linguistic structures,[56] and his conviction of the similarity of these structures to those of his own language and values, led him to see translation as a means of reconciling what time and distance might otherwise estrange.

In the prologue to his *Quart Livre* of 1548, Rabelais had defined *le Pantagruélisme,* that product of his own adoption of Greek values, as "[une] certaine gayeté d'esprit conficte en mespris des choses fortuites" ["a certain jollity of mind, pickled in the scorn of fortune," as the Urquhart-Motteux translation has it]. It could surely have been no accident that Estienne, reflecting on the links between French and Greek, and on the even more mysterious bonds between a people and its language, was brought to speculate that a similar force might be at work,

soit que les premiers auteurs de la nostre [langue] ayent ainsi parlé à l'imitation des Grecs, soit que par une mesme gayeté d'esprit ils se soyent entrerencontrez en ces mesmes façons de parler. (*Conformité,* p. 26)

[whether because the earliest authors of (the French tongue) spoke thus in imitation of the Greeks, or whether, because of a like jollity of mind, they met on common ground in these selfsame ways of speaking.][57]

# Kenneth Lloyd-Jones

## Notes

1. Jacques Espagnolle, *Le vrai Dictionnaire étymologique de la langue française* (Paris: Klincksieck, 1896), p. i.

2. All translations are my own, unless otherwise indicated.

3. J. De Boisjoslin, "Rapport sur *La Clef du vieux français* par M. l'Abbé Espagnolle," in *Revue de la Société des Etudes Historiques* (1891), p. 205.

4. Just as Espagnolle was to condemn the "philologue habitué à ne voir partout que du latin" [the philologist used to seeing only Latin everywhere] and appeal to "le linguiste libre de tout préjugé" [the linguist free from all prejudice], who would accept that such words as *vie, or,* and *taureau* [life, gold, bull] come, not from *vita, aurum,* and *taurus,* but from βίος, αὖρον, and ταύρος (*La Clef du vieux français* [Paris: Leroy, 1890], p. 3).

5. For an excellent anthology of *apologiae* from the first half of the sixteenth century, see Claude Longeon, *Premiers Combats pour la langue française* (Paris: Librairie Générale Française, Livre de Poche Classique, 1989). Longeon remarks that if, in the latter half of the century, other vernaculars constituted the main threat to French, "l'adversaire est le latin" (p. 6) [the opponent is Latin], between 1500 and 1549. He goes on to point out that in 1501, for example, of eighty books published in Paris, eight are in French and seventy-two in Latin (p. 7).

6. This question is explored by Colette Demaizière, "Deux Aspects de l'idéal linguistique d'Henri Estienne: Hellénisme et Parisianisme," in *Henri Estienne* (*Cahiers V.-L. Saulnier no. 5, Collection de l'E.N.S.J.F. no. 43* [Paris: Presses de l'E.N.S.J.F., 1988]), pp. 63–75.

7. Guillaume Budé, *Commentarii Linguae Grecae* (1529) [*Commentaries on the Greek Language*], in *Opera Omnia*, vol. 4 (Basel: Froben, 1557), col. 1419.11.

8. François Rabelais, *Pantagruel* [1532], ch. 8.

9. For Budé, see in particular Marie-Madeleine de la Garanderie, *Christianisme et lettres profanes (1515–1535): Essai sur les mentalités des milieux intellectuels parisiens et sur la pensée de Guillaume Budé,* 2 vols. (Paris: Champion, 1976). For a discussion of the

295

# The Theoretical Writings of Henri Estienne

prolongation into the seventeenth century of the Renaissance debate over the superiority of Greek to Latin, see Jean-Claude Margolin, "La bataille des 'latiniseurs' et des 'helléniseurs' au XVII^e siècle à propos du P. Philippe Labbe et du *Jardin des Racines Grecques*," in *Acta Conventus Neo-Latini Guelpherbytani: Proceedings of the Sixth International Congress of Neo-Latin Studies: Wolfenbüttel, 12 August to 16 August 1985*, ed. Stella P. Revard, Fidel Rädle, and Mario A. Di Cesare (Binghamton: M.R.T.S., 1988), pp. 437–67. For a general background, there are some useful contributions in *Les Humanistes et l'antiquité grecque*, ed. Mitchiko Ishigami-Iagolnitzer (Paris: Editions du C.N.R.S., 1991).

10. For example, the teaching endeavors of Dorat, Lambin, and Turnèbe. For an overall review, see Olivier Reverdin, *Les Premiers Cours de grec au Collège de France* (Paris: P.U.F., 1984); for a discussion of Amyot's contribution to the teaching of Greek, see Christiane Lauvergnat-Gagnière, "Amyot et l'étude du grec en France au XVI^e siècle," in *Fortunes de Jacques Amyot: Actes du Colloque International (Melun, 18–20 avril, 1985)*, ed. M. Balard (Paris: Nizet, 1986), pp. 57–66.

11. For example, Ronsard, Du Bellay, and Belleau: see in particular Isidore Silver, *Ronsard and the Hellenic Renaissance in France*, new ed. (St. Louis and Geneva: Washington University Press and Droz, 1987). See also Marc Bizer, "Ronsard the Poet, Belleau the Translator: The Difficulties of Writing in the Laureate's Shadow," in this volume.

12. Above all, Amyot: see, in particular, René Sturel, *Jacques Amyot, Traducteur des Vies Parallèles de Plutarque* (Paris: Champion, 1908), and Robert Aulotte, *Amyot et Plutarque: La tradition des Moralia au XVI^e siècle* (Geneva: Droz, 1965). Aulotte fully brings out the socio-cultural dimensions of Amyot's undertaking: "Recréer, tel est bien le propos d'Amyot. Recréer non pas comme un auteur qui rebâtirait une oeuvre sur nouveaux frais, mais comme un acteur créant ou recréant un rôle" (p. 282) [To recreate, such is Amyot's purpose. To recreate, not like an author who would construct a new work starting entirely afresh, but like an actor creating or recreating a role]. For Amyot, the good translator "doit tenir compte du public, de ses besoins, et de ses goûts," and must exemplify the "vulgarisateur honnête homme, soucieux de ne pas choquer, de ne pas être obscur, de ne pas dépayser" (p. 284) [(He) must take account of the public, of its needs and of its tastes, (and must exemplify) the popularizer and "wellborn man of judgment, taste and experience," careful not to shock, not to be obscure, not to lead the reader into

296

uncharted terrain]. (I owe the translation of *honnête homme* to Donald M. Frame, *Montaigne's "Essais": A Study* [Englewood Cliffs, N. J.: Prentice Hall, 1969], p. 99). It is not to belittle Amyot's work to state that he perfectly embodies the notion of translator as domesticator. As such, he stands at the polar extreme from Estienne.

13. Chiefly, Louis Le Roy: see Werner Gundersheimer, *The Life and Works of Louis Le Roy* (Geneva: Droz, 1966); see also Jean-Claude Margolin, "Le Roy, traducteur de Platon, et la Pléiade," in *Lumières de la Pléiade: IX<sup>e</sup> Stage International d'Etudes Humanistes, Tours, 1965* [*sic*: sc. *1964*] (Paris: Vrin, 1966); and Jean Jehasse, "Loys Le Roy, maître et émule de Jean Bodin," in *Etudes sur Etienne Dolet . . . publiées à la mémoire de Claude Longeon,* ed. Gabriel-André Pérouse (Geneva: Droz, 1993), pp. 251–64.

14. For general information on Estienne, see Louis Clément, *Henri Estienne et son oeuvre française* (Paris: Picard, 1898); see also the individual essays in *Henri Estienne, Cahiers V.-L. Saulnier no. 5* (see n. 6 above).

15. Henri Estienne, *Artis Typographicae Querimonia, De Illiteratis quibusdam Typographicis, propter quos in contemptum venit* (Paris [?]: H. Stephanus, 1569) [*Complaint lodged by the Art of Printing, concerning certain illiterate printers, because of whom it has fallen into disrepute*]. Current citations are taken from the edition in *De Vitis Stephanorum . . . Dissertatio,* T. Jansson (Amsterdam: J. Wasserberg, 1683), pp. 138–47.

16. It should be noted here that all Latin and vernacular quotations from Renaissance texts are reproduced *verbatim,* except that conventional nasal abbreviations have been resolved, and *i* and *u* reproduced as *j* and *v* where appropriate, in accordance with modern usage. Greek is also quoted as it is in the original, except that the positioning of breathings over diphthongs and the selection of grave or acute on the *ultima* have generally been brought into line with modern usage: I have, however, made a very small number of silent corrections, where to preserve the original could only lead to confusion.

17. Henri Estienne, *Herodoti Helicarnassei historiae lib.ix, & de vita Homeri libellus. Illi ex interpretatione Laur. Vallae adscripta, hic ex interpret. Conradi Heresbachii: utraque ab Henr. Stephano recognita . . .* [*Nine Books of Histories by Herodotus of Helicarnassus, and a Brief Book on the Life of Homer, the Former from the Translation Attributed to Lorenzo Valla, the Latter from the Translation of Conrad Heresbach: Both Revised by Henri Estienne . . .*] (Geneva: H. Estienne, 1566 [Bib. Nat., Paris: J 629]).

297

# The Theoretical Writings of Henri Estienne

18. Henri Estienne, *Project du livre intitulé De La Precellence du langage François* [*Prospectus for the Book (To Be) Called "On the Preeminence of the French Language"*] (Paris: Mamert Patisson, 1579 [Bib. Nat., Paris: X 9714]), fols. 2ᵛ–3ʳ: (Geneva: Slatkine Reprints, 1972, same pagination). This enterprise was destined to remain at the stage of a "project."

19. The question over whether poetry should be translated into verse form is an important one in the Renaissance, but more germane to the field of poetics than to the kind of philological translation discussed here, in that it involves theories of *imitatio* and *mimesis.* See Joachim Du Bellay, *La Deffence et illustration de la Langue Françoyse* [1549], ed. Henri Chamard (Paris: S.T.F.M., [1948] 1966), Bk. 1, ch. 5–6. See also Graham Castor, *Pléiade Poetics: A Study in Sixteenth-Century Thought and Terminology* (Cambridge: Cambridge University Press, 1964), pp. 63–76: Castor usefully distinguishes between "the extreme of [Aristotelian] 'true mimesis' [and] the extreme of false mimesis . . . the predominantly philological interests of the early Humanist editors, who stressed above all else in the ancient literatures the perfection of form and expression. For them style was the element in a literary work which was most worthy of imitation" (p. 73). Our study of Estienne, even though his interests were more linguistic than literary, shows that this remains true for Humanist editors of his generation too.

20. This desire to allow his translations to be as eloquent as possible may well be why Estienne does not cite the original Greek and Latin. Given his careful approach to the requirements of philological editing, such omission is unusual, but we may suppose that it is justified here by a desire not to allow the presence of the originals to deflect from the rhetorical thrust of his own versions.

21. Henri Estienne, *Deux dialogues du nouveau langage françois: italianizé et autrement desguizé . . .* [*Two Dialogues on the New French Language, Italianized and Otherwise Disguised*] (Geneva: H. Estienne, 1578); current quotations are taken from the edition by Pauline M. Smith (Geneva: Slatkine, 1980).

22. Among other solecisms, we may note Philausone's use of *mostret* or *pouves* (Estienne prefers older forms like *monstroit* or *pouvois*): also, adjectives corresponding to the It. *-esco* ending ("le langage *courtisanesque*," p. 36), or *-ico* ("la religion *christianique*," p. 339), and the "italianate" confusion of l/r ("garbe" for "elegance," < It. *galba*: cf. "sgarbatement" for "gracelessly," < It. *sgarbato*, p. 36). Estienne makes sure we realize

# Kenneth Lloyd-Jones

his intentions a little later, in his "AVERTISSEMENT au Lecteur" (p. 64) ["CAUTION to the Reader"]: "Sçachez, lecteur, que ce n'est pas sans cause que vous avez ici les mesmes mots escrits en deux sortes, asçavoir non seulement 'françois,' mais aussi 'frances': et non seulement 'je disois' . . . mais aussi 'je dises' . . ." [Know, reader, that it is not without cause that you have here the same words written in two ways, namely not only 'françois,' but also 'frances': and not only 'je disois' . . . but also 'je dises' . . .].

23. Estienne was not, of course, alone in this view: see James Romm, "More's Strategy of Naming in *Utopia*," *Sixteenth Century Journal* 22 (1991): 173–83: "Like his fellow Humanists, Thomas More was deeply interested in both philology and semiology, and in particular in the ways these two disciplines overlapped. For him, Greek and Latin, or language in general, could at times become a kind of code, the meanings of which could be extracted only imperfectly or not at all" (p. 173). Thus, it is argued, More undermines "the assumption that language can convey consistent or unambiguous meanings."

24. The references are to Herodotus, 1:126, 4:8, and 5:92.γ (*Deux Dialogues,* ed. Smith).

25. The presence of a Greek letter in a word set in roman characters reveals a further attempt at replication without deviation. It is no doubt in a similar spirit that Estienne occasionally preserves the different vowel lengths in his Latinized transcriptions of Greek words: see for example his *Sexti Philosophi Pyrrhoniarum hypotypωseωn libri III . . .* (Paris: H. Stephanus, 1562). Although somewhat uncommon, the insertion of Greek font, and even Greek punctuation, into roman type is found elsewhere in Renaissance printing: for a full discussion, see Robert Proctor, *The Printing of Greek in the Fifteenth Century* (Oxford: The University Press, 1900).

26. See Kenneth Lloyd-Jones, "Humanist Debate and the 'Translative Dilemma' in Renaissance France," in *Medieval Translators and their Craft,* ed. Jeanette Beer, Studies in Medieval Culture 25 (Kalamazoo: Western Michigan University, 1989), pp. 347–71. The chief texts in question are Desiderius Erasmus, *Ciceronianus, sive De Optimo Genere Dicendi* (Basel: Froben, 1528), ed. and trans. Betty I. Knott, *The Collected Works of Erasmus,* vol. 28 (Toronto: University. of Toronto Press, 1986); and Etienne Dolet, *Dialogus, De Imitatione Ciceroniana, adversus Desiderium Erasmum Roterodamum* (Lyon: S. Gryphe, 1535), ed. Emile V. Telle (Geneva: Droz, 1974).

# The Theoretical Writings of Henri Estienne

27. Glyn P. Norton, *The Ideology and Language of Translation in Renaissance France and their Humanist Antecedents* (Geneva: Droz, 1984), p. 14: quoted in Lloyd-Jones, "Humanist Debate," p. 367.

28. See, in particular, Olivier Reverdin, "Henri Estienne à Genève," and Elizabeth Armstrong, "Les Rapports d'Henri Estienne avec les membres de sa famille restés ou devenus catholiques," in *Henri Estienne, Cahiers V.-L. Saulnier*, no. 5 (see n. 6 above). Both Henri and his parents, along with some younger brothers and sisters, settled in Geneva and declared their allegiance to Calvinism. In contrast, his uncle Charles remained in Paris as a Catholic and published a large number of texts under his own imprint.

29. Juvenal, *Satires*, 10:365–66 (*Deux Dialogues*, ed. Smith). The version quoted is how Estienne has it. Modern readings favor the following:

nullum numen habes, si sit prudentia: nos te,

nos facimus, Fortuna, deam caeloque locamus.

[You have no godly power, if prudence is present. It is we, oh

Fortune, who make a goddess of you and situate you in the heavens.]

(*Satires*, ed. A. E. Housman [Cambridge: Cambridge University Press, 1931], p. 101.) This correction does nothing to invalidate Estienne's use of the text; if anything, it reinforces it.

30. Henri Estienne, *De latinitate falso suspecta, Expostulatio Henrici Stephani* [*A Complaint by Henri Estienne, Concerning Latinity Falsely Held Suspect*] (Geneva: H. Stephanus, 1576 [Bib. Nat., Paris: X 17721]; also, Geneva: Slatkine Reprints, 1972). In spite of his allegiance to the superiority of Greek among the classical languages, Estienne is not above praising Latin when it suits him, as a means of furthering his claims for the superiority of French among the vernaculars. His thesis here is in direct contradiction to that of his *Conformité du langage françois*, discussed below. As we have noted, however, consistency is not allowed to hinder patriotic aims: "Il lui suffit d'avoir rattaché le français tout à la fois au grec et au latin, pour avoir atteint le but qu'il visait" [It was enough for him to have tied French to both Greek and Latin to have reached the aim he was after], Clément, *Henri Estienne*, p. 206 (see n. 14 above).

31. The whole question of Estienne's approach to etymology is analyzed in detail by Colette Demaizière, "Les Réflexions étymologiques d'Henri Estienne de la *Conformité* (1565) aux *Hypomneses* (1582)," in *Discours étymologiques: Actes du Colloque inter-*

*national organisé à l'occasion du centenaire de la naissance de Walther von Wartburg,* éd. J.-P. Chambon and G. Lüdi (Tübingen: Niemeyer, 1991), pp. 201–10.

32. See the *Greek-English Lexicon,* ed. H. G. Liddell and R. Scott, rev. H. S. Jones et al. (1843, 1925; Oxford: Clarendon Press, 1966) [cited hereafter as Liddell-Scott].

33. Alfred Ernout and Antoine Meillet, *Dictionnaire étymologique de la langue latine* (1932; Paris: Klincksieck, 1967), p. 523.

34. H. M. Hubbell, for example, finds that "It exhibits a roughness and at times obscurity of style," and goes on to note its "confusion of thought," in his edition and translation of the text, Loeb Classics, no. 386 (Cambridge, Mass. and London: Harvard University Press and W. Heinemann, 1976), p. 350.

35. For a good analysis of the translation principles put forward here and, in particular, their rhetorical aspects, concerned with such technical matters as *numerus* and *pondus* and the different treatment to be accorded to *verborum exornationes* and *sententiarum exornationes,* see Albert Yon, intro. to Cicero, *De optimo genere oratorum* (Paris: Les Belles Lettres, 1964), pp. 97–105.

36. See, for example, the well-known statement of Jesus in John 8: 12, ἐγώ εἰμι τὸ φῶς τοῦ κόσμου, clearly meaning a light for "the people of the world"; see William F. Arndt and F. W. Gingrich, *A Greek-English Lexicon of the New Testament and other Early Christian Literature . . .* (Chicago and London: University of Chicago Press, 1979).

37. Liddell-Scott, p. 1285.

38. See the *Oxford Latin Dictionary,* ed. Peter G. W. Glare et al. (Oxford: Clarendon Press, 1982), p. 1133.

39. Guillaume Budé, *Le Livre de l'institution du prince* [*The Book of the Education of the Prince*] (Paris: Jehan Foucher, 1547 [Bib. Nat., Paris: *E 3136]), fol. 15ʳ. The text was composed ca. 1519 and circulated in manuscript until 1547; see Claude Bontems, *L'Institution du Prince, de Guillaume Budé: Le Prince dans la France des XVIᵉ et XVIIᵉ siècles* (Paris: P.U.F., 1965); and Marie-Madeleine de la Garanderie, "Guillaume Budé, Prosateur français," in *Prose et Prosateurs de la Renaissance: Mélanges offerts à M. le*

# The Theoretical Writings of Henri Estienne

*Professeur Robert Aulotte* (Paris: S.E.D.E.S., 1988), pp. 39–47.

40. Henri Estienne, *Traicté de la conformité du langage françois avec le Grec . . . avec une preface remonstrant quelque partie du desordre & abus qui se commet aujourdhuy en l'usage de la langue françoise* (Geneva: H. Estienne, 1565 [Bib. Nat., Paris: X 9732]) [*A Treatise on the congruence of French and Greek . . . with a preface remonstrating against something of the disorder and misuse which is found nowadays in the French language*], *fol. 4ʳ. As Estienne notes, "En une epistre Latine que je mi l'an passé audevant de quelques miens dialogues Grecs, ce propos m'eschapa . . ." [In a Latin epistle which I placed last year at the head of some Greek dialogues of mine, I ventured the following remark. . .].

41. Henri Estienne, ΘΗΣΑΥΡΟΣ ΤΗΣ ΕΛΛΗΝΙΚΗΣ ΓΛΩΣΣΗΣ. *Thesaurus Grecae Linguae ab Henrico Stephanos constructus . . .* , 6 vols. (Geneva: H. Estienne, 1572–73), re-ed. C. B. Hase, G. R. L. de Sinner, T. Fix, 9 vols. (Paris: F. Didot, 1831–65.). The reference is to Robert Estienne's great *Thesaurus Linguae Latinae* (Paris: R. Estienne, 1531). In his *Conformité du langage françois avec le grec,* Estienne reminds us that his knowledge of Greek is not that of a "clerc d'armes" (*fol. 16ʳ) [a junior clerk], for his father had taught him the language as a child—even before Latin, "comme je conseilleray tousjours à mes amis de faire instituer leurs enfants . . . combien que la coustume soit aujourdhuy autrement" [which is how I will always advise my friends to have their children taught . . . although the usual way is the opposite today]. *O tempora, o mores. . . .*

42. For a broader discussion of some of the "genealogical" values underlying the Humanist cult of Greek, see Kenneth Lloyd-Jones, "The *Apologia* for Hellenism in the French Renaissance," *Romance Languages Annual, 1991,* ed. Jeanette Beer, Charles Ganelin, and Anthony J. Tamburri (West Lafayette: Purdue Research Foundation, 1992), pp. 72–77.

43. Clément, *Henri Estienne*, p. vii (see n. 14 above), indicates the existence of over 160 volumes with Henri Estienne's imprint, in Hebrew, Greek, Latin, and French, as well as a further 89 either projected or now lost.

44. Henri Estienne, *De abusu linguae grecae, in quibusdam vocibus quas Latina usurpat, ADMONITIO Henrici Stephani* [*An Admonition by Henri Estienne on the mistreatment*

# Kenneth Lloyd-Jones

*of the Greek language, regarding certain words and expressions which Latin has taken over*] (Geneva: H. Estienne, 1573 [Bib. Nat., Paris: X 24854]).

45. Estienne cheerfully passes over the similar shift between Latin and French, whereby, for example, *gaudium* > *gaudia* > *joie*. Once again, the patriot inspires the philologist. For a serious analysis of the issues involved, see Demaizière (see n. 31 above).

46. Henri Estienne, *Hypomneses De Gall. Lingua . . . Inspersa sunt nonnulla, partim ad Graecam, partim ad Lat. linguam pertinentia, minime vulgaria* [*Treatise on the French language . . . containing some matters bearing on Greek, some on Latin, and not at all common knowledge*] (Geneva: Typis Henr. Stephani, 1582 [Bib. Nat., Paris: X 11523]): ὑπόμνηεσις = treatise, discussion.

47. See François Moureau, "Henri Estienne et l'orthographe du XVI<sup>e</sup> siècle," in *Henri Estienne, Cahiers V.-L. Saulnier no. 5*, pp. 55–61 (see n. 6 above).

48. See n. 40 above: the text is also available in Slatkine Reprints, Geneva 1972.

49. Thucydides, *History of the Peloponnesian War*, 5.2.4 and 5.3.2. Without a full reading of the original, Estienne's concern might not be clear. It has to do with the fact that the Greek indicates the old wall was breached in only one place, whereas the translations Estienne has in mind leave open the possibility of a number of points of penetration. Such a distinction is important not only as fact but also for its implications regarding the military tactics employed. The question is clearly fresh in Estienne's mind, since he had just published his own edition, *Thucydidis . . . de bello Peloponnesiaco libri octo, . . . ex interpretatione Laurentii Vallae, ab Henrico Stephano recognita* [*Eight books on the Peloponnesian War by Thucydides, . . . in the Translation of Lorenzo Valla, Revised by Henri Estienne*] (Geneva: H. Estienne, 1564), in which the title page once again stresses his view of the importance of *correctio* for translation

50. In addition to the examples discussed we might add here some of Estienne's more fanciful etymologies at the start of Book Three: he suggests, for instance, that *chef* ("head,"< *capitem*) comes from κεφαλή, which through syncopation gave *κέφ. More winning, perhaps, is: "Caca, mot des petis enfans, κακᾶν: comme Papa, de πάππα, Maman, de μαμμᾶν."

303

# The Theoretical Writings of Henri Estienne

51. *Iliad* 1:218 (Achilles is answering Athene). Modern editions have ὅς κε θεοῖς ἐπιπείθηται. . . .

52. Efforts to represent the ethical dative in English tend to be unsuccessful: something like "and right there, under your nose" would capture the sense in which the reader is implicated, but would, of course, demolish any effort at preserving the stylistic register.

53. See, for example, the *Rhetorica ad Herennium* 4:14.

54. *Conformité,* p. 8; the Place Maubert was the heart of "popular" Paris, and the site of criminal executions in the sixteenth century. Students of the Renaissance will recall that the other great French Humanist theoretician of translation, Etienne Dolet, was put to death there in 1546.

55. English seems quite inadequate to the task here. Estienne's reference to the preterite indicates that he is using "être éveillé" perfectively, rather than descriptively (i.e., as the verb *to be* governing a predicate). Although it could in fact be argued that "je suis éveillé" is actually a present passive, Estienne appears to want to align it with the verbs conjugated with *être* in the perfect, like *aller* ("il est allé" = "he has gone"), in which considerations of aspect and tense are to some degree blurred: cf. English "he is gone."

56. It is a well-known gibe that Aristotle made philosophy out of Greek grammar, but it does seem fair to wonder, for example, how different the Western perception of reality might have been if Greek had not had the capacity to make neuter nouns out of present participles of the middle voice, like τὸ φαινόμενον.

57. This study of Estienne's theoretical writings is meant to complement Kenneth Lloyd-Jones, "The Tension of Philology and Philosophy in the Translations of Henri Estienne," *International Journal of the Classical Tradition* 1/1 (1994): 36–51.

304

# The French Translation of Agrippa von Nettesheim's *Declamatio de incertitudine et vanitate scientiarum et artium: Declamatio* as Paradox

## Marc van der Poel

The *Declamatio de incertitudine et vanitate scientiarum et artium atque excellentia verbi Dei* [*Declamation on the Uncertainty and Worthlessness of the Sciences and the Arts, and on the Excellence of the Word of God*], written in 1526 and published in 1530 by Heinrich Cornelius Agrippa von Nettesheim (1486–1535), is a good example of a Latin humanist text so popular that it was translated into several vernaculars during its own century. An Italian translation was published in 1547, an English translation in 1569, and a French one in 1582.[1] Written in the political and religious turmoil of the age of Christian humanism, Agrippa's *Declamatio* was controversial from the moment of its publication. Its author was already known as an enthusiastic student of magic and occultism, and as a neoplatonist who professed that the Hermetic was compatible with orthodox Christian theology. Now, in the *Declamatio*, he was seen to be attacking both clerical and secular authorities. Because of the severity of its criticism of the Roman Church and its apparent inclination toward Lutheranism, the *Declamatio* was, immediately on publication, placed on the index of forbidden books by the Faculty of Theology at the Sorbonne. In its turn, the Faculty of Theology at Louvain investigated the *Declamatio* at the request of Margaret of Austria, then governor of the Low Countries, and subsequently identified a number of passages as heretical and offensive to Catholics. Agrippa was to defend his *Declamatio* against these charges in two separate works,[2] but its publication alienated him from the Imperial court at Malines, which had

305

Marc van der Poel

hitherto employed him as archivist and historiographer.

Throughout the sixteenth century, the *Declamatio* continued to appear on lists of books forbidden to the faithful.[3] Judging from the large number of editions, however, it would seem that the various condemnations of the *Declamatio* did not prevent its circulation. Unfortunately, these various editions have not yet been studied in detail, nor have the expurgations in the Latin editions from ca. 1540 onwards. The purged editions omit, in fact, some twenty-one passages, varying in length from a few words to a number of sentences and treating, for the most part, theologians, friars, or the Roman Church as a whole.[4] It is my intention here to discuss the 1582 French translation (which was based on the full version of the Latin text and meant to be read in French aristocratic circles) and to address the dual questions of how well the French translator followed the Latin text and whether his translation envisaged the same function as the original.

At the time of its translation, the *Declamatio* had a well-defined reputation in France. Agrippa, who had published a study on magic, *De occulta philosophia* [*On Occult Philosophy*], shortly after the *Declamatio,* was portrayed as a diabolical magician and an atheist in such works, destined for the general public, as the biographical dictionary published by André Thevet in 1584.[5] Such a negative judgment reflects the bulk of sixteenth-century Christian thinking toward magic and the esoteric tradition. This philosophic tradition must, however, be taken into account to determine the full purport of the *Declamatio,* even if its evaluation was never developed in this perspective during the Renaissance itself, and we shall see that the French translation bears the mark of the Church's condemnation of magic and Hermetic philosophy. On the other hand, the *Declamatio* had some notoriety in intellectual circles as a sceptical and fideistic text. Thus, Montaigne uses some ten quotations from the *Declamatio* in his *Apologie de Raymond Sebond* [*Justification of Raymond Sebond*] (1580), the famous essay in which he criticizes human reason and the sciences.[6] But, at the same time, other

306

writers claimed that Agrippa was a charlatan and his *Declamatio* a paradox, essentially a rhetorical exercise not intended to convey any serious
thought. In France, this judgment was voiced by Jacques Tahureau
(1527–55) in his *Dialogues*, published posthumously in 1565.[7] The title
of the 1582 French translation indicates that it, too, presented the work
in this manner: *Declamation* (changed into *Paradoxe* from the second
edition onward) *sur l'incertitude, vanité et abus des sciences. . . .
Oeuure qui peut proffiter, & qui apporte merueilleux contentement à
ceux qui frequentent les Cours des grands Seigneurs, & qui veulent ap-
prendre à discourir d'une infinité de choses contre la commune opinion*[8]
[*Declamation* (later *Paradox*) *on the Uncertainty, Worthlessness and
Misuse of the Sciences. . . . A Work Which Can Be Profitable and Which
Will Bring Satisfaction to Those Who Frequent the Courts of the
Nobility, and Who Wish to Learn to Reason on an Infinity of Topics
against Commonly Held Opinion*]. We shall see that this manner of
qualifying the text is, in fact, in conflict with Agrippa's intention.

Before turning to the textual analysis of the French version, it will
be helpful to say something about the contents of Agrippa's *Declamatio*
and on the translator himself, Louis Turquet de Mayerne. The scanty
biographical information available on this latter scholar can be summed
up in a few sentences. He was born in Lyon around the middle of the
century and was among those Huguenots who fled to Geneva after the
Saint Bartholomew massacre in 1572. On March 16, 1573, he was
registered as "habitant" [resident] of Calvin's Commonwealth. At some
time between 1587 and October 1591, he returned to France and settled
once more in Lyon, where he was an elder of his church, and later in
Paris, where he died in 1618.[9] His works include a general history of
Spain, the first edition of which was published in 1587,[10] and a study on
state constitution, published in 1611.[11] This last work was sharply criticized, and Turquet subsequently published an *apologia* shortly before he
died.[12] In addition to these original works, he translated a Spanish rhetorical work by the humanist Antonio de Guevara, against court life and

307

in praise of country life, and Juan Luis Vives's well-known Latin work *Institutio feminae Christianae* [*Education of the Christian Woman*].[13] Little is known about Turquet's ideas and his motivations as writer and translator. He was one of many Huguenots who were to leave France after 1572, but his original writings, as well as his translation of Agrippa's text, suggest that even in exile he remained a patriot and a supporter of the French monarchy. His 1611 political treatise, however, published some twenty years after his return from Geneva, suggests something of a change of mind: Turquet dedicated his work to the States General of the Republic of the Seven Provinces, and his dedicatory letter contained severe criticism of the Catholic monarchies in general.

As for Agrippa's *Declamatio*, it is divided into 102 chapters and an epilogue. It is, in part, an encyclopedia of the arts and sciences and, in part, a rich sociological study, albeit with a strong polemical tone. Agrippa is especially critical of those who hold social power, namely church officials and nobility, and it was mainly for this reason that the book gained support in humanist circles. The starting point of Agrippa's argumentation, expressed in the first chapter, is the observation that the sciences are neither good nor bad in themselves; it is man's innate wickedness, conditioned by original sin, that makes their outcomes harmful. The structure of the work as a whole is somewhat loose but, nonetheless, carefully planned. A careful reading allows us to discern two principal sections: the first 53 chapters constitute a survey of the arts and sciences, following roughly the traditional scheme of the seven liberal arts, while the remainder, chapters 54 to 102 and the epilogue, is a sociological study based on the detailed observation of political, ecclesiastical, and economic institutions.[14]

Throughout the book, Agrippa's outlook is highly critical of human behavior, in both its intellectual and social contexts. This attitude leads to a theological tenet, which he expresses in the last few chapters of his work, in which he directly addresses his intellectual peers, the "scientiarum professores" [those who profess the sciences]. Only firm belief in the word of God, as expressed in Scripture, helps man overcome his depravity and provides him with a key to truth and sure knowledge. This exhortation to rely on the Bible is accompanied by an appeal for spiritual introspection. The precise philosophical and theological roots of Agrippa's ideas are not always clear, but they are obviously connected with the complex and not yet fully studied question of the relation between Renaissance magic and Christianity in the sixteenth century.

Turquet's translation of the *Declamatio* is neither inaccurate nor inflexible, but, as we shall see, he does not hesitate to manipulate his transfer of the original.[15] A common feature, evident on virtually every page, is paraphrase by means of binomials: e.g., "ratio" [system] (A, fol. Bv$^r$)[16] to "raison & fondement" [system and foundation] (T, p. 18); "tam solicite" [so carefully] (A, fol. Bv$^r$) to "tressoigneux & aduise" [most carefully and circumspectly] (T, p. 19); "De Herculis laboribus" [on the labors of Hercules] (A, fol. Ci$^r$) to "des trauaux & forces d'Hercules" [on the labors and energies of Hercules] (T, pp. 30–31); ("super fumo machinari omnia" [to invent all kinds of vain things] (A, fol. Cij$^v$) to "faisans sur tout estat & prattique de fumee & vaine ostentation" [executing everything in the form of smoke and empty show] (T, p. 34); "seuerissimis legibus" [with the most severe laws] (A, fol. Ciij$^v$) to "sous grandes & rigoureuses peines" [under extensive and rigourous penalties] (T, p. 37); "argumentis" [with arguments] (A, fol. Cvi$^v$) to "par raisons & arguments" [with reasons and arguments] (T, p. 47); "ciuilibus officiis" [to civic duties] (A, fol. Cviij$^r$) to "aux charges & affaires publiques" [to public responsibilites and business] (T, p. 51); "intellectualem naturam" [intellectual nature] (A, fol. Dij$^v$) to "nature spirituelle & intellectuelle" [intellectual and spiritual nature] (T, p. 60); "templa" [churches] (A, fol. Mvi$^v$) to "temples, cloistres" [temples, cloisters] (T, p. 269); "pugnant pro" [they fight for] to "valident &

approuuent" [they confirm and approve]; "dirimunt" [they break up, dissolve] to "rompent & separent" [they break and separate]; and "prouentus" [outcome, profit] to "proffit & commodité" [profit and benefit] (A, fol. Nviij$^v$; T, p. 300). In the chapter on painting, paraphrase turns the maxim "cumque ars summa sit, ingenium tamen vltra artem est" (A, fol. Eviij$^r$) [although technical skill is of the highest importance, talent is even more so] into a long statement concerning painting: "Et combien que l'art, l'industrie, & exercice de la peincture soit excellent & de grand aduantage à celuy qui en fait estat, si est ce que le naturel luy sert encor dauantage, & est pardessus tout" (T, p. 104) [And although skill, industriousness, and practice in painting are excellent and greatly advantageous to whomever makes a career of it, the fact remains that natural talent is more useful to him, moreso than anything else]. As we can see, this style of translation subjugates neither target to source nor source to target. The recourse to binomial forms not only gives the translator a free hand in the exploration of the semantic richness of the source language but also helps to make the sentence rhythms of the target language more flowing and, thus, contributes to a more pleasing style.

Turquet frequently alters the ordering of items. Thus, "in solo vsu maiorum autoritateque" [according to the sole usage and authority of our elders] (A, fol. Bv$^r$) becomes "en l'autorité & vsage" [the authority and usage] (T, p. 18); "vtrum Aristotelis anima scribi debeat endelechia per delta vel entelechia per tau" [whether Aristotle's (word for) "soul" should be written *endelechia* with a delta, or *entelechia* with a tau] (A, fol. Bvi$^r$) becomes "si l'ame d'Aristote doit estre escrite Entelechie par t, ou Endelechie par d" [whether Aristotle's "soul" must be written Entelechie with a *t,* or Endelechie with a *d*] (T, p. 21); "blandiri, & res suas enarrare" [to flatter, and to detail one's business] (A, fol. Cvi$^v$) becomes "donner à entendre ses affaires, de flatter quand il est besoing" [to give account of one's business, and to flatter when it is necessary]

(T, p. 47); "pronuntiationem, memoriam" [pronunciation, memory] (A, fol. Cvi$^v$) becomes "la mémoire, la prononciation" [memory, pronunciation] (T, p. 47); "haeccaeitatibus, instantibus" (A, fol. Diij$^v$) becomes "instants, hecceïtés" (T, p. 62)[17]; "Polymestrem & Saccadam Archiuum" (A, fol. Dviij$^v$) becomes "Sacadas Argien et Polymestres" (T, p. 80)[18]; and "sacerdotum monachorumque collegia" [colleges of priests and monks] (A, fol. Mvi$^v$) becomes "colleges de moynes, & chanoines" [colleges of monks and canons] (T, p. 269). These changes in word-order contribute to the enhancement of the rhythm and harmony of the target text, but at little or no cost to fidelity to the original. Thus they further illustrate a degree of stylistic or linguistic sensitivity on Turquet's part. Such refusal to be too tightly bound by the semantic dictates of the source text exemplifies the concern for both accuracy and flexibility mentioned earlier.

Single words or groups of words are sometimes omitted: e.g., "quam ars" [than an art] (A, fol. Bi$^r$; cf. T, p. 6); "deque variis impedimentis constructionis" [on the various impediments of grammatical construction] (A, fol. Bvi$^r$; cf. T, p. 21); "isonomiam" [equality of political rights] (A, fol. Bvi$^r$; cf. T, p. 22); "saepe" [often] (A, fol. Bvi$^v$; cf. T, p. 22); "semper" [always] (A, fol. Cvii$^v$; cf. T, p. 51); "sero admodum" [rather late] (A, fol. Dv$^v$; cf. T, p. 69); "regi" [to the king] (A, fol. Dvii$^v$; cf. T, p. 75); and "quam plurimos" [as many as possible] (A, fol. Kij$^v$; cf. T, p. 208). In some instances, Turquet makes what we may suppose to be an unintentional mistake, as when he translates "Pleton" [Gemisthus Plethon, the Byzantine philosopher who died in 1452] as "Platon" [Plato] (A, fol. Ivi$^r$; T, p. 195), or "rhetoricam" [rhetoric] as "republique" [republic] (A, fol. Cviij$^v$; T, p. 53). However, in the chapter on common courtiers, where mention is made of the murder of Phocus, the Greek eponym of Phocis, we find that Turquet corrects the source text, in which Agrippa had written "Proteus" (A, fol. Pv$^r$), identified in the *Odyssey* as a god of the sea: Turquet rightly changes this to "Pelee"

311

[Peleus] (T, p. 338). Occasionally, a translation is somewhat vague: "in bonorum cognitione" [in the knowledge of good things] (A, fol. Bi$^v$) becomes "en la cognaissance du bien" [in the knowledge of the good] (T, p. 7); "loquendi regulas videlicet constructus, regiminis & significatorum" [the rules of speech, that is, of the construction of words, of grammatical requirements, and of meanings] (A, fol. Bv$^r$) becomes "des reigles pour sçavoir accompagner les dictions par certain ordre, & selon certaines significations" [rules to know how to group sayings together in a certain order, and according to certain meanings] (T, p. 17); and "de terminorum passionibus" [on the properties of terms] (A, fol. Diij$^v$) becomes "des passions, des termes" [on passions, on terms] (T, p. 62). Most of these omissions and free translations are opportune in that they avoid unnecessary difficulties and make for greater readability. The controlling factor continues to be essentially rhetorical in nature—the desire to produce a text sufficiently respectful of the norms of the target language to please and inform the French reader.

Concern for the readership is evinced in other ways. Various changes suggest that the translator attempts to accommodate the reader who is less familiar with the fields of scholarship and the learned languages. Difficult terms may be defined: "theses, hypotheses" [theses, hypotheses] (A, fol. Cvii$^r$) to "theses ou questions generales, & particulieres ou hypotheses" [theses, or general questions, and particular questions, or hypotheses] (T, p. 48); "quiditates" [quiddities] (A, fol. Dij$^v$) to "quidités (c'est l'essence propre de ce que lon veut demonstrer)" [quiddities, that is, the particular essence of what one wants to demonstrate] (T, p. 59); "arithmetica haec" [this art of arithemetic] (A, fol. Dvij$^r$) to "ceste science d'Arithmetique ou des nombres" [this science of Arithmetic, or numbers] (T, p. 73); "tricolus" [a game of chance, making use of numbers] (A, fol. Dvij$^r$) to "le tricole, ou trois poincts" [the *tricolus*, or triple-point] (T, p. 75); "Aborigines" [aboriginals] (A, fol. Gvij$^r$) to "Aborigenes, ou originaires Latins" [aboriginals, or the original Latins]

(T, p. 151); "augurum collegium" [college of augurers] (A, fol. Gvij$^v$) to "vn college, cour, ou compagnie d'un certain nombre d'augurs" [a college, court or company of a certain number of augurers] (T, p. 151); "goetia atque theurgia" (A, fol. Hiiij$^r$)$^{19}$ to "ces impostures que les Grecs appellent Goëtie & Theurgie" [these shams that the Greeks call *goetia* and *theurgia*] (T, p. 166); and "circa membranam epicranidem" [around the membrane of the brain] (A, fol. Iv$^v$) to "autour de la taye qui couure le test, qu'il appelle membrane epicranide" [around the skin which covers the head, which he calls the epicranial membrane] (T, p. 194). Other words are more amply explained: "prima artium illarum (sc. the *trivium*) elementa instrumentaque" [the first elements and instruments of the *trivium*] (A, fol. Biij$^v$) to "les petits commencements & instruments d'icelles, a sçavoir les lettres A, B, C, D etc." [the small beginnings and instruments of the *trivium*, namely the letters A, B, C, D and so on] (T, p. 13); "in obeliscis" [on obelisks] (A, fol. Biij$^v$) to "en leurs esguilles ou colonnes pyramidales" [on their needles or pyramidal columns] (T, p. 14); "praenestinas tesseras & talos, & aleas" [die-cubes used in the town of Praeneste, knuckle-bones used for games, and dice] (A, fol. Dvij$^r$) to "le sort ou diuination qui se fait par le iect de dés, comme anciennement en la ville de Palest[r]ine, lors dite Preneste, par les tales, qui cstoyent presque ressemblans aux osselets des pieds des animaux" [the fortune or divination done with a throw of the dice, as formerly in the town of Palest[r]ina, then called Praeneste, with "tales," which were almost like the knuckle bones from animal feet] (T, p. 73); "Anapaesto pede" [in the anapaestic meter] (A, fol. Ei$^r$) to "deux breues et vne longue, tă ră tām" [two shorts and a long: tă ră tām] (T, p. 81); and "spondeo pede" [in the spondaic meter] (A, fol. Ei$^r$) to "le pied & la mesure de deux longues" [the foot and the beat of two longs] (T, p. 82).

In the chapter on grammar, Agrippa had lamented that grammatical issues have sometimes led to religious problems. He cites the example of the heresy of the Antidicomarianites (A, fol. Bvij$^r$), according to

313

which certain people believed that Mary had lost her virginity after the birth of Christ because the gospel says of Joseph "et non cognoscebat eam donec peperit filium suum" [(he) had no intercourse with her until her son was born] (Matt. 1: 25).[20] Turquet inserts a comment explaining that the heretical interpretation of *donec* is based on Hebrew sources: "suyuant la maniere de parler & phrase des Hebrieux, à laquelle ils se sont arrestés" [according to the manner of speech and phrasing of the Hebrews, which they adopted] (T, p. 23). Unfamiliar names may be given a more familiar form: "Philo" (A, fol. Biij$^v$) becomes "Philon Iuif" [Philo the Jew] (T, p. 13); "Simonides Melicus" (A, fol. Biij$^v$) becomes "Simonides poëte lyrique" [Simonides the lyric poet] (T, p. 13); "Stephanus Graecus" (A, fol. Ciiij$^r$) becomes "Estienne Grec, qui a faict le catalogue des villes" [Stephen the Greek, who catalogued the cities] (T, p. 40); "Berosus" (A, fol. Fij$^v$) becomes "Berose Chaldee" [Berosus the Chaldean] (T, p. 112); "Morus anglicus" [More the Englishman] (A, fol. Gij$^v$) becomes "Thomas Morus" (T, p. 138); "Firmianus" (A, fol. Iij$^v$) becomes "Lactance" (T, p. 185)[21]; "Galenvs Pergamenus" (A, fol. Iiiij$^v$) becomes "Galien le medecin" [Galen the doctor] (T, p. 191); "Thomas" (A, fol. Ivi$^v$) becomes "Thomas d'Aquin" (T, p. 197); and "Aeneas Syluius" (A, fol. Niiij$^r$) becomes "Eneas Sylvius, qui fut depuis Pape" [Aeneas Sylvius, who was later Pope] (T, p. 286). In one case, there is a substitution: Agrippa's list of famous lovers (Lancelot, Tristan, Euryalus, Pelegrinus, and Calistus) is modified by Turquet to Lancelot, Tristan, and Amadis of Gaul (A, fol. Niiij$^v$; T, p. 287). Elsewhere, scholarly attributions are omitted, e.g., "vt Auerroistae contendunt" [as the Averroists claim] (A, fol. Bi$^v$; cf. T, p. 8); "in Priorum resolutionum lib." [in the books of (Aristotle's) *Prior Analytics*] (A, fol. Bij$^v$; cf. T, p. 10); "ut ait Cicero" [as Cicero has it] (A, fol. Dvi$^r$; cf. T, p. 70); "Apollinaris" (A, fol. Ivi$^v$; cf. T, p. 196); "quae Platonicorum opinio est" [which is the position of the Platonists] (A, fol. Ivii$^r$; cf. T, p. 199); and "teste Plutarcho" [according to Plutarch] (A, fol. Qi$^r$; cf. T, p. 349).

A general consideration of the varieties of textual amendment discussed hitherto allows us to see that Turquet adapts his material with the non-scholarly reader in mind. There is a clear pedagogical purpose to his definitions and paraphrasing of technical terms, his explanations by recourse to etymology, and his insertion of explanatory remarks on learned authors with whom the readership could be assumed to be unfamiliar. In combination with the previously illustrated strategies aimed at securing stylistic fluency, such adaptations indicate that many of Turquet's techniques are essentially linguistic in inspiration. They seem generally to aim at making the thought of the original more accessible to readers who, in their ignorance of the source language, could not be expected to grasp the associative values that could be taken for granted when writing for those competent in Latin.

Of more far-reaching substance, however, we find an important number of what we might term conceptual, rather than linguistic, changes in certain passages containing controversial political or religious judgments. Like many of the linguistic changes detailed above, they might seem relatively minor if considered in isolation, but taken together they reveal an undisputable and dramatic shift in the hermeneutic process. What we have seen so far reveals a translator sufficiently respectful of the source text to make of his translation strategies a means of contextualizing Agrippa's thought for readers unfamiliar with either the Latin language or the cultural assumptions that automatically go with it. We shall now review cases in which the translator becomes more an audacious agent of change than a deferential agent of transfer, as he tampers with the thought of the original for what we can assume to be ideological or doctrinal reasons. And it is modifications of this type, ultimately more seditious and far more destructive of the source text than those of the earlier kind, that enable us to sense not only Turquet's linguistic approaches to translation but also his appreciation of translation as a rhetorical strategy. In his hands, the Latin *Declamatio*, which had issued such a major intellectual and spiritual challenge to its

315

scholarly readers, is converted into a kind of parlor-game, a conventional "paradox," little more than an unequivocal, unoffensive, and entertaining book for the upper class French reading public invoked on its title page.[22]

First, Turquet intervenes in two passages containing derogatory remarks about the French monarchy and the Court, once by altering the text and once by placing a critical note in the margin. In the chapter dealing with court life, Agrippa had claimed that courtiers are usually very poor political advisors because of their obsequious attitude toward the king. One of his examples referred to the contemporary situation. He pointed out that the French monarch followed the bad advice of his counsellors and engaged in a calamitous conflict with the Emperor (A, fol. Piiij[r]). Turquet omits this criticism of the French diplomatic policy of the 1520s and writes simply that Royal courts have poor counsellors, as much in France as elsewhere (T, p. 334). The other passage occurs in the chapter on the origins of the nobility and the monarchies in contemporary society. Agrippa had mentioned the violent ascent to power of the medieval king Hugh Capet and had added that he was popular with the population of Paris because of his valor, even though he was not of noble birth (A, fol. Si[r]). Turquet translates this passage in full, but comments in a marginal annotation that this story is not believable and has been corrupted by those who hate the French monarchy (T, p. 397). Although Turquet lived in exile during the eighties, the dedicatory letter to Henry III in the first edition of his history of Spain, published in 1587 (that is, five years after our translation), suggests that he remained even in exile loyal to France and a firm supporter of the monarchy. We can also surmise that Turquet was fearful of the unfavorable reception of his translation in France if it included such remarks as these, which might be taken as an expression of his disapproval of the system of monarchy. The polemic that was to surround his political treatise of 1611, in which he did in fact propose that the monarch be removed from the center of political institutions, shows that such a fear would not have been without foundation.

Second, Turquet intervenes in a number of passages that were critical of the Protestants, or that he considered inappropriate in a work destined for the general public. In particular, he abridges or expunges three passages containing critical remarks on the opponents of the Roman Church. In his chapter on rhetoric, Agrippa had pointed out that eloquence was often used by unscrupulous people for evil purposes, especially in the fields of politics, jurisprudence, and religion. One example of unprincipled men in the domain of religion had related to contemporary issues: are not all the leaders of the German heretical sects, so numerous today since the appearance of Luther, eloquent men both in speech and writing, Agrippa had asked rhetorically (A, fol. Di$^v$). Turquet omits this harsh judgment of Luther and the Protestant movement in Germany (T, p. 56). Later, Agrippa's mention of Martin Luther as an unremitting heretic is deleted from a sentence referring to Luther's views on the rules for marriage (A, fol. Oi$^v$; T, p. 302). Turquet further suppresses the last two sentences of the chapter on images, in which Agrippa had condemned the various forms of superstition related to images, such as the excessive worship of relics. In the omitted passage, Agrippa had pointed out that the contrary of this fault (the excessive disrespect of relics) also led to the adoption of heretical positions, and he had mentioned as examples of the victims of such heresy the contemporary participants of the German Protestant movement (A, fol. Lv$^{r-v}$; T, p. 241).

Other altered passages have a less specific thrust, and we can assume that Turquet probably altered or deleted them in order to avoid raising questions concerning orthodoxy among his readers. A few such cases have bearing on magic and Hermetism: in the chapter on various forms of trickery ("De praestigiis") [On Impostures], Agrippa had spoken of those who misused magic, a field in which he himself had been active

Marc van der Poel

during his entire life. After proclaiming that he wished to recant whatever erroneous opinions he had held during his youth, Agrippa added:
"Tandem hoc profeci quod sciam quibus rationibus oporteat alios ab hac
pernicie dehortari" (A, fol. Iij$^r$) [Now I have made such progress, that I
know on which grounds I must dissuade others from this calamity].
These grounds are specifically mentioned and amount to a definition of
the conditions under which the practice of magic is permissible: "Quicunque enim non in veritate, nec in virtute dei, sed in elusione
daemonum, secundum operationem malorum spirituum, diuinare &
prophetare praesumunt, . . . aeternis ignibus cruciandi destinabuntur" (A,
fol. Iij$^{r-v}$) [For whoever dares to divine and prophesy, not in truth and
in the power of God, but, through the trickery of demons, in keeping
with the operation of bad spirits . . . , will be tormented by eternal fire].
Turquet, however, did not translate the crucial words *quibus rationibus*
[on which grounds] and, thus, changed the qualified and conditional tone
of the original into a flat rejection of magic and an outright condemnation of its practitioners. Similarly, in the chapter containing the praise of
the ass, to which I shall return later in some detail, Turquet omits a passage referring to the second-century author Apuleius and his *Metamorphoses* (or *The Golden Ass*). In this novel, the main character, Lucius,
is metamorphosed into an ass before his initiation into the mysteries of
Isis. Apuleius (whose name can be found in some indices of forbidden
books) was further supposed to be the author of the Hermetic dialogue
*Asclepius*, and we may suppose that Turquet's suppression of reference
to him here is chiefly motivated by Christianity's negative attitude toward magic and the Hermetic tradition in general.

  There are also instances of the translator's intervention in some of
the numerous passages in which Agrippa had mentioned Holy Scripture
or had referred to a specific Biblical passage. It seems likely that Turquet considered the use of the Bible to be too liberal for the context in
question. In the chapter on grammar, Agrippa had discussed the fate of

Saul, the first king of Israel, rejected by God for disobeying the divine command to destroy utterly the Amalekites. In Agrippa's interpretation, Saul had misunderstood God's meaning, taking the word translated in the Vulgate as "memoria(m)" [memory] for "mares" [males].[23] Turquet translates this passage in full but adds a marginal note rejecting the pertinence of Agrippa's remark and, at the same time, denying altogether his integrity as a scholar (A, fol. Bvi[v]; T, p. 22): "Ce passage est mal à propos amené par Agrippa en ce lieu, comme il est coustumier de corrompre les passages de tous auteurs, & les faire seruir à son propos" [This passage has no bearing on the topic discussed here by Agrippa, just as he habitually corrupts passages in all the authors, and makes them subservient to his own purposes]. This negative appraisal of Agrippa serves to confirm his reputation as a charlatan and echoes the judgment of such writers as Tahureau and Thevet.[24]

Elsewhere, in a passage on the lack of good morals at court, Agrippa had written, paraphrasing Scripture : "vix maritis ipsis vxorum meretricatus curae est, modo vt ait Abraham ad Saram, bene sit illis propter illas, uiuantque laute ob gratiam illarum" [Even husbands do not care whether their wives fornicate, provided, as Abraham says to Sara, they are doing well thanks to their behavior and are living in prosperity on account of their credit] (A, fol. Pij[v]).[25] Here, Turquet has erased the identification of the quotation as a Biblical one (T, p. 329). Elsewhere, in the chapter on the Word of God, Agrippa had argued that to know the Bible is not only of importance to theologians but also that it "(pertinere) ad omnem hominem, siue vir, siue mulier, siue senex, siue iuuenis, siue puer, siue indigena, siue aduena, siue proselytus . . ." (A, fol. Zviij[v]) [concerns every one, whether male, female, old, young, child, native, foreign, or a convert (proselyte)]. Here, Turquet mentions only men ("l'homme"), women ("la femme"), old people ("les vieils"), adolescents and children ("les ieunes & enfans"), and native or foreign peoples ("estrangers, ou naturels"; T, p. 533). He omitted "converts," thus evading

319

the need to introduce the theological controversy as to whether non-Christians are allowed to study Scripture. Such manipulations of Agrippa's use of the Biblical references reveal a certain degree of circumspection. In order to make his work function as a vehicle for little more than entertainment, Turquet no doubt felt that passages which could be taken as contemptuous of Scripture or which left room for theological argument must be rendered uncontroversially. Excision, adaptation, and marginal annotations are the means to that end.

The same principles are operative when Turquet makes some important modifications to the chapter containing the praise of the ass ("Ad encomium asini digressio"), a text that was one of Agrippa's most challenging and controversial writings. It contains the principal theological idea expounded in the *Declamatio*, setting out to justify Agrippa's reference in the preceding chapter to the Apostles and all the true followers of Christ as asses. It argues that the ass is not only a useful animal but also, in the Hebraic tradition, the symbol of strength, patience, and clemency and, thus, according to Scripture, is held in great esteem by God. This praise also echoes the Hermetic tradition, in which the ass symbolizes the inspired ignorant.[26] In one passage in particular, Agrippa apostrophized his intellectual peers and urged them to become like asses, that is, to practice Christian purity and simplicity (A, fol. Aiiij$^r$). Turquet does not translate the personal pronoun "vos" that occurred twice in this passage and, thus, omits the author's direct call for spiritual and intellectual humility (T, pp. 541–42). In the margin at the head of the chapter, the reader is advised that the Latin text is not rendered in its literal form, because it is blasphemous: "Ce chap. est quelque peu different du Latin, parce que l'auteur se iouë trop irreverement de l'escriture: partant a esté aucunement addouci par le traducteur" (T, p. 540) [This chapter is somewhat different from the Latin, because the author too irreverently makes fun of Scripture. Therefore it has been slightly softened by the translator]. This note refers to the following passage, entirely omitted by Turquet (the omission is indicated by a separate marginal note[27]):

> Hunc [sc.asinum] (quae constans fama est), Christus suae natiuitatis testem esse voluit, in hoc a manibus Herodis saluari voluit, atque ipse asinus etiam contactu corporis Christi consecratus est, crucisque signaculo insignitus: nam Christus ipse pro redemptione humani generis triumphaturus ascendens in Hierusalem, testibus euangelistis, hunc vectorem conscendit, sicut id magno mysterio per Zachariae oraculum praedictum fuit: et ipse electorum pater Abraham asinis tantum equitasse legitur. (A, fol. Aiij$^v$–Aiiij$^r$)

> [There is unanimous consent that Christ chose an ass to be witness to his birth, that He chose to be saved from Herod's hands sitting on an ass, and even that the ass is consecrated by the touch of Christ's body and marked by the sign of the cross. For as the evangelists testify, Christ himself, when he entered Jerusalem in order to triumph on behalf of the redemption of humanity, mounted on an ass to carry him, following the prophecy of Zachary foretold in great mystery. And we read that Abraham himself, the father of the chosen people, used to ride only an ass.]

Agrippa also refered to the prophet Balaam's ass, which saved its master from an angel (Num. 22), and claimed that this ass was gifted with a prophetic spirit, stressing the fact that it spoke in human language (A, fol. Aiiij$^v$). Turquet omits both of these observations from his translation (T, p. 543).

Finally, Turquet omits a passage containing a legendary episode from the life of Saint Germain, a fifth-century bishop who died a martyr and whose relics were an object of veneration in France.[28] Agrippa had related that Saint Germain once called back to life an ass (A, fol. Aiiij$^v$–Av$^r$). According to Agrippa, this episode constituted proof that the ass participates in life after death. It seems reasonable to surmise that this unorthodox claim was sufficient to merit suppression of the passage in Turquet's eyes.

It will be apparent from the preceding discussion of changes in language and content that Turquet's translation must be appreciated independently of its original. We can group our conclusions around two focal points. First, the *translator* has clearly left his mark on the text. Indeed, not only has Turquet translated in a flexible manner in order to produce an agreeable text for his French readership, he has also allowed himself to make changes of substance. It seems safe to ascribe these to Turquet's political and religious feelings. We have also seen that he has left his personal mark on the text, in the form of marginal notes in which he usually gives a negative appraisal of Agrippa's scholarship, thus underscoring the latter's contemporary reputation as an impostor. Second, Turquet's consideration of *the prospective readership* has resulted in a number of modifications. It is clear that he has aimed to produce a stylistically fluent translation, to be enjoyed by the general reader, rather than a *verbum pro verbo* translation that scientifically reproduces Agrippa's words. Various textual changes suggest that he did not entertain any extensive scholarly expectations of his readers. Additionally, a number of passages show that Turquet has taken into consideration the favorable attitude toward the monarchy that might be expected of his prospective readership. Turquet also eliminates or changes a number of passages that could give rise to problems of orthodoxy, passages that he doubtless judged to be unsuitable for an entertaining work destined for a general public not trained to deal with theological niceties.

Turquet's translation redefines the function of Agrippa's text. What was a *declamatio* has become a paradox, and the consequences of this shift of rhetorical focus are important for our assessment of the relationship between source and target texts. In spite of its condemnation by the theologians and his subsequent alienation from his patron, the Emperor, Agrippa never disavowed the *Declamatio* or dismissed it as a literary trifle. In his *Apologia*, written in response to the charges of the Louvain theologians, Agrippa first pointed out that they had failed to understand the fundamental thesis set forth in the *Declamatio*. He explained that what he had sought to argue was that reliable and true knowledge belongs to the realm of theology and is to be found in Scripture: he denied in so many words that his book contains a flat rejection of human knowledge.[29] He went on to explain that he saw the genre of the *declamatio* as a rhetorical text presenting arguments in a disputatious and polemical fashion. He thus pointed out that the positions the theologians had found offensive should not have been condemned as scientific pronouncements, but ought to have been refuted in a countering declamation ("declamaturus partem diuersam"), as invalid arguments in support of the main thesis.[30] In a letter to his friend and protector Lorenzo Campeggio, Agrippa clearly repeated his desire that his opponents challenge his work in open debate, either in the form of a rhetorical text or a public disputation.[31] The French translation, in contrast, places Agrippa's *Declamatio* in a wholly different hermeneutic context. In this version, published some fifty years after the original, the status of a text that brings refined critical discussion and rhetorical reasoning to the religious and political issues of its day is degraded to that of a literary trifle on a conventional theme, intended to do little more than amuse the reader. Literary play and ostentation take the place of disputation and polemic. Turquet's French text serves to confirm in a fairly trivial manner the commonly held social opinion that arts and sciences do, in fact, lead to sure knowledge and do have real worth. Further research is needed to establish whether the paradox of the worthlessness of the arts and sciences was, indeed, a topic discussed in the circles mentioned on the title page and whether Agrippa's work played a part in that debate; the numerous reprints of Turquet's translation between 1582 and 1630 would certainly justify such a study. We should also remember that the genre of the paradox, to which Agrippa's *Declamatio* is assigned in its French version, does, in fact, allow for a satirical function.[32] Since Turquet chose to work from an unexpunged version of the *Declamatio* (that is, a version containing passages criticizing the Catholic Church) and then omitted the passages containing criticism of the Protestants, it is certainly possible that he meant to have his readers believe he was translating a satire against Catholic society.[33] But even if this is so, it still remains to be shown that the translation was actually taken in this manner by the non-learned French reading public, which was surely overwhelmingly Catholic. In this context, we need further research not only into the public reaction to Turquet's translation but also, more generally, into the function of the sixteenth-century paradox as a vehicle of satire.

It must be emphasized, however, that Turquet did not share Agrippa's outlook, even if it was one of Agrippa's intentions to write critically about Christian society and the Roman Church. Unlike his translator, Agrippa never joined the Protestant Reformation, and the criticism directed by him and by many other humanists of his generation against Church and politics was ultimately intended to restore the unity of Christendom rather than promote the schism resulting from the actions of Martin Luther. In the hands of its French translator, the *Declamation on the Uncertainty and Worthlessness of the Sciences and the Arts* surely became a very different composition.[34]

# The French Translation of Agrippa Von Nettesheim

## Notes

1. There is no modern bibliography of the works of Agrippa. The translations are listed in Christoph Gottlieb Von Murr, "Conspectus omnium editionum operum Henrici Cornelii Agrippae ab Nettesheym," *Neues Journal zur Litteratur und Kunstgeschichte*, vol. 1 (Leipzig, 1798), pp. 73–76.

2. *Apologia aduersus calumnias propter Declamationem de Vanitate scientiarum, & excellentia uerbi Dei, sibi per aliquos Louanienses Theologistas intentatas . . .* [*Justificatory Response to the Calmunies Concerning the Declamation on the Worthlessness of the Sciences, and the Excellence of the Word of God, Undertaken by Certain Louvain Theologians . . .*] (s.l. 1533). The second work, which will not be discussed here was entitled *Quaerela svper calmunia, ob eandem Declamationem, sibi per aliquos sceleratissimos sycopantas, apud Caesaream Maiestatem nefarie ac proditorie illata,* and published in the same volume as the *Apologia*.

3. The *Declamatio* appeared on both the 1531 and 1544 *indices* issued by the University of Paris, on the 1546, 1550, and 1558 *indices* issued by the University of Louvain, and on the 1551and 1559 *indices* of the Spanish Inquisition; see *Index de l'université de Paris 1544, 1545, 1547, 1549, 1551, 1556,* in J. M. De Bujanda et al., eds., *Index des livres interdits*, vol. 1 (Sherbrooke: Centre d'Etudes de la Renaissance, Editions de l'Université de Sherbrooke; Geneva: Droz, 1985), pp. 88, 124; *Index de l'université de Louvain 1546, 1550, 1558,* in vol. 2 (1986), p. 131; *Index de l'inquisition espagnole 1551, 1554, 1559,* in vol. 5 (1984), pp. 258, 365.

4. A useful survey of the various Latin editions of the *Declamatio* is provided by Von Murr (see n. 1 above), pp. 59–73, and by David Clément, *Bibliothèque curieuse historique et critique ou catalogue raisonné de livres dificiles* [*sic*] *à trouver*, vol. 1 (Göttingen: J. G. Schmid, 1750), pp. 81–87. Clément lists the twenty-one expunged passages in his note 88.

5. *Les Vrais Pourtraits et vies des hommes illustres grecz, latins et payens . . .* (Paris, 1584), fols. 542$^r$–544$^v$.

6. See Pierre Villey, *Les Sources et l'évolution des essais de Montaigne*, vol. 2 (Paris: Hachette, 1933), pp. 168–71.

7. See Villey (see n. 6 above), p. 167; Jacques Tahureau, *Les Dialogues: non moins profitables que facetieux,* critical edition by Max Gauna (Geneva: Droz, 1981), pp. 199–203. Throughout the *Dialogues*, Tahureau's opinions are voiced by "le Democritic."

8. The first edition was published in 1582 by Jean Durant (or Durand), probably in Geneva; see *Index Aureliensis. Catalogus librorum sedecimo saeculo impressorum*, vol. 1, part 1 (Aureliae Aquensis [Baden-Baden] and Geneva: Fondation Index Aureliensis, 1962 [1965]), no. 101.902. The second edition was published in the same year (ibid., no. 101.903). Later editions were published in 1603, 1608, 1617, 1623, 1630 (all without printer's name or place of publication), and 1688 and 1715 (Amsterdam). For Durant (Durand), see Hans Joachim Bremme, *Buchdrucker und Buchhändler zur Zeit der Glaubenskämpfe. Studien zur Genfer Druckgeschichte, 1565–1580* (Geneva: Droz, 1969), pp. 152–54.

9. Biographical data from *Biographie universelle (Michaud) ancienne et moderne*, nouvelle édition, vol. 27 (Paris: chez Madame C. Desplaces and Leipzig: Librairie de F. A. Brockhaus, s.a.; reed. Paris: Delagrave, 1840–1900); Eugène and Emile Haag, eds., *La France protestante*, vol. 7 (Geneva: Slatkine, 1966); and Alex. Desplanque, *Mézières en Brenne et la famille Turquet de Mayerne. Etude historique* (Paris, 1864), p. 29, n. 1. The date of Turquet's registration as "habitant" in Geneva is recorded in Paul Frédéric Geisendorf, *Livre des habitants de Genève, 1572–1574 et 1585–1587*, vol. 2 (Geneva: Droz, 1963), p. 76. The approximate date of his return to France is deduced from his *Epistre au Roy. Présentée à sa Majesté au mois d' octobre 1591* (Tours, 1592); the phrasing of his address to the King in this letter suggests that it was written after Turquet's return from exile.

10. *Histoire générale d' Espagne* (Lyon: J. de Tournes, 1587). The letter of dedication to Henry III, dated 15 August 1586, is written from exile. Second and third editions of this work, both containing additional material, were published in 1608 and, posthumously, in 1635. For an assessment of Turquet's historical work, see B. Sánchez Alonso, "Mayerne Turquet y los historiadores españoles del siglo XVI," *Estudios dedicados a Menéndez Pidal*, vol. 1 (Madrid: Consejo Superior de Investigaciones Científicas, 1950), pp. 589–99.

# The French Translation of Agrippa Von Nettesheim

11. *La Monarchie aristodemocratique, ou le gouvernement composé et meslé des trois formes de legitimes republiques* (Paris: J. Berjon, 1611). On this work, see Roland Mousnier, "L'Opposition politique sous Louis XIII: Louis Turquet de Mayerne," in *Bulletin de la société d'histoire moderne*, 9e série, no. 9, a. 53 (January–March); Suppl. to *Revue d'histoire moderne et contemporaine* (1954): 7–10; and Roger Soltau, "La monarchie aristo-démocratique de Louis Turquet de Mayerne," *Revue du XVI<sup>e</sup> siècle* 13 (1926): 78–94. The work of Soltau includes an assessment of the polemic surrounding this work.

12. *Apologie contre les détracteurs des livres de la monarchie aristodémocratique* (s.l., 1617).

13. *Le Mépris de la cour,* 1574; a 1591 edition is mentioned by Gustave Moeckli, *Les Livres imprimés à Genève de 1550 à 1600. Nouvelle édition revue et augmentée* (Geneva: Droz, 1966), pp. 130–31. *Livre de l'Institution de la femme chrestienne, tant en son enfance, que mariage et viduité, aussi l'office du mary, le tout composé en Latin et nouvellement traduit en langue françoise par L. T.* (Lyon: B. Rigaud, 1579). It has not been possible to consult these works.

14. For a detailed survey of Agrippa's *Declamatio,* see Aug. Prost, *Les Sciences et les arts occultes au XVI<sup>e</sup> siècle. Corneille Agrippa, sa vie et ses oeuvres,* vol. 1 (Paris: Champion, 1881–82; repr. Nieuwkoop: De Graaf, 1965), pp. 91–114; and Roland Crahay, "Un Manifeste religieux d'anticulture: le *De incertitudine et vanitate scientiarum et artium* de Corneille Agrippa," in Jean-Claude Margolin, ed., *Acta Conventus Neo-Latini Turonensis* (Paris: Vrin, 1980), 2: 893–96.

15. Reference are to the following editions:
A = *De incertitudine et vanitate scientiarum declamatio inuectiva . . .* (Coloniae: M.N. [Melchior Novesianus], 1531); see *Index Aureliensis* (see above, n. 8), no. 101.840; copy of the Royal Library, The Hague, shelf mark 226 J 21.
T = *Declamation sur l'incertitude, vanité et abus des sciences . . .* (s.l. [Geneva]: Iean Durand, 1582); see *Index Aureliensis,* no. 101.902; copy of the Bayerische Staatsbibliothek, Munich, shelf mark H.lit.U.29.

16. Following standard binding techniques, the volume (in 8°) conists of five numbered folios followed by three unnumbered ones: I flag the latter with an asterisk.

# Marc van der Poel

17. These are technical terms taken from the specialized vocabulary of scholastic logic: *haeccaeitas* [the quality of being this, "this-ness"] denotes the relation of individuality, conceived as a positive attribute; *instantia* is a counter argument, showing that a given argument is ineffective.

18. Polymestres (more correctly, Polymnestos) and Sakadas of Argos were two ancient Greek musicians.

19. These are two different kinds of sorcery: "goety" is the invocation of evil spirits; "theurgy" the invocation of beneficent or divine spirits.

20. Biblical translations are taken from *The New English Bible* (Oxford and Cambridge: The University Presses, 1970).

21. Elsewhere, however, "Firmianus" (A, fol. Giiij$^v$) is rendered as "Firmien" (T, p. 143).

22. It should be noted that the *paradox*, or paradoxical encomium, is a form of mock eloquence, devoted to the praise of an unworthy or trifling object or to the defence of a thesis that goes against commonly held opinion. As such, it was a highly popular form of writing during the Renaissance; the most famous example is, of course, Erasmus's *Praise of Folly*. See Henry Knight Miller, "The Paradoxical Encomium with Special Reference to its Vogue in England, 1600–1800," *Modern Philology* 53 (1955–56): 145–78; and A. E. Malloch, "The Technique and Function of the Renaissance Paradox," *Studies in Philology* 53 (1956): 191–203.

23. "Dixit autem Dominus ad Mosen, 'Scribe hoc . . . *Delebo enim memoriam Amalech sub Caelo*'" [The Lord said to Moses, "Record this in writing . . . 'I am resolved to blot out all memory of Amalek from under heaven'"] (Exod. 17: 14). Agrippa notes in his discussion of this matter the fact that the Hebrew word used in the original allows for both meanings.

24. Two other marginal notes confirm Turquet's negative opinion of Agrippa's learning: T, p. 431 (cf. A, fol. Tiiij$^v$), and T, p. 477 (cf. A, fol. Xiiij$^v$–Xv$^r$).

25. The reference is to Genesis, 12: 10–13: "When he (Abram) was approaching Egypt, he said to his wife Sarai, 'I know very well that you are a beautiful woman, and that

when the Egyptians see you they will say, "She is his wife"; then they will kill me but let you live. Tell them that you are my sister, so that all may go well with me because of you and my life may be spared on your account'."

26. See the brief remarks of Frances Yates on Giordano Bruno's dialogue *Idiota triumphans*, in *Giordano Bruno and the Hermetic Tradition* (London: Routledge and Kegan Paul, 1964), pp. 296–98; and Vincenzo Spampanato, *Giordano Bruno e la letteratura dell' asino* (Portici: E. della Torre, 1904).

27. "Il se iouë de l'escriture en cest endroit au Latin, qui est obmis" [He makes fun of the Bible in the Latin text, and this is ommitted] T, p. 541.

28. His relics were still venerated in Amiens during the eighteenth century: see Johann Heinrich Zedler, *Grosses Vollständiges Universal-Lexikon,* vol. 10 (Halle-Leipzig, 1735, repr. Graz: Akad. Druck und Verlagsanstalt, 1961); and Abbé Pétin, *Dictionnaire hagiographique*, vol. 1 (Paris, 1850) (= *Première Encyclopédie théologique,* vol. 40, ed. J. P. Migne).

29. *Apologia* . . . , fol. Ciij$^v$.

30. See the revelant passages in *Apologia* . . . , fol. Cviii$^r$ and Iv$^v$.

31. *Epist.* 7.12, in *Opera* . . . , vol. 2 (Lugduni, per Beringos fratres, s. a.; repr. Hildesheim: Olms, 1970), p. 1010. The letter probably dates from 1532.

32. For the characterization of the paradox in Antiquity, see Arthur Stanley Pease, "Things without Honor," *Classical Philology* 21 (1926): 27–42, esp. 34–35.

33. Paola Zambelli has suggested that the popularity of the *Declamatio* could possibly be explained by the fact that it could be used for satirical purposes ("A proposito del *De vanitate scientiarum et artium* di Cornelio Agrippa," *Rivista critica di storia della filosofia* 15 [1960]: 166). A comparision could be made with Henri Estienne's vast *Apologie pour Hérodote*, a satire of Catholic society published in Geneva in 1566.

34. This study was made possible by a grant from the Dutch Royal Academy of Sciences.

329

# Reading Monolingual and Bilingual Editions of Translations in Renaissance France

## Valerie Worth-Stylianou

In recent years much scholarship has been devoted to translation in the French Renaissance. Bibliographical studies have revealed the quantity of translations published in the sixteenth century;[1] historians of ideas have demonstrated the role of translations in formulating and disseminating currents of thought;[2] and the status of translations within the broader spectrum of imitative writings has been acknowledged.[3] Like other published works of the period, Renaissance translations prompt a number of questions about their reception and, in particular, the relationship among translator, printer, and public. For each member of the triangle, we may seek to establish identity and motives, while recognizing that the precise degree of collaboration between translator and printer may be difficult to determine. The identity of the translator and the printer is usually known,[4] but that of the readership may, at best, be putative.[5] As to the motives, even if we can rely on the evidence of prefatory materials from the translator and/or printer, we rarely have testimony from the reader. In all three cases we are, however, able to draw certain hypotheses from the concrete artefact itself. The exact form in which a translation is presented is indicative of the way in which it was expected to be read, that is to say how the translator/printer conceived it, or the grounds on which it attracted specific categories of readers.[6]

If we examine a selection of original editions and reprints of sixteenth-century translations, a number of features recommend themselves to our attention. Beyond the text of the translation, what preliminary and concluding material is provided? Apart from prefatory remarks by translator or printer, we may find an index, tables, glossaries, notes, etc. For example, Jean Collin translates several of the philosophical works of Cicero (published in 1537 and 1541).[7] In each case, in the margin of the translation the proper names from the text are repeated—in their Gallicized form—to indicate that a glossary entry is given at the end of the volume. The glossaries, in fact, constitute a small encyclopaedia on classical culture, many entries running to several pages of explanation.[8] The information given does not presuppose a close acquaintance with the classics. To take as an example one of the shorter entries from the *Songe de Scipion,* referring to Numantia:

> Numance estoit une ville en Espaigne, devant laquelle les Romains ont tenu le siege quatorze ans, laquelle à la fin a esté destruicte et rasée par Scipion Aphricain le Myneur, duquel est le songe que descript Ciceron, dont il a aussi esté appellé Numantius. (fol. 118[r])

> [Numantia was a town in Spain, which the Romans besieged for fourteen years, which was finally destroyed and razed to the ground by Scipio Africanus the Younger, whose dream is described by Cicero, and as a result of which he is also known as Numantius.]

A slightly longer example, the entry under *Consul,* provides substantial material that goes beyond the context of the translation. In particular, Collin comments on the etymology of the term and offers a summary history of the office. We may assume that the entry would satisfy the inquiries of most readers, for while Collin names his classical authorities, Sallust and Livy, he does not give any precise references to enable the reader to pursue the subject:

> Les Consulz ont esté faictz apres que les roys ont esté expulsez hors de Rome, et sont appellez Consulz, pource qu'ilz conseillent et pourvoyent à la republique. Les premiers consulz ont esté Lucius Junius Brutus, et Lucius Tarquinius Collatinus, lesquelz ont eu toute la charge et administration de la republique, et autant de puissance,

comme s'ilz eussent esté roys, fors que quand il estoit question de juger quelqu'ung à mort, il y avoit appel d'eulx au peuple. Par chacun an les Romains faisoient et eslisoient nouveaulx consulz estimantz, que par ung tant brief temps, qui estoit d'une seule annee aulcun ne deviendroit insolent en ceste dignité et puissance, comme dict Salluste. Les enseignes des consulz estoient, que douze hommes alloient devant eulx, et portoient des haches d'armes, ou hallebardes, à l'entour desquelles estoient liées des verges, comme dict Livius, qui signifioit, qu'ilz avoient puissance de punir et occir, tous deux ensemble n'usoient de ces enseignes, mais en ont usé l'ung apres l'aultre, de paour que le peuple n'estimast, que pour ung roy il en avoit deux, et Junius Brutus le premier eu ces enseignes du consentement de Tarquinius Collatinus son collegue et compaignon. (fols. 93$^v$–94$^r$)

[The Consuls were created after the kings were expelled from Rome, and are called Consuls because they counsel and administer the republic. The first consuls were Lucius Iunius Brutus and Lucius Tarquinius Collatinus, who had full responsibility for and administration of the republic, and as much power as though they had been kings, except that when someone was to be sentenced to death they consulted the people. Each year the Romans created and elected new consuls, believing that over such a short period, that of only one year, no-one would become arrogant in the position of power, as Sallust says. The insignia of the consuls were that twelve men walked in front of them, and carried axes, or halberds, around which were tied rods, as Livy says, which showed that they had the power to punish and put to death. The two consuls did not use these insignia together, but used them one after the other, lest the people should think that in place of one king they had two, and Iunius Brutus was the first to have these insignia by the agreement of Tarquinius Collatinus, his colleague and partner.]

In contrast, a re-edition in 1584 of Etienne de la Planche's earlier translation of Tacitus also offers a glossary (entitled "Annotations") at the end of the work.[9] However, in this case the notes are brief, many of the items referring the reader to other classical or neo-Latin authors, as seen in the following examples:

> *Fueillet I. lig. 12. Dictatures,* l'origine de ce magistrat seul souverain a Rome durant méme la liberté, est escrite au 2. livre de la 1. Decade de T. Live, et sa puissance par Pluta. en la vie de Fabius Maximus.

> [*Fol.I. line 12. Dictatorships,* the origin of this officer, absolutely supreme in Rome even during her freedom, is described in the second book of the first *Decade* of T. Livy, and its power by Plutarch in the life of Fabius Maximus.]

> *Fueill. 9 li. 7. Cirque,* estoit ung long espace comme une lice, environné de sieges, où volontiers l'on faisoit courir des chevaux seuls, ou trainans des coches. Plut. en Paul-Emile. Les esbats du Cirque sont escrits au 5. Livre Variarum epistol. de Cassiodore.

> [*Fol. 9 line 7. Circus,* was a large area, like a jousting arena, surrounded by seats, where horses were frequently made to race on their own or pulling coaches. Plutarch in *Paulus Aemilius.* The games at the circus are reported in the 5th Book of the *Various Letters* of Cassiodorus.]

Jean Collin's translation was, doubtless, primarily addressed to non-Latinists, whereas the re-edition of de la Planche's version may also have served those with some degree of competence in the classics. This is the central focus of the present chapter: should we assume that translations are read by those totally or almost totally unversed in the foreign language, or might they also—in some cases primarily—be aimed at those with varying degrees of bilingual competence?

It is useful to start by gathering visual evidence. First, are any illustrations included, and if so where and how frequently? Broadly, illustrations may be indicative either of a desire to produce a luxury object or, more frequently, of a wish to make the text appear more accessible. They are generally uncommon in translations of classical works, particularly after the first third of the sixteenth century, and, thus, it is their presence rather than their absence that is deserving of comment.[10] Since illustrations break up an unrelieved mass of text, they can make a classical work appear less rebarbative to a non-scholarly public. One such example is Hélisenne de Crenne's prose translation of the *Aeneid* that Denys Janot published in 1541. It is divided into chapters, many of them headed by a woodcut.[11] Immediately, the *Aeneid* takes on the outer form of a novel, like the popular romances of the period, and, indeed, an analysis of Hélisenne's ornate paraphrastic technique of translation confirms this visual impression.[12] The famous opening three words, *Arma virumque cano* . . . , of Virgil's epic are embellished almost beyond recognition in Hélisenne's twenty-word paraphrase:

> J'ay proposé d'exhiber par mes escriptz, la ruyne et extermination de la tresinclyte et populeuse cité de Troye. . . . (*Les Quatre Premiers Livres des Eneydes,* fol. ii^r)

> [I have undertaken to show in my writings the ruin and extermination of the very famous and populous city of Troy.]

When she comes to render the final speech of Dido to Aeneas, Hélisenne effectively uses the Latin text as no more than a foundation on which to build a tragic romance of her own composition. Under the mantle of Virgil's authority, she introduces familiar rhetorical arguments as to the fickle nature of men and the fidelity of women:

> Nec te noster amor, nec te data dextera quondam,
> Nec moritura tenet crudeli funere Dido? (*Aeneid,* 4:307–08)

335

O homme sçelere et prompt à mutabilité, l'amour fidele et cordiale que je te porte, n'a elle peu meriter de reciproque et mutuelle affection estre recompensée? As tu mis en oblivion que lors que ta main dedans la mienne mise fut, de perpetuelle alliance me feiz promesse? Helas moymesmes Dido qui de brief es dangers de l'inexorable Atropos succumberay, n'ay je peu vaincre ton cueur. (*Les Quatre Premiers Livres des Eneydes*, fol. lxxxviii[r])

[O wicked man prone to fickleness, has the faithful and warm love which I bear you been unable to earn reciprocal and mutual affection as it deserves? Have you forgotten that when your hand was placed in mine, you promised me eternal union? Alas, have I, Dido, who am shortly to succomb to the dangers of inexorable Atropos, been unable to win your heart?]

The combined textual presentation and idiosyncratic style adopted by Hélisenne turn the *Aeneid* into romance rather than epic.

Second are questions of the type of print that is used and how the text is presented on the page. The choice of print fonts is probably the printer's responsibility rather than the translator's, but it provides an effective means of conveying an initial statement about the text. Features such as the shift from Gothic in the earlier sixteenth century to roman and italic later, or the increasing tendency over the first half of the century to space texts more generously, are common to many printed books, including translations. Of more significance are cases of either different print types and layout being used within a single text or divergences between several versions of the same classical text that were published around the same time.

When one looks to the text itself of a translation, two features stand out in determining how a given version or edition might have been conceived and read: the annotations that appear in the margin and the inclusion of part or the whole of the original text alongside the French version. Some translations, of course, have no notes in the margin. For example, Du Bellay's version of the fourth book of the *Aeneid,* published in 1552 by Vincent Certenas, offers only the French text.[13] As a result, this version stands as a piece of poetry in its own right, implicitly inviting the reader to judge it on its merits, without constant justification by reference to its source. Other translations of both prose and poetry are accompanied by notes in the margin that seek to mediate the reception of the classical text. It is helpful to divide annotations that are characteristic of Renaissance translations into four categories: philological, contextual, rhetorical, and moral. Some versions combine annotations from two or more of these categories; others include only one type. In most cases, if the comments appear in the first edition of the translation, we may assume they are provided by the translator rather than the printer, particularly where they explicitly relate to difficulties of translation. Occasionally, such annotations may occur only in subsequent, even posthumous, editions, and here we may suppose that the printer is interposing his own reading of the text.

Philological comments are those that refer to a difficulty either in establishing a correct reading of the source text or of providing an adequate transposition into French. In both cases, the translator is reminding the reader that the vernacular version is not entirely congruent with the source text and that translation is a task of exegesis fraught with its own difficulties. In drawing the reader's attention to such a problem, the translator is seeking not to underline or impose a single reading of the text in question, but, on the contrary, to caution against allowing the target text to circumscribe the fuller potential meaning of the original. An example is Etienne Dolet's version of Cicero's *Tusculanae Disputationes,* printed at his own press in 1543.[14] Dolet makes only sparing use of marginal annotations, preferring to allow his version to stand as an independent text. However, linguistic discussions within the Latin text pose an insuperable challenge to the translator seeking to provide a target text free of commentary. Hence, when Cicero draws on several

Valerie Worth-Stylianou

meanings of the Latin verb *carere* [to lack, to be short of] to discuss whether loss of sensation at death can be considered as a deprivation, Dolet warns the reader in the margin:

> *Carere.* Prends garde, en quelle perplexité je suis, pour te bien exprimer la signification de ce verbe, carere: et pour te rendre facile l'intention de Cicero. (*Questions tusculanes*, p. 65)

> [*Carere.* Note what a difficulty I face in expressing properly the sense of this verb *carere,* and in making Cicero's meaning clear to you.]

Dolet's practical solution within the translation is to use a number of different French terms to approximate the sense of the different idiomatic usages in Latin. The tenor of the margin comment does not assume that the reader of Dolet's version will have any degree of competence in Latin, but the inclusion of the term from the source text (*carere*) would allow a more scholarly reader to return to the original text if he chose. Etienne de la Planche encountered a similar problem in his translation of the term *principes* in the work of Tacitus, but adopted a different solution:

> *Feuill. 31 pa. 2. lign. 3.* principes, le mot a double signification, car il se prend pour les dignitez et membres de l'armee: et pour un lieu du camp. C'est pourquoy je l'ay laissé Latin, pource il doibt estre appellé en François Principes.

> [*fol. 31. para. 2. line 3. principes*, the word has a double meaning, for it is used for the senior ranks and members of the army: and for a position in the camp. This is why I have left it in Latin, because in French it must be called *principes.*]

Whereas Dolet drew attention to the theoretical problem in his margin gloss, but sought to neutralize it in his translation, de la Planche's use of a foreign term ensures that readers remain aware of the difficulty. In both cases, it is the act of translating into the vernacular that leads to an awareness of the insufficiencies of the French language and, thus, prompts the translator to enrich its resources, either through paraphrase or through Latin borrowings. In a period when the French language is developing rapidly, translation becomes one of the stimuli for the growing *copia* of the vernacular.

Contextual annotations are commonly supplied by Renaissance translators, including Dolet and de la Planche. We have already seen that in some cases a single word is highlighted in the margin, referring the reader to a detailed entry in a glossary. Alternatively, shorter explanations may be supplied at more or less regular intervals in the margin itself. Such annotations allow us to gauge the degree of competence presumed of the reader. As an extreme example, Hélisenne de Crenne's version of the *Aeneid* in 1541 reminds the reader of the identity of common mythological figures, such as the Muses:

> Les Muses sont filles de Juppiter et de Minerve, et sont déesses des chantz, et de melodie: elles sont neuf, qui selon philosophie nous representent les neuf instrumens requis a vociferation, et parolles, cest a scavoir, la gorge, la langue, le palais, les quatre dentz, et les deux lebvres. (*Les Quatre Premiers Livres des Eneydes,* fol. ii^v)

> [The Muses are daughters of Jupiter and Minerva, and are goddesses of song and melody: there are nine of them, who according to philosophy represent the nine instruments required for producing sounds and words, that is to say, the throat, the tongue, the palate, the four teeth, and the two lips.]

In contrast, some translations give contextual explanations in the form of cross-references to classical authorities, thereby supposing that some readers at least will be familiar with other classical texts and, indeed, able to verify points of detail in the Latin original. Etienne Dolet's version of Cicero's *Epistolae ad Familiares,* appearing in 1542 from his own press, on three occasions refers the reader to other Latin or neo-Latin authorities: Aulus-Gellius, Vegetius, and Budé.[15] In all probability these notes are destined for a particular section of his readership: students, for whom the *Epistolae ad Familiares* were frequently required reading. Such students might use a vernacular translation as a guide, rather than a substitute for the Latin text. Were similar readers envisaged for a version of Caesar's *Commentarii belli gallici* characterized by a very unusual translation or editorial policy, namely Estienne de Laigue's *Commentaires de Jules Cesar de la guerre civile,* appearing in 1539?[16] Annotations on points of context are given in the margin in either French or Latin, with no observable criteria governing the choice of languages. For example, on the same page we find three successive annotations, two in French, then one in Latin:

> Pisaure est une ville quon appelle a present Folie pres du fleuve de Isaure.
> [Pisaurum is a town which is now called Folia near the river Isaurus.]
>
> Tigre est a present appellee saincte Marie saint George.
> [Tigrum is now called St. Maria-St.George.]
>
> Hic est Thermus cuius meminit Luca. libro ii.
> [This is the Thermus spoken of by Lucan Book II.]
>         (*Commentaires de Jules Cesar,* fol. vii<sup>r</sup>)

Perhaps the Latin commentaries should have been translated into French and were only left in Latin as an oversight. At all events, the references as they stand could only have been pursued by a reader with bilingual competence.

Both philological and contextual annotations provide the reader with additional information to facilitate his factual understanding of the text.

They do not, however, impinge significantly upon the reader's qualitative evaluation of the work. Moral and rhetorical annotations, in contrast, offer a form of commentary designed to highlight certain features of a text, ultimately directing the reader's appreciation of it. In this sense they are more didactic or prescriptive. Extensive moral commentary on a translation is most common in the early part of the century, when the influence of medieval allegorizing was still strong. An obvious example is *La Bible des poetes,* a prose translation (or, more strictly, paraphrase) of Ovid, of which six editions appeared between 1484 and 1531.[17] It was accompanied by a French version of the detailed allegorical interpretations of Pierre Bersuire, interspersed in the text under the headings *gloses, sens moral,* and *allegories.* These offered physical, historical, moral, and spiritual allegories, of the kind familiar to late medieval readers. Following the paraphrase of the episode of Jason, Medea, and the Golden Fleece, at the start of Book VII of the *Metamorphoses,* for example, the "Sens moral" [moral allegory] commences thus:

> Ceste ysle dont parle icy Ovyde est situee en la mer mediteriane ou frixus fut par le mouton ou veau dor apporte comme dit a este. Lequel il dedia et sacrifia au dieu mars. Par laquelle toison dor nous pouvons entendre les richesses temporelles, et mesmement celles deglise, cestassavoir prebendes, benefices et aultres dignitez, celles sont les richesses de laignel ou veau dor: cest de Jesuchrist: laquelle est ordonnee aux vestementz des povres et indigentz. Par jason jentens le bon prelat qui veult acquerir ceste toison: cest a dire qui veult parvenir aux offices et prebendes ecclesiastiques. Par les beufz enflambez jentendz les cruelz tirans. Par le dragon veillant j'entends le dyable qui jamais ne dort. (*La Bible des poetes,* fol. M ii^r)

> [This island of which Ovid speaks here lies in the Mediterranean Sea, where Frixus was borne by the golden sheep or calf, as has been related. He dedicated and sacrificed it to the god Mars. By this golden fleece we may understand temporal riches, and particularly

those of the church, that is to say prebenderies, benefits and other honors, these are the riches of the lamb or calf of gold: that is of Jesus Christ: which (the golden fleece) was intended for the clothing of the poor and indigent. By Jason I understand the good prelate who wishes to acquire this fleece: that is to say who wishes to accede to the ecclesiastical titles and prebenderies. By the flaming oxen I understand cruel tyrants. By the watchful dragon I understand the devil who never sleeps.]

The gloss passes quickly from contextual information (the island's location) to moral allegory. First, a universal parallel is drawn between the golden fleece and the pursuit of temporal wealth, but the focus is soon narrowed to an extended analogy between characters in Ovid's narration and medieval or Renaissance clerics' ambitions. What is most noteworthy about this kind of allegory is its reductive and prescriptive character. Each item of a fable has a direct correlation with a "truth" in the real world. The text is decoded for the readers, who need search no further for themselves. In her study of *Ovid in Renaissance France,* Ann Moss shows that allegorical readings of Ovid continued to find a place in introductions to some subsequent French translations even in the mid-sixteenth century, but they no longer punctuated the text as annotations. As she comments,

> Perhaps it was felt that vernacular readers needed preliminary guidance on how to understand the fables, whereas the more homogeneous public for the Latin editions, well schooled in reading the fables as moral *exempla* by their humanist teachers, could be left to cope intelligently with the text of the *Metamorphoses* plain and unadorned.[18]

Translations of prose histories or works of philosophy in the mid-sixteenth century might still admit intermittent moral annotations, sometimes several on nearly every page, sometimes only occasional remarks.

The most common form taken by such annotations is that of *sentences*: brief statements of a general moral truth. Obviously this relates to the Renaissance practice of the commonplace book, in that readers would keep a record of instructive and apposite *sententiae* that they had encountered. Students, or older readers still mindful of their *collège* training, could rapidly scan the margins of a translation provided with moral annotations for such material, and some translations even provide a list of *sentences* at the end of the volume. This type of annotation suggests that the translator/printer was either directly anticipating the requirements of one kind of reader and/or using the technique to emphasize his own reading of the author in question. It is important to establish whether moral annotations accompany all editions of a given translation or are added or omitted at a later date. In the latter case, a printer may be covertly annexing a translation to which to attach his own interpretation of the source text. An excellent example of the degree of intervention possible is provided by Simon de Goulart's revised editions of Amyot's translation of Plutarch's *Vitae*. In a careful comparison of different editions, Jacques Pineaux has shown how the almost unannotated text of Amyot is supplied with extensive margin comment in Goulart's edition of 1587.[19] A Protestant pastor, Goulart draws Calvinist lessons from Plutarch, especially concerning Providence. Thus, in the life of Romulus, Goulart introduces the following comment on the foundation of Rome:

> L'origine de celle qui a esté l'abregé du monde et maistresse de tant de peuples une si longue espace d'années estant si peu cognue, aprend à tous de bien considerer l'incertitude et vanité des choses qui semblent estre les plus fermes en ceste vie et d'adorer aussi la providence eternelle qui sur des fondemens si petits et obscurs a basti puis apres une si puissante monarchie.[20]

> [The origin of the town which was the centre of the world and mistress of so many peoples for such a long period of years being so little known, teaches all to consider well the uncertainty and vanity

of things which seem to be the most secure in this life and also to adore the eternal Providence which on such small and obscure foundations thereafter built such a powerful monarchy.]

As Pineaux observes, "Le Plutarque de Goulart est un Plutarque moralisé, et la lecture des *Vies* proposée par l'éditeur est une lecture providentielle" (p. 335) [Goulart's Plutarch is a moralised Plutarch, and the editor's reading of the *Lives* is a providential one]. The reader of the 1587 edition would, therefore, be perceiving Plutarch through a kind of double refraction: Amyot's humanist translation and Goulart's Calvinist commentary.

Rhetorical annotations drawing attention to the form or expression of ideas in the source text are found less commonly than moral annotations. One reason may be that translators are often aware of the difficulty of capturing the full stylistic force of the source text in their version, and any rhetorical commentary invites a critical scrutiny of the exact phrasing of the target text. When rhetorical annotations do occur, they do so most frequently in translations of the middle third of the century, coinciding with the renewed interest in rhetoric and poetics in the vernacular. An example of a translation provided with an unusually generous number of rhetorical annotations is Claude Chaudière's version of Cicero's first Verrine Oration, which appeared in 1551.[21] The very choice of a prime example of Ciceronian forensic oratory lends itself to Chaudière's approach. The margins of his translation provided the student of Latin rhetoric, or the aspiring French lawyer, with a brief handbook on how to make an effective case. Chaudière identifies techniques of *dispositio,* such as the proper use of the *exordium,* and figures of *elocutio,* such as *amplificatio.* Furthermore, he provides brief comments on why Cicero adopts certain strategies, as, for example:

En ce commencement Ciceron demonstre n'avoir accusé personne en jugement, ains tousjours defendu. (fol. 7ʳ)

344

[In this opening Cicero shows that he had never accused anyone on trial, but on the contrary always spoken in defence.]

and:

Ciceron dit ce, a celle fin que les Siciliens ne se faschent de si grande louenge qu'il prent envers les autres, et n'aient peur.(fol. 16$^r$)

[Cicero says this in order that the Sicilians should not be angered by his great praise of others, and that they should not be afraid.]

Just as Goulart's moral annotations directed the reader of Plutarch toward the text in a certain way, so Chaudière's rhetorical annotations identify what he considers the significance of the source text. In each case, the translation is presented in a prescriptive framework, leading readers towards the translator's interpretation. In an age so conscious of the power of rhetoric, works of translation, like so many other forms of writing, manifestly seek to control their impact on their public.

From the discussion of the range of possible annotations, it is clear that while many translations were addressed simply to the French-speaking non-Latinist, in other cases translators/printers were expecting a readership with some degree of competence in Latin. This assertion is equally borne out by a number of translations that include part or all whole of the source text in the margin alongside the translation. Again, we need to ask what information this feature can provide about the way in which a given translation was perceived by printer, translator, and reader.

Since far more translations appear in a monolingual than a bilingual format in the Renaissance, we may start from the premise that the inclusion of part or all of the source text is a deliberate policy adopted by translator and/or printer. In the earlier part of the century, there are various forms in which editions provide extracts from the source text. At a minimal level, the first words of a new section may appear in Latin. This is the case in the 1530 edition of Guillaume Michel de Tours's translation of Suetonius, printed by Pierre Leber.[22] Each chapter of the translation is given a title, below which there are the opening words in Latin, a symbol denoting a new section of text, and then (with no break or change of type) the French translation. For example:

> Annum agens Caesar sextum decimum patrem amisit etc. Du temps que Julius Cesar dictateur eut attaint son seiziesme (an) de son aage florissant, son pere qui estoit a Romme preteur mourut a Pise de mort soubdaine. (fol. i$^r$)

> [On reaching his sixteenth year, Caesar lost his father etc. At the time when Julius Caesar the dictator had reached the sixteenth year of his youth, his father who was a praetor at Rome died a sudden death at Pisa.] .

Other translations may give a greater amount of the source text, as in the case of Octovien de Saint-Gelais's popular translations of Virgil, where approximately one third of the Latin text appears—this time in the outer margin, alongside the translation, and in a smaller type.[23] Thus, Octovien's translation of the opening eleven lines of the *Aeneid,* which runs to thirty lines in French, is accompanied by lines 1–3 and line 8 of the Latin text. Visually, the French version dominates. What is the function of a partial reproduction of the source text? No doubt to allow the reader the option of following the Latin in a parallel copy. The student seeking some assistance might use this system, or the older reader who had some Latin, but not enough to feel confident enough to tackle the original unaided. In such editions, the presence of the Latin reminds the reader that the translation has not displaced the source text entirely, but rather provides a convenient means of access to it.

The relationship between source and target texts is brought to the fore in the case of complete bilingual editions. Textual layout often provides an indication as to whether the French translation is an important, but secondary, commmentary on the Latin text or whether the Latin text is a parenthetical check on the translation. We should observe which text comes first or occupies the center columns of the page; which is printed in the larger type; and whether the type faces are differentiated. The evidence of the appearance of the text needs to be weighed against the translator's practice: in particular, does the presence of the complete source text correspond with a more literal style of translation that might seek to reaffirm the relationship between model and imitation?

Observations on complete bilingual translations can be usefully divided between editions of an essentially pedagogic nature and those offered to a wider market. From the 1530s, a number of printed books bear witness to the role in some Renaissance school curricula of what is now termed comparative linguistics.[24] The contribution of Robert Estienne is outstanding, not only through his succession of bilingual dictionaries[25] but also through primers such as *La Maniere de tourner toutes especes de noms latins en nostre langue francoyse*.[26] The title page of this last work states that it was specifically conceived "A lutilité des jeunes enfans, estudians es bonnes lettres" [For the use of young children, studying the classics], and the contents (categories of nouns, basic conjugations, etc.) are suitable for elementary students of Latin. Of most interest here is the format: explanations of particular items are given in French and then illustrated by Latin examples (in roman type), with the corresponding French translation opposite (in italics). The layout is identical to that adopted in many bilingual editions of classical works. For example, under the heading *Nomen* [Noun], Estienne defines the grammatical category and then draws attention to the absence of the article in Latin as opposed to French, before setting out his paradigms:

Voyla que c'est du nom.
Et quant au tourner d'iceluy, convient scavoir, que nostre langue
francoyse ha sur ce quelque felicite semblable à la grecque,

principallement aux noms appellatifz, desquelz nous mettrons
tantost les especes. car quant et [*sic*] lesdictz noms, et au
devant diceux, tousjours nous mettons ung article, qui ayde
moult à exprimer la signification diceulx, et sont lesdictz
articles, le, la, les: du, de la, des: comme pour exemple,
En singulier pur [*sic*] les trois gendres.

| Magister | *Le maistre* |
| Scientia | *La science* |
| Scamnum | *Le banc* |

En pluriel pour les trois gendres.

| Magistri | *Les maistres* |
| Scientiae | *Les sciences* |
| Scamna | *Les bancz* |

En singulier pour les trois gendres en genetif cas.

| Magistri | *Du maistre* |
| Scientiae | *De la science* |
| Scamni | *Du banc* |

En pluriel pour les trois gendres au genetif.

| Magistrorum | *Des maistres* |
| Scientiarum | *Des sciences* |
| Scamnorum | *Des bancz.* |

[This is what a noun is:

And as for translating the aforesaid, it is important to know that our
French language has in this regard some advantage similar to Greek,
principally in the case of concrete nouns, of which we shall shortly
give the categories. For as to these nouns, and in front of them, we
always put an article, which greatly helps to convey the meaning of
them, and these same articles are "le, la, les," "du, de la, des," as for
example,
In the singular for the three genders:

| Magister | *The master* |
| Scientia | *The science* |
| Scamnum | *The bench* |

In the plural for the three genders:

| Magistri | *The masters* |
| Scientiae | *The sciences* |

Scamna          *The benches*
In the singular for the three genders in the genitive case:
Magistri        *Of the master*
Scientiae       *Of the science*
Scamni          *Of the bench*
In the plural for the three genders in the genitive:
Magistrorum     *Of the masters*
Scientiarum     *Of the sciences*
Scamnorum       *Of the benches.*]

It is probable that Estienne's primers both reflect and encourage human-ist teaching practices, in particular, the need to pay close attention to the original when translating into the vernacular. The parallel arrangement of Latin and French draws the student's attention to significant points of translation technique, such as, here, the need to include the article in French.

Another humanist aware of the pedagogic value of bilingual texts was Robert Estienne's friend, Mathurin Cordier, an early teacher of Jean Calvin.[27] Two bilingual editions of Cordier's selections from Cicero's *Epistolae ad Familiares* were first published in 1542 and 1545.[28] The presentation of the texts suggests the way in which they were used. First the reader finds the entire Latin text of a letter; then the text is repeated, divided into small sections, each accompanied by the French translation and, sometimes, also by a Latin paraphrase. For example (the symbols reproduced here are those dividing the sections in Cordier's text),

Equidem // Quant est de moy.
Ego praetermisi neminem // je n'ay point laisse passer homme du
    monde.
Quem quidem // lequel certes.
Ego putarem) arbitrarer // je pensasse.
Esse perventurum ad te) ad te usque venturum // qu'il allast jusques a
vous.

349

Cui) sub ad te.

Ego non dederim literas // par lequel je ne vous aye escript.

(*M.T.C. Aliquot epistolae* [1542], p. 6)

[As for myself, I have not let any man pass who I thought might be coming your way, without my writing to you.]

The French translation is presented as a commentary on the Latin, facilitating and controlling the student's understanding of it. The translation precisely renders every phrase in Latin, but the style tends towards paraphrase ("neminem" [no-one], "homme du monde" [no-one in the world]; "dederim literas" [I gave a letter], "je ne vous ay escript" [I did not write to you]) where this makes the sense of the original clearer. In this way, the French translation has a role similar to contextual annotations in monolingual translations.

Cordier was himself the author of several Latin textbooks designed to help younger students of Latin, and some were reprinted subsequently with the addition of French parallel texts. A letter from the printer Estienne Michel to the readers of his 1579 edition of the *Colloques de Mathurin Cordier*[29] makes it clear that, in publishing a parallel text, he was following standard teaching practice:

> L'on m'a incité (amy Lecteur) à faire traduire ces Colloques en François, pour le bien et profict des enfans, lesquels peuvent avoir en iceux ample matiere d'apprendre à parler Latin, et consequemment de cognoistre en nostre langue vulgaire et commune la conception de l'Auteur d'iceux. Ce qui leur sera à mon advis un grand soulagement, ayans devant les yeux ce que les maistres leur pourront avoir familiairement interpreté: et aux maistres un grand plaisir et contentement, de voir que si les enfans n'ont retenu l'exposition de ce qu'il leur aura esté leu, ils peuvent avoir recours à la traduction Françoise de leur leçon. (p. 3)

[I have been encouraged, dear Reader, to have these Conversations translated into French for the good and benefit of children, who may find in them plentiful material to learn to speak Latin, and thereby to know in our common, vernacular tongue the ideas of the Author of this work. Which in my opinion will be a great comfort to them, having before their eyes what their teachers may have explained to them informally: and for the teachers it will be a great pleasure and satisfaction to see that if the children have not remembered the oral explanation of what was read to them, they can have recourse to the French translation of their lesson.]

The presentation of the parallel texts makes the pre-eminence of the Latin obvious by the use of a larger, roman type, while the French is in smaller, italic type. The Latin text always precedes the French translation, which, as in Cordier's versions of Cicero, tends to paraphrase and explanation. When François Forest's press reprinted this popular work in 1593, however, the translation was revised, not only to rectify glaring inaccuracies[30] but also to move towards a more literal style. The printer explains the pedagogic motives to the reader:

Nous avons mis peine qu'ils ayent esté plus fidelement traduits, et mesmes qu'on se soit accommodé à la phrase Latine, pour donner l'intelligence des mots aux enfans moins avancez. (fol. 2$^r$)

[We have taken pains that they should be more accurately translated, and even that the Latin sentence structure should be respected, in order that the less advanced children may follow word by word.]

Close in spirit to Robert Estienne's bilingual primers, the Forest edition of Cordier's *Colloques* offers a basic textbook in comparative linguistics. The re-editions of such bilingual textbooks bear witness to their success and highlight the pedagogic role of translation into the vernacular.

For bilingual editions not specifically aimed at schools, a broader market existed. For example, Louis des Masures translated the twelve books of the *Aeneid* and published them in installments between 1547 and 1560. The French verse translation is accompanied in the margin by the complete Latin text. Du Bellay praised des Masures's version of the first two books as "fidele et diligente,"[31] and the bilingual edition confirms this judgment. Des Masures is not seeking to rival Virgil's poetic mastery but, rather, seeking to provide a competent rendering that can be consulted either in its own right or as a means of access to the Latin. The earlier complete translation of the *Aeneid* by Octovien de Saint-Gelais had responded to similar criteria in providing regular extracts from the source text, but des Masures's version goes further in obviating all need for the reader to hunt out a Latin text.

The practical attraction of parallel texts in a single volume was well understood by the Lyonnais printer Guillaume Rouillé. Among the parallel texts from his press are Latin and French versions of part of the Old and the complete New Testaments, Alciati's emblem book, and Cicero's *Epistolae ad Familiares*.[32] The title pages of these works highlight the parallel texts, with, for example, the 1558 edition of the *Psalms* and *Book of Proverbs* bearing the description,

> Le tout traduit de l'Ebreu en Latin et en Francoys et reduit par versetz, respondant l'une version à l'autre.

> [The whole text translated from Hebrew into Latin and French and set out verse by verse, with parallel translations.]

The practical advantage of combining source and target texts in one volume is spelled out in Rouillé's prefatory letter to the reader of his 1561 re-edition of Etienne Dolet's translation of the *Epistres Familiaires:*

> Et ce pour l'utilité de . . . ceux aussi qui bien souvent sont fort empeschez pour expliquer quelque passage, tenant en chasque main un livre, assavoir en l'une le latin, et en l'autre le francoys.

352

[And this for the benefit of . . . those also who are often much
inconvenienced when explaining some passage, holding in each hand
a book, namely in one hand the Latin and in the other the French.]

Another interesting point to emerge from this prefatory letter is the
existence of a particular group of readers served by bilingual translations,
those using them in order to learn French via Latin. In a cosmopolitan
city such as Renaissance Lyon, foreign scholars and students would have
been good clients. A similar use of a bilingual format is seen in a 1612
re-edition in Frankfurt of the translations of Tacitus's works by Estienne
de la Planche and Claude Fauchet. The printer Nicolaus Hoffmann
explains in the letter of dedication to Albert John Smirzicio, that he has
added the French translation alongside the Latin text because he knows
his patron loves things French and has recently travelled in France.[33]
Here we can be sure of the correlation between the policy of the printer
and the tastes of one particular reader.

What this edition and Rouillé's of the *Epistres Familiaires* have in
common is that printers are imposing the format of the parallel text
retrospectively, to meet their perception of the requirements of a new
group of readers. There is no comment as to whether this reflects the
translators' view of their task. In the case of Dolet's version of Cicero,
at least, we may have reservations.[34] Dolet's theoretical comments on
translation are well documented and suggest he wanted the target text to
stand in its own right, in place of the source text. For example, in the
third of his five precepts for good translation in *La Maniere de bien
traduire d'une langue en autre*,[35] he discourages an over-literal attention
to Latin word order:

Et par ainsi, c'est superstition trop grande (diray je besterie ou
ignorance?) de commencer sa traduction au commencement de la
clausule. Mais si, l'ordre des mots perverti, tu exprimes l'intention
de celuy que tu traduis, aucun ne t'en peult reprendre. (*La Maniere
de bien traduire*, pp. 15–16)

[And in this way, it is too scrupulous (should I say folly or ignorance?) to start one's translation at the beginning of the sentence. But if, having changed the word order, you express the meaning of the author you arc translating, no-one can reproach you for it.]

The French text is to distance itself from the original ("l'ordre des mots perverti"), a recommendation that sits uneasily with a bilingual format. When translations passed into the public domain of the printed book, however, the translator relinquished absolute control. A new printer was at liberty to present the text differently. The introduction of margin annotations or a bilingual format defines the new perspective from which a translation is viewed. Research on Renaissance translations has rightly emphasized that the translator, by his approach to his task, mediates the reception of the source text. Similarly, the form given to the concrete artefact of the printed edition, whether this form be imposed by the translator or the printer, is a significant factor influencing Renaissance readers' perceptions of classical and neo-Latin texts.

## Notes

1. See, most recently, Paul Chavy, *Traducteurs d'autrefois: Moyen Age et Renaissance. Dictionnaire des traducteurs de la littérature traduite en ancien et moyen français (842–1600)*, 2 vols. (Paris and Geneva: Champion-Slatkine, 1988).

2. See, for example, Robert Aulotte, *Amyot et Plutarque: La tradition des "Moralia" au XVI^e siècle* (Geneva: Droz, 1965); and Christiane Lauvergnat-Gagnière, *Lucien de Samosate et le lucianisme en France au XVI^e siècle: athéisme et polémique* (Geneva: Droz, 1988).

3. See the comprehensive survey of Renaissance attitudes to translation in Glyn P. Norton, *The Ideology and Language of Translation in Renaissance France and their Humanist*

*Antecedents* (Geneva: Droz, 1984).

4. However, a minority of Renaissance translations were published anonymously, especially if the translator was unsure of the reception his work would receive: e.g., *Epistre de Cicero envoyee a Octavius, du temps que la Republique estoit troublee* (Paris: Conrad Badius, 1546 [B.N., Paris: Rés. p. Z.80]). I give the location of all sixteenth-century texts cited, since variants even within a press-run were frequent at this period.

5. Specific references to the translations that Renaissance readers consulted are rare. A famous exception is Montaigne's praise of Amyot's version of Plutarch (Book 2, *Essai* 4, "A demain les affaires").

6. Unfortunately, none of the bibliographies of Renaissance translations to date (such as Chavy's; see n. 1 above) includes a description of textual presentation, much less an analysis of the style of each translation. It is, therefore, not possible to give statistical data on the frequency of a particular feature.

7. *Le Livre de amytié de Ciceron* (Paris: Anthoine Bonnemere, 1537 [B.N., Paris: *E1474]); and *Les Trois Livres des loix de Ciceron. Le Songe de Scipion* (Paris: Denys Janot, 1541 [B.N., Paris: Rés. p. R.773]). In quotations from these and other sixteenth-century texts, I follow the original spelling and punctuation, except that abbreviations are resolved, and *i/j* and *u/v* are distinguished.

8. For example, in the glossary appended to the *Songe de Scipion,* the entry under "Legion" runs to two pages and includes a discussion of the etymology of the term, the standard composition of a legion, and examples of how legions functioned in battle.

9. *Les Oeuvres de C. Cornelius Tacitus . . . le tout nouvellement mis en françois avec quelques annotations necessaires pour l'intelligence de mots plus difficiles et remarquables* (Paris: Abel L'Angelier, 1584 [Bodleian Library, Oxford: Douce TT 50]). At the start of the *Annotations*, the reader is advised that Justus Lipsius's revisions to the Latin text of Tacitus have been consulted in the 1581 edition by Plantin—further evidence of the scholarly nature of this work.

10. One notable exception to this trend is provided by generously illustrated versions of Ovid's *Metamorphoses,* notably the edition published in Lyon in 1557 by Jean de

Tournes. For an excellent survey and bibliographical description of sixteenth-century French translations of Ovid, see Ghislaine Amielle, *Recherches sur les Traductions françaises des métamorphoses d'Ovide illustrées et publiées en France à la fin du XV^e siècle* (Paris: Editions J. Touzot, 1989).

11. *Les Quatre Premiers Livres des Eneydes du treselegant poete Virgile* (Paris: 1541 [Bibliothèque de l'Arsenal, Paris: fol. B.613. Rés.]).

12. See the comparative study by Christine Scollen-Jimack, "Hélisenne de Crenne, Octovien de Saint-Gelais and Virgil," *Studi Francesi* 78 (1982): 197–210. This study looks at the extent to which Hélisenne used Octovien's translation alongside the Latin text in composing her own version.

13. *Le Quatriesme livre de l'Eneide de Vergile,* Paris, 1552: reproduced in Joachim Du Bellay, *Oeuvres Poétiques,* vol. 6, *Discours et Traductions,* ed. Henri Chamard (Paris: Droz, 1931).

14. *Les Questions tusculanes de M. T. Ciceron* (Lyon, 1543 [B.L., London: C.107.a.20]). For a fuller study of this aspect of the translation, see Valerie Worth, *Practising Translation in Renaissance France: The example of Etienne Dolet* (Oxford: Clarendon Press; New York: Oxford University Press, 1988), pp. 176–82.

15. *Les Epistres familiaires de Marc Tulle Cicero* (Lyon, 1542 [B.N., Paris: Rés. Z.2145]).

16. Paris (Galiot du Pré), 1539 (Bodleian Library, Oxford: 8 C 2 Art).

17. My comments and example are drawn from *La Bible des poetes de Ovide Methamorphose (*Paris: Philippe Le Noir, 1531 [Bodleian Library, Oxford: Douce O.191]).

18. *Ovid in Renaissance France. A Survey of the Latin editions of Ovid and commentaries printed in France before 1600* (London: The Warburg Institute, University of London, 1982), p. 38.

19. Jacques Pineaux, "Un continuateur des Vies Parallèles: Simon Goulart de Senlis (S.G.S.)," *Fortunes de Jacques Amyot: Actes du colloque international (Melun 18–20*

*avril 1985)* (Paris: A.-G. Nizet, 1986), pp. 331–42.

20. Quotation cited by Pineaux, "Un continuateur," p. 334.

21. *Premier Livre des accusations de M.T. Ciceron, contre Caius Verres, nommé Divination* (Rheims: Claude Chaudière, 1551 [B.N., Paris: Rés. X. 1081]).

22. *La Tresillustre et Memorable Vie, faictz, et gestes des douze Cesars* (Paris: Pierre Leber, 1530 [Bodleian Library, Oxford: Douce S 509]).

23. See, for example, *Les Eneydes de Virgille* (Paris: Antoine Verard, 1509 [B.N., Paris: Rés.g.Yc.318]).

24. See Norton, *Ideology and Language of Translation* (n. 3 above), pp. 140–42.

25. Notably his *Dictionaire francoislatin* (Paris: Robert Estienne, 1540).

26. Paris: apud Franciscum Stephanum, 1540 (Bodleian Library, Oxford, Rawl. 8 943).

27. See Charles E. Delormeau, *Un Maître de Calvin, Mathurin Cordier: l'un des créateurs de l'enseignement secondaire moderne, 1479–1564* (Neuchâtel: Editions H. Messeiller, 1976).

28. *M. T. C. Aliquot epistolae cum latina simul et gallica interpretatione* (Paris: Prigentius Caluarinius, 1542 [B.N., Paris: S.21817]); and *M. Tul. Ciceronis epistolarum familiarium liber secundus. Aliquot item epistolae ex caeteris libris, tum ad Atticum, tum ad alios, selectae in gratiam iuventutis. Cum latina et gallica interpretatione* (Paris: Charles Estienne, 1545 [B.N., Paris: Rés.Z.2122]). Delormeau, *Un Maître de Calvin* (n. 27 above), p. 81, believes that an ex-student of Cordier produced these editions from class notes, without Cordier's authorization.

29. Lyon: Estienne Michel, 1579 (Bodleian Library, Oxford: Douce C.14).

30. See the printer's prefatory letter: *Les Colloques de Maturin Cordier*, 1593, fol. 2[r] (Bodleian Library, Oxford: Ashm. B.12).

31. Du Bellay, *Oeuvres Poétiques*, 6: 250.

32. For a detailed bibliographical description of these works, see le Président Baudrier, *Bibliographie lyonnaise* (Paris: J. Baudrier, repr. 1964), vol. 9.

33. *C. Cornelii Taciti Opera latina, cum versione gallica* (Frankfurt: Nicolaus Hoffmannus, 1612 [Bodleian Library, Oxford: 8 T 22 Art.]).

34. See Valerie Worth, "A Bilingual Edition of Cicero's *Epistolae ad Familiares,*" *Bibliothèque d'Humanisme et Renaissance* 50/1 (1988): 77–80.

35. Lyon: Etienne Dolet, 1540; repr. by J. Tastu for Téchener, Paris, 1830.